THE
TRANSFORMATION
OF EARLY AMERICAN
HISTORY

The Transformation of Early American History

SOCIETY, AUTHORITY, AND IDEOLOGY

Edited by JAMES A. HENRETTA,
MICHAEL KAMMEN, *and*
STANLEY N. KATZ

Alfred A. Knopf

NEW YORK

1991

THIS IS A BORZOI BOOK
PUBLISHED BY ALFRED A. KNOPF, INC.

Library of Congress Cataloging-in-Publication Data
The transformation of early American history: society,
authority, and ideology / edited by James A. Henretta,
Michael Kammen, and Stanley N. Katz. — 1st ed.
p.   cm.
Includes bibliographical references and index.
ISBN 0-394-58147-4
1. United States—History—Colonial period, ca. 1600–1775.
2. United States—History—Revolution, 1775–1783.
3. Bailyn, Bernard.   I. Henretta, James A.   II. Kammen,
Michael G.   III. Katz, Stanley Nider.
E188.5.T73   1991
973.2—dc20   90-43248   CIP

Manufactured in the United States of America

FIRST EDITION

CONTENTS

ACKNOWLEDGMENTS

This *festschrift* was the work of many hands. The conference at which some of these papers were originally presented was organized by a committee of Bernard Bailyn's former graduate students. Its members were Richard D. Brown, Richard L. Bushman, Philip J. Greven, James A. Henretta, Michael Kammen, Stanley N. Katz, Pauline R. Maier, Mary Beth Norton, Gordon S. Wood, and Michael Zuckerman.

Susan Hunt of the Charles Warren Center at Harvard University efficiently handled a multitude of conference arrangements in Cambridge, while Padma Seetharam and Susan Oetkin smoothly managed a mass of correspondence at the Department of History, University of Maryland, College Park. The conference was funded by contributions from those attending and support from the Newhouse Foundation, the Charles Warren Center, and two anonymous donors. The final manuscript was expertly prepared by Rosemary Crew at the University of Maryland.

The editors would like to thank all of these individuals and institutions for their contributions to this project, and Jane Garrett of Alfred A. Knopf for her continuing encouragement and assistance.

THE
TRANSFORMATION
OF EARLY AMERICAN
HISTORY

Bernard Bailyn, Historian and Teacher

AN APPRECIATION

MICHAEL KAMMEN *and*

STANLEY N. KATZ

ALL OF THE ESSAYS in this volume have been written by men and women who received their graduate education in early American history at Harvard University under the principal guidance of Bernard Bailyn. The authors are now themselves practicing historians who teach or have taught at diverse colleges and universities throughout the United States. Many of them, like Professor Bailyn, have also lectured and taught as visiting faculty members at universities overseas. The authors as well as the editors were markedly influenced by Bernard Bailyn as a teacher, by his charismatic yet enigmatic personality, and above all by the compelling example of his own scholarship.

Each of us is delighted to take this opportunity, as Bernard Bailyn approaches retirement at Harvard University—retirement from the classroom, that is, though not from his spacious but book-packed workshop in Widener Library J—to participate in a joint enterprise that honors his impact upon our collective understanding of American origins. Just as we were once privileged to study under his tutelage, we are now privileged to collaborate in conveying to him our admiration and deepest appreciation.

Bernard Bailyn is one of the most innovative and eminent historians in the world. He certainly stands among the most influential practitioners of the craft in the United States today. Although his publications have concentrated upon the seventeenth and eighteenth centuries, students of the "modern" period are invariably familiar with his writings. Even though we have not checked the most recent citation indexes, it is abundantly clear that Bailyn's work has enjoyed remarkable impact and visibility. One of his classic essays, for example, "Politics and Social Structure in Virginia," has been anthologized and reprinted in *at least* seventeen collections of essays; and another, "Political Experience and Enlightenment Ideas in Eighteenth-Century America," has been reprinted in twenty-three such anthologies.

The significance of his scholarship has received considerable recognition in the form of prestigious awards: a Pulitzer Prize and a Bancroft Prize for *The Ideological Origins of the American Revolution* (1967), a National Book Award for *The Ordeal of Thomas Hutchinson* (1974), a second Pulitzer Prize and an Immigration History Society Prize for *Voyagers to the West: A Passage in the Peopling of America on the Eve of the Revolution* (1986). In 1980–81, at the age of fifty-nine, he served as president of the American Historical Association.

The excitement and interest that Bernard Bailyn generates beyond the historical profession, and even beyond academe, is demonstrable even though it is difficult to calibrate. Two different sorts of illustrations may suffice. In 1971, following the furor aroused by publication of the Pentagon Papers, Anthony Lukas published an article in *The New York Times Sunday Magazine* about Daniel Ellsberg. Recounting various topics discussed in the course of their interviews, Lukas describes a moment when Ellsberg reached into his briefcase and pulled out a well-thumbed paperback copy of Bailyn's *Ideological Origins of the American Revolution.* Lukas continues:

> Turning to the last paragraph, he [Ellsberg] asks, "Have you ever read that? I've read it a dozen times, but it still moves me so much I can't read it out loud without weeping." I begin reading from the point marked by his long index finger:
> "But some, caught up in a vision of the future in which the peculiarities of American life became the marks of a chosen people, found in the defiance of traditional order the firmest of all grounds for their hope for a freer life. . . . It was only where there was this defiance, this refusal to truckle, this distrust of all authority, political or social, that institutions would express human aspirations, not crush them."[1]

For the second illustration, here is a brief but enthusiastic account (written in a letter during May 1988) of a new course on the origins of the Constitution of the United States that Bailyn introduced that spring semester at the Harvard Law School:

To the delight of other Harvard faculty members,
Bernard Bailyn pokes some fun at Prince Charles.
BOSTON *Globe* STAFF PHOTO/FRANK O'BRIEN, SEPTEMBER 5,1986.

The "student" body ranged from brilliant freshmen to diligent
seniors swatting up summas to bright but slightly bewildered
law students to senior Boston lawyers, foreign experts on comparative constitutionalism, and the law dean's wife.[2]

Another measure of Bailyn's magnetism and impact can be seen in
terms of the more than sixty Ph.D.s that he has trained over the past
thirty-five years at Harvard. Many of those doctoral students did not
come to graduate school intending to specialize in either colonial history
or the history of American education. But they were attracted by Bailyn's
brilliant lectures and his stimulating seminars. He has never sought converts. Rather, drawing disciples has been one "price" that he has had to
pay for the dynamism of his personality and the intriguing example he
supplies of the human mind profoundly engaged by challenging issues
and historical problems.

Most of those sixty-some students now hold professorships or administrative positions at universities and learned institutions throughout the
United States and Canada. Late in October of 1987 (on Halloween,

actually) they gathered in Cambridge, Massachusetts, to honor Bailyn with a two-day conference on the occasion of his sixty-fifth birthday. The conference turned out to be just as rigorous, lively, and stimulating as its organizing committee had hoped. Bailyn, who has never been known as a shrinking violet, participated in all of the discussion sessions with characteristic gusto. His former students, who have not hesitated to disagree with him on varied matters of method, emphasis, and interpretation, "gave as good as they got," so to speak.[3] As the conference drew to a close, those whose viewpoints differed from Bailyn's or from one another's, agreed to disagree and ended the conference in the traditional Cantabrigian manner: with sherry, assorted munchies, animated conversation, and the renewal of old friendships.

BERNARD BAILYN was born and raised in Hartford, Connecticut, and concentrated upon literature and philosophy as an undergraduate at Williams College (A.B. 1945). He reacted quite negatively to one dominant teacher there, however, an ethereal philosopher enamored of Hegel and Emerson, and consequently Bailyn was "driven into positivism," as he puts it, by the compelling belief that for scholarship to have integrity it must be verifiable.

During the Second World War he served in the Army Signal Corps and in the Army Security Agency. He subsequently lived in Paris for a year and has retained a fondness for certain French writers as well as vivid memories of postwar Paris.

> I once lived on the Rue de la Huchette. What a gang we had there—1 whore, 1 male stenographer at the American embassy, and a friend of mine, a classics major at Harvard. The classics major was a flaxen blond, and "Blondie," as the whore was called, had thick peroxide yellow hair and was ferociously jealous of my friend, a timid soul, whom she used to terrify by stroking his head. *Voilà.*[4]

Bailyn began graduate study in history at Harvard in September 1946 and received his Ph.D. there in 1953. He recalls that in 1946, before leaving the U.S. Army, he jotted down three intersecting "areas of interest" that he intended to pursue:

> The first was the relation between European and American life. The second was the transition between the pre-modern and modern worlds, a period of history close enough to the modern world to show palpable continuities between past and present

but distant enough for effective historical perspective. And the third was the interplay between social history and cultural or intellectual history.[5]

At Harvard he specialized in early American social and economic history, as well as medieval (especially French) and Roman history. The mentors who influenced him most were Oscar Handlin, then a young social historian, and Charles Taylor, a medievalist. "Both presented history," Bailyn recalls, "as a mode of complex analysis; both stressed social and institutional history in its intersections with people's perceptions and subjective experiences." He also learned from Samuel Eliot Morison's written work, particularly the "Admiral's" manner of weaving into a single, coherent narrative a "large-scale, complex series of events."[6]

In 1949 Harvard appointed Bailyn an instructor, in 1953 an assistant professor of history, in 1958 an associate professor with tenure, and three years later he was promoted to full professor. In 1966 he was named Winthrop Professor of History, and in 1981 he became Adams University Professor. In 1983 Bailyn began a term as director of the Charles Warren Center for Studies in American History. From 1962 until 1970 he served as editor in chief of the John Harvard Library, an extensive series of modern editions of classic works by various sorts of American writers. He has also been the co-editor of *Perspectives in American History* (an annual collection of essays published by the Warren Center), in 1967–77 and 1984–86.

Beyond the confines of Cambridge he has been active in the American Historical Association, serving as its president in 1981. He is also an elected member of the American Academy of Arts and Sciences, the American Philosophical Society, the National Academy of Education, the Royal Historical Society (U.K.), and the Mexican Academy of History and Geography, as well as a corresponding fellow of the British Academy. Closer to home, and to his chosen area of specialization, Bailyn has served four terms as a member of the Council of the Institute of Early American History and Culture, based in Williamsburg, Virginia: in 1959–62, 1964–67, 1971–74 (chairman), and again in 1981–84.

BERNARD BAILYN's most enduring intellectual preoccupations are embodied in the bibliography of his published work, listed at the end of this volume and assessed from two different yet complementary perspectives in the essays by Gordon S. Wood and Jack Rakove that follow this one. Several of his interests and concerns are somewhat less obvious or visible, however, and they deserve brief notice here. He is intrigued by the divergent public roles that intellectuals play in various sorts of societies—particularly the notable differences between France, Germany, Austria, and the United States—and he has always been concerned about the creative function of "mind," of intellection, both in times past and as a critical feature of the historian's vocation.[7]

Reading through the corpus of Bailyn's major work, one might not readily guess that he is deeply conversant with the social sciences and even with the natural sciences as modes of scholarly inquiry and enterprise. It is rare, indeed, to encounter in Bailyn's prose a phrase like "functional integration,"[8] and rarer still to find in his footnotes any citations at all to works by sociologists, social psychologists, anthropologists, or political scientists. The fact remains, however, that his wife, Lotte, not only has worked with Bailyn on several of his own projects, but is an astute social psychologist herself;[9] that his father-in-law, Paul F. Lazarsfeld, was a remarkably wide-ranging and extremely influential sociologist;[10] and that an erudite, scholarly book-length "joke" written by Robert K. Merton, a giant in the field of sociology, takes the form of an open letter to "Dear Bud," which is what Bernard Bailyn is called by his friends.[11] (As a child in Hartford he was "Buddy.")

When it became quite trendy to design "interdisciplinary" projects during the 1960s and '70s, and when that modifier became a buzz-word in academe, Bailyn held his peace in public; but privately he had harsh words for the artificiality of contrived collaborative situations, such as "interdisciplinary seminars."

> Interdisciplinary seminars are boring. Anything rigged to accomplish some meta-purpose, like bringing disciplines together, can only be artificial, hence boring. The trick is to get into real, not meta, problems which need work from all directions; then one forgets about boundaries in trying to find solutions with help from wherever it can be found. Here's where the scientists are so good. [Molecular biologist James D.] Watson's group in Cambridge used half a dozen "disciplines"—and he himself had to bat up a few areas quickly just to take the next step. Biophysics was invented in that way. And I remember our asking Watson whether Harvard should set up a *department* of biophysics, when it was a hot new area—he said no, don't freeze it with administration, but let it keep finding its own natural shape. Not that he is such a genius at organization; but he had a point there. Why is it the humanities and social sciences have to be flogged all the time to keep getting interdisciplinary? Maybe because so many of the problems they keep working on

are so routine and arid and so little impelled by the need to know real things that make any difference.[12]

The first two essays in this volume discuss the intellectual development, coherence, and professional context of Bernard Bailyn's work. They examine the corpus of his writing in a systematic way. A few pages are appropriate here, however, concerning certain motifs and interests that have been pervasive throughout Bailyn's career and are essential components of his distinctive signature as a historian—motifs and interests that have directly influenced his students and directly or indirectly the many thousands of professional colleagues, student readers, and members of the general public who enjoy significant and serious books about American history. In the paragraphs that follow we have chosen to italicize certain "key words" that recur with striking regularity in his writing.

Bailyn has long been fascinated by the *transmission of culture* from the Old World to the New: what happened to traditional notions and functions of the family and the school, to churches and to the structure of society when they were transplanted to a new and quite different setting. Second, and closely related, he has increasingly called attention to various manifestations of the transmission process as historical events that are different in character from conventional events such as an election, or an economic depression, or a political rebellion. The latter are *manifest* events, evident to participants and contemporaries. The former he calls *latent events*; and what is most striking about them is that contemporaries may have been only partially aware of them, if at all.

In discussing these *latent events*, and the *transformations* of which they were a part, Bailyn invariably stresses hesitant human responses, such as confusion or inner conflict. Important historical changes often occur even though no one actually seeks them; "unexpected developments" are responsible for "bewildering struggles," social dysfunction or political disjunction. Only gradually and tentatively could people make sense of their new experiences, discern patterns, ascribe meaning, and plan for the future accordingly.[13]

Quite often innovations take place despite the wishes or the intentions of people—most of whom actually prefer stability or inertia to change and the awkwardness of deviating from the norms of tradition. The larger configuration of events has a way of whizzing ahead of anyone's expectations, with *transformational* consequences that are dramatic or profound precisely because they become so comprehensive. Thus the original (1965) title of Bailyn's best-known book, *The Ideological Origins of the American Revolution*, was *The Transforming Radicalism of the American Revolution*. And in *The Peopling of British North America*, one of his most recent works, he refers to the great population movements of early modern times as a "transforming phenomenon":

> the movement of people outward from their original centers of habitation—the centrifugal *Völkerwanderungen* that involved an untraceable multitude of local, small-scale exoduses and colonizations, the continuous creation of new frontiers and ever-widening circumferences, the complex intermingling of peoples in the expanding border areas, and in the end the massive transfer to the Western Hemisphere of people from Africa, from the European mainland, and above all from the Anglo-Celtic offshore islands of Europe, culminating in what Bismarck called "the decisive fact in the modern world," the peopling of the North American continent.[14]

By dint of dealing with transatlantic colonies in various developmental and transformational phases, Bailyn often uses a general framework of *core and periphery*, or metropolitan center and its derivative, primitive, outlying dependencies. He is necessarily a well-informed comparativist, deeply knowledgeable about early modern Europe in general, and about the continent as well as developments in Great Britain. Given his constant preoccupation with transmission, transformation, and historical innovations—both deliberate and inadvertent—Bailyn is very clearly a believer in the distinctiveness of American civilization. Although he rarely, if ever, uses the phrase "American exceptionalism," he repeatedly insists upon the "distinctive characteristics of British North American life."[15] He has argued, in his most widely read works, that the process of social and cultural transmission resulted in peculiarly American patterns of education (in the broadest sense of the word); and he believes in the unique character of the American Revolution.[16]

We repeat: these are not the claims of some parochial chauvinist. American culture is not superior because it is distinctive. Nor does Bailyn deny the absence of any parallels or shared patterns at all. In discussing the anomaly of human callousness on the part of American revolutionaries who struggled for freedom and equality in public life, Bailyn wrote the following, highly representative, passage:

> None of this was unique to America. These were common characteristics of the *ancien régime*, pre-modern in its social concerns and conditions. But while America shared these characteristics of eighteenth-century society, its way of life was unique. The colonists lived in exceptional circumstances and shared a peculiar outlook. Unlike the inhabitants of the British Isles, they were not located at the center of their culture looking outward

toward exotic margins. Their experience was the opposite. They lived on the far periphery looking inward toward a distant and superior metropolitan core from which standards and the sanctioned forms of organized life emanated. They lived in the outback, on the far marchlands, where constraints were loosened and where one had to struggle to maintain the forms of civilized existence.[17]

Bailyn is drawn to historical *anomalies* like a moth to a candle. Or, to alter the image quite radically, one might almost say that when the historian's compass spins wildly out of control, as it so often does, Bailyn seeks to pinpoint *anomalous situations* in order to understand why the compass is whirling so crazily. He has frequently noted the anomalies in eighteenth-century American politics. In scrutinizing the genesis of higher education in the colonies, he saw that subtle and critical elements in "the story of Harvard's origins emerge from the observation of anomalies: that is, of gaps, peculiarities, and inconsistencies which do not explain themselves. To see such anomalies one must start with a picture of what a predictable straight-line development would have been for an informed person at the time."[18]

Bailyn takes particular pains to differentiate between the genuine anomalies that so intrigue him and the historiographical ones that result from the clutter of our modern, disparate scholarly literature. In a book review, for example, Bailyn faulted an author whose book "takes its shape from an anomaly in historians' interpretations rather than in the historical data themselves."[19]

Although Bailyn does not seem to relish the task of book reviewing, and has done less and less of it over the years, his reviews are notable because they invariably call attention to a transcending problem of methodology, or of the state of the literature concerning some significant issue. His review of new biographies of Charles McLean Andrews and Carl Becker provided the pretext for a mini-history of the role of early American stereotypes in American popular culture. His review of a book about the *Annales* school of historians in France became the occasion for a discussion of differences between the public roles of American and French intellectuals. And his review of a new *Historical Atlas of Canada* supplied an opportunity for a succinct discussion of the potential as well as inherent limitations of the historical atlas as a research tool.[20]

Needless to say, Bailyn's own work has been reviewed very widely: usually in a highly positive manner, sometimes in a systematic and dispassionate way,[21] and more recently by occasional critics who have dissented strenuously from his chosen emphases, more particularly

concerning those segments of early American society that have *not* figured prominently in his work.[22] In 1975, when the International Con-
gress of Historical Sciences held its (once-every-five-years) meeting in
San Francisco, Soviet historians of the United States took issue with
Bailyn for what they perceived to be excessively sympathetic treatment
of the Loyalists in the American Revolution (Bailyn's biography of
Thomas Hutchinson had appeared in 1974), and for insufficiently ac-
knowledging socioeconomic conflict as a primary cause of the Revolution.
In its lengthy coverage *The New York Times* reported that "Professor
Bailyn took the criticism equably."[23]

LOOKING BACK as a teacher, Bailyn has said that training Ph.D.
candidates was vastly easier than preparing lectures for undergraduate
courses. Be that as it may, he brought to both levels of instruction an
enthusiasm, an earnestness, and certain enigmatic qualities that made
him a memorable presence in any kind of classroom. His lectures, which
most graduate students attended, were not routinely entertaining, and
they were not exquisitely timed fifty-minute showpieces. They offered
a topical and probing analysis of major issues and problems in seven-
teenth- and eighteenth-century American history, with considerable reference to Europe, and especially to Britain. They were delivered in a
hesitant yet highly articulate manner that left listeners with an awed
sense of being in the presence of intense, almost agonized cerebration
of the most serious sort—agonized because of Bailyn's determination to
rethink old problems and render them intelligible in new ways, a task
that required him to be precise, to say *exactly* what he meant clearly yet
economically.

His reading assignments tended to be archaic, such as volumes one
and two of Edward Channing's *A History of the United States* (1905 and
1908), and we may never know why he didn't give us a peek at some of
the more recent writings of the 1950s and 1960s. Perhaps he mistrusted
the interpretive "stuff" written after World War II, whereas Channing
and Max Farrand just gave us the naked, unencumbered facts. Perhaps.

Taking a research seminar with Bailyn developed into a droll yet
apprehensive guessing game. He made no attempt to supply a syllabus
for purposes of systematic coverage, or to introduce us to the current
essential literature. Instead, each book that we were asked to read and
discuss (some of them fairly exotic) had been selected because it exemplified and provided a springboard for discussing some vital aspect
of the historian's craft—*e.g.*, a book whose very organization defeated
the goal of its argument; or a book whose interpretation simply could

not be persuasively demonstrated because of the type or types of sources used; or a smorgasbord of essays assigned in order to display diverse styles of expository prose by historians—the advantages and especially the *dis*advantages of each style—and the covert ways in which style shapes the communication of substance.*

The anxiety of preparing for a session of Bailyn's seminar lay in the realization that you never *really* knew why you had been asked to read a particular book; and discussions often consisted, in part, of a series of cheerful put-downs on his part, usually deft jabs, such as "So?" or "So what?" or, finally, when he began to explain what he had in mind (with about ten minutes remaining): *"Look!"*[24] Or a more wordy interjection when someone had made an oral presentation based upon his or her research: "How do you get a handle on this material?" Or, referring to a historical problem: "How do we get from Time One to Time Two with this stuff?"

By the end of a graduate course with Bailyn one had learned at least four enduring lessons, and none of them had very much to do with the substance of the past. One learned to read the work of others with a very critical eye. One learned that posing significant historical problems (rather than filling a gap) was the proper point of departure for research. One learned that the presentation of an essay, a dissertation, or a book *must* have two key ingredients: focus and explanatory power. Finally, perhaps some of Bailyn's students decided that the ultimate secret of pedagogical success was: keep 'em guessing. Simply to be perverse? Not at all. Rather, if you don't reveal all, they keep wondering, worrying, and, above all, thinking. "So what?" meant, Dig deeper. And so we did. Or at least we tried.

BERNARD BAILYN is a man who protects his privacy. He also has a playful mind and spirit—often absolutely exuberant—and occasionally he permits a glimpse of the inner, highly opinionated, blithe but controlled spirit beneath the public persona of a Harvard professor. When he was congratulated in 1968 for winning the prestigious Bancroft Prize of $4,000 for *The Ideological Origins of the American Revolution*, he replied

---

*Close readers of Bailyn's own work know that he is partial to metaphors drawn from natural science and technology, such as a satellite or an electronic switchboard, and that he has an affinity for vivid and active modifiers like explosive, hurtling, swirling, propulsive, "a milling factionalism," and "an almost unchartable chaos of competing groups." He particularly favors the word "profound," as in "a profound disorganization of European society in its American setting." It also amuses him to see just how long he can sustain a complex sentence without allowing its syntax to become incorrect in any way. (Or at least, it *used* to amuse him to do so.)

that it was "a nice surprise all around, and a nice bundle of cabbage, too. . . ." In the autumn of 1970, a few months into his tenure as chairman of Harvard's Department of History, he wrote the following to a former student:

> The chairmanship here proves to be a very surprising job. So far I have signed several hundred pieces of paper that Harriet Dorman [for many years the department's administrative "secretary"] has produced and otherwise have served mainly as master of the revels, having, with a fine show of efficiency and administrative verve, arranged one cocktail party and delegated (isn't that what administrators are supposed to do?) two dinners for visiting firemen. I have also rearranged the furniture in the office (Harriet soon put them back again) and told a professor that he could not have another fifth of teaching fellow time (though frankly I could not myself see why not, but I figured that chairmen are supposed to say no to these kinds of things). I am now slowly recovering from this great effort, and am looking forward to the Thanksgiving vacation.[25]

Most of Bernard Bailyn's students were initially captivated by his sheer enthusiasm for history as an intellectual discipline and by early American history because that was the period to work in if one wished to have Bailyn direct one's dissertation. When it came time to "direct," however, he didn't. Or not exactly. He achieved instead a delicate balance between detachment and cordial support. We were left alone to define our own topics and develop suitable strategies for research. We never felt that our work was merely an extension of his own or, worse, a footnote to his own. If we strayed from "focus," he let us know. If we stayed on track, he remained warmly supportive. If we failed to recognize some important implications or aspects of our own work, he made written comments accordingly, and then we were on our own once again.

It is not easy to explain just how or why we feel such a sense of gratitude to a mentor who gave us quite so much autonomy. He edited our work very little, and at times, when we sought advice about professional matters, he could be maddeningly nondirective. We were treated as young yet entirely independent historians. We knew that he was a shrewd perfectionist, that he cared passionately about the quality and intellectual integrity of his own work, and that he cared about the quality of ours —not because it would reflect well or ill upon him, but because our work, like his own, ultimately mattered.

Perhaps the enigmatic aspect of Bernard Bailyn's temperament can best be explained in terms of Thomas Reed Powell's characterization many years ago of a man "who leaned neither to partiality on the one hand nor to impartiality on the other."[26] There has never been a more engaged historian than Bernard Bailyn, nor one any more detached than he. Perhaps that is why he remains one of the most respected and influential scholars of our time.

The Creative Imagination
of Bernard Bailyn

GORDON S. WOOD

I N A RECENT LECTURE entitled "History and the Creative Imagination," Bernard Bailyn has defined the modern creative historian
as someone who has enriched "a whole area of historical investigation by redirecting it from established channels into new directions,
unexplored directions, so that what was once dark, vague, or altogether
unperceived, is suddenly flooded with light, and the possibilities of a
new way of understanding are suddenly revealed."[1] He selected four
twentieth-century historians who he believes have been truly creative in
this way—Perry Miller, Charles McLean Andrews, Sir Lewis Namier,
and Sir Ronald Syme. In their respective fields each of these scholars,
says Bailyn, made a permanent difference in the writing of history. They
did not necessarily write "the most widely read kind of history, the most
commonly cited, or even the most generally admired." What they did
write, however, was the kind of history that "permanently shifted the
direction of historical inquiry not by exhortation or fashionable trend-
setting but by substantive and enduring discovery." Bailyn believes there
are several reasons for the creativity of these four historians.

They were, first of all, old-fashioned professionals, dedicated to the
craft of history-writing and its ways. They were masters of facts, of masses
of information. "All had the capacity to locate, control and absorb very
large quantities of hitherto unused or underused data," and it was their
immersion in this new or freshly examined data that enabled them to

think creatively. They were alert to oddities, to surprises, to discrepancies in the data, and out of their detection of these anomalies they found the sources for their imaginative reconstructions of the past.

All these creative historians had technical skills, of course, and often great narrative powers, but in the end what really distinguishes such historians from many others with longer bibliographies, says Bailyn, is their imaginative power, their "capacity to conceive of a hitherto un-glimpsed world, or of a world only vaguely and imperfectly seen before." Not just to define a new issue here or to uncover a new problem there, but to create of the past "a verifiable world of interconnections, of re-lationships which together add up to a different and better picture of the whole—more comprehensive, deeper, closer to the grain of reality —than had been seen before"—that is the true mark of a great creative historian.[2]

If so, then Bailyn is surely one as well. In fact, Bailyn fully fits his own definition of the modern creative historian. He has made a difference —a permanent difference—in his field of early American history. He has transformed every aspect of the subject he has touched—from the social basis of colonial politics to early American educational history, from the origins of the American Revolution to, it seems likely, early American immigration. Indeed, few if any American historians in the modern era of professional history-writing have dominated their par-ticular subject of specialization to the degree that Bailyn has dominated early American history in the past thirty years.

This would be a notable accomplishment at any time, but more im-pressive is the fact that it has taken place during a period when the subject of colonial history itself has virtually exploded in knowledge and significance. Early American history, Bailyn has recently said, was "once a neatly delimited field of study," but now it seems "boundless." It has come to involve the histories of Western Europe and Africa as well as that of the New World. And the field now includes interesting and ever-proliferating studies by scholars in other disciplines—geographers, economists, econometricians, theologians, philosophers, literary schol-ars, anthropologists, and sociologists.[3] Indeed, so powerful, so extensive, so far-ranging has been this explosion of knowledge of colonial America that only the monographs of hundreds of scholars could account for it. Discoveries in historical scholarship, Bailyn has written, "can at best be only small adjustments in the immense and ever enlarging map of his-torical learning, the whole of which—the old information and the latest discoveries—must be absorbed anew by every historian."[4] Yet Bailyn's discoveries over the past generation, it seems fair to say, have been much more than small adjustments to what we know about the origins of

America. He has in fact redrawn whole sections of the map of our historical knowledge of early American history and has greatly broadened and deepened our understanding of America's colonial past—generating by himself schools of scholarship. And more: at the very moment when many other historians might think of retirement, he has launched an ambitious transnational project involving worlds in motion over two centuries—not simply to tell a story about the origins of America but also to bring under some sort of narrative control the ever-enlarging forces of current scholarship, indeed, nothing less than "the whole world of cultural-anthropological, social structural, and demographic history which lies scattered in hundreds of books and articles written over the past quarter century by scholars in several disciplines pursuing separate paths of inquiry."[5]

Remarkable as Bailyn's achievement has been (and will continue to be), what may be equally remarkable is that we who were his students at the beginning of his career a generation ago already knew the future and predicted the achievement, even saw the seeds, of what has become the gargantuan Peopling of British North America project.

Like others of Bailyn's graduate students, I arrived at Harvard in 1958 with no intention of working in colonial history. I was prepared to study modern European history or modern American history, perhaps diplomatic history—everything and anything but early American history. Like other graduate students, I considered the colonial period of American history to be simply a quaint prologue to the main story, an abridged mishmash of myths and folklore with no historical significance. I thought John Smith and Pocahontas, the Pilgrim Fathers and Squanto, belonged in the story-telling of elementary school where I had last learned about them. For me colonial history meant Chippendale highboys, cobbled streets, and milk-paint houses, not serious historical reality. My undergraduate teacher in the survey in American history had actually skipped through the colonial portion of our Morison and Commager textbook in a week, telling us that the period was not as important as what came after. And Richard Hofstadter's *American Political Tradition*, one of the books I most admired in the 1950s, ignored the century and a half of colonial history altogether and began with an essay on the Founding Fathers. The colonial past did not seem like the rest of America's past, and historians tended to condense and telescope it in strange ways. For example, one of the most popular and authoritative of American history textbooks in the 1950s and early 1960s squeezed into a single paragraph accounts of Bacon's Rebellion in 1676 and the uprising of the Paxton Boys in 1763–64 as incidents of colonial violence. The authors, distinguished historians all, no doubt could not have imagined lumping together for the national period discussions, say, of the Whiskey Rebellion in 1794 and the march of Coxey's Army on Washington in 1894. But apparently they considered time in the colonial period as shorter and more compressible.[6] Although in the 1950s this neglected first half of American history, under the leadership of the Institute of Early American History and Culture and its expertly edited journal, *The William and Mary Quarterly*, was already emerging as the most exciting and lively field in the country, I didn't know that then.[7] In the fall of 1958 I had no interest whatsoever in colonial history and had no desire to take any courses in it.

But I had to take a research seminar, and like other beginning graduate students I sought advice not from the professors but from other graduate students, particularly those only a year ahead of us who were still young and unjaded enough to talk to the graduate students following them. At a Henry Adams Club get-together on the evening before we had to decide our courses, these older, more experienced students enthusiastically advised a group of us to take Bailyn's seminar. We were skeptical: we had never heard of him and had no interest in colonial history. It was true, they said, that Bailyn was relatively new and young, but he had just gotten tenure and was going to be prominent. More important than that, these students told us, Bailyn was exciting: his seminar was like no other, and we would learn something about history, not just early American history, but history.

So about a dozen or more of us, all from different places and with different degrees of preparation, signed up. Unlike most of the other seminars given at Harvard, in Bailyn's seminar we were assigned reading that seemed to have little or no connection to the subject of the seminar, which was colonial politics. We read books on slavery, on colonial cities, on Puritanism; we even read W. B. Weeden's 1890 volumes on the social and economic history of New England—all the time shaking our heads and wondering what on earth did he want us to read this for. We usually found out in the subsequent seminar discussions, which were always intense. Bailyn had a knack for leading those discussions that is not easily duplicated or even described. At times it seemed little more than his being interested in what each of us was saying and then responding with "So?" At any rate, he forced us to draw out the significance or the lack of significance of each of our statements, and in the process we learned about history. Despite all the history courses I had taken as an undergraduate, I had never really known what the discipline of history was about. Bailyn taught us that. He taught us, without actually saying so in so many words, that historical-mindedness was not merely the accumulation of knowledge about the past but, more important, a mode of understanding, a way of perceiving reality.

Indeed, of all the American historians at Harvard Bailyn seemed the most self-conscious about the discipline: self-conscious, however, not in the manner of a philosopher of history, but self-conscious, as he later put it at a 1962 symposium on philosophy and history, in the manner of a "working historian." Unlike Charles Beard and Carl Becker, who in their American Historical Association presidential addresses of the 1930s had excitedly relayed to their mostly inattentive colleagues the latest philosophical relativism and epistemological skepticism coming out of Europe, Bailyn remained cool to the philosophy of history and its concerns. Although at one point as head tutor he arranged for Morton White to talk to all the Harvard history concentrators about the philosophy of history, I don't believe he himself was ever captivated by such lofty matters. Indeed, he has never hidden his deep contempt for historians who have "endless scholastic debates on theory" but do not actually produce any substantive history.[8] His seminar in 1958 suggested to us, as his later comments at the New York University symposium in 1962 made explicit, that historians had little or no need to arrive at precise answers to the questions that enthralled philosophers—"questions of objectivity and subjectivity, the nature of fact, etc."—in order to do their work in history.[9] Instead, in the seminar we concentrated on the more immediate, down-to-earth problems of the working historian —about the nature of historical problems, about good and badly posed historical questions, about the sufficiency of historical proof, about the importance of literary presentation. In the seminar we began to learn about the writing of history. It was an exhilarating experience that I believe none of us, even those who went on to other specializations and periods of history, ever forgot.

Outside of Harvard few as yet knew of Bailyn, so we graduate students did the best we could to spread the word throughout the profession. I recall telling in 1960 a skeptical graduate student from a Midwestern university whom I'd met at the Connecticut Historical Society that he had to read Bailyn's new book on education in early America; but the student shook his head and sniffed at the possibility of anyone's making the subject of education in the colonial period interesting. Already, of course, with Harvard's decision to grant Bailyn tenure—an extraordinarily prescient and uncharacteristically venturous action for Harvard, based as it was on only a slim monograph on the New England merchants in the seventeenth century and several essays—others elsewhere had become curious about this young historian who had gotten a position coveted by some of the brightest luminaries of the profession. I remember a fellow graduate student who had been an undergraduate at Berkeley going home on vacation and having his former teacher, a distinguished professor of colonial history, ask to look at the student's notes from Bailyn's lecture course—no doubt anxious to find out what this upstart from the East was about.

Whatever Harvard's reasons for his appointment, we graduate students were confident of his future achievement. It was not the amount Bailyn had written in 1958, for his publications were as yet meager. It was not his command of technical skills, for he had not yet demonstrated, as he would shortly—in 1959 with the aid of Lotte Bailyn—that he could intelligently use computers, or what were in fact only crude tabulating machines, before most other historians knew what they were.[10] And it was not that he wrote with rare clarity and elegance, for his mature style was not yet revealed. No, it was none of these characteristics that made us in 1958 confident that Bailyn would become a distinguished historian. What gave us confidence, what made us realize that we were witnessing an exceptional historical mind emerging, was his remarkable capacity to imagine and re-create his own cosmos: a transplanted European social order radically transformed by a New World environment.

But it was not just the vastness and elegance of his colonial world that impressed us; that would never have been enough. What really overawed us was the extraordinary way he rooted this world in the hundreds if not thousands of rather ordinary scholarly articles and monographs written over the years, and in ever-increasing numbers in the 1950s, by countless rather plodding colonial American and early modern British historians. We were reading some of these scholarly articles and monographs at the same time we were listening to Bailyn's lectures, and occasionally we could locate the sources from which he had drawn and formulated his material. But it was the fresh and exciting way he transformed all this seemingly trivial and boring scholarship that dazzled and astonished us. Bailyn's imagination created a society that was strikingly different from that portrayed in the monographic historical scholarship of colonial America while at the same time it remained firmly grounded in that scholarship. He had the uncanny ability to reach both high and low at the same time, to bring imaginative life and historical movement into the technical and the often obscure and dreary productions of historical scholarship. He even managed to make his assignments of several volumes of Edward Channing's old-fashioned history seem bearable to us.

Suddenly the colonial period did not appear quaint and parochial any more. Bailyn always tried, sometimes strained, to bring the broadest, most cosmopolitan perspective to bear on what he said—as, for example, in his comparison of the mammoth modern editions of the writings of the Founding Fathers with Theodore Besterman's edition of Voltaire's writings, P. S. Allen's *Letters of Erasmus*, or Mommsen's great editions of

Latin and Greek inscriptions.[11] Always the aim was to lift us out of our parochialism, to acquaint us with the largest possible intellectual world. In fact, as he has suggested in a recent lecture at the German Historical Institute, he sought to pass on to us something of the cosmopolitan perspective that he himself had gotten from "the least parochial people" he has known—the 1930s Jewish exiles from the German-speaking world, some of whom he knew personally through his wife's family.[12]

To us he was a historian's historian, a professional's professional, and we were awed by his dedication to the craft. He did nothing by halves. The editorial expertise and the breadth and depth of annotation and documentation that he brought to the first volume of his edition of *Pamphlets of the American Revolution* rival Julian Boyd's.[13] There was nothing in his chosen field, it seemed, that he did not know about; and if we mentioned to him a book, an article, or a source that he had not heard of, we could be sure he would immediately investigate it. He looked down on historians who worked only with secondary sources and reveled in his involvement in the archives and his command of the concrete details of the past.[14] He had no interest whatsoever in using history as a form of social criticism. Bailyn had nothing but scorn, as he later wrote, for the "self-conscious intellectual posturing" and the "pretentiousness and pomposity" of those, like the French *Annales* historians, who sought to be "intellectuals" instead of working historians.[15] He turned down opportunities to write or review in the popular or intellectual press (as he still does), and he has remained freer of the enticements of the larger society and more committed to the exclusive world of scholarship than any historian of his rank and renown whom I have ever known.

He always seemed to be thinking synthetically, trying to make sense out of what other historians were producing. Bailyn's presidential address to the American Historical Association in 1981 and his Peopling of America project were there at the beginning—waiting to be born. In 1951, while still a graduate student, he wrote a penetrating critique of Fernand Braudel's monumental study *La Méditerranée et le monde méditerranéen à l'époque de Philippe II*. He concluded his review by saying that Braudel's book was not, as Lucien Febvre and others had claimed, "a revolution in historical method but rather a summary in three parts of a large body of knowledge."[16] It was an extraordinary statement for a mere graduate student to make about what others were already calling a European masterpiece, and its audacity still takes the breath away. Despite Bailyn's devastating criticism, however, Braudel's work, which was not translated into English until two decades later, went on to become a worldwide historical classic. As Jack Price in the early 1970s put it to me in his droll way, Bailyn's critical review of Braudel in 1951 apparently had not hurt either man's subsequent career.

Even in this early review of Braudel, Bailyn revealed the breadth of his historical vision and the depth of his historical consciousness—and something of his historical ambition. Already in 1951 he foresaw the "avalanche of specialized monographs" that threatened to overwhelm our ability to write history. Modern historians, said Bailyn, have a "deep need" for a "subtler historiography" than past generations possessed; "they felt more keenly perhaps than Henri Berr the need for new principles of *synthèse*."[17] Already Bailyn had a vision of putting together a world that, unlike Braudel's static three-tiered structure, would be truly historical: where its capacity to make "man's past intelligible" would lie in "its movement, which is to say its life."

Bailyn chose as his historical subject the American colonial past—a seemingly unlikely choice given the nostalgic and trivial character of the colonial period in the minds of many twentieth-century Americans. Still, many of America's greatest historians—from George Bancroft to Carl Becker and Charles Beard—wrote much of their history about early America. The colonial period, wrote Bailyn in 1956, contains "for Americans the roots of the present" and "provides and has long provided basic points of reference for national self-awareness. And not merely for scholars or devotees of history. At each stage of our history, popular attention has demanded and received some vital understanding, however ill-informed, of colonial origins."[18] Bailyn has said that his choice of subject, made when he left the army in June 1946, was particularly dictated by the fact that America's early history was where several different historical developments intersected—where the premodern world became modern and where Europeans became Americans. The colonial period was an ideal area for concentration because, said Bailyn, it is "close enough to the modern world to show palpable continuities between past and present but distant enough for effective historical perspective."[19] As the recent "creative ferment of scholarship" in this period of early modern Western history has shown—"a wealth of research and writing concentrated on a relatively short period of time that is perhaps unique in western historiography"—he could scarcely have selected a more exciting point of conjunction.[20]

Bailyn entered the study of colonial history with an acute sense that his "generation finds its starting point in what it considers to be the limitations of its predecessors' work." Bailyn thought that his predecessors, particularly Charles McLean Andrews, whom he selected as one of his great creative historians, had left out of their early American history both movement and social life. "What is missing from Andrews' image of the past," said Bailyn, "is politics and society. Government is there in abundance, but nowhere in his writings can one find a description of the informal structure by which social groups competed for state power."

Andrews was simply incapable of conceiving of society itself as a legitimate historical subject. To the end of his life Andrews remained convinced, as he said in a posthumously published essay, that social history was either "a sort of chaos of habits and customs, ways of living, dressing, eating, and the performance of duties of existence" without rhyme or reason, or else "social science" concerned not with movement through time but with the laws of human behavior. Consequently, said Bailyn, Andrews's history of formal structures and constitutional and legal institutions, grand and imposing as it was, was "a history limited in depth."[21]

Bailyn began his career with a sensitive understanding of the social sciences and their usefulness for history. In this he was obviously indebted to his mentor, Oscar Handlin, whose exciting and engaging deadpan lectures on the whole of American social history we were listening to at the same time we were hearing Bailyn. Bailyn, like Handlin, clearly saw the constructed nature of both personality and society, and in his lectures and writings he sought to untangle the diverse ways by which society and its structures—whether those of family, the economy, or politics—molded men and events. Society was not something given, taken for granted, but problematic, formed, shaped, developed over time. The colonial period was fascinating precisely because it, unlike any other period of American history, saw the creation of society virtually de novo. Perhaps nothing more distinguishes Bailyn from Charles McLean Andrews and Thomas J. Wertenbaker, or historians of the past half century from their predecessors, than this capacity to conceive of society itself as the central subject of study and analysis. Of course, in the 1920s and 1930s Arthur M. Schlesinger, Sr., and Dixon Ryan Fox had promoted their History of American Life series as social history. But lacking any clear conception of society as a formed and developing entity, many of the authors of the books in the series saw social history, in G. M. Trevelyan's famous words, simply as "the history of a people with the politics left out." Such social history often became little more than descriptions of the daily lives of people in the past, their conditions of work and leisure, the circumstances of their families and households, the forms of their religious and artistic thought, their customs and local folkways—interesting stuff, no doubt, but essentially antiquarian and trivial. Such old-fashioned social history remained peripheral, superficial, without any central theme or coherence.

Only with the increasing borrowing of conceptions from the social sciences were historians eventually able to conceive of social history as the history of society—a history that lay at the heart of their endeavor. Such social history was not an aspect of sociology, as some historians in the mid-1960s still seemed to think.[22] Social history does not try to establish predictive generalizations or any sort of laws of social behavior. Like all history, social history is concerned with particular societies in particular places at particular times in the past. Although social historians and sociologists may both treat society "as an organism, with functionally related parts, with coherent groupings, with structures more essential than formal institutions," they ask different questions and have different purposes.[23] Despite his intimate knowledge of social theory and the pervasive use of sociological conceptions in his work, Bailyn never mixed up what sociologists do with what social historians do; indeed, in his lectures and writings he scrupulously avoided explicit references to all sociological conceptions or terms, and in reading our papers or chapters he was quick to cross out any Parsonsian jargon that might have crept into them. Nevertheless, Bailyn (and Handlin, who for many of us was the only teacher at Harvard who matched Bailyn in imagination and creativity) taught us that society as a structured, functioning, evolving entity was the proper subject of the historian.

Bailyn saw that once society was grasped in this sociological way, then a reappraisal of the whole of early American history became possible. This assumption that society itself was the proper subject of historical study and analysis undergirded all of Bailyn's early work; it was what enabled him to penetrate beneath Andrews's administrative and institutional world into the hurly-burly of social life without at the same time being overwhelmed by the triviality that had pervaded much of the previous work in colonial history. And it allowed him to connect otherwise discrete events and to make generalizations across the seemingly very different colonies. But more: the conception by Bailyn (and other historians) that society was the proper subject of historical study saved the colonial period from collapsing into mere antiquarianism. Even at the beginning Bailyn was keenly aware that what he has recently called "the most venerable structure of Anglo-American history," which was "known in its narrowest form as the 'whig' interpretation" and "which explained the present in terms of an inferior but improving past," had long been "so severely eroded that the turning points and the overall contours of the story have almost entirely disappeared."[24] With its disappearance, society had to become the central organizing principle of historical study in the colonial period—if the period were to have any coherence at all.

No period of American history has benefited more from the rise of modern social history than has the colonial period. For in the colonial period there are few headline political events to hang a narrative line on. There are no presidents, no congresses, no supreme court decisions, no national elections to write about, which is one reason why the colonial period always seemed so mythical and free-floating, so easily telescoped and foreshortened. Yet during the past generation in which modern social history has flourished, this lack of palpable political events and national institutions in the colonial period has become an advantage. The headline events and political institutions that preoccupied historians of the national period were not present to divert the attention of social historians; they were not there to get in the way of long-term analyses of society.

Colonial historians therefore were freer than national historians have been to concentrate on the *longue durée*, on social and cultural developments that extend longer than a few years or even a few decades. It is not surprising that the modern study of American demographic and family history began first in the colonial period (and by a Bailyn student); or that one of the earliest studies of American attitudes toward death concentrated on the colonial period. Historians cannot trace such enduring social and cultural subjects over only a decade or two; they need long stretches of time. Colonial historians, unlike national historians, were used to dealing with long periods of time and thus were more likely to be attracted to the new social and cultural history.

Bailyn himself has not generally been identified with the new social history that arose in the 1960s and 1970s, though many of his students have been. Nevertheless, new social history, or the history of society, was what he (and Oscar Handlin before him) was writing in the 1950s. In his first book Bailyn tried to chart the rise of merchant groups in seventeenth-century New England and to uncover the personal and informal means by which these merchants conducted their activities. Historians, said Bailyn, may have described the commercial system of the seventeenth century in "abstract, geometrical terms," but for people at the time it was "not something impersonal, existing above men's heads, outside their lives, to which they attached themselves for purpose of trade. . . . Trade was the creation of men and . . . the bonds that kept its parts together were the personal relationships existing among them." In his study of the New England merchants Bailyn laid bare an incredibly complicated web of personal and kinship connections tying the Atlantic trading community together.[25]

Bailyn's book was less economic history than it was social history. Throughout he was not as much interested in describing the economic activities of the merchants as in demonstrating the ways these economic activities shaped the character of colonial urban development and the structure of colonial society. Bailyn was especially fascinated by the distinctions that commercial arrangements and governmental connections bred—between cosmopolitan urban entrepôts and backward villages, between privileged insiders and resentful outsiders, between the fashionable and established Samuel Shrimptons and the Puritan and provincial Samuel Sewalls. Society and the persons who composed it were —and still are—the subjects of his scholarship.

The title of his second book—*Education in the Forming of American Society*—more explicitly revealed his understanding of society: as a collective entity that is formed, molded, developed over time.[26] But Bailyn probably best disclosed his conception of the way society could be written about historically in his 1959 article "Politics and Social Structure in Virginia." This essay has been widely republished and cited and became one of the most influential short pieces ever written in American historiography. Underlying the essay and making it possible was Bailyn's understanding of the peculiar organization of social life in the seventeenth century. "All of the settlers in whatever colony presumed a fundamental relationship between social structure and political authority." Authority and superiority of all sorts were indivisible; "there was not one hierarchy for political matters and another for social purposes." Consequently, state and society were identified and thought to be one. For seventeenth-century Englishmen the state "was not an abstraction existing above men's lives, justifying itself in its own terms, taking occasional human embodiment." Rather, Bailyn saw the state, just as he had seen the economy in his study of the merchants, as "indistinguishable from a more general social authority; it was woven into the texture of everyday life."[27] Suddenly Bacon's Rebellion and a number of other events made sense in new ways. Bacon's Rebellion had been previously interpreted as a struggle for liberty by oppressed yeomen, as a forerunner of the American Revolution, as a reaction to the government's limitation on western expansion; but no one before Bailyn had described the rebellion as a response to the ways Virginia's society was maturing and stabilizing in the last quarter of the seventeenth century.[28] Only such a historically sensitive understanding of the peculiarities of early America's social development could make coincident sense of the series of rebellions and insurrections that erupted in most of the colonies during the last quarter of the seventeenth century.

Even his book *The Origins of American Politics* was really social history. In his preface, Bailyn quotes Woodrow Wilson's recollection of going into his colonial history exam "crammed with one or two hundred dates and one or two thousand minute particulars about the quarrels of nobody knows who with an obscure Governor, for nobody knows what. Just think of all that energy wasted! The only comfort is that this mass of information won't long burden me. I shall forget it with great ease." In Bailyn's conception of history as the history of society, however, these minute particulars and obscure quarrels threw off their meaninglessness and triviality; they became the consequences of politics whose history became the history, not of government, but of the ways men have used the instruments of government, "the history of the struggles for authority, hence of the rivalries, factions, and interests that swarmed through and about the agencies of government."[29]

This short book on colonial politics, the culmination of a decade or more of work, rested on Bailyn's long-held assumption that politics was distinct from government and was best understood as society operating upon government. Too often historians had neglected or misunderstood this point and had written their political history as a history of formal governmental institutions or as a history of public transactions or public events. Bailyn's achievement in this book, as it had been in his article on Virgina in the seventeenth century, was to combine society with politics, to penetrate beneath the surface of government and lay bare the underlying social reality that molds political institutions and gives life to public events. Bailyn spends much of the book leading the reader through excavations into what he calls "the substratum of politics," into the "social conditions" that political events on the surface of life only "reflected." Consequently, the reader gets a picture of a structured but dynamic society with depths below depths, each layer more deeply rooted and more fundamental than the other. One of Bailyn's favorite literary devices in this book, as in his earlier work, was to describe some underlying social condition to account for, say, political factionalism, then to go on and write, "but the sources of factionalism lay even deeper than this."[30] Such imagery of probing and digging conveyed a sense of discovery and an explanatory power that no surface narrative, no mere description of the quarrels between the colonial assemblies and obscure governors, could have done. Nevertheless, despite the predominantly social character of this book on colonial politics, its achievement as social history was overshadowed by what many took to be the book's preoccupation with issues of political culture, issues drawn from what has become to date the most famous of Bailyn's works—*The Ideological Origins of the American Revolution*—which was published almost simultaneously with *The Origins of American Politics*.

It is ironic, to say the least, that Bailyn should be best known for this book on ideology and that he should be accounted the leading exponent of the so-called "idealist" or "ideological" interpretation of the American Revolution. The fate of that book—the way it was fed into what came to be called the "republican synthesis," which has been used for present partisan purposes by a variety of scholars and social critics at both ends of the political spectrum—is an object lesson in the unanticipated consequences of purposive action. Bailyn could scarcely have foreseen how his book would be read and used and how he would come to be seen as an exclusively "ideological" or "intellectual" historian. We who were his students in the late 1950s and early '60s can only shake our heads at the wondrous ways of the profession. For the Bailyn we all knew at the beginning was not someone preoccupied with the power of ideas. Far from it. Back then Bailyn seemed to us to be preoccupied with Sir Lewis Namier and with a Namierite approach to reality.

Namier, who is another one of Bailyn's great creative historians, revolutionized history-writing about eighteenth-century English politics. Namier was certainly as important to twentieth-century British historiography as Charles Beard was to twentieth-century American historiography, and he was a far better and more sensitive historian to boot. And Namier's tough-minded view of human nature and social reality makes Beard's seem sentimental and weak by comparison. Namier, like other historians writing in the first part of the twentieth century, was very much influenced by Marx, Freud, and behaviorist psychology. To Namier human reality lay not in men's ideas, in their reasoned statements, in their professed principles and purposes; it lay beneath the surface, in their psyches, in their passions and interests. Ideas—speeches in Parliament, newspaper essays, the pronouncements of political leaders—were not what moved people; they were really only the epiphenomenal consequences, the *ex post facto* rationalizations, of behavior determined by other forces. "What matters most," said Namier in a concise summary of his position, "is the underlying emotion, the music, to which ideas are a mere libretto, often of a very inferior quality." Namier devoted much of his history-writing career to challenging his whig predecessors' tendency to overrate "the importance of the conscious will and purpose in individuals." He urged historians "to ascertain and recognize the deeper irrelevancies and incoherences of human actions, which are not so much directed by reason, as invested by it *ex post facto* with the appearances of logic and rationality."[31] Namier's approach to history tended to squeeze the intellectual content out of what men did. Ideas setting forth principles and purposes for action, said Namier, did not count for much in the movement of history. Ideas were not part of Namier's understanding of "reality."

Bailyn introduced us to Namier in his seminar. Not only did we read some of Namier's work and that of his followers, but the seminar topics that Bailyn suggested for us to work on were infused with Namierism: they dealt with patronage, with interests, with kinship, with personal connections of all sorts in the intimate world of colonial and Anglo-American politics. We were excited. We thought we were getting beneath the formal surface of early American political life into the nitty-gritty of reality where we could see how things actually happened, where having a friend on the Admiralty board in London might be far more important in getting a position in the colonies than any American sources of influence.

In his 1958 seminar Bailyn also had us read Herbert Butterfield's recently published criticism of Namier and the Namier school. In this devastating critique Butterfield showed the static and atomizing limitations of Namier's "structural analysis" and made a plea for "the operative force of ideas" in history and for the need to retain some semblance of old-fashioned narrative if we were to make sense out of the structurally analyzed and microscopic pieces of the past.[32] Despite reading Butterfield's criticism, however, we believed Bailyn's heart still lay with Namier, with "structural analysis," and with "in-depth" social history. We knew that Bailyn was keen on maintaining motion and life in history, but we had little doubt that the book Bailyn was then writing on colonial politics would deal with an underlying social reality and would be filled with Namier-like assumptions and findings, with interests, connections, and patronage—not with the rational purposes, conscious calculations, and reasoned ideas that appeared on the surface of political life in speeches and formal writings. Hence our surprise in 1965 at Bailyn's apparent retreat from hard-boiled Namierism in the attention he gave to ideas in his introduction to the volume of Revolutionary pamphlets.[33]

It is true that in 1960, in a paper presented to the XI International Congress of Historical Sciences, Bailyn had devoted a good deal of attention to the role of ideas in the American Revolution. But despite this attention, Bailyn's treatment of ideas in his paper was very much governed by Namierite assumptions about the separation between ideas and what Namier called a "changing reality." Both Namier and Bailyn in this address to the International Congress, later published in the *American Historical Review* as "Political Experience and Enlightenment Ideas in Eighteenth-Century America," assumed that ideas exist apart from experience, that ideals, forms, and procedures—the mental worlds of people—tend to outlive the conditions that gave rise to them and thereby tend to continue a disembodied existence independent of an underlying dynamic and changing reality. Hence, as Namier put it in one of the best short essays on history ever written, "maladjustment in human affairs is a concomitant of change." History saw an "ever-recurring divergence between fixed ideas and a changing reality." Names and words linger on long after the experience that gave them meaning has been transformed. "Caught in the perennial tangle of names, ideas, and reality," wrote Namier, "man plays with them, and they play with him."

Then at times, "when the burden of the past becomes unbearable," people suddenly seek to bring their ideas into line with their widely divergent reality. These become moments of dramatic change, of revolution.[34]

In his understanding of the relation of ideas to social change, Bailyn was at the same time influenced by the work of another of his creative historians, Perry Miller, especially his *Colony to Province*. Miller, of course, never believed that counting votes or selling fish ever constituted any sort of reality worth writing about. But in his second volume of *The New England Mind*, as Bailyn noted in a perceptive review in 1954, Miller did try to tell the story of the accommodation of Puritan thought to what Bailyn called "the unexpected realities of American life." To narrate this change, said Bailyn, Miller "devised a brilliant technique," which consisted of explaining the inherited intellectual heritage, pointing out its ambiguities and weaknesses, "and then as it were, pouncing upon the precise moment when thinkers, impelled by the changing world about them, blinked their eyes and suddenly saw the familiar thought in a new way." Suddenly for the Puritans, said Bailyn, the glass was half empty instead of half full. Their doctrine remained unchanged, their inherited structure of thought still intact. But in those moments of "altered comprehension" were revealed "the source of changes" that would, "ultimately, determine the total transformation."[35]

In his 1960 paper for the International Congress, Bailyn used to great effect both Namier's and Miller's conceptions of the relation between ideas and experience. They helped him explain what he thought was the apparent paradox between the seriousness with which the American revolutionaries took radical British and European Enlightenment ideas and the lack of any appreciable radical reform during the Revolution. Bailyn resolved the paradox by arguing that most of what the revolutionary leaders "considered to be their greatest achievements during the Revolution—reforms that made America seem to half the world like the veritable heavenly city of the eighteenth-century philosophers —had been matters of fact before they were matters of theory and revolutionary doctrine." American society was radically changed—but not at the moment of Revolution and not by imported European ideals. It was changed "by the mundane exigencies" of the colonists' experience over the previous century and a half. The American colonists in their political, social, and religious lives had been forced, not by any adherence to ideas and principles but "by the circumstances of life in a wilderness environment," to deviate gradually from their inherited ideas and from their English and European norms. "Major attributes of enlightened polities," wrote Bailyn, "had developed naturally, spontaneously, early in the history of the American colonies, and they existed as simple matters of social and political fact on the eve of the Revolution." "Behavior had changed—had had to change—with the circumstances of everyday life; but habits of mind and the sense of rightness lagged behind." What the Revolution—and its Enlightenment ideals—did was catch up with the experience; it explained, justified, symbolized, formalized, and legitimated these social and political matters of fact—this "changing reality"—that had developed over the previous century and a half. "The glass was half full, not half empty."[36]

It was a dazzling performance—to compress so much in a six- or seven-thousand-word essay—and its central thrust was undeniably powerful: not only did it account for a growing body of post–World War II historical writing and nicely fit Bailyn's (and Handlin's) conception of America emerging out of a European confrontation with a wilderness environment; it was at the same time able to maintain the radical significance of the American Revolution—even if the Revolution had now become essentially an affair of the mind, "more than elsewhere . . . a matter of doctrine, ideas, and comprehension."[37] Despite Bailyn's stress on the importance of ideas in the Revolution, his essay, like his earlier review of Miller's book, still presumed in a Namier-like fashion that hard reality—the real stuff of life—lay not in the colonists' minds at the moment of revolution but in their shared experience over the previous century and a half. Only with his subsequent work on the pamphlets of the Revolution did that presumption begin to change.

Bailyn says he began his study of the revolutionary pamphlets as "a divergence" from his investigation of colonial politics.[38] Howard Mumford Jones, then editor in chief of the John Harvard Library, invited him to prepare a collection of pamphlets of the American Revolution for publication in that series. Bailyn did not think the project would be particularly burdensome, and it was related to his continuing study of colonial politics. Thus at the outset he had little inkling of either the magnitude or the momentous implications of what he was getting into. His interpretation of the pamphlets, initially published in 1965 as an introduction to the first volume of the pamphlets and later enlarged and published in 1967 as the *Ideological Origins* book, eventually infused and transformed not only his understanding of colonial politics but as well his reputation and position in the field of early American history. From that moment on he became identified as the leader of the "ideological" school of historians who were presumably averse to a socioeconomic interpretation of the Revolution and who stressed the conservative nature of the Revolution.

Bailyn himself, it is true, supplied some basis for this label. In his preface he wrote that "study of the pamphlets confirmed my rather old-fashioned view that the American Revolution was above else an ideological, constitutional, political struggle and not primarily a controversy between social groups undertaken to force changes in the organization of the society or the economy."[39] Not that Bailyn wanted to be identified with the so-called "consensus" school of historians of the 1950s, who had denied that eighteenth-century Americans had had a revolution at all and who had interpreted what happened as an essentially conservative movement to preserve American democracy and rights from a fumbling if not tyrannical British imperial government. Bailyn never thought that the Revolution was simply a colonial rebellion: there was too much evidence that the revolutionaries themselves thought they were involved in a real revolution, that they were introducing a new era in human affairs, and that they took deliberate steps to reshape institutions in light of the most advanced Enlightenment ideas. By 1965 Bailyn began to find even more radicalism in the Revolution than he had in 1960, but again it seemed largely confined to the realm of ideas.

More than his International Congress address of 1960, Bailyn's general introduction to his volume of pamphlets emphasized the dynamic and transforming character of the Revolution; indeed, he entitled his introduction "The Transforming Radicalism of the American Revolution." "In no obvious sense," he wrote, "was the American Revolution undertaken as a social revolution. No one, that is, deliberately worked for the destruction or even the substantial alteration of the order of society as it had been known." Yet, said Bailyn, the social order was transformed—not through the confiscation and redistribution of loyalist property or through economic dislocations, but through "changes in the realm of belief and attitude," in "the views men held toward the relationships that bound them to each other. . . ."[40] Again, whatever was radical about the Revolution was confined to the mind or to some future time. Bailyn seemed extremely reluctant to admit that the Revolution might have had social sources or that the revolutionaries in 1776 might actually have worked to alter substantially the order of society as it had been known.

In the book, published two years after the introduction, Bailyn further stressed his belief that, however radical the leaders of the revolutionary movement were, "they were eighteenth-century radicals concerned, like the eighteenth-century English radicals, not with the need to recast the social order nor with the problems of economic inequality and the injustices of stratified societies but with the need to purify a corrupt constitution and fight off the apparent growth of prerogative power." In his 1973 essay "Central Themes of the American Revolution," Bailyn continued to underline his conviction that "the Revolution was not the result of social discontent, or of economic disturbances, or of rising misery, or of those mysterious social strains that seem to beguile the imaginations of historians straining to find peculiar predispositions to upheaval." And in his 1975 paper for the XIV International Congress of Historical Sciences, he was as thorough and as explicit as he has ever been in his denial that the Revolution originated "in social and economic dislocations and in the strivings of deprived segments of the population to improve the condition of their lives," or that it intended in any way to change the Americans' social order.[41] The Revolution seemed to have sprung from people's minds and to have had little or nothing to do with the society.

Bailyn says he began his exploration of the intellectual world of the revolutionaries without a "fascination with ideas as such" and without "an *a priori* assumption that beliefs and ideas are the prime movers of history."[42] But as he became increasingly preoccupied with the colonists' political culture, Bailyn seemed to take less and less interest in the underlying social conditions, the social substrata, that earlier he had thought were the principal sources explaining political and intellectual events on the surface of life. More and more, in fact, he applied his geological imagery of subterranean layers not to the society but to the culture, to the structure of thought and ideas. It was almost as if he had chosen to write what J. G. A. Pocock referred to, in relation to his own investigations into "the concepts, assumptions, and languages" of politics, as "a Namierism of the history of ideas."[43] Bailyn now posited layers below layers, depths below depths, in people's thoughts and ideas. Repeatedly he referred to "the underlying motivations and mood," the "deep-lying sense," the "substratum of belief," the "deep-lying implications," and drew distinctions between the surface and substance of ideas, the foreground and deep background of people's minds, the vocabulary and grammar of thought, the dominant mood and the undercurrents of the culture.[44] These metaphors of layers, as Jack Rakove has pointed out, were more often than not eclipsed by images of "territorial exploration," with ideas pressing against or penetrating the "boundaries" and "frontiers" of conventional thought, which better suited Bailyn's eventual identification of people's "middle-level beliefs and ideas," their ideology, with what the cultural anthropologist Clifford Geertz called "maps of problematic social reality." Ultimately the colonists' ideology—their values, beliefs, and attitudes, not their social conditions, not their social circumstances—was what Bailyn "understood to have lain at the heart of the Revolutionary outbreak and to have shaped its outcome and consequences."[45]

It has been an extraordinary development in American historiography. Here was a historian who began his career, indeed, defined his relationship to his predecessors, by becoming a historian not of ideas, not of politics, not of economics, but a historian of society—the only kind of historian, it seemed in 1958, one could or ought to be. Yet in his interpretation of the greatest event in the period of his interest—indeed, the greatest event of all American history—he has been apparently unwilling to entertain any sort of social interpretation of the Revolution, any sort of explanation that concentrates on underlying social conditions, on the social substratum. Although Bailyn had never accepted a crude Namierite or behaviorist view that ideas were only epiphenomenal rationalizations for events shaped by other forces, nevertheless in his early work he had often implied that the most important springs of action lay in the social circumstances of people. The Boston merchants, for example, who backed Anne Hutchinson in the Antinomian controversy of 1636–37 "with striking uniformity" were not simply responding to her theology. So too the rebellion of 1689 in Massachusetts "divided the northern merchants on lines not of ideology but of interests defined by the degree of proximity to officialdom." And the participants in Bacon's Rebellion may have talked about unfair land-distribution and Indian pressures, "but behind these issues lay deeper elements related to resistance against the maturing shape of a new social order."[46]

Although these references to "interests" and "deeper elements" in Bailyn's early work actually resemble "those mysterious social strains" that he later expressed so much contempt for, Bailyn's involvement in the revolutionary pamphlets apparently made him less willing than he had been to probe beneath the surface of events and ideas in order to uncover underlying social conditions more determinative of what happened. Since his discovery of ideology, Bailyn has repeatedly denied that the Revolution had social origins and social impulses and has gone out of his way to refute those historians who have tried to find any.

Bailyn's apparent aversion to entertaining any social interpretation of the Revolution, despite his commitment to being a social historian, has confused and troubled even some of his former students, not to mention others in the profession. The explanation of this aversion is not easy. Bailyn has said that his view that the primary cause of the Revolution lay in the ideology of the Americans is no more "intellectual" or "idealist" than "locating the origins of World War II in the fear and hatred of Nazism."[47] If that is indeed the case, if that is all he meant by his elaborate description of the revolutionaries' political culture and his statements that this political culture lay at the heart of the Revolution and shaped its character and consequences, then all the controversy over *The Ideo-*

logical Origins has been a tempest in a teapot. For at the high level of generality suggested by his analogy, no one could quarrel with his argument about the origins of the Revolution, any more than anyone could quarrel with his statement about the origins of World War II lying in the fear and hatred of Nazism.

But Bailyn seems to have meant more than what is implied by his comparison of the Revolution with World War II; for in both cases his general statement about people's beliefs being at the heart of what happened in no way precludes other, more deeply lying social explanations. Just as social historians might agree with his statement about the origins of World War II without believing that such a general statement prevents them from positing more specific, more fundamental, and more socially based explanations for the war, so might Bailyn have easily entertained social explanations of the Revolution that were fully compatible with his interpretation of the revolutionaries' political culture. But for several reasons Bailyn seems to have developed a particular antipathy to social interpretations of the Revolution.

Part of the explanation surely lies in the changed scholarly atmosphere of the 1960s, with its hermeneutic challenge to both a Parsonsian functionalism and a Marxism that had made culture seem to be merely a crude reflection of social structure. A sensitive historian would have to have been living in a capsule not to have been affected to some degree by the heightened scholarly emphasis on language, ideology, and symbolic action that has taken place in all disciplines since 1960.

No doubt too, part of the explanation for Bailyn's aversion to any social interpretation of the coming of the Revolution lies in his deeply felt conviction, expressed as early as his 1960 paper presented to the International Congress of Historical Sciences, that the substantial changes in American society had already occurred in the course of the previous century and a half of colonial history and that the Revolution was in a sense only an intellectual catching-up with the new American social circumstances. Only some version of this view could give the colonial period the great importance and relevance in the whole story of America's development that Bailyn believes it deserves.

But there seems to be more to Bailyn's uneasiness with social interpretations of the Revolution than these considerations. A more important part of the explanation has to do with his view of the peculiar way ideas oscillated throughout the entire revolutionary period. He believes that in the pre-revolutionary period the ideology of Americans—their ideas, fears, and hopes—had a special potency and explosiveness, an "intellectual dynamism," that not only brought on the Revolution but had a contagious effect on American attitudes toward slavery, religion, and the traditional social order. All the impassioned events of the years leading up to the Declaration of Independence, including even changes in social relationships, he says, can be best understood in ideological terms, in terms of "belief and attitude."[48] In the decades following 1776, however, conditions changed, and "the approach that allowed one to understand the main events of the earlier years no longer serves for the later: a different kind of analysis and a different focus are required." The ideological passions of the pre-revolutionary years "slowly filtered through the ordinary activities of life" and were cooled. "Ordinary life reasserted itself and cultural, sectional, and social differences . . . became important." Ideas lost their potency. "In the 1780s and 1790s the essential themes of American history became more complicated than they had been in the years before 1776, and they cannot be understood in essentially ideological terms." Somehow "the inner lives of people's minds, beliefs, and sensibilities" no longer counted as much as they had earlier.[49]

Bailyn's notion that ideas are ascendent and important at particular ideologically exciting times in the past—until social conditions reassert themselves—suggests a kind of seesawing up-and-down fluctuation between ideology and social behavior that, I believe, does violence to the full reality of human action. What Jack Rakove has called "the classic antinomies of historiography"—interests and ideas, base and superstructure, society and culture—are artificially if not falsely posed.[50] Ideas and social circumstances are not polarities and can never be mutually exclusive. Even Geertz, who has sought to construct an independent science of symbolic action and whom Bailyn quotes approvingly in his "Central Themes" essay, has never really been able to insist intelligibly that ideology and cultural symbols are by themselves constitutive of persons, structures, and events.[51] Although historians for practical or heuristic purposes may choose to emphasize either one or the other in their writing, both consciousness and social conditions are always equally important constituents of human action and reality. Hegel and Marx were both right.[52] Indeed, not only does every moment in human affairs, however ordinary, placid, and cool, involve both ideas and social forces, but moments of ideological passion, like those of pre-revolutionary America when the colonists were struggling to find new meanings to explain or justify what was happening, are precisely those moments when social conditions are most dynamic and turbulent—most in need of being made meaningful by the historical participants. So the very excitement and exhilaration of the colonists' ideology in the years leading up to the Revolution are the best indicators that something interesting and momentous was occurring in the society. At the same time, however, it is clear that ideology can never be construed simply as a reflection of the social structure.

Yet it is not only Bailyn's belief that the pre-revolutionary period can be best, if not exclusively, understood in ideological terms that has made him averse to social explanations of the Revolution. It is also the way the historiographical polemics over the Revolution have evolved during the past several decades that helps explain his reluctance to consider any social interpretation of the Revolution.

Not that Bailyn is concerned merely with defending what some might call his turf within the profession as the leader of the so-called "ideological" school. Bailyn has a longer and grander view of the past, and his role in interpreting it, than any such narrowly self-interested professional concern suggests. Yet there is no doubt that the historiographical polemics have affected Bailyn's unwillingness to entertain social explanations of the Revolution. The manner in which the conflicting sides of the historical debate over the American Revolution have developed in the twentieth century makes it difficult for any historian sensitive to the differentness of the past and to the nature of the discipline to concede much to the "social" explanation of the Revolution, because any such explanation is likely to be identified with what has been called the "neo-Progressive" interpretation of the Revolution. And, for very good reasons, Bailyn finds this interpretation very wrongheaded.

Bailyn's antipathy to the neo-Progressive interpretation does not stem from personal or political conservatism, or from any lack of sympathy with the present strivings of blacks, women, or any other deprived persons who seek to better their condition. His antipathy comes rather from a deeply felt belief that this interpretation is essentially unhistorical: it violates the historian's central concern for the authenticity of the past, and it breeds anachronism—what Marc Bloch called "the most unpardonable of sins" that a historian can commit.[53]

Bailyn, of course, is fully aware of the present's need to relate to the past and of the power of this need in stimulating historical inquiry and writing. "There is always," he writes, "a need to extract from the past some kind of bearing on contemporary problems, some message, commentary, or instruction to the writer's age, and to see reflected in the past familiar aspects of the present." But without "critical control," this need, says Bailyn, "generates an obvious kind of presentism, which at its worst becomes indoctrination by historical example." Unfortunately, says Bailyn, too much of the historical search for social and economic roots and purposes in the revolutionary movement is presentist; it reflects "the assumption that the impulses to revolution in eighteenth-century America must in some way have been analogous to impulses that account for modern social protests and social revolutions." These present-minded historians have brought to the study of the Revolution many of the concerns of modern life—"concerns involving race relations, inequitable wealth distribution, impoverishment, social discontent, mass protest, malevolent economic policies, oligarchical political systems." No doubt, says Bailyn, their historical writing has enriched our understanding of colonial life in a multitude of ways, "but the neo-Progressive purposes that empower and shape much of this writing—to portray the origins and goals of the Revolution as in some significant measure expressions of a peculiar economic malaise or of the social protests and aspirations of an impoverished or threatened mass population—have not been fulfilled." These purposes have not been fulfilled because, says Bailyn, they attempt "to answer what Lucien Febvre . . . called 'une question mal posée.'" They are essentially anachronistic; they are based on a modern conception of what causes a revolution. This neo-Progressive writing is "oriented to the present at least in the issues it recognizes if not in the problems it formulates and the conclusions it reaches. . . . It arises from an instinct to find unity and continuity in American life," to find something familiar in the eighteenth-century origins of the nation.[54]

Bailyn recognizes that this is not an unworthy instinct. Indeed, the use of "origins" in several of his titles expresses a desire to find some continuity between then and now. When pushed too far, however, this desire to find continuity and connections between the past and the present results in what English-speaking historians commonly call "whiggism"—the anachronistic foreshortening that makes the past a mere anticipation of our present.[55] Despite his own wish to find continuity between the colonial period and the rest of American history, Bailyn has run little risk of writing whiggish history. In some cases the titles of his books alone have had to bear the enormous burden of bridging the distance between lost and unfamiliar colonial worlds and the familiar worlds of later American history.

His book *The Origins of American Politics*, for example, seems to be about everything but those origins, as he himself admits in the preface. The colonists' political system in the mideighteenth century had "no climax in the state and national party politics of later periods of American history. There is, consequently, no obvious eventuality to point to, and as a result no self-evident, pre-established principle of relevance for the historian to bring to his work. . . . The story of politics in the colonial period is not that of a distinct evolution toward the modern world: the evidences of growing modernity are delusive." Thus, instead of describing the roots of modern American democratic politics where organized political parties compete for votes among a large and relatively egalitarian electorate, Bailyn's book re-creates a peculiar political world of grinding factional conflict in which narrow and shifting oligarchies tied together by family or patronage struggled for power in a variety of political arenas. We know what he means by his use of "origins" in the title—that this American political world was different from the eighteenth-century English political world and in that difference lay the sources of a future American politics.[56] But those sources are oblique and distant, to say the least. Despite the reference to "origins," therefore, the emphasis in that book, and in all of Bailyn's work, is on the disparities between then and now, between past and present, not on the continuities.

Bailyn has always known that what is crucial for historical understanding is an acute sensitivity to the strangeness and differentness of the past. The unforgivable flaw of the early-twentieth-century historians of education, he wrote in his *Education in the Forming of American Society*, was their assumption about the nature of history. For these historians "the past was simply the present writ small. It differed from the present in the magnitudes and arrangement of its elements, not in their character." Historians with such an assumption about history inevitably fall into anachronism or whiggism. Historians of this sort, said Bailyn, have "no capacity for surprise." They lack what should be instinctive to a historian—the belief that the world we currently live in—its institutions, its ideas, its social forms—may not have existed at all for people in the past, may "in fact have been inconceivable to them."[57]

Therefore, to be a creative historian, Bailyn suggests, is to emphasize the differences between then and now and to exploit those differences in an imaginative re-creation of a lost past world. Bailyn has in fact been criticized for being too good a creative historian. In his book *The Ideological Origins* "the Revolution," it has been said, "appears as an episode essentially of the eighteenth century, devoid of subsequent significance."[58] Although this charge is scarcely accurate for *The Ideological Origins*, it is true that Bailyn has sometimes recently carried his passion for the pastness of the past almost to the point of embracing antiquarianism. In a commentary on a 1984 collection of historical writings on seventeenth-century New England, Bailyn praised the essays in the volume precisely because they were "nostalgic, backward looking—and correctly so," for they had recaptured "the stance the people of the time took to the greater world." They were "contextualist essays, in their approach the very opposite of that optimistic whiggism that refers events to eventualities and that therefore can never contain surprises." Even the word "frontier" in discussing the early American settlements is to be avoided, "for 'frontier' implies an advance toward a goal, a positive march forward, a leap ahead." Indeed, it suggests a movement toward a future American society of self-sufficient frontiersmen and thus anachronistically distorts the actual meaning that the seventeenth-century settlements had for the colonists living not on such a "frontier" but on the far outer periphery of the British-Atlantic world.[59]

Yet this fervor for "contextualist" history, this desire to describe the past only in its own terms, when carried too far can indeed undermine the historian's ultimate obligation, which is after all to explain how that unfamiliar past grew into a future world none of the historical partici- pants intended or anticipated. Bailyn of course is aware of the problem and understands that "the very possibility of historical explanation lies in the differences between the perspective and range of knowledge of participants and those of the historian."[60] Nevertheless, in his desire to escape from the present-centeredness of much recent historical writing he seems at times reluctant to admit that the past he describes had a future at all. So in his analysis of the debates over the Constitution he goes out of his way to stress the pragmatic conservatism of the Federalists. In designing and defending the Constitution, the Federalists, he says, "had no intention of creating new ways of thinking"; they only wanted to take older inherited ideas and where necessary rephrase, reinterpret, and reapply them to new circumstances. "They would have been aston- ished to hear that they were discarding one paradigm—something called civic humanism or republicanism—and creating another—something called liberalism. They could not have conceived of the distinction."[61]

All this may be true enough, and given the ways recent historians have distorted the past for the sake of the present—have unsubtly and un- critically imposed on the past paradigms and categories of their own creation—Bailyn's contextualism, his emphasis on what past actors ac- tually thought and intended, is a healthy antidote, to say the least. But to stress only the pastness of the Federalists, only their intentions, only what they knew and could have conceived of, is ultimately to evade the historian's responsibility to connect the past with what came after. The historian needs to recover not just past meaning but also the future significance of that meaning, not just past intentions but also the un- anticipated future consequences of those intentions. The Federalists may not have intended to create new ways of thinking (though even that is arguable), but, intentionally or not, they certainly contributed to new ways of thinking about government and politics. No American in 1787–88 set about to create something that modern scholars call "lib- eralism," but nonetheless a liberal democratic world soon emerged as a consequence at least in part of what Americans in 1787–88 did and thought.

For a historian to describe the ways in which the future was created by the ideas and actions of the past does not necessarily have to lead to sloppy anachronistic present-centered history. It is a question of degree, of getting the balance right, of properly locating one's historical account on the spectrum between extreme whiggism on the one hand and extreme antiquarianism on the other. Bailyn realizes that these "differences of approach" between present-minded and past-minded historians "may at times be narrow, mere shadings of emphasis; but they can also be gross."[62] And for him grossness is what is at present palpable in American historiography: so often and so crudely have recent historians shaped their explanations of the past in direct response to the issues and values of our own time that he has concluded that a good historian cannot err too much on the side of past-minded history. One can hardly blame him—not when some engaged historians (his own students, no less) have criticized his work for being too exquisitely attuned "to the temper of an earlier time" and thus for failing, "finally, to address the dilemmas of its own day." His desire to re-create the past authentically is said to be "politically charged" because, *mirabile dictu*, it "gives priority to the beliefs of historical actors" over our present beliefs, "thus inhibiting a critical dialogue between past and present values." With presentism so blatantly blowing in the wind, it is not surprising that Bailyn wants to hunker down and cling as tightly as possible to historical contextualism.[63]

All four of the historians Bailyn selected as creative—Miller, Andrews, Namier, and Syme—are contextualists; that is, all "sought to understand the past in its own terms: to relocate events, the meaning of documents, the motivations of historical actors in their original historical sockets." All directed their greatest suspicions and vigilance at anachronism. All were excited by the differences between past and present, not the similarities. And all were sensitive to "the time-bound limits that circumscribed the knowledge, understanding, and range of action of figures in the past."[64]

Only through such contextualist history, Bailyn suggests, are we able to approach what he calls the "ultimate stage of maturity in historical interpretation where partisanship is left behind, where the historian can find equal humanity in all the participants, the winners and the losers. . . ."[65] By the early 1970s Bailyn thought that such a stage of maturity had been reached in our interpretation of the American Revolution. And therefore he thought we were ready finally to understand the principal victims and losers of the Revolution—the loyalists.

His 1974 study of the most important loyalist of them all, Thomas Hutchinson, was designed to probe "the origins of the Revolution as experienced by the losers, and thereby restore, in some small degree, the wholeness of that event." *The Ordeal of Thomas Hutchinson* is in my opinion the most elegant and artful of Bailyn's works, yet it aroused the most controversy and was the one most bitterly received. It was published at a passionate moment in American life, and it was regarded even by some of Bailyn's own students as a apology for the "establishment" and even for the Nixon administration. In 1975 I heard one otherwise sensible scholar argue in all seriousness that Hutchinson was really Richard Nixon and the Hutchinson letters whose public exposure helped destroy Hutchinson were really the Nixon tapes. Bailyn in his preface tried to dispel any suggestion that his book was a tract for the times—emphasizing that "the structure and substance of the book, and the issues it discusses, developed from considerations of Hutchinson's time, not of our own"—but he soon came to realize that the effort, at least for some readers, had been futile.

No doubt there is truth in the charge that Bailyn's book defends Hutchinson. It meant to do that; it intended to make clear why a sensible and well-informed person could have opposed the Revolution. It deliberately set out to look at the Revolution from the point of view of "the most important loyalist of all" in order to make "the story whole and comprehensible."[66] It is an extraordinarily sympathetic study. To be sure, Bailyn ultimately stresses the limitations of Hutchinson's thought—his inability in the end to comprehend the aroused moral passions and idealistic aspirations of the revolutionaries—but throughout the book he portrays a man who understood better than his contemporaries what was happening. Hutchinson, in his "Dialogue between an American and a European Englishman" (1768), said Bailyn, "anticipates with remarkable clarity the ultimate drift of opposition thought. . . . Above all, he saw more clearly than any writer of the time that persistence in the claims of a moral basis for resistance must end in revolution—a revolution that history might justify if it succeeded, but not because it was in an objective sense more moral than the establishment it overthrew. For the relationship between law and morality, he saw, was ambiguous, and only success could be a final arbiter."[67]

The drama of Bailyn's book lies in Hutchinson's struggle with the circumstances impinging on and limiting him, circumstances that he understood better than his contemporaries but never sufficiently, never fully enough, for him to overcome them. It was ironic therefore that critics should have thought that *The Ordeal of Thomas Hutchinson* was a tract for the times. For Bailyn believed that his Hutchinson book was the least whiggish of his books, the least concerned with the origins and issues of the present. The understanding and the compassion he was able to show for Hutchinson flowed from the ultimate stage of maturity that he believed the historical literature on the American Revolution had reached. "At this point," he wrote, "the distance has become so great, the connections so finely attenuated, that all of the earlier assumptions of relevance, partisan in their nature, seem crude, and fall away, and in their place there comes a neutrality, a comprehensiveness, and a breadth of sympathy lacking in earlier interpretations." At this ultimate stage of interpretation the historian is no longer a partisan. "He has no stake in the outcome. He can now embrace the whole of the event, see it from all sides. What impresses him most are the latent limitations within which everyone involved was obliged to act; the inescapable boundaries of action; the blindness of the actors—in a word, the tragedy of the event."[68]

No one has more succinctly described the character of history as a humanistic discipline. To have a sense of the tragedy of life, to have neutrality, comprehensiveness, and breadth of sympathy for people in the past, to understand their blindness and folly, to see the extent to which they were caught up in circumstances over which they had little control and yet struggled against those circumstances, and to realize the degree to which they created results they never intended—to understand all this is to have a historical sense.[69]

Bailyn's more recent work likewise reflects a heightened awareness of the underlying social conditions in the past that circumscribed and shaped people's lives, and it shows an increased sensitivity to the complicated ways in which people in the aggregate bring about results that no single one of them ever intended. "We are all Marxists," Bailyn said in his 1981 presidential address to the American Historical Association, "in the sense of assuming that history is profoundly shaped by underlying economic or 'materialist' configurations and by people's responses to them"; though he adds that "few of us are Marxists in the doctrinal sense of believing that these forces and these responses alone are sufficient to explain the course of human affairs."[70] In his Peopling of British North America project he has returned to social history with a vengeance and has reminded us that he is still the social historian he always was.[71]

Because of the extraordinary discoveries of the new social and quantitative history during the past several decades, Bailyn has become more than ever mindful of the presence in the past of what he calls "latent events" that conditioned and set boundaries to what people did. These latent events were "events that contemporaries were not fully or clearly aware of, at times were not aware of at all, events that they did not consciously struggle over, however much they might have been forced unwittingly to grapple with their consequences, and events that were not recorded as events in the documentation of the time." Modern social history with its new statistical and quantitative capacities is discovering large-scale aggregate patterns—demographic movements, economic series, family cycles—that few contemporaries, or even later historians, ever knew existed. Indeed, so profuse and complicated have the findings of modern social history become that the earlier confidence that society itself could be the subject of historical study has been shaken. "Studies of aspects of 'society' in the past—classes, estates, communities, families—have now so increased that the subject, even within that definition, seems to be beyond comprehensive control." The only way we historians can now view these "large-scale systems of events operating over various areas" is to enlarge our perspective. Even a bird's-eye view will no longer do: "to see the whole of the entire set of interrelated systems that impinged on preindustrial America one would have to circle the globe like a satellite," which is one perspective Bailyn has used in his Peopling project.[72]

From such a high altitude it would be very easy to fall into the pathetic mood of Fernand Braudel that sees the individual "imprisoned within a destiny in which he himself has little hand, fixed in a landscape in which the infinite perspectives of the long term stretch into the distances both behind him and before."[73] And much of Bailyn's introduction to his Peopling of British North America project offers just such high-level descriptions of the patterns of population migration or the workings of labor markets in which nameless aggregates of people were moved by forces no one of them understood. But Bailyn has no intention of confining himself to such a Braudelian perspective, which tends to drain all movement and life out of history. " 'Peopling,' " he says, "means motion, process, evolution in time, but it is not abstract: it concentrates on individuals and their fortunes."[74] What he wants to do in his history is relate and combine these large-scale impersonal latent events with what he calls "manifest events," that is, "events that contemporaries were clearly aware of, that were matters of conscious concern, were consciously struggled over, were, so to speak, headline events in their own time even if their causes and their underlying determinants were buried below the level of contemporaries' understanding."[75] The goal of history-writing, says Bailyn, is not to separate out and isolate these events of different dimensions, these manifest and latent events, but rather to bring them together and integrate them in a developing story in much the way Ronald Syme did in his *Roman Revolution*—a book which Bailyn says he has "gone back to time and again," and which he considers "a master demonstration of what can be done in combining analysis and narrative."[76] For Bailyn, "the essence and drama of history lie precisely in the active and continuous relationship between the underlying conditions that set the boundaries of human existence and the everyday problems with which people consciously struggle."[77] George Eliot or Thomas Hardy or Henry James could not have described better what they were doing in their novels.

Such tragic history is not the sort of present-centered, instrumentalist history that many American historians want to write, which is the source of much of their quarrel with Bailyn's work. Those historians view history exclusively through the categories and values of the present and seek to use it directly to solve our present problems. They want history to empower people, to help them develop self-identity, to enable them to break free of the past. They do not want to hear about the unusability and pastness of the past or about the latent limitations within which people in the past were obliged to act. They do not want to hear about the blindness of people in the past or about the inescapable boundaries of their actions. Such a history has no immediate utility and is apt to remind us of our own powerlessness, of our own inability to control events and predict the future. And it is the future that these historians are primarily concerned with, even some of those who are interested in the differentness of the past. Many who today call themselves historians are not really historians at all. To be sure, some of them investigate "the past as a foreign country," but they do so primarily as anthropologists or social critics, seeing in the strange ideas and behavior of past peoples either alternatives to or object lessons for a present they find oppressive and objectionable. "Their vision of the past turns them toward the future," wrote Nietzsche of such make-believe historians; they "hope that justice will yet come and happiness is behind the mountain they are climbing. . . . They do not know how unhistorical their thought and actions are in spite of all their history."[78]

But a historical sense, the tragic sense that Bailyn talked about in the Hutchinson book, is not for climbing mountains and controlling the future. Unlike sociology, political science, psychology, and the other social sciences, which try to breed confidence in managing the future, the discipline of history tends to inculcate skepticism about people's ability to order their destinies at will. History that reveals the utter differentness and discontinuity of the past tends to undermine that crude instrumental and presentist use of the past that Americans especially have been prone to. And history that shows that the best-laid plans of people in the past often went awry and that most people struggled against forces which they never clearly understood and over which they had little control tends to dampen that naïve conquer-the-future spirit that Americans above all other peoples possess. All of which explains why Americans, despite their enormous investment in exploiting the past, are notorious for their lack of a historical sense.[79]

At the same time, however, such a historical or tragic sense need not be deterministic or fatalistic. It does not deny the individual's responsibility for his or her actions; indeed, by making people aware of the circumstances impinging on and limiting them it makes true freedom and moral choice—and wisdom—possible. And, as Bailyn's recent work shows, it is not necessarily pessimistic.

In fact, in Bailyn's latest book, *Voyagers to the West*, the moving and inspiring tone with which he concluded *The Ideological Origins of the American Revolution* is back, stronger than ever. *Voyagers to the West*, as more than one reviewer has pointed out, exuberantly pays tribute to the dynamism and exceptionalism of America, its freedom and promise, its enterprise and boundlessness. The book is a *tour de force* of historical presentation—combining between two covers five different methods of presentation: descriptive exposition, quantitative tabulation, structural analysis, graphic representation, and narratives of selected individuals and families. In the expository, statistical, and analytical sections of the book, Bailyn tries to keep his satellite-like distance in his descriptions of the structural circumstances and of the latent events in which the historical participants struggled. But in the micro-narratives encompassing nearly half the book, Bailyn comes down to earth and gets remarkably close to the manifest events in the lives of some ordinary and not-so-ordinary migrants.

In these detailed accounts of the fortunes of particular individuals and families, it becomes clear that Bailyn did not write this volume as if he had "no stake in the outcome" of the history it presents. Indeed, in *Voyagers to the West* Bailyn sounds more like his mentor Oscar Handlin than ever before—indeed, even going beyond Handlin at times in unalloyed celebration of the uniqueness of America and the aspirations of the people who came to it. "The colonists," says Bailyn, "lived in exceptional circumstances and shared a peculiar outlook." They inhabited a strange borderland world "looking inward toward a distant and superior metropolitan core from which standards and the sanctioned forms of organized life emanated."[80] Yet, unlike Handlin in *his* early immigrant studies, Bailyn does not focus on what, in reference to those studies, he has elsewhere described as the "subjective experience of people uprooted from their origins, tossed about in a tumult of disorienting transitions, and settled into awkward, bewildering, often despairing communities in which hope was transferred from the present to future generations."[81] Although *Voyagers to the West* describes some spectacular failures among the migrants, Bailyn's emphasis overall is not on their bewilderment and despair over what was lost but on their hopefulness and excitement over what was gained. They came, he says, by the tens of thousands, to "an open country, full of promise," to "that loose, ill-organized, world on the margin of European civilization," to a new society "far less intricate, structured, and continuously interactive than the one they left behind, but one that allowed them autonomy," "a more open world" befitting

their "expansive energies, a world where difficulties could be bypassed
. . . and where the imagination was released." Colonial America, Bailyn
concludes, was "a risky world where one lived not in a dense and elaborately nuanced human environment . . . but in a loose, still forming
society where it was possible to proceed alone, free of encrusted burdens
and ancient obligations."[82]

Reviewers have criticized Bailyn's celebration of American exceptionalism and risk-taking enterprise in *Voyagers to the West* because such a
celebration seems to make America "the culture of reference for the rest
of the world" and to be ungenerous toward other peoples shoved out
of the way or left behind in the scramble for success. In particular, it
seems to concentrate on "the experience of independent white men . . .
the ambitious, self-improving winners" in the story, and to slight "the
inherently circumscribed lives of middle-class women, encrusted with
the burdens of families and children, and those of slaves and indentured
servants, trapped within new forms of ancient systems of obligation."[83]
But not only is such criticism essentially anachronistic—asking the past
why it cannot be more like the present—but it also inverts the proportions of the story. What is significant in the context of the middle and
late eighteenth century that Bailyn is describing is not that many people,
including African-American slaves and nearly all women, remained burdened and trapped within traditional systems of obligation, but that so
many others, even though only white males, were eager and able to seek
and find release and independence from those burdens and obligations.
The achievements of many white males in the late-eighteenth-century
Atlantic world in fact made possible the eventual strivings of others for
their freedom, independence, and prosperity. There is nothing ethno-
centric or teleologically inevitable about this story; as events in our own
time make only too obvious, it has to be one of the great achievements
of world history.

As Bailyn suggests, the eighteenth-century Anglo-American world by
no means took freedom and personal independence for granted; many
people, including many white males, were still unfree and dependent,
and the colonists, like Englishmen in general, "remained remarkably
insensitive to the human consequences of deprivation"—deprivation of
all sorts, including chattel slavery. Yet fundamental social movements,
like the migrations of tens of thousands of people, were changing all
that. Indeed, it seems evident, though the connections in the book are
as yet indirect, that Bailyn's *Voyagers to the West* actually suggests some
of the groundwork for what eventually could become a sophisticated
social explanation of the origins of the American Revolution—an upheaval based not on the class-ridden nature and the oppressive strength
of the *ancien régime* but rather on its increasing weakness and openness.

Not that Bailyn's voyagers of the 1770s became themselves revolutionaries or in any direct sense were involved in the Revolution; indeed, many of his migrants became loyalists. But their migrations were often symptomatic of the same kinds of social forces that lay behind the Revolution. There were many people in the Anglo-American world of the late eighteenth century who were willing to risk all, even their lives, for the opportunity to get rich and live free and independent. But their willingness "to forsake a known present for an unknown future" was not based on poverty or on any sense of hopelessness. Quite the contrary: for reasons that historians have still not made entirely clear, the prospects of ordinary people in the late-eighteenth-century Anglo-American world —in fact, in the entire Western world—were higher, their expectations more aroused, their hopes for the future more promising than at any time in history, so much so that all traditional obligations inevitably came to seem burdensome and arbitrary and all changes in their lives threatening and frightening, for they could not really know what the future held for them.[84]

Those Highland tenant farmers from Sutherland County, Scotland, who left for the New World in the early 1770s—and who are described by Bailyn in loving detail—were by no means poor and desperate people; indeed, they were composed of "some of the most secure small farmers" and were led by some of "the most prominent" tenants-in-chief of the region. Although these farmers were suffering economic distress, they were not impoverished; and despite charges that their landlords were like "Egyptian taskmasters," they must have known, says Bailyn, that the major landlords were "responsible, concerned, and conscientious." Indeed, so free of the Scottish landlords' paternalistic control had the tenants become that the landlords' belated efforts to reinstate traditional personal services were naturally resisted as "arbitrary." It was the same with other changes in their lives—rent increases, grain shortages, decreases in the prices of their produce: the tenant farmers found themselves "caught up in changes they could not control, changes that, by any sensible projection into the future, threatened to debase their settled way of life." So these Scottish farmers, "experienced people not likely to abandon security for delusive dreams," suffering "not present ruin but the fear of future deprivation," risked what they had, which was substantial, and took off for an unknown future in the New World— leaving those who stayed behind confused and puzzled by their apparent "madness."[85]

The same puzzlement would be felt, the same charges of madness would be made, about those colonists who participated in the American Revolution. What, it was asked in 1776 and after, could ever have possessed the American people—as prosperous and free as any in history—to engage in what the bewildered loyalists described as "the most wanton and unnatural rebellion that ever existed"?[86] But is it not possible that many eighteenth-century Americans, experiencing, like those Highland Scots, disruptions in their lives and changes they could not fully comprehend or control, were likewise willing to pull up their substantial stakes in settled communities and set off, as they did, in treks of hundreds and even thousands of miles—to Vermont, to Maine, to North Carolina, to the Mississippi Delta—to better their prospects; or, more startling still, when the occasion arose in 1775 were even willing to engage the greatest power in the world in a long and bloody war in order to protect and further the opportunities this New World offered to them and their children of being free and independent? We will have to await the subsequent volumes of the mammoth Peopling of America project to see how the story turns out. One can glimpse, however, out of the rich particularities of this largest and most thoroughly documented of the works of this distinguished and imaginative historian just how the social and ideological sides of his *oeuvre* might at last be brought together and made whole.[87]

"How Else Could It End?"

BERNARD BAILYN AND THE PROBLEM

OF AUTHORITY IN EARLY AMERICA

JACK N. RAKOVE

T HERE ARE FEW historians whose collected works are less amenable to ready summary than those of Bernard Bailyn. The problem is not merely that his writings range over the entire landscape of early American history, nor even that the divergent approaches he has pursued in his books and essays make it impossible to categorize him simply as an economic or political or intellectual historian. The greater difficulty stems from Bailyn's conception of the historian's enterprise and his fascination with solving highly specific problems of research. "True historical problems," Bailyn once wrote, are those that arise from "questions raised by the observation of (1) anomalies in the existing data, or (2) discrepancies between data and existing explanations."[1] Nothing better demonstrates the undiminished force of his commitment to monographic history and the solution of the "technical" problems it entails than the extraordinary research evident in *Voyagers to the West*, his most recent (and notably his longest) book.[2] At a point in one's career when most scholars would venture to write little more than reflective restatements of previous work (whether their own or others'), Bailyn has embarked on a major project of staggering dimensions. In this sense, then, a proper evaluation of Bernard Bailyn's historical scholarship should assess each of his works on its own terms as a solution to a particular puzzle.

Yet his contribution to historical scholarship obviously amounts to more than the sum of the puzzling "anomalies" and "discrepancies" he has examined. For Bailyn has never been content to solve a problem on its own terms without also attempting to derive more evocative or suggestive insights that would somehow link the immediate subject to some larger context. From the start of his career, and in virtually all his writings—essays as well as books—Bailyn has sought to find meanings that carry his interpretations well beyond the immediate bounds of the narrative.[3] *The New England Merchants in the Seventeenth Century*[4] does not merely describe the growth of a commercial economy in that region; it also offers a powerful critique of the concept of class as it had often been applied to the structure of colonial society. Or again, *The Ordeal of Thomas Hutchinson*[5] not only explains how Hutchinson's astute grasp of the issues of the Anglo-American controversy led ineluctably to the very catastrophe he hoped to prevent; it also proposes a powerful model of the psychology of Loyalism—a model drawn not from facile readings in contemporary theory but rather from Bailyn's immersion in the evidentiary record of Hutchinson's own turmoil.

Even Bailyn's lesser works and essays—and one uses the adjective advisedly—have exerted significant influence over the entire field of early American history. What other introduction to an annotated bibliography has had the seminal impact of *Education in the Forming of American Society*?[6] What other essay has provided a more suggestive synthesis than "Politics and Social Structure in Virginia," which by one authoritative survey has been reprinted at least seventeen times?[7] Even the highly technical study (with Lotte Bailyn) of *Massachusetts Shipping, 1697–1714*[8] holds a special place in the annals of quantitative history for its pioneering use of the counter-sorter.

The one place where Bailyn is at his most suggestive is, of course, *The Ideological Origins of the American Revolution*,[9] his best-known and most influential work. The impact that this book has had on the historiography of the Revolution and, indeed, of American politics from the late colonial period to the Civil War, needs little elaboration here. In his discovery of the colonists' prior absorption of the political ideas of English radical whigs, Bailyn provided a powerful explanation of the concerns that impelled them to interpret British actions after 1765 in the most sinister light possible. More than that, *The Ideological Origins* allowed other historians—beginning most notably with the concurrent work of Bailyn's student Gordon S. Wood—to reconstruct and recover an entirely new range of meanings in the constitutional experiments of the Revolutionary era and the party conflicts of the early national period (and beyond). Finally, by deploying the social scientists' concept of ideology to mediate the longstanding conflict between historians who regarded formal ideas as sufficient explanations of behavior and those who saw them as "only epiphenomenal, superstructural," Bailyn set an exemplary precedent that numerous historians have followed since.[10] (All this was the outgrowth of an editorial project that began, Bailyn tells us, "as a divergence" from a projected study of colonial politics.)[11]

Yet in a curious way, the very success of *The Ideological Origins* has made it more, not less difficult to assess its place in the Bailyn *oeuvre*, or even to perceive the larger argument of the book as a whole. There is nothing especially surprising about this: every author learns that readers can always use and abuse a text in unanticipated ways, or that even sympathetic critics will attribute to it meanings one never intended to convey. Something of this fate has afflicted Bailyn's preeminent work. Many of the scholarly disputes it helped to foster have moved well beyond the arguments that Bailyn actually offered while ignoring some of its most important elements. References to *The Ideological Origins* have acquired something of a perfunctory character, typically taking the form of an introductory note lining up the usual "neorepublican" suspects.[12]

Released from the historiographical pigeonholes in which it has been confined, Bailyn's interpretation of the Revolution can be seen as the centerpiece of a broader and more complex argument about the development of American society from the first settlements to its "swift emergence as a distinctive society in the early nineteenth century." Within this larger context, the specific explanation of the coming of independence reveals only one facet of Bailyn's interpretation of the Revolution—and by his own, perhaps understated account, arguably not the most important. The ideological interpretation, Bailyn has observed, "merely explains why at a particular time the colonists rebelled and establishes the point of departure for the constructive efforts that followed." The deeper significance of the Revolution rests elsewhere: in its challenge to received assumptions about the nature of authority and the relation between society and the state; on the occasion it provided for Americans to "complete, formalize, systematize, and symbolize" developments that had already taken place during the previous century and a half of colonization; on the way in which it "molded permanent characteristics of the culture that would develop within" the new republic it created.[13]

The central issue, then, was authority, not independence. The crucial problem is stated in the final paragraphs of *The Ideological Origins*, where Bailyn allows the Loyalist critique of the Revolution to bring his own interpretation of the meaning of that event to its powerful and moving conclusion. What the opponents of independence ultimately feared, Bailyn argues, was not only the cost of separation from Britain but the "harvests of licentiousness" that must inevitably flow from the subversive challenge the Revolution posed to all established authority. "How else could it end?" Bailyn has the Loyalists ask.

> What reasonable social and political order could conceivably be built and maintained where authority was questioned before it was obeyed, where social differences were considered to be incidental rather than essential to community order, and where superiority, suspect in principle, was not allowed to concentrate in the hands of the few but was scattered broadly through the populace?

Explaining how this situation came to pass—why established authority had grown so weak in colonial *and* Revolutionary America, and more important, how the revolutionaries "found in the defiance of traditional order the firmest of all grounds for their hope for a freer life"—is the great issue that Bailyn's writings collectively and cumulatively strive to resolve.[14] The concluding question of *The Ideological Origins* thus states the one sustaining theme that best enables us to view Bailyn's work as a whole, to see how approaches to seemingly discrete historical problems build upon one another, and to identify the recurring motifs and organizing principles of the remarkable enterprise that is Bernard Bailyn's contribution to the study of early American history.

THE STARTING POINT for Bailyn's own analysis of the critical transition in the structure of authority in early America can be readily described. At the outset of colonization, Bailyn noted in his essay "Politics and Social Structure in Virginia," all of the settlers "presumed a fundamental relationship between social structure and political authority. Drawing on a common medieval heritage" that took the hierarchical ordering of society as a given, "they assumed that superiority was indivisible; there was not one hierarchy for political matters, another for social purposes." The local gentry thus embodied the public authority of the state in the most vivid manner: "the state was not an abstraction existing above men's lives, justifying itself in its own terms"; rather, "it was indistinguishable from a more general social authority; it was woven into the texture of everyday life." This image of the unitary character of traditional authority—of the received "assumption that superiority was indivisible, that social eminence and political influence had a natural affinity to each other"—recurs in key passages elsewhere in Bailyn's work. And it was also revealingly echoed in the oft-quoted passage in *Education in the Forming of American Society* where Bailyn portrayed the traditional family as being so closely integrated with the larger community "that it was at times difficult for the child to know where the family left off and the greater society began." The discipline learned within family and community "introduced the youth in a most significant way to a further discipline, that of government and the state."[15]

The anomaly or transformation that Bailyn seeks to explain obviously involves the erosion of this traditional conception of authority and the establishment of a new order where "authority was questioned before it was obeyed." But this change in the very character of authority has two distinct aspects. The first and more conspicuous centers on the nature of leadership in American society and the conditions that first undermined the habits of deference that were so vital a feature of aristocratic regimes and then encouraged the revolutionaries to abandon the ideal of a mixed regime of fixed social orders for the more modern and realistic sociology that we associate with James Madison. But this sapping of the status and power of elites finds a parallel in the weakening of the authority of the state itself, in its inability to define and advance transcendent notions of the public good distinct from those sought by particular interests within the society. It is this transformation that Bailyn also evokes, though often in allusive terms, to suggest how the events of the Revolutionary era marked both a culmination and realization of tendencies rooted in the colonial past, and an explosive transition that shaped the emergence of the open and democratic society of the nineteenth century. And, further, it is this emphasis on the altered character of the state that enables us to see just how closely Bailyn's work should be linked with that of his own teacher, Oscar Handlin, and especially with the classic monograph (written with Mary Handlin) *Commonwealth*.[16] The liberal state of the Handlins' *Commonwealth* is the distant objective which lies just over the horizon of Bailyn's own explorations in the history of the long struggle between liberty and power.

Between these two very general poles of traditional authority and the emerging liberal state there lies, of course, an enormous space within which one can imagine numerous lines of historical development to be traced. (And, indeed, it was to identify just how many lines deserved exploration that the Handlins wrote *The Dimensions of Liberty*, their brilliantly synoptic overview of the history of liberty in America.)[17] But the paths that Bailyn has followed in his own analysis are clearly marked, and so, too, are the vantage points where he has paused en route to sketch the most salient features of the landscape he has observed.[18]

The first axis of exploration—and the one that most closely links Bailyn's writings from *The New England Merchants in the Seventeenth Century* to *The Ordeal of Thomas Hutchinson*—centers on the character of the provincial elites that had coalesced in the colonies by the early eighteenth century and their role in the politics of the Anglo-American empire. A second line of inquiry, pursued only briefly but leading nonetheless to some provocative observations, describes the pressures that certain conditions of settlement—especially denominationalism—placed upon the role of the state. A third ascending path allows Bailyn to view the ground the colonists had previously covered from the heights to which the Revolution unexpectedly led them. From this vantage point Bailyn surveys the broad sweep of early American history to point out prominent features of the colonial environment whose significance the colonists had ignored in their provincial eagerness to cast their gaze back over the water to England. And while "the details of this new world were not as yet clearly depicted,"[19] the general shape that American attitudes, ideas, and institutions would henceforth take were all, in Bailyn's view, deeply affected both by the exhilaration of the Revolutionary climb and, as potentially dangerous heights were reached, by the growing caution that led the more careful (like James Madison) to look for exposed ledges, loose boulders, and slippery handholds.

A metaphor that sets Madison to climbing any mountain other than Jefferson's Monticello has obviously been indulged too long.[20] What do these general lines of inquiry contribute to our substantive understanding of Bailyn's work?

The principal way stations in Bailyn's mapping of the elites of colonial America are easily plotted. In *The New England Merchants* and in the brilliantly synthetic essay "Politics and Social Structure in Virginia," Bailyn traced the emergence over several generations of the groupings of merchant and planter families who constituted the upper classes of their respective regions. Both studies end with the formation by the late seventeenth century of creole elites whose "social character" reflected local circumstances of settlement and economic interests, but whose political authority now lay vulnerable to the externally imposed demands of an empire "whose purposes were obscure, whose direction could neither be consistently influenced nor accurately plotted, and whose human embodiments were alien and antagonistic." Although a measure of stability was restored after the various risings and rebellions of the 1670s and 1680s, Bailyn concludes,

> the divergence between social and political leadership at the topmost level created an area of permanent conflict. The political and social structures that emerged were by European standards strangely shaped. Everywhere as the bonds of empire drew tighter the meaning of the state was changing. Herein lay the origins of a new political system.[21]

The intellectual elision between "the origins of a new political system" and *The Origins of American Politics* is hard to ignore.

In *The Origins of American Politics*, Bailyn moved ahead in time to examine this "area of permanent conflict" between imperial officials and creole elites as it operated in the age of Walpole and Newcastle. In large part, of course, these three lectures served to establish an evidentiary foundation for the central argument of *The Ideological Origins.* By explaining how the radical whig ideas that influenced American resistance so decisively *after* 1765 had been absorbed intact in the colonies much earlier, Bailyn also sought to blunt the predictable objection that revolutionary ideology was no less manipulable than the inflated claims of rights that the Progressive historians had dismissed as so much propaganda. But again, Bailyn's analysis of the weakness of authority is closely linked to his explanation of the "brittleness" of colonial politics.

The conflicts of the eighteenth century took the familiar form of struggles between executive prerogative and legislative privilege, driven by the inability of colonial governors to buttress their exaggerated claims of formal powers with the practical tools of influence that were the stuff of Georgian politics in England. But constitutional disputes were, in one sense, merely the occasion of controversies rooted in what Bailyn calls "the social substratum of politics." The deepest layers of instability that Bailyn ultimately uncovers lie at the level of fundamental differences in "the nature of leadership" and, "deeper even than this," in "the role of government in society." In Britain the whig aristocracy was so "successful" in its rule, so manifestly endowed with the natural advantages that "wealth, education, and leisure" were presumed to bestow, that its conduct as a governing class only "perpetuated and reinforced the ancient assumption, still very much alive in the eighteenth century, that superiority should be unitary, that leadership in politics should fall to the leaders of society." And the preservation of its rule was further enhanced, Bailyn concludes, by the "very restricted role" that contemporaries expected government to play in society—especially in the wake of the settlement of the great constitutional and religious controversies of the preceding century.[22]

Far different, Bailyn argues, was the situation in America. In certain colonies, provincial elites did attain something of the unquestioned social superiority that the whig aristocracy "at home" enjoyed as a matter of course. But elsewhere "the identity of the natural political leaders was seldom beyond contest." Competition among aspiring families was sharpened by the intrusive presence of imperial officials who could whet but never slake the political ambitions of the upper level of colonial society. But leadership was unstable for a more fundamental reason. The development of new regions of settlement, "the openness of the economy," and the instability of such "groupings" of interest as did exist made it impossible "to re-create in America the kind of stable interest politics" that operated to such effect in Britain. And this newness turned decisions that would have been regarded as routine and noncontroversial in Britain into sources of bitter public dispute and private rivalry in America. The active role that government itself played in the development of the economy and in the organization of public institutions made its own decisions "a source of conflict" and thus "tended to intensify controversies that otherwise existed."[23]

A few of those who opposed particular exercises of state power found themselves driven, Bailyn concludes, "toward a mode of understanding altogether new, altogether modern"—toward both the "interest group theory of politics" that James Madison would propound in the Tenth *Federalist* and acceptance of the legitimacy of opposition to government. In this movement Bailyn attributes special importance to William Livingston. Implicit in the arguments with which Livingston opposed the chartering of an Anglican college in New York during the 1750s lay the recognition "that there was no impartial interest of the state that stood above the conflicts of ordinary interests; that the state itself did not exist other than as a faction or party in the everyday competition of power." The colonists had first perceived the alien character of the state in the imposition of imperial authority external to their own society; but now some were coming to sense that what was problematic was the role of the state itself, rather than the personification of its power in particular governors and their cliques.[24]

This appeal to a Madisonian conception of politics might suggest that Bailyn equates the "origins of American politics" with the acceptance of a pluralist conception of the state. But in the concluding pages of *The Origins of American Politics*, he draws back from this formulation—which runs at least a mild risk of anachronism—to emphasize instead the "latently revolutionary" character of the ingrained fears of ministerial power that would finally detonate after 1765. Taken by itself, the existence of an "area of permanent conflict" between local elites and imperial officials was not a sufficient condition of revolution. As Bailyn noted elsewhere,

> The Anglo-American political community could have continued to function "dysfunctionally" for ages untold if certain problems had not arisen which were handled clumsily by an insensitive ministry supported by a political population frozen in glacial complacency, and if those problems had not stirred up the intense ideological sensibilities of the American people.[25]

How those ideological sensibilities were inflamed to forge a "logic of rebellion" was the great subject of the first half of *The Ideological Origins of the American Revolution*. But arguably it was in *The Ordeal of Thomas Hutchinson* that Bailyn brought his analysis of the problem of authority in colonial America to its critical conclusion—and with an explanatory power and narrative detail that in some ways exceed the relevant but highly compressed concluding chapters of *The Ideological Origins*.

Bailyn's Hutchinson embodies everything an American aristocracy had become—and might long have remained—had the empire held to its happily "dysfunctional" course. As the most celebrated descendant of a family which offers "almost an ideal type" of Bailyn's seventeenth-century New England merchants, he personified both the potentialities and the limitations of the colonial elite.[26] By securing for himself and his endogamous family the fruits of access to the Anglo-American political world, Hutchinson had mastered, as well as any colonist could hope to master, the challenge that his forebears faced when "the bonds of empire drew tighter." In this success he represented—as well as any colonist could represent—the traditional fusion of political and social authority: distinguished public servant and wealthy merchant, a man equally attentive to the good of New England and the empire. And the coexistence of these loyalties, Bailyn suggests, further allowed Hutchinson to view the issues dividing Britain and American with an objectivity that few of his contemporaries attained.[27] At the same time, Hutchinson's career exemplified recurrent motifs in Anglo-American politics. The fierce jealousy to which he and his clan were exposed at bottom differed little from the resentment that Nathaniel Bacon and his allies had directed against Governor William Berkeley and his circle in Virginia a century earlier; the problems that Hutchinson encountered in unruly Massachusetts mirrored the embarrassments that had beset countless other colonial governors in earlier decades.

Yet for all this, as avatar of a colonial aristocracy Hutchinson remains more than a little manqué. His success was the success of a provincial bourgeois whose innate prudence, calculation, and restraint precluded his attaining that ease of command which is the mark of traditional superiority. Hutchinson could never be at home in the world of the whig aristocracy so brilliantly captured in David Cecil's *Melbourne*. However much he identified with the demands and benefits of empire, he remained a New Englander to the bone—and never more pathetically so than when his exile in England forced him to measure the personal cost of his loyalty.

Some historians have questioned how well Bailyn's account of Hutchinson's individual failure explains the general phenomenon of Loyalism, or whether he succeeds in treating the winners and losers of the Revolution with the mature objectivity he has claimed—the implication being that Hutchinson gets off too easily, or is depicted too favorably. On the first of these counts, Bailyn seems well aware of the risk he has run when he alludes to the "essential if rather elusive characteristic, or set of characteristics" that, in his view, gave a degree of (one might say) ideological unity to a movement whose sources were otherwise diverse.[28] But the second reservation is ill founded. For notwithstanding all the virtues that Hutchinson is shown to possess, his inadequacies remain, in the end, more potent and historically more important than his strengths.

It is even more important to recognize, however, just how vital, indeed necessary a place *The Ordeal of Thomas Hutchinson* occupies in Bailyn's overall interpretation of the Revolution, not only because that story would indeed be incomplete without it, but also because of the multiple ways in which Bailyn uses Hutchinson to illustrate, personify, and finally symbolize the meaning of that struggle. At the most obvious level, it is easiest to link Hutchinson to the sequence of events that drove "the logic of rebellion" described in *The Ideological Origins* to its conclusion. Viewed from this angle, Hutchinson appears as the arch-conspirator whose acts of betrayal provided the proverbial smoking pistols that agitators like Samuel Adams needed to sway public opinion to the side of resistance. Because Massachusetts played so central a role in the politics of resistance, and Hutchinson so critical a role in Massachusetts, it is almost impossible to imagine how one could explain the Revolution without him. So, too, Hutchinson's career perfectly illustrates the anomalies of the Anglo-American empire that Bailyn analyzed in *The Origins of American Politics*: the difficulty of using patronage to build governing coalitions, the lack of consistent or informed guidance from London, the continual problem of maintaining influential connections "at home."

But one has to look further to explain why this biography has such exceptional power. In using Hutchinson to personify the fate of authority in late colonial America, Bailyn emphasizes the two liabilities that made him the "preeminent victim" of the Revolution: the enormous personal hatred he engendered, and his simple incapacity to perceive or comprehend, much less master, the deepest sources of the abuse to which he was subjected. In accounting for these dual failings, Bailyn presents an argument that transcends the specifically political aspects of Hutchinson's career to evoke more fundamental sources of weakness in the structure of authority in early America.

Not by chance does Bailyn give John Adams the first word in both the opening pages of the biography, which ask why Hutchinson was so despised, and the epilogue, which diagnoses the critical defect of character that led to his doom. For suspicion and hatred of Hutchinson had been "ruling passions" of Adams's life for fifteen years, Bailyn notes, after which they were merely "obsessive." It is easy enough to locate Adams's fears in the bitterness of the struggling attorney resenting the appointment of the untrained Hutchinson to the chief-justiceship, but as early as his 1962 essay reviewing "Butterfield's Adams," Bailyn suggested that a force more elemental was at work. Adams's hatred of Hutchinson "flowed," Bailyn wrote, "from his general resentment of the unassailable social superiority that existed in the world he was seeking to conquer." What these two representative protagonists of the opposing sides of the Revolution shared, Bailyn implies, was in many ways more striking than the extreme differences in their politics. Bailyn presents both as products of a culture still Puritan, in its residual asceticism if not its formal religious beliefs. Hutchinson's response to a visit to the country estate of Lord Hardwicke "is almost interchangeable with . . . John Adams's response to wealth and elegance." Perhaps most notably, the constitution which Adams wrote for Massachusetts "exhibited to perfection the ideal of balance achieved through the independence and separation of powers which, in an older context, Hutchinson had struggled to retain."[29] Why, then, did hatred and suspicion of Hutchinson become Adams's "ruling passions"?

What Hutchinson represented to Adams was an authority that seemed arbitrary simply because it was authority. Differences in ambition or social position are not what distinguish the two men, but rather the differences in attitude and temperament that flowed from the particular stations they occupied in provincial life. And this, in turn, is what enables Bailyn to isolate "the elusive characteristic" which best explains why "so prudent, experienced, and intelligent a man" as Thomas Hutchinson could neither comprehend nor control the forces arrayed against him. In the final analysis, Bailyn argues, Hutchinson failed because his ingrained acceptance of traditional notions of dependence and superiority left him incapable of understanding the raw resentment that all forms of superiority inspired among those, like Adams, who felt that their own path to advancement lay barred not by the higher merit of others but by arbitrary distribution of mere ascriptive privilege. The resentment that established hierarchies evoke among newcomers and outsiders lay entirely beyond Hutchinson's ken.

> Committed to small, prudential gains through an intricate, closely calibrated world of status, deference, and degree—the Anglo-American political world of privilege and patronage and of limited, arbitrary access—he could not respond to the

aroused moral passion and the optimistic and idealist impulses that gripped the minds of the Revolutionaries and that led them to condemn as corrupt and oppressive the whole system by which their world was governed. . . . [H]e did not sense the burdens of the system within which he lived so deeply, nor the frustration it engendered in those who lived outside or at the margins of its boundaries, nor the moral indignation it could provoke.

It was this lack of imagination and empathy—far more than differences of principle or even interest—that led Hutchinson and others like him to underestimate the source and intensity of the forces arrayed against them, and thus to pursue courses of action which inflamed rather than quelled the suspicions that led the colonists from resistance to revolution.[30]

In each of these ways, then, Hutchinson provides a fitting conclusion for major themes in Bailyn's earlier writings on colonial elites and Anglo-American politics. But even this does not exhaust the interpretive uses to which his career may be put. For it is through Hutchinson that Bailyn restates and elaborates the great question that brings *The Ideological Origins* to its conclusion—*viz.*, "what reasonable social and political order could conceivably be built and maintained where authority was questioned before it was obeyed?"

Far more than Thomas Bradbury Chandler or Jonathan Boucher or Daniel Leonard—the leading Loyalist writers upon whom Bailyn drew in the last section of *The Ideological Origins*—it was Hutchinson who most clearly grasped the intellectual challenge posed by the arguments of the Revolutionary leaders, even as he failed to comprehend "the moral indignation and meliorist aspirations" from which those arguments had taken rise. "Within his own terms of reference," Bailyn observes,

within his own assumptions—which were ordinary assumptions of the age taken to a high degree of refinement—his arguments were irrefutable: which is why ultimately they became the revolutionaries' chief target. They mark the boundaries of traditional thought, and they therefore establish the point of departure for what became, to posterity, the innovative and creative thought of the time.

And again, Bailyn notes, Hutchinson's reconstruction of the contending positions (especially in his "Dialogue between an American and a European Englishman") is remarkable not only for its fairness to both sides or the cogency of its defense of ministerial policy, "but because it goes beyond all of the immediate controversies to the outer boundaries of the issues involved, elevating the discussion to a level of universality that was unique for its time"—most notably in moving beyond the ostensible issue of parliamentary jurisdiction to ponder more fundamental issues "of the nature of subjectship and allegiance" in a political community operating without a fixed constitution or any determinate means of testing the legitimacy of acts of government. What Hutchinson ultimately feared was the corrosive effect that defiance of legally constituted authority would have on obedience to law itself. A revolution, if successful, could establish a new set of moral claims as the foundation upon which law and obedience would thereafter rest; but no existing system could accede to such claims without forfeiting its capacity to use law to command obedience. So acute was his insight into the consequences of his opponents' claims that Hutchinson actually anticipated "the ultimate drift of opposition thought," even while those consequences remained "vague and doubtful even to the most imaginative leaders of the opposition"—and even though the very rigidity to which his temperament and political predicament drove him was also what "would in fact lead the Americans across the frontiers of the *ancien régime* to the modern political world."[31]

Boundaries and *frontiers*: The controlling images that Bailyn regularly deploys to describe how the Revolution transformed American life evoke intellectual efforts that variously mark, touch, probe, press against, burst, sweep past, and propel themselves beyond "the boundaries of traditional thought," "the boundaries of received political wisdom," "the frontiers of eighteenth-century political culture."[32] And those boundaries lay, he repeatedly suggests, where familiar assumptions about authority still taught men to think of sovereignty as a unitary power vested in the state, and the right to exercise it as the natural possession of those who enjoyed the combined "attributes of the favored—wealth, wisdom, and power." To move beyond the first of these boundaries, the colonists had to abandon accepted notions of constitutions and sovereignty, "to think of constitutions as objective, fixed, ultimately written documents," and "to conceive of organs of government specifically empowered to rule on the constitutionality of the government's actions."[33] To move beyond the second, they had to rethink not only the entire theory of mixed government, but also fundamental assumptions about hierarchy and superiority and the demands of deference.

There was nothing irrational in Hutchinson's adherence to these assumptions. It was the revolutionaries, "demanding a responsiveness in government that exceeded the traditional expectations of the time," who were "impelled by aspirations that were no recognized part of the world as it was." In the biography, Bailyn allows the sources of these demands and aspirations to remain obscure because Hutchinson himself could see them only as "irrational," "politically pathological," and ultimately incomprehensible. Yet elsewhere in his writings—most conspicuously, of course, in *The Ideological Origins*, but also in important ways in several of his essays—Bailyn makes it clear that the specific shortcomings that left Hutchinson and his class so vulnerable to attack merely exemplified one aspect of a more pervasive and powerful, though conceptually more elusive, phenomenon.

In Bailyn's sketch of John Adams, it appears in the elision through which the "social animosities" he first directed against the Hutchinson-Oliver clan "took fire and became the source of a flaming hatred of state authority." In the essay on *Common Sense*, it explains how the "dominant tone . . . of rage" that Paine expressed against all forms of authority "sparked into flame resentments that had smoldered" among the colonists for years. In Bailyn's restatement of "The Central Themes of the American Revolution," it is identified as "the belief that through the ages it has been privilege—artificial, man-made and man-secured privilege, ascribed to some and denied to others mainly at birth—that, more than anything else except the misuse of power, had crushed men's hopes for fulfillment." And in his wide-ranging essay on the *annus mirabilis* 1776, it is summarized in terms of the impatience with which Americans and like-minded Britons viewed the "inept, inefficient, irrational" performance of the major institutions of British public life.[34]

Yet for all the interpretive emphasis and rhetorical power that Bailyn invests in these sentiments, the sources of this pervasive resentment of privilege and the authority of the state seem at times to be not so much described or traced as simply posited. The closest Bailyn comes to explaining the origins of this broad-based resentment is in his treatment of the idea of class. In *The New England Merchants*, for example, he argues that there was no merchant class as such but rather a continuous spectrum of "merchant types descend[ing] from the high-church officialdom group . . . to the lowest reaches of the group where tradesmen, peddlers, shopkeepers, mariners, and fishermen gathered together their resources, invested in a few voyages overseas, and gradually came to think of themselves as merchants."[35] Elsewhere in his writings he has repeatedly held that the most significant aspect of the early American social structure was the relative narrowness of social distances and the differences between the contiguity and fluidity of colonial society, on the one hand, and the rigidity and fixed legal statuses of traditional European society, on the other. And the most conspicuous difference lay at the top rather than the bottom of the social scale. Long before the Revolution, "the colonial aristocracy had become a vaguely defined, fluid group whose power—in no way guaranteed, buttressed, or even recognized in law—was competitively maintained and dependent on continuous, popular support."[36]

Privilege and status were thus resented not because they were potent and oppressive, but because they were vestigial and pretentious. The formulation seems classically Tocquevillean in its emphasis on relative egalitarianism as a more explosive force for social resentment than established and secure distinctions between legally defined classes. But again, the reader may wonder whether the weakness of the state derived from any sources other than the political weakness and ineptitude of those who struggled to wield its power on behalf of an empire perceived as alien and intrusive.

There are, however, two other areas where Bailyn does discuss the atrophying of the inherent authority of the state in ways that go beyond his central fascination with the role of elites in Anglo-American politics. One involves the issue of religious establishment; the other, the settlement of the "marchlands" whose peopling he explores in his most recent work.

The place of religion in American life is central to Bailyn's overarching interpretation because it is here that he locates the beginnings of the liberal state whose development after the Revolution was the great subject of the Handlins' *Commonwealth*. In their account of the emergence of the liberal state, the Handlins had emphasized the gradual erosion of the traditional notion that the state, acting in behalf of public or quasi-public purposes, could bestow preferential privileges of incorporation on select groups of private citizens. The ability of the state to define transcendent purposes or even "the common interest" was sharply compromised, the Handlins argued, as the multiplication of grants of privilege to particular local interests made it difficult to identify the greater public good that was ostensibly being served.[37] But the same development that the Handlins located in nineteenth-century questions of economic policy was to some extent anticipated, Bailyn argues, in disputes over the nature and extent of religious establishments that had figured so prominently in mid-eighteenth-century provincial politics. For here, too, efforts to use the authority of the state to bestow legal privileges on particular sects or to enforce notions of orthodoxy met such widespread opposition that the entire principle of religious establishment entered the Revolutionary era already gravely damaged.[38]

Bailyn has reportedly described the Virginia Statute for Religious Freedom—and not the Declaration of Independence or the Constitution or the Tenth *Federalist*—as the "most important document in American history, bar none."[39] But its significance does not rest on what it actually accomplished, for here as on so many other points, Bailyn sees the formal enactments of the Revolution more as legitimating what had already come to pass than as requiring radical changes in practice and behavior.[40] Its significance rests instead in its attempt to deny the state any right to act in an area always regarded hitherto as a vital dimension of civil policy. The general principle of delegated power that lay inherent in the act of writing new constitutions did not by itself impose effective limitations on the authority of the state (or more to the point, the legislative powers of the states). As James Madison noted in his "razor-like" analysis of the general problem of protecting rights, the powers of legislation were either so plastic or, in the case of laws regulating property, so unavoidably intrusive on particular claims of rights, that specific limitations on the powers of government were likely to be unavailing or impracticable. Government had no choice but to regulate the "various and interfering interests" of which even eighteenth-century societies were composed; but in religion, where matters of opinion only were at stake, its authority could be safely abrogated. The idea of disestablishment thereby illuminated the first area in which it was possible to envision "charters of power granted by liberty" substantially reducing the scope of the responsibilities exercised by the state.[41]

The second great area in which Bailyn has attributed a general suspicion of the state to masses of the population may seem, at first glance, far more problematic. In the three elegant lectures that make up *The Peopling of British North America*, and in the massive *Voyagers to the West*, Bailyn appears to have left his concern with revolutionary ideology and elite politics far behind. As one reviewer has provocatively (though not necessarily correctly) noted, this new project can be seen as Bailyn's response to those who accused him of writing purely elitist or idealist history; if you want social history, these books announce, here it is "with a vengeance."[42] One can readily see in *Voyagers to the West* a return to themes that had engaged Bailyn at the start of his career, most notably in its emphasis on entrepreneurial functioning in a world as Atlantic as that which the first generations of Hutchinsons had set out to master a century earlier.[43]

Yet in two essential respects, *Voyagers to the West* fits perfectly within the schema of Bailyn's writings on Anglo-American politics. The evidentiary core of this book is found in the remarkable surveys of motives for emigration that officials at the exit ports were asked to keep once their superiors grew alarmed at the upsurge of population movement to America just before the Revolution. These surveys have a dual political significance. For all their bureaucratic earnestness, they testify to the feebleness of the British government's response to the surge of voluntary emigration to America, to the sheer incapacity of any authority at the time to fathom, much less channel or dam a population movement so massive in scope, yet involving the decisions of countless thousands of individuals and families. As Bailyn observed at an early point in his research:

> one thing is clear: this massive, infinitely complex movement of people from all over the British Isles and the Rhineland, from every corner of the older American settlements to almost every region of the unorganized, wild cis-Mississippi universe —all of this frantic peopling of half a continent—was beyond the control, indeed the comprehension, of those who managed the British government.[44]

Allowances are, of course, to be made for the incapacity of any eighteenth-century government to cope with forces so profound and complex. Yet the problem was taken seriously enough to lead the British government not only to order the surveys Bailyn has mined but even to consider prohibiting future emigration to America. Such a policy could be justified on narrow mercantilist grounds—the received wisdom whose boundaries Adam Smith and other innovative thinkers would soon cross. But it took equal inspiration from the self-interested calculations that led the Anglo-Irish landlord and first secretary of state for America, the Earl of Hillsborough, to reckon the costs of emigration in the highly personal terms that the loss of tenants could pose to his own estate. One is again thrown back to "the Anglo-American political world of privilege and patronage and of limited, arbitrary access," and its ingrained tendency to equate the protection of its own interests with the public good.

Bailyn sees Hillsborough through the eyes of Benjamin Franklin, who (like Hutchinson) knew a thing or two about how to operate the levers of influence, but whose cumulative despair of "the incapacity of the British government and the narrowness of its vision" finally led him— as Hutchinson could not have been led—to " 'apprehend more mischief than benefit from a closer union' " between Britain and America.[45] Yet Bailyn can hardly use the cosmopolitan Franklin's repudiation of the corruptions of England to illustrate the *popular* attitudes toward authority that he wishes to evoke. It is rather the plight and motives of the emigrants themselves that provide the link between Bailyn's atomistic account of emigration and the public events of the late eighteenth century. For whether one thinks of the luckless, unattached, sometimes desperate farm workers, journeymen, and convicts who, for want of other opportunity, became eligible for recruitment as indentured servants, or the

more substantial provincial families whose emigration involved calculations of generational mobility, Bailyn's account of the sources of the
"dual migration" to America presumes unhappy encounters with existing
structures of authority and privilege.

The point is not that every immigrant became a patriot in some crudely
telescoped variation of Crèvecoeur's account of the conversion of battered peasants into new Americans. What Bailyn conveys, or even simply
implies, is an extraordinarily powerful image of experiences shared by
masses of colonists which helps to make explicable or comprehensible
to us what observers in the eighteenth century could only barely detect,
if at all. The "manifest event" of the American Revolution, Bailyn observed in his presidential address to the American Historical Association,

> will not be obscured by discoveries of events of another order,
> but explanations of the origins, development, and consequences
> of the Revolution are beginning to take on quite different forms
> in the light of latent events that are now being uncovered. For
> the extraction of quantitative information from records that
> were never intended to provide such data makes it possible to
> detect events in the population and migration history of the
> pre-Revolutionary years that profoundly affected government
> policy, settlement policy, and attitudes to authority, all of which
> helped shape the origins and outcome of the Revolution.[46]

This observation will probably not assuage those who persist in doubting
whether or how deeply revolutionary ideology penetrated among the
general population; nor, again, is it meant to explain in any simple way
issues of political allegiance.[47] Like Gordon Schochet's study *Patriarchalism in Political Thought*, which "relates a key concept in political
thought to deep-lying social attitudes shared as interior experiences by
whole populations in the seventeenth century," this experience of migration and mobility, with the attenuation of loyalties that it both pre-
supposes and reinforces, thus offers a way of integrating the "manifest"
changes in notions of allegiance and authority that the Revolution
wrought with the "latent" events in population history that only the
historian can fully recover.[48]

A formulation that links the history of liberty in America to the "inner
lives" of immigrants—however imaginatively reconstructed—can only
remind us how closely the work of Bernard Bailyn should be linked with
that of his teacher, Oscar Handlin. More could be written on this subject,
and not merely in terms of a common agenda of research and writing,
but also by asking how Handlin and Bailyn have conceived of the processes of historical change (getting from A to B). When the history of

American historical writing in this era comes to be written, the influence that these two gentlemen have exerted not only over those who were fortunate enough to be their students, but over the prevailing conceptions of virtually the whole of the American past, will surely deserve explanation. Not the least of their achievements, it will be discovered, will have been to demonstrate how fundamental questions of the nature of authority and the sources of voluntary obedience within the liberal state have been tied to the issues of social history upon which much of their scholarship has centered.

Colonization and the Common Law in Ireland and Virginia, 1569–1634

DAVID THOMAS KONIG

W HEN THOMAS JEFFERSON began his description of the "Laws" for Query XIV of *Notes on Virginia*, he stated un-equivocally that the first colonists immediately "adopted" the laws of England. "Under this adoption," he confidently explained, "the rule, in our courts of judicature was, that the common law of England, and the general statutes previous to the 4th of James [1607], were in force here. . . ." Good lawyer that he was, Jefferson was simply acknowl-edging the well-known King's Bench opinion of 1693 in *Blankard* v. *Galdy*: "In case of an uninhabited country newly found out by English subjects, all laws in force in England, are in force there. . . ."[1] But Jefferson was a better lawyer than historian, for it was not at all clear in 1607 that the colonists—either by the "consent" or "practice" he cited—had adopted the common law, or that they wanted to. The law as practiced in the king's courts in London had many challengers for the role of shaping society in England's distant marchlands across the sea. Physical adversity, personal ambition, and administrative confusion would all play a role in delaying the ascendancy of the common law. As general factors in shap-ing Virginia's early history, each has been given its due. Virtually ig-nored, however, has been the powerful impact of contemporary events in England's other wild and hostile overseas possessions. Driven by many of the same economic impulses and shaped by many of the same political considerations, the lessons learned in England's marchland experience

in Ireland, and before that in Wales and the North, would play a major
role in Virginia.

Jefferson could not admit such a delayed reception or unenviable
kinship, however. His view of the transfer of English rights across the
Atlantic required him to place the common law with all its rights among
the baggage taken in Christopher Newport's fleet in 1607, just as he had
placed Anglo-Saxon liberties among the possessions brought to England
from the forests of Saxony by Hengist and Horsa more than a thousand
years earlier.

Yet the expansion of the realm had been conducted under legal aus-
pices quite hostile to the common law. Beginning in Wales and the North,
it rested firmly on the extension of the royal prerogative; Henry VIII
and Elizabeth therefore made much use of conciliar administration, by
which they appointed local barons to "councils" with broad and great
judicial powers outside the common law. In theory an attempt to extend
Tudor absolutism into the rough marchland regions, conciliar rule in
practice never escaped the inherent tension produced when power is
projected over great distances. The Tudors, aware of their inability to
obtain full obedience from far-off border barons who dominated the
outlying marchland areas of the realm, learned to strike a compromise
between their ideal of centralization and the reality of "lords marcher"
whose loyalty was as tenuous as their own ambitions were great. It made
sense to Henry VIII, as well as to his daughter Elizabeth, to accept reality
and to permit such men to continue exercising their enormous local
powers in exchange for carrying out the basic goals of Tudor policy.
Local marchland power, blessed with the imprimatur of a royal commission, thereby satisfied both crown and magnate.[2]

Not surprisingly, the shape of justice as actually administered in the
marches followed local inclinations rather than royal imperatives. Henry
VIII created his conciliar courts in the North and West simply by royal
commission, without statutory authorization and without placing precise
limitations on their operation. Commissions to presidents and councils
provided only the most general and open-ended guidance to those who
held them. Not until early in the seventeenth century were conciliar
instructions even enrolled; until then, reported Sir Edward Coke, they
remained "kept . . . in private."[3] Conciliar justice was swift and virtually
beyond accountability; it did not employ juries, and its proceedings were
not bound by the protections of regular common law prosecutions or
the slowness of process in civil litigation. Where judicial authority was
conferred by charter, as in grants to the Stannaries of Devon and Corn-
wall, no writ of error lay to common law courts. For redress of judicial
grievance, suitors were left to "the custome of the same courts without

let or impeachment of any writ or writ of error, or of false judgement sued or to be sued in any of the courts of the kings bench or common pleas." Such, commented Coke, was the extent of franchisal autonomy.[4] Whatever was happening in the courts at Westminster, justice in the Welsh and Northern marchlands operated in ways unknown to the common law; there, the needs of borderland justice allowed a simplified system of unrestrained justice to expedite procedure and exaggerate judicial power. The Crown was forced to tolerate and even support these legal outrages as a necessary part of maintaining its control, however thus limited, in the marchlands.[5]

Ireland's unhappy experience in the sixteenth and seventeenth centuries remains the clearest example of how this process first extended across the seas.[6] Ireland stood not only as a strategic threat (that is, as a steppingstone for a Spanish invasion), but it also loomed as an attractive opportunity for the expansion of England's landed aristocracy. For reasons equally selfish and nationalistic, then, England's landed elite and mercantile community both eagerly embraced the Irish venture. Recognizing the value of a mutually beneficial enterprise, Elizabeth's principal secretary of state for foreign matters, Lord Burghley, set the model for Tudor expansion: "He would harness private greed," one scholar has put it, "for public gain."[7]

Many of the resident Anglo-Norman, or "Old English," elite warmly embraced the concept. Roman Catholics descended from the twelfth-century invaders of the island, they welcomed Elizabethan conciliar government as a way of accommodating Tudor imperatives while at the same time retaining their local sway. They expected the new councils planned for Ireland to be less an agent of outside control than a vehicle for their own advancement. The councils, they hoped, would be placed in their hands with a distinguished local lord—perhaps even a bishop —as president.[8] Beyond the Pale, the area surrounding the English presence at Dublin, many local Gaelic nobles and clan chiefs accommodated the English intrusion while hoping for continued autonomy, too. Nominally giving allegiance to the Crown and freeing their clansmen of loyalty obligations, they accepted English titles of nobility and vast tracts of land confiscated from the Roman Catholic Church.[9]

Government in Ireland therefore followed the pattern already well established in England's West and North; as in those frontier regions, magnate cooperation and reliability meant far more than the imposition of any particular form of local law or justice. Moreover, as the cumbersome mechanisms of the common law proved to be ill-adapted to the needs of the frontier administration, the Tudors abandoned them and replaced them with conciliar justice. Elizabeth responded to local pressures by circumventing them: for Connaught in 1569 and Munster in 1571 she established the swifter, simpler, and more discretionary system of conciliar justice.[10] As a result, the law as practiced in the queen's courts at Westminster would have little practical influence on conciliar justice in Ireland.[11]

Administrative structures naturally followed in conformity with the needs and goals of exploitative expansionist ventures. Conciliar justice placed enormous powers in the hands of officials whose courts wielded powers greater than those generally available to English judges, whether common law or prerogative. Far from Westminster, marchland conciliar courts remained outside the mainstream of English legal change, which saw the limiting of prerogative powers and the dispersal of judicial function into more specialized courts. While in England the Star Chamber and Privy Council had divided their powers and assumed separate jurisdiction over matters pertinent to each of them, conciliar courts such as the president's court in Ulster retained them as a unified jurisdiction.[12]

Accountability had little limiting role in the operation of conciliar courts; they enjoyed vast powers adapted to the needs of their special jurisdictions, and their judges were not reluctant to employ them or, where necessary, corrupt them.[13] From the most basic level of government on up to that of viceregal administration, therefore, justice in Ireland acted with little or no external constraint. Manorial organization, for instance, permitted landlords to conduct their own courts leet where royal officials could not interfere and where, of course, the common law did not apply. If even these formidable powers failed, there always remained the potential for imposing martial law out of dire necessity. To Captain Thomas Lee in Munster,

> martial law is very necessary, and (in my opinion) ought to be granted to all governors of remote and savage places where your majesty's laws are not received . . . until such time as the people shall become civil, and embrace the laws, and peaceable living.[14]

Yet martial law, however unexceptional in the marchlands, was seen only as an emergency expedient, and was not even necessary in the normal course of events, so adaptable and powerful were the more ordinary instruments and procedures of marchland justice. This was so because judicial simplification affected process, too, and thereby strengthened judicial administration. Conciliar courts dispensed with the complicated writ system of the common law courts and used instead a simple bill of complaint that produced a subpoena summoning the defendant to court without naming a charge. Usually not employing a jury, cases proceeded with written pleadings, sworn depositions, and witness examinations, and then to judgment and court order.

For all its impressive background of success in Wales and the North, conciliar rule failed in Ireland. And it failed spectacularly, as rebellious Irish repeatedly rose in the closing decades of the sixteenth century to oust the unwelcome intruders. The loyalty of the Gaelic lords proved to be ephemeral, and Elizabeth repaid their rebellion in kind, producing a bloodbath that has continued for centuries. Ill-advised and insensitive Tudor conciliar justice also played a major role in this collapse. The presidency courts, like other legal institutions reaching down to the grassroots of Irish society, had contributed to this failure by arousing both disappointment and outrage. Unlike the powerful barons who ruled in Wales and the North, the men available as presidents in Ireland often lacked the stature needed to command obedience; when Sir Henry Sidney appointed Warham St. Leger to the Munster presidency, he had to obtain a knighthood for St. Leger so that he might bring adequate rank to the office.[15] Notwithstanding this *ad hoc* elevation, St. Leger caved in to local influence. At the opposite extreme, presidents failed by ignoring local interests completely.[16] Ignoring Sidney's efforts, English presidents generally did not include the native elite—whether Gaelic or Anglo-Norman—in their councils. Rather, they rapaciously pursued their own goals, exploiting local labor and subverting the power of the native nobility.[17]

Controlled by a small clique of outsiders and inaccessible to local powerseekers, conciliar justice offered little to assure acceptance among the native population. When, as happened occasionally, local magnates served on the councils, so great was local resentment at the courts' actions that they lost all popular support.[18] The Irish rejected conciliar justice as emphatically as they repudiated Protestantism. "St. Patrick is of better credit than Christ Jesus," commented an English observer of the Irish; "and they fly from the laws as from a yoke of bondage."[19] As an alternative to traditional jurisdictions, conciliar justice made few converts. Sir William Pelham, a high judicial officer in Ireland, reported to London in 1580, "There is such a settled hatred of English government that the best disposed of the Irish do make profit of the time to recover their accustomed captainries and extortions."[20]

Conciliar rule ironically fell short of satisfying English colonists, too. If English law was ever to support a reliable colonial society in Ireland, it must serve the vital purpose of preserving the most fundamental support of the English social order—landholding. Subjugation by the sword, so self-evidently a failure despite its frequent application, would never assure the peace and civility that the English sought for Ireland.

Unless land titles could be secure, English adventurers would not risk their lives and fortunes in the violent world across the sea. Conciliar justice, however, was a poor guarantor of titles, limited to possessory jurisdiction that prevented violence by conferring temporary possession without title. Only the common law, as practiced by the king's courts at Westminster, could award title and provide the security of tenure that a stable provincial society required.[21]

Sir Peter Carew discovered the limits of conciliar justice when he sought to oust Sir Christopher Chyvers from lands near Dublin in 1568. Chyvers met Carew's challenge frontally when sued before the Lord Deputy and his council. That forum, Chyvers argued, "was no ordinary court for the trial of lands, and therefore the Lord Deputy and Council were no competent judges." Maintaining that "no person should be impleaded for any lands but by the order and course of the common law, and not otherwise," Chyvers and his counsel concluded that "the common law being every man's inheritance, no man ought to be abridged thereof." To Carew's dismay, the two common law judges sitting with the council agreed.[22]

Carew finally bullied the council into accepting his claim, but only by invoking the queen's prerogative and claiming that he "could not have his just trial at the common law, and therefore his matter was determinable before the Lord Deputy and Council." Though successful for Carew against Chyvers and another victim, this argument revealed its own weakness: it had acknowledged the supremacy of the common law in property matters, and it had left a cloud of uncertainty hanging over others who might try to use conciliar courts in this way.[23]

If land claims were to be firmly based and serve as an inducement to colonization, the common law would have to be established in Ireland no less clearly than in metropolitan England. The common law was not just the law of the land; it was the law *of* land: it settled the course of descents, defined the nature of estates, and established the procedures and substance of land acquisition and transfer.[24]

The Tudors had converted Irish tenures to English legal forms, but rights required enforcement, and with few exceptions only common law courts could make final judgments on real property. Presidency courts might begin cases by taking depositions, but their authority was strictly limited beyond that.[25] Once shires were created—a process underway in Ireland—they were "governed by the laws of England, and not by the discretion of the president and councell," wrote Coke; "and this were to bring their inheritances, goods, etc, *ad aliud examen*." The common law referred land claims *ad aliud examen* [to another trial] for the same reason it issued prohibitions against ecclesiastical courts in other matters:

rights such as those touching property must not be tried "by a jurisdiction or manner of process disallowed by the laws of the kingdom."[26]

Exceptions to this rule remained anomalous and *ad hoc*. On two occasions, in 1588 and 1592, royal commissioners traveled from London to Dublin "to hear and determine all pretended claims" sent to them after preliminary hearing ("chiefly upon the deposition of witnesses") at presidency courts, but Coke, speaking for the increasingly influential common lawyers, regarded such proceedings as irregular. At best, these were expedients demanded by necessity "when one of the parties or both were poor, who are ever most clamorous." Otherwise, he made clear, "actions real and personall were not to be heard and determined by commission, but according to the laws of the realm."[27]

As early as the 1570s—even as conciliar rule was just being established in Munster and Connaught—critics saw its deficiencies. In the short run, overbearing *arriviste* presidents were antagonizing local lords; in a longer-term perspective, conciliar justice failed to create the security of landholding and property transfer needed for social stability. But not all Elizabethan colonizers saw fit to acknowledge this yet, and Elizabeth yielded to those calling for bloody repression by way of "a strong hand to contain [the Irish] in their loyalties" rather than to "pamper them with favours and rewards."[28]

The accession of James I marked a significant shift of emphasis in colonial policy. Promoters still used much the same language of firmness, but contained within it was a new approach. Order must be established, wrote Edmund Spenser in 1608, "yf not by Lawes and Ordinaunces, [then] by the sworde; for all those evills muste firste be Cutt awaie by a stronge hande before anie good Cane be planted." But Spenser, despite having been an eyewitness to the atrocities at Munster in 1598, was not calling for a policy of systematic brutality. Rather, he envisioned that the Irish must be "prepared by the sword." In their present uncivilized condition the Irish were not ready for the common law, but they might be brought round to it "by the sworde for the ymposinge of the Laws uppon them." "[B]y the sworde," he explained, "I meante the Royall power of the Prince, which oughte to stretche it selfe forthe in her Chiefe strengthe to the redressinge and Cuttinge of all those evills which I before blamed, and not of the people which are evill: for evill people by good ordinaunces and government maye be made good."[29]

Critics like Spenser saw the variety and independence of local jurisdictions as an obstacle to the effective imposition of English rule in far-off areas. Sir John Davies, attorney general for Ireland, blamed England's medieval failures on such grants and used them as a foil for criticizing its present difficulties in 1612; by contrast, he vigorously advanced common law institutions as the proper strategy for effecting colonial control. Describing King Edward III's efforts but clearly referring to recent decades, he asked his readers to "see what inconveniences did arise by these large and ample grants of lands and liberties to the first adventurers in the conquest." The common law had not figured in that enterprise, not only because of the king's preference for treating the island as a conquered territory under his prerogative, but also for a more immediately instructive reason: local magnates—whether the "Old English" Anglo-Norman or recently transplanted "New English" —saw the common law as a rival to their private jurisdictions. The common law, Davies explained, "would have abridged and cut off a great part of that greatness which they had promised unto themselves."[30]

Proposals for reviving common law institutions languished under Elizabeth, but under James I the arguments of common lawyers such as Davies and Sir James Ley, chief justice in Ireland, would have considerably more influence.[31] The new Stuart monarch expressed indignation at "how much our goodness, and bounty, hath bene abused; our Intentions, and directions eluded; and many things doone, that must be reformed." Sympathetic to the new thrust of colonization and impressed with English local government—he even introduced justices of the peace in Scotland—James began by heeding the advice to invigorate the Irish common law courts of King's Bench, Common Pleas, and Exchequer.[32] Since the 1580s, if not before, Irish lords-deputy were receiving criticism of those courts as "weak," and as poorly representative of Crown interests. "The officers that now are, being Irish, are so greatly affected to their own countrymen, that doing one for another they little regard the Queen's profit," advised one report to Lord Deputy John Perrot from Dublin in 1585. Irish judges, it continued, "sit in such unseemly order that there is no accompt made of a court there, but as a petty hundred court in the country, nor no reverence at all used by them."[33]

Irish judges alone would not suffice. The availability of jury trial at common law meant that English interests would require English jurors; Irish jurymen, complained Spenser, "make no conscience to perjure themselves in their verdicts and damn their souls"; often, these men had been compelled by their lords to lie. Not only English judges, but an adequate population of English jurors, must be available if Ireland was to be brought to "goodnes and Civilitye." Ultimately, the program would succeed in Ireland as it had succeeded in England:

> I Cannot see how that maie be then by the discipline of the
> Lawes of Englande, ffor the Inglishe weare at firste as stout
> and warlike a people as ever weare the Irishe And yeat yee see

> are now brought unto that Civilitye that no nacion in the worlde
> excelleth them. . . .[34]

Aptly suiting James's own preference to conciliate rather than crush, this would be the approach he adopted to colonization. James's own antagonistic relationship with the common law at home did not deter him from imposing it as an instrument of centralization across the sea in Ireland. As a perverse and ironic punishment, in fact, James even ordered Sir Edward Coke—exemplar of the common law—to Ireland in 1623.[35]

Common law administration had a greater attraction to ambitious colonizers and land-hungry residents in Ireland. Davies keenly perceived the impulse to acquire land and, more importantly for James's own immediate goals, the link between secure land tenures enforced in common law courts and social stability. "Again, in England and all well-ordered commonweals men have certain estates in their lands and possessions," he wrote, "and their inheritances descend from father to son, which doth give them encouragement to build and to plant and to improve their lands, and to make them better for their posterities." Lord Deputy Sir Henry Sidney had converted tenures from the "uncertain" Irish customary law of gavelkind and tanistry into "a course of inheritance according to the course of the Common Law"; now common law courts must be available to guarantee common law interests.[36]

The shiring of Ulster in 1605 exemplified the process by which James would ultimately impose English forms in Ireland and transmit the common law. English justices in assize visited on circuit twice yearly and, with the aid of English sheriffs and English magistrates, began to bring the common law to the Irish countryside.[37] James was particularly concerned to extend its rights to his Scots colonists in Ulster because as aliens they suffered serious legal disabilities. Under common law, a Scots subject's title to land was always defeasible (open to challenge), and he could neither inherit nor bequeath to his children. To remedy this, James that same year made all Scots in Ireland denizens of both England and Ireland, a status that allowed a landholder's children to inherit if born after his denization.[38]

The real beneficiaries of James's policies were those who could penetrate or manipulate the common law courts as they operated and then bend them to their own goals. The Scots and "New English" took full advantage of the legal system to amass large estates through a common law system that they, as landholders and petty officials on the scene, controlled. With little hope of ever gaining influence in the oligarchically controlled conciliar courts, these men now filled the midlevel offices that handled the escheat of rebel lands and the discovery of concealed Crown interests; with such powers, a land-hungry official might become, as one adept practitioner has been described, a "grantee-cum-escheator-cum-surveyor." Far from oversight by London officials, and working with minutiae that defied centralized supervision, they corrupted royal policy. Allied to corrupt juries and complaisant sheriffs, they solidified their control.[39] Skillfully manipulating the courts, an adventurer might invite a tenant to sue him at common law for title to land held by lease, lose the cause, see the court award title to the tenant, and then simply resume possession and receive a virtually indefeasible title from the collusive plaintiff.[40]

Under the protection of the common law, a new breed of colonial adventurer had gained power and wealth at the expense of the Crown in Ireland.[41] Royal commissioners might grumble, but early Stuart colonization policy needed a loyal—that is, equally self-interested—class of colonial landholders as a way of subduing a tragically violent borderland. If allowing this to happen under the common law was preferable to conciliar institutions, then James was prepared to support the common law. When he drastically overhauled the Irish parliament by enfranchising forty Protestant boroughs, opponents of English rule saw this, too, for what it was: the empowerment "of a few . . . under the name of burgesses" to protect Crown interests while pursuing their own.[42]

The replacement of conciliar machinery with the more broadly dispersed structures of common law administration did not necessarily elevate judicial proceedings to a higher standard of justice—nor was it intended to. But it did serve other vital purposes. For one, the common law was gaining a well-deserved reputation as a protector of private property, especially land. Commerce, too, benefited from common law ascendancy, as Coke and his allies in Parliament were successfully using it as an instrument of private economic freedom.[43] Its institutional dispersal of authority also offered advantages to an ambitious adventurer class that might be counted on to be loyal to a Crown that had bestowed such an opportunity.

Even independent of the substantive law involved, therefore, the common law served to solidify control among a new colonizing adventurer class capable of operating largely on its own. Numerous London companies received large grants of Ulster land on which to settle colonists and operate their own local institutions. Local plantations were run by representatives of the companies of Ironmongers, Skinners, Drapers, Salters, Mercers, and Haberdashers. Such companies, whether doing business in Ireland or Virginia, had to place considerable autonomy in the hands of those on whom they had to rely for supervision of their lands. They were no less reluctant (or more able) to intervene in abuses of legal authority than the crown was toward those on whom it had conferred distant authority.[44]

The example of the Ironmongers in Coleraine, where George Canning had been granted 3,210 acres in Agivey as "undertaker by lease,"[45] aptly illustrates the legal remoteness of the marchland. Canning had a tenant, Samuel Pidgeon, from whom he took both land and chattels at will. According to Pidgeon's desperate and "clamorous petition" of April 1627,[46] Canning had Pidgeon arrested "without any matter or cause offered" (since none was required) and then used the authority of the court to send his "menne" (a term used generically to describe liveried retainers) to Pidgeon's tenancy; there, they seized cattle worth, by Pidgeon's account, £33. Canning's men had them appraised, however, at £14, and before Pidgeon could replevy the cattle, they hid the livestock and sold them off. Old-fashioned riot in another era, it now had the legal justification of a court order. Although legal mechanisms existed for the suppression of riot, Canning, as "Farmer, or undertaker by lease," controlled local judicial institutions and inflicted even worse troubles on poor Pidgeon. The landlord's men took more cattle (beating Pidgeon's wife in the process) and when Pidgeon tried to obtain a warrant for the men's arrest, Canning had him arrested on a debt demand of £30. Pidgeon languished in "prison" five days before he could raise bail, only to be arrested again on another £30 demand. By the time he gained his liberty, Canning's men had driven off his milking cows and then had impounded them as strays, leaving them in the pound until they "were dryed upp."[47]

Men like Canning had learned to exploit a situation where traditional social networks did not exist, traditional avenues of community control were impossible, and where, when asked by his victim why he behaved so, a man could answer simply "that he hath noe freind but his purse and the Lawe." Back in Dublin, officials of the Ironmongers' Company addressed their inquiry to Canning, but limited it to the weak comment that "we hope [it] is untrue, yet we desire you to write" and "answer thereof." No further record exists of this controversy.[48] Like that of other acquisitive undertakers, Canning's success exemplified a pattern of colonial expansion driven by a self-interested adventurer class capable of gaining control of their own mechanisms of law and authority. If royal control were threatened, of course, a swift return to martial law or the use of inquisitorial methods in the Court of Castle Chamber would demonstrate the power of the Crown to any challengers—witness the Earl of Strafford's policy of "thorough" after 1634; but successful colonization required successful colonists, and such men found in the common law their own instrument of control.[49]

.   .   .

REALITY, IDEOLOGY, AND EXPERIENCE would combine to rep-
licate many aspects of the Irish experience in Virginia. Despite the vastly
differing climates English adventurers confronted in Ireland and Virginia, the limits of premodern technology and the scarcity of tractable
labor in a wild terrain would force colonial settlement into roughly similar patterns.[50] A common contempt for the native populations worked
a powerful influence on English colonists in each,[51] and many of the
same men who had invested money and effort in the Irish conquest
would be intimately involved with the American enterprise.[52]

Another important similarity would obtain, too. As in Ireland, competing notions of law and judicial administration would struggle for
control in Virginia. The eventual triumph of the common law as the
basis of Virginia's legal system occurred no more smoothly nor automatically than it had done in Ireland, and for many of the same reasons.

Jefferson was correct in locating a common law impulse in the founding of Virginia. The "Articles, Instructions, and Orders" issued for the
colony on November 20, 1606, specified that for "the good government
of the people" the colony's laws be "as neer to the common lawes of
England and the equity thereof as may be."[53] Sir Edward Coke, who as
attorney general had a major role in drafting the "Articles," was no less
concerned than James I to assure the loyalty of far-off marchland
colonists. As with the king, experience and considerations of policy
led him to emphasize the common law as an instrument of successful
colonization.

But mention of these "common lawes," seen in context, would not
prevent local liberties from arising under Virginia Company authority. The concept of "the common lawes of Englande" was a capacious
one still in flux in the early seventeenth century. Especially in the
provinces—such as Ireland—the substance of the common law was less
consistent than its growing prestige would indicate. Moreover, the common law held within it principles that contributed to its own mutability
and adaptability. For example, it gave wide interpretive latitude to charters and opened the way for considerable manipulation by those possessing liberties under them. Coke gave this principle renewed life in
his *Second Institute*: charters, he wrote, were "to be construed *secundum
earum plenitudinum*, that is, as fully and beneficially as the law was taken
at that time when they were made. . . ."[54] Accordingly, there remained
within the common law a powerful tradition of judicial discretion as well
as acquiescence in local variation.

Interpretive latitude in the common law tradition, then, added to the
built-in tensions within marchland justice. While the Company Council

in London remained under the control of its treasurer and stockholders, the colony's *resident* leaders in Virginia were nothing other than a march-land council closely akin to that of Wales, the North, or Ireland. The charter made it clear that justice was in the hands of the resident council. True, the charter provided that all colonists and their children "shall have and enjoy all liberties, franchises and immunities within anie of our other dominions to all intents and purposes as if they had been abiding and borne within this our realme of Englande or anie other of our saide dominions."[55] But these rights, it will be observed, included "all liberties, franchises, and immunities"—the language of local privileges and the enjoyment of local law beyond the common law. Notwithstanding the Company's goal of protecting its costly investment with potent legal mechanisms that would impose order and guarantee business success, the latitude inherent in the charter contained within it a tension—the very same tension inherent in the Irish enterprise, where the pressing necessities of survival and profit, with the same geographical dispersal and aggressive acquisitiveness of landowners, forced the devolution of authority and a distribution of powers sufficient to render central authorities helpless from afar.

Even before population growth and the tobacco boom burst the bonds of compact settlement, therefore, the justice system of colonial Virginia offered two powerful models—conciliar and common law—for the ambitious Company adventurers to exploit for their own advancement. Conciliar justice, with its potential for self-aggrandizement through the exercise of vast and unspecified powers, obviously had a great attraction, and the first leaders of the colony did not hesitate in assuming the mantle of lords marcher on the Chesapeake. Seeking to eliminate rivals, they ignored common law principles of criminal justice. George Kendall was brought to trial without a grand jury indictment for spying (and was later executed) in 1607, and John Smith was summarily condemned on a charge of murder early in 1608. The charge was based, not upon any common law or statutory definition of the crime of murder, but rather upon the Biblically derived notion of Smith's responsibility for the lives of men lost under his command. Only the return of Captain Christopher Newport that same day saved his life.[56]

As governor in 1610, Sir Thomas Gates was empowered to take possession of all prior letters patent and instructions and "dispose of them in the future according to your discretion." Gates, who assumed control of the colony after the experiences of the first years had demonstrated the perils of divided conciliar leadership, was given enormous discretionary power in being told to proceed "rather as a Chauncelor then as a judge." He was authorized to create his own personal guard and to appoint lesser officials—unspecified as to powers or number—as needed. The Company, acknowledging the protean nature of a frontier settlement, authorized him, too, to "make, adde or distinguishe any lawes or ordinances at your discretion. . . ." Although the instructions hedged such a grant by specifying laws "accordinge to the authority limited in your Comission," the Company concluded its order to Gates by giving him a typically wide-ranging commission as council president: other than limiting his authority to name a successor, the Company explained that

> we doe by these our lettres instructions binde you to nothinge so strictly but uppon due consideration and good reason and uppon divers circumstances of time and place wherein we cannot here conclude you may in your discretion departe and Dissent from them and Change alter or establishe execute and doe all ordinances or acts whatsoever that may best conducte the glory of god, the honor of our Kinge and nation and the good and perfect establishement of our Colony.

Gates's instructions, a Magna Carta for baronial tyranny, would remain in spirit as the dominant force behind the colony's legal development in its first decades, and would prevent the implementation of the rival common law system.[57] Gates was soon succeeded by Sir Thomas West, Lord De la Warr, whose arrival was praised in London and welcomed at Jamestown. Continuing the drift toward a marchland style of rule, the new governor strode into church followed by his own armed, liveried retainers.[58]

By the time Gates had resumed control of the colony in 1611, however, settlement already had spilled over from Jamestown Island into several other "forts" and "hundreds," as John Smith described them.[59] Stretching from Point Comfort at the tip of the peninsula to the falls of the James, they also reached across the river and penetrated southward to the Nansemond River basin.[60] The structure and operation of these settlements has eluded historical description because they have, quite simply, left almost no records. Contemporary accounts are few, as most descriptions that have come down to us are the product of the fierce factional squabbling that afflicted the management of the colony. We have indictments aplenty of oppressive acts by councilors, as their opponents appealed to the Company in London for support in gaining the upper hand over the colony. But we have much less indication of how conciliar power translated into practices and power wielded beyond Jamestown.

Perhaps we will never obtain such knowledge, but enough information can be gleaned to suggest some tentative answers. In the first place, the unit of local administration was not so strictly defined as to have any one name even to describe it. Its purpose was military as well as economic, and for that reason Smith chose to label them "forts" and "hundreds." Their leaders, therefore, fell into two categories: military commanders and manorial lords. While the commanders could—and did—apply martial law, the proprietors possessed the broad instruments of franchisal justice—that is, to conduct courts for their own profit (from fees) and for the protection of their interests as landlords. Franchisal courts possessed extensive discretion; by English legal practice, they were limited only by their adherence to the terms granted them, the broadly construed notion of public welfare, and consistency with royal interests.[61] Despite the undoubted authority of the governor and council, these subunits—like those run by George Canning of Coleraine for the Ironmongers—possessed considerable autonomy and, it is likely, went their own way with regard to any system of justice.

One settlement, though probably exceptional in the degree to which this process was exploited, offers considerable support to such speculation, especially if interpreted with Ireland as backdrop. The enterprise was the work of John Martin, son of a London goldsmith and backer of Sir Francis Drake. Captain Martin had visited Roanoke in 1585 while sailing with Drake's fleet; renewing his interest in colonization, he ventured to Virginia aboard the *Godspeed* with Christopher Newport's fleet in 1607. When the Company's instructions were opened on arrival at the Chesapeake, Martin was named as one of the colony's first councilors. Well acquainted with the potential of the New World, Martin was the lone dissenter opposing the abandonment of the enterprise after the "Starving Time" in 1610. And well he should have clung to the New World, for Martin had quickly seized the potential of the colony's isolation and the opportunity for independent aggrandizement. Dubbed by John Smith "refining Captain Martin" for his lust after gold, Martin was instrumental in getting a governor deposed and a rival councilor shot to death. With that accomplished, he and John Ratcliffe assumed virtually unchallenged control of the colony until Lord De la Warr arrived and promptly removed him from the council as "a most unworthie person."[62]

Martin's significance lies not only in his high-handed style as councilor; rather, his subsequent career is worthy of closer examination because it reveals the way in which someone might use the inherently centrifugal force of English local development to erect for himself a secure and autonomous marchland enclave. It took Martin several years, but in 1617 he finally attained the kind of autonomous local authority that put him, for all practical purposes, beyond accountability.

Undoubtedly through the influence of his brother-in-law Sir Julius Caesar, Martin obtained a patent that enabled him to set out on his own to exploit the human and natural resources of the region. He received the right to "free trafick in the Bay and Rivers"—an extraordinary grant, inasmuch as it allowed him to create an alternative economy beyond the control of the Company—and broad legal powers over his servants. According to the patent, Martin was free to run his plantation "in as large and ample manner and to all intents and purposes as any Lord of Mannor here in England." Martin's Brandon was even put beyond the administrative control of the council in all but the most serious of matters, military necessity: he was free, as the patent said,

> to govern and comand all such person or persons as at this time
> he shall carry over with him or that shall be sent him hereafter
> free from any comand of the Colony except it be in aiding and
> assisting the same against Foreign or Domesticall Enemy.[63]

Martin put his privileges to good use and turned his estate on the south side of the James, Martin's Brandon, into a notorious haven for men seeking to elude the council—to frustrated authorities, it became "a receptacle of vagabonds and bankrupts and other disorderly persons," a refuge "where such as are indebted do shroud and rescue themselves under his protection."[64] Martin, as fully as any who wielded the diverse powers of a lord marcher in Ireland, successfully resisted, with force, the efforts of colony officials to serve writs on his property.[65]

Martin's grant was truly unique, yet its exceptional nature is illuminating for suggesting a contrary and competing tendency that would emerge ascendant in the 1630s. Martin's Brandon represented the persistent aggrandizement of independent authority along marchland lines. By contrast, the so-called "greate Charter" of 1618 (actually a series of commissions issued by the Company to Sir George Yeardley) would overhaul the organization and management of the colony and set it on a different course of local governance. Often credited with bringing the common law to Virginia—a highly problematical contribution, given the protean nature of that term—the charter of 1618 can be credited with something scarcely less significant in the modernization of justice in colonial America. Certainly, it swept away the military regime of Sir Thomas Dale; such a fact is significant, but in itself must not be over-emphasized. "Dale's Laws" were not a sharp departure from contemporary marchland practice,[66] and their suspension must be seen as an attack on *all* extraordinary jurisdictions. That assault on private justice is what gave greatest lasting importance to the commissions of 1618. Significantly, Yeardley was directed to organize the colony's existing plantations into a uniform system of "four cities or burroughs" and to consolidate the varied settlements "into one body corporate . . . under equal and like law and orders with the rest of the colony."[67] Never given credit for what this properly accomplished, this clause ended forever the formal, legal basis for proprietary justice or private judicial franchises and pushed the colony toward public jurisdiction.

The Company also now provided for the establishment of "particular plantations" organized by independent adventurers. Enterprises of this sort had existed before, including those owned by such men as Argall and Martin, and as franchisal units their courts probably had exercised a jurisdiction as divergent as any in Ireland. But the charter of 1618 introduced a new and radical departure by barring these settlements from going their own way legally. They might no longer do justice as they pleased, for "equal and like law" would apply there, too. Such justice might be harsh and brutal, but it would have to have the approval of Jamestown. The grant to John Smyth of Nibley and others in 1619 spelled out this new limitation: their enterprise at Berkeley Hundred might "frame and make orders ordinances and constitutions" for its inhabitants, but these must conform to English law and—pointedly— "to the forme of governement by the said Treasorer Counsell and company to be established."[68]

At the same time, the more conventionally accepted significance of the creation of an assembly takes on new meaning, for it tied to the Company—or at least to a central institution—the self-interest of the powerful local landowners. The first meeting of the assembly on July 30, 1619, was a "Who's Who" of Virginia, but not of any traditional elite. Rather, it consisted of new men who—like their Irish counterparts recently enfranchised as burgesses for the Dublin parliament of 1613— had carved wealth and power out of the wilderness and were intent on protecting it from outside control. They were the new leaders of the colony, ensconced in plantations on both sides of the river, from the falls to Point Comfort, all of them eager to share in the spoils of political dominion.

Central to the transformation of politics was the "equal and like law" provision, for it began Virginia's transition from marchland to Anglicized province. As in Ireland, ambitious adventurers had thrown in their lot with a source of law and power that would guarantee their own collective ascendancy against rival local factions or individuals. The "equal and like" clause contributed, too, to a linking of political power with the economic order as it was relentlessly emerging in Virginia, rather than as an externally imposed marchland instrument of control.[69] Opening the way to a wave of home-grown leaders in the 1630s, it would force them into a new arena of competitive efforts to recast the relationship between social and political status.

Nonetheless, the arrival of the 1618 charter did not end attempts to circumvent Company control and erect private preserves. It was natural, perhaps, that Captain John Martin should challenge the new principle, and he did so by attempting to send two representatives from Martin's Brandon to sit at the newly convened House of Burgesses. Unwilling to seat anyone who posed a threat to the laws and authority of the assembly they controlled, the Burgesses asserted the right to be the sole judge of who might sit among them and refused to admit Martin's men. Sending to England for confirmation of this authority, the Burgesses requested an end to his extraordinary privileges and asked that the Company abolish all private liberties that would "diverte out of the true course the free and publique current of justice." Martin's patent they attacked as a precedent by which "the uniformity and equality of lawes and orders extending over the whole Colony might be impeached."[70]

Martin's patent threatened to return the colony government to the tumultuous marchland status of its first years, and to slow the creation of a landed-gentry form of provincial society. Neither the Company nor the newly constituted oligarchy of Burgesses and Councilors (joined unicamerally as the General Assembly) could tolerate such a loss of mastery. Both the Company and the General Assembly recognized a common interest in placing justice under public rather than private jurisdiction. Whenever Virginia law was to be scrutinized for conformity to English law, therefore, it would be the *king's* law against which it was to be measured—"It beinge not fitt," said the Company in 1620, "that his Majesty's subjects should be governed by any other laws then by such as shall receave influence from his Majesty."[71] Everyone was to take oaths of allegiance and supremacy, the Company ordered the next year, and justice was to "bee equallie administered to all His Majesties subjects ther resideing, and as neare as may be after the forme of this realme of England."[72] Consistent with this impulse, the Company also rescinded as improperly obtained Martin's "divers exorbatant pryveledges and transcendent liberties."[73]

Even before the constituting of the Burgesses, Martin's efforts had brought him into direct conflict with men who might show outward loyalty to the Company but who were equally ambitious for their own benefit. Aware of the diminishing potential for private, franchisal autonomy after 1618, they had cannily recognized that the route to their own wealth and power was now through the institutional structure of the Company and its public institutions.

Captain Samuel Argall, for instance, saw in Martin the very spirit of faction-torn marchland disorder that was troubling the Company in London no less than it was bedeviling the king; it also stood in his way as a rival source of power and profit in the colony. Citing Martin, he advised the Company to cease offering broad private trading privileges, on the ground that otherwise the colony magazine (a subsidiary trading company for marketing all tobacco) could not prosper. Consistent with his efforts to reestablish the primacy of the Company over individual members as well as over unruly laborers, Argall also reinstated the rigor of Dale's martial code, compelled attendance at church (on pain of being "a slave" for a week), and outlawed private trade with the Indians.[74]

Having moved forcefully to elevate the powers of the governor, however, Argall himself soon proceeded to demonstrate the tenacity of the lord-marcher model of self-aggrandizement. Acting under his authority as governor, he disseized landholders to his own advantage, took Company cattle as his own, acted "under pretence of being Admirall" to confiscate hides, used Company employees on his own plantation, and engaged in the very same private Indian trade barred to others.[75] Erecting his own marchland enclave at Argall's Town upriver from Jamestown, he used—without assembly assent—public power for private gain. Not surprisingly, the new assembly in 1619 swiftly confiscated his property and returned it to public control.[76]

Argall, however, had only been continuing the practice commenced by Yeardley, the man who, ironically, had brought the "greate Charter" to Virginia. Whatever the Company's policy with regard to discouraging independent marcher lordship, Yeardley went his own way and pursued his personal gain shamelessly. Arriving with a freshly obtained knighthood to enhance his power, Yeardley attempted to play the role of lord marcher.[77] According to a petition from William Kemp of Elizabeth City, Yeardley had "turned out," (that is, had disseized) numerous "old planters," including a "wife great with child."[78] Kemp's petition arrived in London amid the bitter factionalism dividing the Company, and his charges never got the undivided attention of the Company and Council. Owing, it is likely, to the intervention of Yeardley's patron the Earl of Warwick, the Company left the burden of proof with Kemp and (in a manner similar to that used by the Ironmongers' Company with Samuel Pidgeon's complaint from Coleraine) sent the matter back to officials in Virginia, so that "any truth" might be discovered.[79]

Yet Argall and Yeardley in employing the office of governor, or the Burgesses in dominating the assembly, had not counted on the wiles of Captain Martin, who had other stratagems to employ in his challenge to centralization of power in the Company. By the 1620s King James was examining Irish land patents for the special privileges contained in them; soon he, and after him his son Charles, would recall many which had been granted in common socage without any obligations, and convert them into knight service with much more onerous burdens.[80] Playing upon James's clear intent to assert royal control in the borderlands, Martin early in 1622 (before the Massacre) proposed his grandest scheme yet. Though impossible of realization even in the confused summer following the Massacre of 1622, the audacity of his request was of such a magnitude that it reveals the continuing lure of marchland aggrandizement. Martin, again with the help of his brother-in-law, petitioned the Crown for the creation in Virginia of a vast tract of land as royal demesne, with "some honorable person"—obviously himself—as "commander thereof," who would be authorized "to give order for plantations thereon for your Majesty's best behoof and profit, giving order also for a justice of oyer and rangers and other officers as shall be thought most convenient for the said forest and plantations." With his associate Captain Robert Hazwell (labeled a would-be "Polonian Lord in his own creating" by the affronted Company), Martin was reaching to erect a vast personal estate under the cover of establishing a royal forest. Not content to create his own private barony, Martin cleverly included the fortress at Jamestown and the residences of the governor and councilors within "the King's forrest," a tract eighty miles in circumference. Martin might have been considering, too, that as chief judicial officer, he would have the vast powers of a justice in eyre to go above or beyond the Company, and to suspend all normal judicial activities.[81]

In the event, however, Martin's efforts failed, for the tide had turned against private justice granted by an outside source, even if under the guise of royal authority. Conversely, Virginians had begun to recognize that their interests were best served by their own collective control of public powers. Their self-serving commitment to the authority of the Company over that of renegades like Martin or Argall became apparent in the desperate days after the Massacre of 1622. With Virginia's first ruling elite dead or departed, the hardy survivors of the dreadful demographic realities of disease, brutality, and opportunism rose to wealth in the colony while the London investors went bankrupt. Uncommitted to the larger goals of the enterprise, these "tough, unsentimental, quick-tempered crudely ambitious men concerned with profits and increased landholdings"[82] now had a blueprint for power drawn by the same impulses and realities that had led to the overhaul of Irish provincial rule. Sent to what they regarded as a godforsaken wilderness far from London, they had learned from their predecessors how to bend the forms of law and administration to suit their needs. They skillfully claimed a legacy of local rule unrestrained by the legal niceties of the metropolis, but nominally justified by the dignity of the king's grant of the common law.

By deciding to recall the Company charter in July 1623, the Privy Council sealed the doom of private jurisdictions and guaranteed the triumph of local magnates seeking to erect a public system that they controlled. In November, Privy Council law officers began *quo warranto* proceedings against the Company charter, and in May of 1624 the court of King's Bench adjudged that no cause had been shown not to revoke.[83] A writ intended, writes Coke, "for franchises which belong to the crown," *quo warranto* was the proper weapon for use "as against the nobles and others of the realme for their liberties, franchises, and priviledges," and its employment in 1624 attested to the king's growing concern about the usurpation of the royal authority in his distant and intractable Chesapeake marchland.[84]

Yet nothing immediately took the Company's place. James's death left all affairs uncertain, and not until March of 1625 did King Charles I proclaim Virginia a royal colony. By another proclamation two months later, Charles made Virginia part of "our Royal Empire" and directly dependent upon the Crown. For the time being, no new company was anticipated, and although Charles planned to create a new London council to run his domain, he never got around to the task. Matters were left to the Privy Council, which quickly lost the will and ability to supervise the enterprise, much as it had failed to direct administration over Ireland's adventurers.[85]

But the effect of the "greate Charter" and James's jealousy of private liberties could not be reversed. Centralization "under equal and like law and orders" offered Virginia's new landed oligarchy the preferred methods of personal aggrandizement and judicial manipulation. These men were not long in setting about the task. Where the council under Company control had once been their rival, it now stood as their opportunity. Gaining control of what had become the highest judicial power in the colony, they punished as seditious all remarks derogatory of their authority and even personal aspersions against them. When Luke Eden, who was owed twenty bushels of corn by the colony treasurer, faced his debtor in the council chamber in May of 1625, his strong demand for repayment was mercilessly quashed. Eden's behavior was deemed "lewd" and his words "unreverent," tending "to the great abuse of the Governor and the rest of the Counsell beinge then in Courte." The council, temporarily unaccountable, ordered that "he shalbe laid neck and heele in the market place," pay two hundredweight of tobacco, and post bond for his future good behavior. No less than Irish councilors, those of Virginia were getting accustomed to using the courts for their advantage.[86] But their power was increasingly becoming a collective force, held jealously and strictly controlled by them as a group. When John Martin managed to obtain appointment in London to the colony's council in 1624, his renegade ambition too directly threatened their purposes; in less than a year (and barely a month after punishing Luke Eden), the council suspended Martin as "a sower of disentions and seditione . . . disobedient to government." Martin's maverick marchland behavior made him "a person exceedinge dangerous to the state and Colonie."[87]

The Virginia councilors recognized that their control, momentarily secure by default from London, might be overturned at a stroke by a reconstituting of the Company or the creation of an entirely new one. Accordingly, they took steps to create a system of locally distributed powers guaranteed by a central body they controlled. In that way, they hoped, the reimposition of centralized power from abroad, by way of Jamestown, would find a well-entrenched local gentry exercising legitimate autonomous powers as in provincial Ireland or England.

Within this context, therefore, the General Assembly in 1624 created monthly courts at Charles City and Elizabeth City. Although the assembly required these courts to keep records and to allow appeals to the Governor and Council, it left them notably vague as to procedures, failing even to make reference to English laws as a model.[88] To their officers, referred to as "commanders," this enactment gave significant police powers and the authority to inflict corporal punishment or assess fines. Ominously, those "persons of quality" who were "not fitt to undergoe corporal punishment" might be "ymprisoned of the discretione of the commander."[89]

The commanders continued to use non–common law methods as a tool to discipline labor. When Governor John Pott issued a commission to commanders in 1630, for example, he conferred on them "full power and authority to doe, execute and performe all such matters and things as are incident and appertayning to the place and office of Commander there."[90] Two years earlier he had alluded to one very significant matter, when he specified that commanders of hundreds should have control over local militia. In addition, courts could draw on the office of provost marshal—an office alien to the common law and criticized in England for its authoritarian origins.[91]

For at least a dozen years after 1618, then, remnants of marchland justice continued to rival the still incomplete application of the common law in Virginia. That Virginians did not establish the common law immediately—or that they twisted it to their purposes when they did— is, however, less significant than the fact that by the 1630s the newly emergent adventurer class was coming to recognize its advantages and to see a system of common laws issuing from Jamestown as their best guarantor of autonomy and security. Unlike the chaotic infighting and disarray that characterized a marchland where legal authority drew its strength from disruptive private grants with no basis in Virginia's society or economy, Virginia's political order would be based on locally achieved and entrenched economic power. Like their predecessors in Ireland, they were erecting a system no less autocratic than that which had preceded it, but it was their creation, and it would be under their control.

Whatever the lingering appeal of the marchland model, the concentration of power under a common system of laws in Jamestown, to be parceled out to the localities under centralized control, steadily gained ascendancy after 1630. As the system of monthly courts expanded farther into "remote parts of this colony" in 1632, the General Assembly ordered that justice be conducted "as neere as may be, accordinge to the lawes of the realme of England." Carefully acting to prevent too great a devolution of authority beyond their control, the assembly also provided that a councilor be a member of the quorum at each court, that records be kept, and that a right of appeal be available. The transition to English common law forms was well underway: commanders were transformed in everything but name into English provincial officials, with authority "to doe and execute, whatever a justice of the peace, or more justices of the peace may doe."[92] Finally in 1634 the assembly put in place the essential elements of the common law system by shiring the colony. Eight counties with their common law courts and officers superseded the monthly courts. Provosts-marshal became sheriffs, and military authority was separated from judicial by the placing of militia matters into the hands of newly created lieutenants. Like justices in assize, councilors were not merely named to the quorum, but were expressly required "to have notice to attend and assist in each court of the shire."[93]

That the earliest English settlers of Virginia did not choose to apply the common law in the first years of colonization reveals a great deal about their purposes and tactics in the vanguard of marchland expansion. Why they ultimately did choose to establish the common law suggests even more about the way that ambitious Englishmen successfully transformed a typical marchland, controlled from abroad, into an English provincial society dominated by its own local elite. As elsewhere in England's expansion overseas, the malleable nature of the law played a vital role in that transformation.

"Some Root of Bitterness"

CORPORAL PUNISHMENT, CHILD
ABUSE, AND THE APOCALYPTIC IMPULSE
IN MICHAEL WIGGLESWORTH

PHILIP GREVEN

LONG BEFORE Jonathan Edwards warned sinners of the dangers of being in the hands of an angry God, Michael Wigglesworth shaped the public consciousness of impending doom as did no other poet or writer in seventeenth-century New England: the images of judgment, destruction, and torment that faced every living person who had not become a child of God, a true saint, one of the few who would escape the punishments of Hell that would endure forever.* In both England and New England, the sense of the imminent end of the world was widespread, with many people convinced that Jesus could return at any moment, that the Day of Judgment was fast approaching, and that the Apocalypse would soon bring the world to its appointed fiery end. Historians, however, have not yet explored the psychological and experiential roots of this apocalyptic impulse, nor have they sought out the hidden and usually forgotten memories of pain and hurt, of physical violence and abuse in the name of discipline and parental authority that underpinned the anxieties, fears, and sufferings of the adults whose consciousness was marked by a keen sense of the approaching Apocalypse. Michael Wigglesworth, too, lived with a sense of expectation

*I am grateful to the following individuals for their helpful and suggestive comments on various drafts of this essay: Rudolph Bell, Paul Clemens, Helen Stokes Greven, James Henretta, and Thomas Slaughter, as well as to the participants at the conference honoring Bernard Bailyn.

and fear. He was an apocalyptic whose imagination provided fantasies and word-pictures that haunted the mental world of seventeenth-century New England. By exploring the persistent themes that emerge from his private writings and his public statements in the poems that were among the most popular ever written in early America, and by examining his life and thought in some depth, it ought to be possible to fathom some of the underlying sources for the apocalyptic impulse among the first generations of New Englanders.[1]

The experience of abuse is embedded at the very center of Wigglesworth's character and life, shaping his feelings, his anxieties, and his beliefs from day to day, from year to year. The suffering and emotional stresses of childhood crippled him so severely as a young man and adult that he ultimately became ill, a prisoner in his own house, unable to take part in the public life of the ministry to which he had been called and to which he devoted his life.[2]

His invalidism as an adult is one of the central clues to his innermost being and the outcome of a childhood shaped by pain and fear—and rage. But the rage was buried, hidden away, and the rebellious spirit that must have been present in the boy whose will was being conquered by the adults who raised him and disciplined him had to be suppressed, denied, repudiated.[3] The effort to bring himself under control overwhelmed him, and he fell ill for many decades. But the impulses that originally shaped the battles over his willfulness never disappeared: they are visible in everything he ever wrote. His private writings, often obscured in shorthand in his diary, and his public writings, in poems read throughout New England, contained the same recurrent preoccupations that reveal the hidden roots of the apocalyptic impulse that underlay the fantasies of *The Day of Doom* and many of his other poems.

What emerges most clearly from an examination of his life and writings is his obsession with affliction, pain, suffering, and punishment. No one knows for certain whether or not Michael Wigglesworth was ever struck physically and suffered the pains of corporal punishment as a child, since no known document proves or disproves this possibility. But his whole life and his entire being provide us with evidence that confirms his preoccupation with corporal punishments and pain, evidence that identifies him as a childhood victim of physical violence and assault by adults. Pain and punishment and afflictions, which are always experienced as forms of chastisement, are the central themes of Michael Wigglesworth's poetry and life. Corporal punishment is the experiential core of his entire theology, fundamental to an understanding of his character and thought.[4]

Fantasies of Punishment

Michael Wigglesworth's obsession with affliction and punishment, his sense of the imminence of doom, the Day of Judgment, and the end of the world marked him as an apocalyptic and formed the central motifs of much of the poetry that he wrote in his late twenties and early thirties. Two of his most famous poems, both written or published in 1662— *The Day of Doom or a Poetical Description of the Great and Last Judgment* and *God's Controversy with New-England Written in the Time of the Great Drought Anno 1662*—captured the imagination of the New England public as did few other writings of any description during the seventeenth century. Both poems were preoccupied with the issue of punishment for the sins both of individuals and of the body politic, the entire covenanted people gathered together in New England.

Physical punishment pervades Wigglesworth's fantasies.[5] Pain and suffering and sustained torments play a decisive role in the dramas of destruction and judgment that were being imagined and set forth for all to read and to anticipate. Wigglesworth created images and scenarios in poetry that captured the essence of punishment and the Apocalypse more vividly and powerfully than anyone else in his generation. The immense popularity of these poems is indicative of the collective resonance throughout New England to these personal obsessions expressed through the motifs of anxiety, terror, and pain embedded in his poems. Many individuals knew from their own experience what it had been like to be physically punished and harshly treated as children.

In *The Day of Doom*, the apocalyptic end comes suddenly, without warning. Few are prepared for the catastrophe that envelops the earth and destroys it by fire, when "God began to powre/Destruction the World upon/in a tempestuous showre." While the saints are being separated from the sinners, the sheep from the goats,

> Lo! Christ begins for their great sins
> to fire the Earths Foundation:
>
> And by and by the flaming Sky
> shall drop like molten Lead
> About their ears, t'increase their fears,
> And aggravate their dread.

But the fires that matter most are not those that consume the earth at the end of time, but the fires that scorch but never consume the flesh of those who are to be damned and suffer in Hell forever. Fire is the medium of God's punishment; the heat and the pain of burning, not dissimilar to the sting of a rod on the flesh, will be the eternal reminders of the price of disobedience to the men, women, and children, including many infants, who are to be damned for their sins while on earth.[6]

According to Wigglesworth, even the Saints who will be spared eternal punishments have been subject to pain and corporal punishments during their lives on earth. Standing next to Christ's right hand on that last day will be

> all Christ's afflicted ones,
> Who being chastised, neither despised
> nor sank amidst their groans:
> Who by the Rod were turn'd to God,
> and loved him the more,
> Not murmuring nor quarrelling
> When they were chast'ned sore.

Even Christ himself, of course, experienced pain and suffering while on earth: "The Cross his pain I did sustain;/ yea more, my Fathers ire/ I underwent, my Blood I spent/ to save them from Hell fire." As Christ says, "But as for those whom I have chose/ Salvations heirs to be,/ I underwent their punishment,/ and therefore set them free."[7]

But it is the goats, standing to Christ's left, whom he has rejected and not chosen for salvation, who murmur and quarrel with the prospects of pain and torments that await them in Hell. These sinners plead for mercy, compassion, and forgiveness, desperate to evade the fate that clearly awaits them for their sins while on earth. For them, though, no such salvation awaits, nor rescue from the punishments to come. Not even their appeals to God's mercy avail:

> Others Argue, and not a few,
> is not God gracious?
> His Equity and Clemency
> are they not marvellous?
> Thus we believ'd; are we deceiv'd?
> cannot his mercy great,
> (As hath been told to us of old)
> asswage his angers heat?

And then Wigglesworth poses the crucial question raised by those whose sins seem slight:

> How can it be that God should see
> his Creatures endless pain,
> Or hear the groans and rueful moans,

and still his wrath retain?
Can it agree with Equitie?
can mercy have the heart
To recompence few years offence
with Everlasting smart?

Remarkably few New Englanders in the seventeenth century ever asked such questions on paper, although many surely must have had similar thoughts prior to their own conversions. But Wigglesworth's Christ responds to such questions and pleas coldly, declaring to the assembled throng that

It's now high time that ev'ry Crime
be brought to punishment:
Wrath long contain'd, and oft restrain'd,
at last must have a vent:
Justice severe cannot forbear
to plague sin any longer,
But must inflict with hand most strict
mischief upon the wronger.

Even infants who die before they sin must suffer damnation as heirs of Adam's fall. Though Jesus might save some, most will be allowed "the easiest room in Hell." As for the rest, Wigglesworth makes clear that God's "wrath is great, whose burning heat/ no floods of tears can slake:/ His word stands fast, that they be cast/ into the burning Lake." The doom they have hoped to evade, to escape, or to be rescued from, is upon them. Their punishment is about to begin, never to end.[8]

All this while, the Saints stand by, watching, listening, experiencing the anguish and torments of those being judged and found guilty and sentenced to perpetual punishments. How do they react? What do they feel? Wigglesworth describes this horrifying scene without pity, without empathy, without remorse:

Where tender love mens hearts did move
unto a sympathy,
And bearing part of others smart
in their anxiety;
Now such compassion is out of fashion,
and wholly laid aside:
No Friends so near, but Saints to hear
their Sentence can abide.

At this penultimate moment in time, families are split apart irrevocably, one person to live in joy forever, another to suffer unimaginable tortures and pains forever.

> One natural Brother beholds another
> in this astonied fit,
> Yet sorrows not thereat a jot,
> nor pitties him a whit.
> The godly wife conceives no grief,
> nor can she shed a tear
> For the sad state of her dear Mate,
> when she his doom doth hear.

Not even the most basic connection between parents and children survives intact in the face of the doom to come:

> The tender Mother will own no other
> of all her numerous brood,
> But such as stand at Christ's right hand
> acquitted through his Blood.
> The pious Father had now much rather
> his graceless Son should ly
> In Hell with Devils, for all his evils
> burning eternally.

This astonishing lack of empathy, this dissociation from the pains and sufferings of those most loved, this capacity on the part of the Saints to feel nothing when they see their own children, kindred, friends, and neighbors consigned to the flames—this is one of the surest signs of having been abused that one can discover.[9]

Yet half a century later, Michael Wigglesworth's own son recalled that Wiggleworth threatened to denounce him on the Day of Judgment if he did not become a Saint, a threat intensified by the fact that his young son had yet to receive evidence of the grace he sought in order to become one of Christ's own, thus remaining in constant danger of damnation. Early in 1711, with his father five years in his grave, seventeen-year-old Edward (who later became Hollis Professor of Divinity at Harvard College) recalled that his parents had "brought [him] up in the Nurture and admonition of the Lord." He acknowledged that "The instructions, Cautions, Counsels and admonitions of my Father, the Ernest Exhortations and tears of my mother, were daily putting [him] in mind of the things which concerned my everlasting peace and wellfare." Although these parental words often "moved [his] affections greatly," he especially recalled being "*terrified* and *astonished* when my father hath been Setting Life and Death before me, and then telling me that if I chose death rather than Life *he would appear as A witness against me in that great and terrible day of the Lord*," the very act his father had imagined others doing in *The Day of Doom* fifty years previously.[10]

For those who are to be damned at the Day of Judgment, Wigglesworth described with sadistic fervor the torments and tortures that they will experience forever. Immediately after being consigned to the flames,

> They wring their hands, their caitiff-hands
> and gnash their teeth for terrour;
> They cry, they roar for anguish sore,
> and gnaw their tongues for horrour.
> But get away without delay,
> Christ pitties not your cry:
> Depart to Hell, there may you yell,
> and roar Eternally.

Wigglesworth then describes the ghastly details of their captivity and torture:

> With Iron bands they bind their hands,
> and cursed feet together,
> And cast them all, both great and small,
> into that Lake for ever.
> Where day and night, without respite,
> they wail, and cry, and howl
> For tort'ring pain, which they sustain
> in Body and in Soul.

When Wigglesworth asks

> But who can tell the plagues of Hell,
> and torments exquisite?
> Who can relate their dismal state,
> and terrours infinite?

the implicit answer is: Only someone who has experienced something comparable while living on this earth, someone who knows from experience what it feels like to be terrorized and tortured, to feel the burning pain of a rod upon his body, and who knows the anguish that a child experiences when being punished by parents. When "Almighty God, whose Iron Rod,/ to smite them never lins [ceases]/ Doth most declare his Justice rare/ in plaguing these mens sins," Michael Wigglesworth could only ally himself with the hand that smote, and create an imaginary scenario, drawn partly from Biblical texts and partly from his own innermost self, that makes most sadistic fantasies seem bland. It is the lurking pleasure that he derives from his descriptions of torture that reveals the secret impulses shaping his fantasies of the apocalyptic end and the Day of Judgment. He is enthralled by God's power, anger, vengeance, and ability to inflict pain on bodies and souls forever, for it is the wicked who capture the reader's attention throughout *The Day of Doom*, not the Saints. The central appeal of this poem is to a sadomasochistic fantasy that rests upon a bed of childhood pain.[11]

Meanwhile, the elect have gone to Heaven, where "they sing unto their King/ a Song of endless Praise:/ They praise his Name, and do proclaim/ that just are all his ways." Having watched the pain and torments of those who were judged and condemned, they have no choice but to justify the ways of God who has saved them from the fires of Hell. They have been rescued; the others, not. For Wigglesworth, Hell was the ultimate expression of the "Iron Rod" of God whose punishments awaited those who would not do his will and obey his rules and commandments.[12]

Long before *The Day of Doom* strikes, however, God often afflicts New Englanders with punishments for their rebellion and their sins. Wigglesworth's famous lament over the declension of New England, *God's Controversy With New-England*, presumes God's use of corporal punishments as the central means of chastising the people "for whose dear sake an howling wildernes/ I lately turned into a fruitful paradeis." As Wigglesworth's God observes:

> Some, that maintain a reall root of grace,
> Are overgrown with many noysome weeds,
> Whose heart, that those no longer may take place,
> The benefit of due correction needs.
> And such as these however gone astray
> I shall by stripes reduce into a better way.

As for "Backsliders," God warns that "Except you seriously, and soon, repent,/ Ile not delay your pain and heavy punishment."[13]

The central theme of the entire poem is filial rebellion: "I children nourisht, nurtur'd and upheld:/ But they against a tender father have rebell'd." And the outcome of their behavior is set forth in explicit detail: "Consider wel & wisely what the rod,/ Wherewith thou art from yeer to yeer chastized,/ Instructeth thee. Repent, & turn to God,/ Who wil not have his nurture be despized." Without the threat of God's rod, and the pain of punishments from their "tender father" who nevertheless beats them into submission to his will and ways, Wigglesworth cannot conceive of anything but disaster. Increasingly, danger and suffering will be forthcoming without true repentance and amendment of their ways:

> Beware, O sinful Land, beware;
> And do not think it strange
> That sorer judgements are at hand,
> Unless thou quickly change.
> . . . Wrath cannot cease, if sin remain,
> Where judgement is begun.

Not only individuals but the people of New England collectively will suffer physical punishments at the hands of their angry God.[14]

Michael Wigglesworth was New England's most ardent apologist for corporal punishment. His intense inner compulsion to justify the most rigorous and brutal forms of physical discipline by his divine Father persisted for years after the composition of his two most famous poems in the late 1650s and early 1660s. In 1669 or 1670, he published another volume of poems that centered around the theme of punishments: *Meat Out of the Eater: Or, Meditations Concerning the Necessity, End, and Usefulness of Afflictions unto God's Children. All Tending to Prepare Them for, and Comfort Them Under the Cross*. In his mid- to late thirties, he transformed his own suffering into poetry that would justify the most anguishing pains inflicted upon their bodies that could be experienced by Christians as the direct will of God, the daily crosses that God's children had to learn to bear and to love. Only Jonathan Edwards, years later, comes close to Wigglesworth in the sustained paean to pain that shapes the voice being articulated in these meditations and poems, a poetry of abuse and physical violence that makes the victims praise their Father no matter what he chooses to do to them, even unto death itself. Wigglesworth's theology requires punishment, and these poems are meant to comfort and sustain those Christians, like himself, who are the subjects of God's discipline.

Suffering, for Michael Wigglesworth, is an inescapable part of being a true child of God. In a meditation entitled "God doth in Mercy scourge His own./ In Wrath he others lets alone," Wigglesworth writes:

> Though various are the Wayes
> And Sufferings whereby
> God doth His Children exercise,
> Correct and also try:
> Yet all must bear the Cross
> Before they wear the Crown;
> All must partake of Chastening,
> Whom God vouchsafes to own.

Wigglesworth insists that

> Great Mercy 'tis to be subdu'd
> By scourging with the Rod.
> My soul be thankful then
> That God thee thus corrects,
> Who might have let thee head long run
> With those whom He rejects.

Pain is essential evidence of being a child of God, for

> Affliction is Christ's School,
> Wherein He teacheth His
> To know and do their duty, and
> To mend what is amiss.
> For though Afflictions may
> Unto the Flesh be painful;
> *David* and other Saints of God
> Have found them very gainful.[15]

In a dialogue between the Flesh and the Spirit, Wigglesworth explores the feelings of the person being punished, articulating the arguments both for and against the infliction of pain by a father's hands. The Spirit notes that

> Fathers may chide and whip
> Their Children till they smart:
> But whil'st their hand Inflicteth stripes,
> They pity with their heart.
> They cast not off a Child,
> Although they angry be:
> Nor doth thy Heav'nly Father mild
> Reject and Cast off thee.

But the body has another view, and the Flesh rejoins out of the felt experiences of anyone who has ever actually been subject to such stripes and whippings:

> OH but I greatly fear,
> My sufferings are not such
> As Childrens Nurture use to be
> But that they differ much.
> They are too great and long
> (I fear) to stand with love:
> Such overwhelming strokes methinks
> Do rather hatred prove.

Here, suddenly and briefly, the secret is revealed: being beaten is not a token of love, but of hate. The Flesh adds, voicing the fantasies and wishes of all abused children:

> Were I a Child of God
> He would more gently deal:
> Nor would he always use the Rod
> But sometimes help and heal.

But the reality is always different:

> But I am day by day
> Afflicted very sore:
> My sufferings have been many years,
> And still are growing more.

For one of the very few times in his life, Wigglesworth allows himself to voice the anxiety and fear of a child who is being beaten, unable to feel the love that is being professed by the father who is causing his pain. The response by the Spirit to this authentic anxiety is to rationalize God's punishments as kindnesses, in the long run, rather than as the severities that the body knows from frequent experience:

> God doth more gently deal
> Than thou considerest well.
> For had he us'd extremities
> Thou hadst been now in Hell.
> He is not so severe
> As thou imaginest;
> For some that were to him most dear,
> Have been much more distrest.

Wigglesworth thus speaks in two voices, one of a child being beaten and suffering pain, the other of an adult justifying the violence and assault in the name of moderation, knowing that even worse could be inflicted, and often is, at the discretion of God the Father.[16]

The most remarkable of Wigglesworth's poems provides an exegesis of corporal punishment that reflects an exquisite sensitivity to a child's experience of abuse: "The Carriage of a Child of God Under his Fathers smarting Rod." The poem is an ode to flagellation, from a child's point of view.[17] Only someone who experienced this personally could know what such a child actually feels when being beaten, and could recall the intense inner conflicts that the rod evokes.

Parents often beat their children in God's name, invoking divine displeasure at the behavior of their children, and claim to be acting as God's arms when they use the rod, or other instruments, for inflicting physical pain upon their children's bodies. Wigglesworth begins his poem by acknowledging that the child whom he is writing about

> . . . sees a hand of God in his Afflictions all,
> And owns it for to be his Rod, Whatever Cross befall.
> For whosoever be th'immediate instrument,
> He knows right well that God himself was the Efficient.

Earthly fathers thus are doing the will of God when they afflict their children with corporal punishments. Wigglesworth notes that

> If . . . the grief be small or the Chastisement light:
> Yet since God finds it not in vain, light strokes he dare not slight.
>
> *   *   *
>
> If greater be the Blow, it doth not him dismay:
> Because he knows a Fathers hand such stripes may on him lay[.]

But if, after conscientious self-scrutiny, "he cannot find the cause/ For which the Lord afflicteth him," he knows, nevertheless, that his sins are such "As God may judge it meet therefore to scourge him all his dayes." Many children are punished for causes or reasons that seem unrelated to anything they themselves have said or done, for often physical violence and pain strike for no apparent reasons. When afflictions come from God, it is not always possible to know the reasons, or to connect them to one's own actions or behavior. But that, Wigglesworth argues, is no defense against the punishments when they are meted out by God the Father.[18]

Wigglesworth knows that a child being punished by a father has no defense against the infliction of pain, no choice, when being beaten with a rod, but to submit to the will of the father who is doing the beating. Like many abused children, this child of God can survive only by identifying himself with the one who is causing him pain, distancing himself from his own self, his own will, his own body, and, most important of all, from his own feelings and thoughts. He has to deny himself in order to survive.[19]

The denial of self and the false humility that arise from the necessity of submission to the pain and the punishment are evident:

> Himself he humbleth under the mighty hand of God:
> And for the sake of that sweet hand doth kiss the sharpest Rod.
> He taketh up his Cross, denieth his own will,
> Advanceth God's above his own, and yieldeth to him still.

Wigglesworth observes the forced passivity of the victim of violence, the utter frozenness that arises when a powerful adult is assaulting a small child with a physical instrument such as a rod: "Unto the yoke of Christ he doth his neck submit:/ He turns his cheek to him that smites, and meekly taketh it."[20]

The crucial moment comes, for Wigglesworth as for all those children who are being beaten in the name of discipline, when the feelings of resistance, rage, and hatred—the most terrifying of all—surge into consciousness, feelings that are too dangerous to be expressed, or even felt. Wigglesworth knows such feelings, because he writes about them with absolute authority:

> Yea when his grief is most, and sorest is his pain:
> He still endeavoureth good thoughts of God for to retain.
>
> *   *   *
>
> His earnest care and prayer when greatest is his smart,
> Is that he never may blaspheme God with his mouth or heart.
> He beggeth Patience in his extremities
> To bear Gods hand, that so his heart may not against him rise.

But the urge and the desire are there, threatening to overwhelm the child and to bring about yet further pain and danger. No wonder, then, that "If murmuring thoughts do rise (or hearts begin to swell)/ He strives to beat them down again; he hates such thoughts like Hell." No defense, no opposition, no escape are possible, not even inwardly. This child has no choice but to deny his own most basic impulses to survive: "God he resolves to love, deal with him as he will:/ And in his mercy to confide *although he should him kill*." Not even his own death from physical assault and pain can make him voice his blasphemous thoughts against the Father who is beating him to death. Such thoughts, Michael Wigglesworth knows, must be suppressed, beaten down, denied. But they are there, at least momentarily, and he knows that as well.[21]

His own experience many years earlier mirrored the point he makes in this poem. In the endnotes to his diary, written sometime in 1653 or 1654, Wigglesworth notes that "the Lord brought me to see all my duties which I had rested in were nothing worth[.] The Lord brought me to resolve with myself though he kill me yet will I trust in him[.] If I must [be] damned yet it shall be in the way of obedience as far as God enabled me. And I was in some measure contented though I should be damned."[22]

Physical violence and potentially murderous assault by an adult upon a child, which is what the poem is actually describing, make it impossible for the child to do anything but submit—or be killed. Carried to its extremity, physical punishment can and too often does cause death, and many children know this even though they survive such life-threatening experiences. The discovery in the early 1960s of the "Battered Child Syndrome" by pediatricians and other physicians has fostered a long-belated recognition of the realities of the dangerous violence and abuse disguised as discipline that Wigglesworth knew so well centuries ago.[23]

Even in his late thirties, Wigglesworth knew what a child feels when being beaten with his father's rod. This knowledge, still vivid and still painful, shaped the insistent inner obsession with punishment and affliction that drove him to write "Carriage of a Child" and many other poems. His ability to write poetry, however, gave him the means to explore the pain that had shaped and misshaped his innermost being from a very early age, and permitted him to confront, in the guise of fantasy and imagination, the feelings that his whole life previously had been designed to obscure and deny.

Affliction and punishment formed the central threads that wove the themes of his psyche and his life together into a coherent pattern, themes that became most visible in the record he kept of his life during his early and midtwenties. By falling ill and becoming an invalid, he was able to keep the source of his suffering a secret, obscured even from his own intense self-scrutiny, while simultaneously revealing it for all to see in the poems that he wrote and published. The apocalyptic impulse, rooted in experiences of assault and abuse and feelings of destructive rage, hostility, and resentment, flowed through his life and thought for half a century.

The Experience of Affliction

Early in 1653, at the age of twenty-one, Michael Wigglesworth began to keep his diary, which provides us with an abrupt and startlingly intimate glimpse of his innermost obsessions, anxieties, thoughts, and experiences. He is suddenly present, in all his complexity and anguish, the themes that obsess him visible on virtually every page: obedience and rebellion, willfulness, a preoccupation with his body and health, a pervasive sense of fear, acute moments of embarrassment and shame, an unending sense of guilt, a mood of almost unceasing melancholy, constant doubt and worry, an abhorrence of anything that gives him a sense of self-worth, be it pride or lust or simply desire and accomplishments. Wigglesworth already was the victim of an anxiety so pervasive, and fears so intense, that the path toward a life of illness and invalidism was being marked out for anyone—other than himself—to see. His life was full of affliction and suffering, despite his youth and accomplishments

—he already had graduated from Harvard College, become a tutor, and, in the course of the next four years was to marry and to become a minister of the gospel at Malden, in the Massachusetts Bay Colony. Michael Wigglesworth was a neurotic young man, whose life bore the marks of pain and affliction and alienation that distanced him both from his father and mother and from his Father in Heaven, the God to whom he devoted his life but whose service, he ultimately discovered, demanded more of him than he was able to give.[24]

Throughout his diary, Michael's relationship with God is that of a child and his father, and his obsessive preoccupation is whether or not he is able and willing to do the will of his Father in Heaven. Willfulness, obedience, and rebelliousness are recurrent motifs throughout his diary. "Behold Lord my pitiful case: remember thou art my father though I be a rebellious child: ah put a childlike spirit into me that I may make thee onely my trust." He immediately adds, however, that he "found much deadness and little brokeness of heart" for his "sins [. . .] and some risings of Atheistic thoughts," which often haunted him, unable to feel the presence of God nor the love of God that he constantly sought in his daily life. "Ah Lord!," he added, "here the groans of thy poor prisoner, who desires to renounce all for thee and thy christ, and caus me not to err from thy wayes nor harden my heart." The following year, he exclaimed that "I desire to obey all thy commandments, subdue my rebellious will that I may become thy willing subject, and strengthen me to do thee more and better service." His persistent fear was that he could not love God, even when he was not being rebellious: "harden not my heart from thy fear and love. I am affraid because I feel so little love to the[e]." The combination of his inability to feel love for his Father and to do his will willingly made punishment necessary: "he onely is my father, able to make me happy willing to make me happy in himself though for my good he disquiet me in the creature, to drive me out of that misery which I haue throwne my self into by over-esteeming the creature and under-valuing him who is my creator and my God." Immediately afterwards, he added his wish "that thou shouldst cross and correct me to teach me wisdom, se[e]ing I should not learn it otherwise," urging God to "joyn instruction to thy correction father. as thou layest on thy rod so put under thy staf to support me. pardon all my sins, giue me thy self and conformity to thy self, that's the great thing that I desire." Here, then, were the fundamental issues that shaped his consciousness and his theology, and underlying all was the constant need for submission to the will of God, the constant rebelliousness that he felt, and the need for punishment that he sought as the child who had not obeyed the commandments of his Father.[25]

The afflictions that Michael experienced at the hand of God and the persistent anxiety that he felt over loving God, being loved by God, and doing God's will, were mirrors of his experiences with his own earthly father, Edward Wigglesworth. Edward Wigglesworth immigrated from England in 1638 with his wife, Esther, and their six-year-old son, Michael (who remained an only child for the first nine years of his life), settling first in Charlestown in the Bay Colony and then moving to New Haven, in Connecticut, where he became a farmer and lived permanently. When Michael was about nine, "God . . . was pleased . . . to visit my Father with Lameness," he recalled, "which grew upon him more & more to his dying Day, though he Liv'd under it 13 yeers." Several times he described his father as suffering from "great weakness of Body," without providing more details concerning the "great & sore affliction" that his father suffered as God willed for so many years. Edward Wigglesworth may have strained his back while working, soon after the birth of his second child and only daughter, Abigail, who was born December 1, 1640, when Michael was nine years old. He also may have been suffering from a progressive neurological disorder. In any case, as a result of his father's affliction, Michael was taken out of school, where he had been learning Latin under the severe tutelage of Ezekiel Cheever. He helped his father farm for three or four years until reaching the age of fourteen, when his father declared him unfit for "husbandry" and sent him back to school. His father remained at home, an object of pity and charity, having been granted a small piece of land near the meeting house to build upon " 'because he is so lame that he is not able to come to the meeting.' " He somehow managed to send his only son to Harvard College, where he "was indeed studious and strove to outdoe" his "compeers, but it was for honor and applause and preferment and such poor Beggarly ends," he later said, since throughout his college years he had "acted from self and for self." By the time that Michael wrote this harsh self-assessment, he already had gone far toward the re-creation of a life similar to that of his own invalided father, whose afflictions burdened him until he was released by death. Michael's bodily afflictions and his subsequent invalidism paralleled the experiences of his father with remarkable faithfulness, since both suffered from symptoms that left them feeling weak and unable to carry out a normal adult life.[26]

For Michael, ill health was the central affliction that he experienced, the primary means that God used to punish him and to cause him to suffer the crosses that continually confronted him throughout his life. His preoccupation with his body and health is evident throughout his diary, indicative of a pervasive hypochondriacal sensitivity to his physical self. His alienation from and distrust of his body, and his obsessive preoccupation with it, suggest a sense of danger and a need to be helped and healed. Ultimately he became both a prisoner in his own house, an invalid unable to work or live an active life, and a physician, who practiced medicine in the community in which he had been called to minister and to teach. Ill health, therefore, is one of the keys to an understanding of his entire life.[27]

From the very first pages of his diary, his extraordinary consciousness of his general state of health and his acute sensitivity to his body are evident. In mid-February 1653, for instance, he wrote that he had "found more sensible weakness of body and pressure by the spleen and flatulent humours this week than for so oft together this winter before," adding that "god still crosses outwardly, and I meet with vexation and rebuke." In March, having visited his parents in New Haven, he prayed that God would "pitty and cure my frail body," observing that "I cannot muse of thee and mourn after the[e] as I should do without overthrowing my bodily health." Immediately prior to making this observation about his own frail health, however, he had recorded a humiliating conflict with his father, whom God had made "an instrument of so discovering my weak and silly management of every business, that he makes my savour to stink in my owne nosethrils," which his father "did most eminently this week immediately after a proud fit of my owne," he acknowledged. He instantly drew the proper lesson from his encounter with his father: "God abaseth the proud!" But he added self-consciously that "My heart as 'tis asham'd of my self so it swells against my father, and cannot conceiv such things to proceed from loue, because that covers a multitude of infirmitys, but this rakes them open to the bottom." His invalid father, though weak in body, thus had turned cruelly upon his only son, who felt humiliated and angered by his father's verbal assault. Immediately, though, he shifted his focus from his father's attack to his own frail body and poor health.[28]

Michael was already in the process of becoming an invalid himself, unloved by his own father, and unable to love him in return. Therein lay the crux of the psychic conflicts that would haunt him for much of the rest of his life. By becoming an invalid like his father, Michael would be able to deny and obscure the feelings of resistance and opposition and rebellion that became the leitmotif of his relationships with both his earthly and his heavenly fathers. Michael's physical problems seemed remarkably similar to his father's, since they involved weakness of the body and vague somatic complaints, although Michael's were focused primarily in his throat and lungs, which made it increasingly impossible for him to speak in public.

From his point of view, ill health was not accidental but purposeful, a direct result of God's willful affliction and punishment. God often visited him "with bodily weakness" to make him conscious of something that he had done, said, or felt. But his illness intensified as a result of his feelings, both conscious and unconscious, associated with his parents. In April 1653, even before his father's death, Michael acknowledged his "want of natural affection to my father, in desiring the continuance of his life *which God ranks among those sins whereto men were given up of God to a reprobate mind.*" And he added: "*Want of honoring my mother yea slight of her speech now the eye that despises his mother the ravens of the valley shall peck it out and the young ravens shall eat it.*" He added, "*Lord I cant stand before thee because of these abominations.*" These two sins were buried, fourth and fifth, in a list of six. He surrounded these two breaches of the fifth commandment with other, less horrible and dangerous sins, ones that would not cause him to be physically maimed because of his alienation from his mother.[29]

On Friday, October 14, 1653, Michael "had some fears . . . about the immutability of gods love in case" he "should fall away from him," but was reassured of "the absolute stability thereof from the scripture." He "met with great diffcultys in my studys and my strength failed me," he observed, while later in the day "God brought to my mind . . . my want of love and dutifulness to my parents, which I beg'd pardon of." The next day he received the news that his father had died on October 1, "whereupon," he said, "I set myself to confess before the Lord my sins against him in want of naturall affections to, and sympathy with my afflicted parents, in my not prizing them and their life which god hath graciously continued so long." The next day he desired "to lay down my soul at christs foot, and to know his wil that I might obey it." Two days later, on his twenty-second birthday, he prayed "*for a right spirit under God's afflicting hand that I might not be secretly glad that my father was gone.*" The previous night, he acknowledged, "*some filthiness in a vile dream escaped me for which I loathe myself and desire to abase myself before my God.*" One week later, "at night in my sleep," he said, "I dream'd of the approach of the great and dreadful day of judgment; and was thereby exceedingly awakened in spirit (as I thought) to follow god with teares and crys until he gaue me some hopes of his gracious good wil toward me."[30]

The apocalyptic impulse had surfaced in the form of a dream, and *The Day of Doom* already was taking shape in his unconscious, one week after the discovery of his secret pleasure in his father's death. A month later, eighth in a list of ten items, was the notation: "want of sence and sorrow for my Fathers death, o Lord forgiue!" Shortly thereafter, he "was assayled with feares in reference to my unsensibleness under gods visitation in my fathers death and I feared least there should be some root of bitterness that I were not willing to part with, unsearched out," but immediately added that "I know none."³¹

From this point onward, Michael's health gradually worsened. At the end of November, a month and a half after his discovery of his father's death, he noted that "I haue scarcely bin wel, nor am yet." The next day he observed that "I found so much trouble of the spleen, as forced me to leav study." He added that God had taken away four men, members of his church, and thought "about this token of the heat of gods great anger, and my own sin kindling thereof." He then catalogued his sins, among them acknowledging "my desert to be kickt out of this world because I haue not had naturall affections to my natural father, but requited him and all my governours evil for good," and he added that he deserved "to be shut out of the world to come, because I haue rebell'd against and dishonour'd and disregarded my heavenly father, been a viper in his bosom where he has nourished me." His inability to love his father or to feel any grief over his death thus continued to haunt him, paralleled at every moment with the sense of an equal alienation from his heavenly Father, against whom he continually rebelled.³²

The death of his father provided no release for Wigglesworth from his inner anxieties and tensions, nor from the obsessive exploration of his own state of bodily health, which always included his sexuality and the functioning of his genitals. His sexuality was as conflicted as the rest of his being, and the sense of alienation from his own most powerful erotic impulses is evident throughout his diary. But his sexual impulses were beyond even his incessant efforts to gain control, and his most poignant plea was to overcome the physical signs of his sexuality that betrayed a degree of self that he found abhorrent and unacceptable. For Wigglesworth, therefore, sex was to become a central expression of the neurotic conflicts that would ultimately imprison him alone with his invalidism.

The roots of his sexual anxieties and fears are evident from the outset of his diary. The first entry immediately noted, in shorthand, the presence of his "*unnatural filthy lust that are so oft and even this day in some measure stirring*" in him after experiencing "the unloving carriages" of his "pupils." Sex, for Wigglesworth, was to become intimately linked to his bodily health and his general state of being, and clearly was to become part of his illness itself. We can track his concerns with his sexuality through the entire diary, particularly those instances, which occur several times, when he experienced seminal emissions both during the day and night. "*I find such unresistable torments of carnal lusts of provocation unto the ejection of seed that I find my self unable to read any thing to inform me about my distemper because of the prevailing or rising of my lusts.*" Several days later, he noted that "*The last night a filthy dream and so pollution escaped me in my sleep for which I desire to hang down my head with shame and beseech the Lord not to make me possess the sin of my youth and give me into the hands of my abomination.*" The sense of shame permeates his diary, but is particularly keen when he experiences "carnal lusts." Filth and pollution, self-loathing, a sense of being "vile," and a pervasive sense of living with "this body of death"—all of these reveal the intense conflicts that Wigglesworth experienced because of his erotic and sexual impulses, over which, despite valiant efforts, he had little or no control. At times, he noted "much distracted thoughts I find arising from too much doting affection *to some of my pupils one of whom went to Boston with me today.*" The homoerotic impulses that arose from his intimate contact with his students surfaced on at least one occasion, when he recorded "*such filthy lust also flowing from my fond affection to my pupils whiles in their presence,*" and confessed that he believed himself to be "*an object of God's loathing as my sin is of my own and pray God make it so more to me.*"[33]

His anxieties over his sexuality were intensified the following year when it suddenly became evident that he might have to become sexually active in a marriage that was being arranged for him. In March 1654, he was still concerned about his sexuality, praying to be delivered "*from carnal lusts These make me afraid when I feel my spirit so prone to close with them.*" Shortly thereafter he received a "*motion of marriage*" which caused him to feel torn between his erotic impulses and needs and his love for God, noting that he "*was ready to be gone awhoring after other loves and to cool in my love to God,*" but found that God helped him to "*loath*" himself. The following July, having gone home to New Haven to visit his mother, he returned to Cambridge, where he soon received a letter from his mother concerning the marriage that was being arranged on his behalf. His reaction was intense: "This report did fill my spirit suddenly with marvellous sorrow and perplexity more then I wel knew how to bear: insomuch that I fear'd least the violence of it should overthrow my bodily health." Although he intended to write "to undoe what was done," he delayed until he heard that the bride chosen for him was to be sent to "England and not to be dispozed of here. At this news," he observed, "my heart was filled with joy." His anxiety thus was quieted, temporarily, when the threat of an imposed intimacy was removed.[34]

The following year, 1655, was a critical year in Michael Wigglesworth's life, decisive in the crystallization of his illness and invalidism because it was the year in which he had to make two momentous decisions: to marry and to work. The emergence of Wigglesworth's invalidism clearly is associated with the anxieties and fears generated by the combined pressures to assume the roles of both a sexually active and a publicly active and assertive adult man. For months prior to his decision to marry, Michael Wigglesworth was obsessed with his body and his state of being but, buried within his obsessions with his health, was a preoccupation with sexual issues surrounding his own dangerousness. Was he to be a danger to himself or to others?

In February 1655, after about two months in which he made no entries in his diary, Wigglesworth resumed his self-examination with an open acknowledgment of the "hard morsel I haue had to chew upon all the winter," entirely alone since "none in these parts have known my afflic- tion" so that he "had none to pitty me, none to pray for me, none to counsel, none to comfort me." He had "even been affraid to pray for my self in this business," being "Affraid to think of my sad condition, because when I haue given way to the thoughts of it, do what I could it was too hard for me and ready to sink me." Thus he could not even pray "for help and health," fearful that he would "be too impetuous" in his "desires." He was in crisis, but totally without help from anyone who might have offered another perspective upon the issues that haunted him.[35]

What was the problem? He believed that he was both in danger himself and dangerous to others because of a sexual disease, which he evidently believed to be gonorrhea. He first wrote about his "weakness," which exposed him "to sin and temptations by day" and to *"dreams and self pollution by night which my soul abhors and mourns for."* At the age of twenty- three, Michael's sexual impulses threatened to overwhelm him and to drive him, he said, "to such a strait as I think few were ever in the like." He then spelled out the conflict in vivid detail:

> To continue in a single estate, Is both uncomfortable many wayes, and dangerous (as I conceiv) to my life, and exposeth to sin, and contrary to engagement of affections, and Friends expectations, and lyable to the harsh sensure of the world that expecteth the quite contrary: To change my condition endan- gers to bring me into a pining and loathsom diseas, to a wretched life and miserable death, the beginnings whereof I do already feel at sometimes, and dread more than death; and conse- quently I fear it would be injurious to another besides my self, whom I least desire to injure.

At this point, he finally sought advice, writing to three distinguished men, two of whom were physicians, and also to Mary Reyner, his first cousin (a relationship that he found uncomfortably close, even possibly incestuous), who had become his prospective bride, warning her "what danger I apprehended, wishing her to be advised and to take counsel, that she may know whom she matches with and have no caus to repent her." His sexual tensions persisted, despite his anxieties and fears, since a week later he noted that "*I found myself much overborn with carnal con-cupiscence nature being suppressed for I had not had my afflux in 12 nights*[.] *Friday night it came again without any dream that I know of. Yet after it*," he added, "*I am still inclined to lust.*"[36]

Throughout this period of tension and anxiety, Wigglesworth noted his bodily afflictions, sometimes the spleen, sometimes flatulence, and sometimes rheum, as well as his general melancholy, which reflects the depressive mood so characteristic of him. He felt that the Lord had been afflicting him throughout the winter, but he had been able to be active nevertheless, preaching periodically at various congregations. But early in April, in an experience that foreshadowed his subsequent life as a housebound invalid, he noted that "having prepared to preach . . . and fully intending it," he "awaked with a very sore throat, so that I perceived my mouth was stop't for that day. . . . I kept hous all that week, being much pained in swallowing my spittle, and so overflowed with rhewm that If I forbare spitting my throat grew painful with drines [dryness]." When he recovered, though, he went to consult John Rogers about his sexual affliction. He then sought further advice from John Alcock, who recommended "marriage" followed by "astringent cordials afterward." Most importantly, Alcock told him that "mine was not vera Gon." As Edmund Morgan observed, "Whether his disease was actually gonor-rhea, of course, no one can say," but it does seem highly improbable, given his celibacy, that his condition was what his hypochondria imagined and feared. He clearly liked the view of Alcock that his "distemper" was the result of "naturalis impulsus seu instinctus irresistibilis." Immediately thereafter, he decided to solve his dilemma by marrying, since it now was "pretty clear to me that god calleth to a speedy change of my con-dition, which I therefore desire to attend as a duty that god calleth unto, leaving my life and health in his hands." God's will, not his own, thus was the evident motivation for marriage. Even in one of the most im-portant decisions of his life, Michael Wigglesworth was unable to take personal responsibility.[37]

Marriage, however, only intensified his anxieties and fears, and his sexuality remained as conflicted and problematic as before. Having mar-ried to preserve his "purity and chastity," he consummated his marriage, presumably through sexual intercourse, and yet almost immediately re-corded, in shorthand again, that he felt "*the stirrings and strongly of my former distemper even after the use of marriage the next day which makes me exceeding afraid. I know not how to keep company with my dearest friend but it is with me as formerly in some days already.*" Very shortly thereafter, he fell ill again. On the second and third trips that he made, he "got a sore cold by preaching at Mauldon" and then "got a surfet, fell into a loosnes" and "was much weakened" at home but, by July 10, he found that his "strength is wel recover'd again." However, he added that "these ilnesses, colds rhewms and keeping the hous so much have made me so tender that I cannot preach but catch a grievous cold. yea these continued colds disable me to any service either in family or in publick."[38]

Sometime prior to July 10, 1655, it is probable that Michael and his new wife, Mary, conceived their only child, Mercy, who was born the following February 22. In late July, he noted his concern with the invitation to preach at Malden, and also acknowledged that *"carnal lusts also exceeding prevailing,"* asking the Lord to *"forgive my intemperance in the use of marriage for thy sons sake."* For one of the few times in his life, he felt happy, however fleetingly, and declared that "I am infinitely indebted unto the Lord that gives me so much comfort in a married estate contrary to my fears; for this I wil prais him whilest I haue a being." Immediately, however, he voiced his concern about "the use of means against my rhewm," which he considered to be his "weakness."[39]

His bodily complaints persisted for many years to come, but it is impossible to know from the diary that survives whether or not Wigglesworth ever was able to enjoy the sexual pleasures of that marriage bed again. The few remaining references suggest the contrary: that, for whatever reasons, he was unable to tolerate the physical intimacy that might have been expected between husband and wife. By September 10, while struggling with the decision over whether or not to accept the invitation to minister at Malden, and already aware that he faced a hard winter without employment and "becaus my weaknes and colds stil continue," he took stock of his position, characteristically making the lists dear to his obsessive efforts to resolve his doubts. The first consideration was, he said, "My present weaknes unfitting me for almost any service, or making it very difficult." Another was the fact that both his mother and fourteen-year-old sister had come to join his household, even though he had no house of his own as yet. The final concern, however, was that it would "be uncomfortable to winter for cold *and especially to me seeing we can't lay severally without obloquy and reproach neither can we lay together without exposing me to the return of grievous disease."* Five days later, he drew in his diary a picture of what Richard Crowder recognized to be "a strangely phallic 'pillar of Ebenezer.'" And the following day, he noted that "some *night pollution escaped me notwithstanding my earnest prayer to the contrary which brought to mind my old sins now too much forgotten (as near as I remember the thoughts that then I had),"* which suggests that he had not been having intercourse with his wife in recent days. They had been married only five months, and she was probably not more than four months pregnant at the time. Intercourse would still seem possible, had he desired it.[40]

After two months of indecision about the invitation to minister to the congregation in Malden, Wigglesworth made up his mind early in October to accept. The first ground involved the issue of his bodily strength: "God requireth and I desire to do service as my strength wil bear; and I feel not such want of strength but that I can preach without prejudice to my body." He also noted that "If they be willing to adventure upon my weaknes, why should not I adventure upon the work." He then observed "some beginnings of amendment by the abatement of rhewm," and getting some good from "the use of the oil against my aptness to get cold." But the fifth reason was that they could not "winter here. Because the hous is too cold, because the room too strait (here is not a private room for me) because also *we must lay together constantly which I can't bare.*" No explanation is offered, but the following February, at the birth of his daughter, he noted in passing that his bed was near his wife's, which confirms that even in their new house in Malden, he did not share a bed with his wife.[41]

The birth of their child was traumatic for both parents. "For so long as my love lay crying I lay sweating and groaning," he acknowledged. His experience paralleled hers: "I lay sighing, sweating, praying, almost fainting through wearines before morning. The next day. the spleen much enfeebled me, and setting in with grief took away my strength, my heart was smitten within me. . . ." After thirty hours of labor, his wife was delivered of her child, and he was informed of the birth, declaring: "oh Let the Lord be magnifyd who heareth the poor chatterings of his prisoners," and noting that "If the dolours of child-bearing be so bitter (which may be onely a fatherly chastizement) then how dreadful are the pangs of eternal death." After witnessing the sufferings of his wife for the next two days, he desired "That I may maintain good thoughts of god while he afflicts amare deum castigantem."[42]

Within the next few years, the pattern for the following two decades of Wigglesworth's life was set: he was becoming an invalid, unable to preach or to speak in public. He ceased keeping his diary on a regular basis after May 1657. By July 1658, his "physical weakness had increased; his wife was in bad health," and on December 21, 1659, Mary died, leaving Wigglesworth, then twenty-eight, with his four-year-old daughter, his mother, and his nineteen-year-old sister living with him in the house in Malden. By 1660, Crowder notes, "His own health went downhill." He was "Mysteriously afficted" and "unable to serve the people," who, in December 1661, considered calling an assistant to their minister.

The following year, 1662, Wigglesworth published *The Day of Doom* and *God's Controversy with New-England* while being "Confined most of the time to his house." His health remained poor, and "his chronic sore throat kept him weak." In the fall of 1663, he took a trip to Bermuda, where he began to study medicine while he hoped to improve his health. Otherwise, he continued to be housebound throughout the 1660s, while he wrote his poetry on affliction, which emerged from several decades of personal suffering.[43]

Even Wigglesworth recognized that the symptoms of his afflictions were open to question and doubt, and acknowledged, in 1662 in the preface to *The Day of Doom*, that many of his friends wondered about the reality of his illness. He declared, however, that after "more than ten years" of "suffering," his readers should know that

> . . . I'm a Prisoner
> Under a heavy Chain:
> Almighty God's afflicting hand,
> Doth me perforce restrain.

He added immediately (having placed the blame for his imprisonment directly upon the intervention and will of God) that

> Yet some (I know) do judge,
> Mine inability,
> To come abroad and do Christ's Work,
> To be Melancholly;
> And that I'm not so weak,
> As I my self conceit.

Indeed, he acknowledged openly, some friends "Do think I nothing ail." He was certain, however, that his afflictions were effectively preventing him from functioning as minister to his congregation.

> Some think my voice is strong,
> Most times when I do Preach:
> But ten days after what I feel
> And suffer, few can reach.
>   *   *   *
> My prisoned thoughts break forth,
> When open'd is the door,
> With greater force and violence,
> And strain my voice the more.
>   *   *   *
> Till I can speak no longer.

He had become a silenced invalid, imprisoned by the afflictions being imposed upon him by God for his own good.

> But why should I complain
> That have so good a God,
> That doth mine heart with comfort fill,
> Ev'n whilst I feel his Rod?[44]

What had he done to deserve such punishments and such pain? What was the source of his afflictions, and why was he being kept prisoner by his Father, unable to preach or to speak out in public? What, indeed, was the "root of bitterness" that warped his life for so many years?

The Meaning of Affliction

From the perspective of the late twentieth century, Michael Wigglesworth's character and life bear the indelible marks of abuse, both physical and emotional, which left wounds that festered for half a century. His obsession with punishment and his persistent anxiety over being punished in Hell forever—calmed but not quelled by the conviction that he had been converted and his soul saved from the fate that terrified him throughout his lifetime—arose from the experiences that he had as a child of two intensely pious parents who must have taken the Biblical injunctions to beat their child with a rod quite literally. The rod is so familiar to him, it springs so readily to his mind and to his lips and pen, that he had to have felt its burning pain often as a child to become so preoccupied with corporal punishments as an adult. The bitterness that he felt for so long was the result of the suppression of feelings of rage and hatred generated by the physical and verbal assaults of the adults who governed his childhood and formed the conscience that would continue their assaults to the end of his life.[45]

The apocalyptic fantasies that shaped his dreams and his poems were rooted in the pains of early childhood, for they were fantasies of retribution and revenge, of torture and pain, of destruction and doom, and they were also fantasies of rescue, forgiveness, and salvation for the elect few chosen by God for eternal life. Had Wigglesworth been confident of his own worthiness for grace and salvation and certain of his own election, it is hardly likely that he would have spent so much of his life in silence, unable to speak out in praise and unable to worship in public the God whom he professed to obey and love. His apocalyptic impulses arose from the buried anger and aggression that had originated in his childhood, when he was forced, in order to survive, to hide his own true self from the two adults who controlled and dominated his life—his father and mother.

Wigglesworth's contemporaries were conscious of the role that "melancholy" played in his illness, and were surely right in their perceptions. But melancholy itself, which now would be called "depression," was believed to be connected to the spleen, which in turn was associated with anger, malice, spite, and other feelings that, turned inward, resulted in the sense of sadness and anxiety Wigglesworth experienced constantly throughout his early twenties. As John Owen King noted, "Melancholy created a conscious sense of criminality that the victim could well consider quite deserved." Wigglesworth's friends thus were correct in their diagnosis of his illness, because it had made him feel like a prisoner for years.[46]

From the perspective of the late nineteenth century, Wigglesworth would have been recognized as a neurasthenic, an invalid who suffered from bodily weakness and vague somatic complaints, unable to live a normal life or to engage in the activities outside the household that others took for granted. But we know now that neurasthenia itself is a response to issues that always focus upon the will of the patient, a form of passive resistance and passive aggression that allows individuals to exert indirect control over their own lives while avoiding the pressures to achieve and to act that their peers believe to be appropriate for adults. Often buried beneath the fatigue and apparent weakness and illness is a powerful, sometimes even murderous, rage whose roots vary but always reach back to childhood. Weakness invariably hides strength, both of mind and of will, but strengths that, unfortunately, are rarely acknowledged or available to the neurasthenic. By a process that psychoanalysts know as "reaction formation," opposites are created out of necessity for survival, and the strong appear to be weak, and illness becomes the disguise for resistance to control and domination from an early age.[47]

Wigglesworth had no self-defense against the assaults he experienced as a child. His whole adult life was spent defending the abuse that he had suffered, for to do otherwise would have made him confront the feelings of rage and hatred for his parents that he clearly found intolerable. The closest he could come was to acknowledge that he did not love his father and was undutiful to his mother. He took refuge in passive resistance, which ultimately became the bodily weaknesses that imprisoned him in his own house. He could not retaliate against his father nor say anything in his own defense when verbally assaulted even at the age of twenty-one. He could not retaliate when his Father in Heaven afflicted him and chastised him, except by falling ill, thus preventing him from carrying out the obligations of public worship that he had assumed as a preacher of the gospel. He certainly could not protect himself against the assaults of his own conscience, which was one of the harshest ever recorded. The only way to survive was through seeming passivity and acquiescence, submission and sadomasochism. The obsessiveness of his quest for salvation and reassurance is itself a mark of his self-restraint, a form of neurotic control that is designed to prevent the free expression of impulses of will and selfhood.

His obsessive character is thus a clue to the origins of his illness, for it often stems from early battles over autonomy and the will, as David Shapiro has made brilliantly clear. But what Shapiro and others have not recognized is that the obsessiveness—which restricts a person's ability to feel and to know what are true desires and impulses, and which controls feelings through doubt and ritual—often arises from the experiences of pain and assault from punishments in childhood. The adult obsession with punishment mirrors the realities of childhood, but the denial of these realities is the root cause of the subsequent illness.[48]

Michael Wigglesworth became an apologist for abuse and punishment of children because he was unable to confront the feelings that he harbored against the parents who had assaulted him and caused him so much pain as a child. Fundamentally, his will and his sense of self were so threatened that, in order to survive at all, he had to deny his own most powerful feelings, impulses, and wishes, a denial that resulted in the appearance of weakness, passivity, and, ultimately, invalidism and illness. Lacking any protection against assault, children learn to survive by identifying themselves with the adults who are assaulting them, as Sándor Ferenczi, Sigmund Freud, Alice Miller, and many others have noted, and as recent studies of abused children constantly confirm. Wigglesworth had to justify the violence done to him by both his parents and his God, since he was unable and unwilling to give voice to his own rage and hatred and aggression. He felt dangerous because of such feelings, and he fell ill to protect his fathers—one on earth, the other in Heaven—and his mother, from such feelings. He denied himself in order to save himself. His will was suppressed, but it was never really broken. His sexuality was suppressed, but it never disappeared entirely. The body seemed to have a mind of its own.[49]

As long as Michael Wigglesworth denied his own feelings and impulses, as long as he continued to assault himself masochistically, as long as he suppressed his sense of self and self-worth, he remained ill. But when, shortly before reaching the age of fifty, he was able to act on his own impulses and to do his own will, he began to recover and to get well. Whether it was the death of his mother or the therapeutic process of writing poetry, or whether some other, unknown factor intervened, he found his own voice again, reclaimed his own sexuality, and began to live the life of an active, assertive, adult man—preaching, teaching, healing, and speaking out against others both in his own community and in the colony at large.[50]

The action that began his recovery of health shocked everyone, and demonstrated, as no other act could have, that he had taken control of his own life at last. Michael Wigglesworth had finally discovered his own "true self," as Alice Miller would say, and began to speak out in his own voice again, no longer an invalid, and no longer imprisoned in his own house. Suddenly, in the spring of 1679, when he was forty-seven years old, he decided to marry his maidservant, Martha Mudge, thirty years his junior. His friends and neighbors were shocked, dismayed, and hostile. The Reverend Increase Mather wrote to denounce this action and to dissuade him from marrying a woman "of obscure parentage, & not 20 years old, & of no church, nor so much as Baptised." "To take one . . . that was never baptised into such neerness of relation," he admonished, "seemeth contrary to the Gospell, especially for a minister of Christ to doe it. The like never was in New England." Nonetheless, despite so much strident opposition by so many people both in his town and beyond, he married Martha Mudge and proceeded to father six children over the next nine years, the first being born in 1681, when Wigglesworth was forty-nine. Three years later, he was offered the presidency of Harvard College, which he declined on the grounds of his "bodily health and strength," but, in September 1685, he went to Cambridge to preach the annual election sermon. At the age of fifty-three, Michael Wigglesworth had recovered his health, spoken out in public again after decades of silence, and resumed an active life as a preacher, speaker, and traveler throughout the colony. He even married a third time after Martha's death, wooing and winning in 1691 the widow Sybil Sparhawk Avery, who was nearly twenty-five years younger. She bore his second son and last child, whom he named Edward, perhaps a sign of an inner reconciliation with his own long-dead father. He died at the age of seventy-four in 1705, having outlived "all his Harvard classmates but one."[51]

Given such achievements and activities, given the remarkable recovery from a life of affliction, invalidism, and self-imprisonment, the words spoken by the Reverend Cotton Mather at Wigglesworth's funeral on June 24, 1705, must have had intense resonance:

It was a surprize unto us, to see a Little Feeble Shadow of a Man beyond Seventy, Preaching usually Twice or Thrice in a Week; Visiting and Comforting the Afflicted; Encouraging the

Private Meetings; Catechising the Children of the Flock; and managing the Government of the Church; and attending the Sick, not only in his own Town, but also in all those of the Vicinity. Thus he did, unto the Last; and he was but one Lords-Day taken off before his Last. But in the Last Week of his Life, how full of Resignation; how full of Satisfaction![52]

What struck Cotton Mather most forcibly about this "Little Feeble Shadow of a Man beyond Seventy" was his astonishing energy and activity, something truly remarkable, given the decades of apparent weakness that had confined him to his house. Perhaps the intense self-scrutiny and self-analysis that characterized Michael Wigglesworth as a young man persisted throughout his lifetime and enabled him, after nearly five decades of life, to tap the hidden roots, not of bitterness, but of strength that had been there all the while. He himself gave credit to the woman whom he married against the will of nearly all who knew him, acknowledging that she had played a crucial role in his recovery. Certainly his reclaiming his sexuality was a major part of his recovery, but by no means all. He also reclaimed his assertiveness and his aggressiveness, and was thus able as a mature adult to take part in life as a whole man again. However he did it, Michael Wigglesworth held the Apocalypse at bay, and the doom that he had anticipated so keenly in his younger years seemed less pressing, perhaps less necessary, as he lived through his fifties, sixties, and seventies. Perhaps the "root of bitterness" had finally become part of the soil that nourished his spirit and freed his energies, enabling him both to be healed and to heal and comfort others. That was the most remarkable achievement of all.

Gender, Crime, and Community
in Seventeenth-Century Maryland

MARY BETH NORTON

E LESABETH LOCKETT, a maidservant charged with bastardy in Kent County, Maryland, in April 1661, could not deny that she had borne a child out of wedlock. But she defended herself vigorously nonetheless, testifying that the child's father, a planter named Thomas Bright, "promised hur Mariege before the Child was gott."* Elesabeth explained to the court that she and Bright had entered into a form of folk marriage by jointly breaking a piece of money. Her claims were supported by several witnesses, among them a male friend of Bright's who revealed that Thomas had admitted "theare wase a peace of Munye Broke betwext hime and Elesabeth lockett." More important was the testimony of the women who had attended Elesabeth as she gave birth. Ann Dabb, Ann Hill, and Catherin Gammer all attested that "when the Childs heed wase in the Birth [canal] Mrs. Blunt tooke the booke

*A portion of this essay was presented at the Seventh Berkshire Conference on the History of Women, Wellesley College, June 1987. I wish to thank the other participants in that session—Cynthia Herrup, Clive Holmes, and Carol Karlsen—for their helpful comments. It was considered in its entirety both at the October 1987 conference in honor of Bernard Bailyn and at the March 1988 conference on women and the law co-sponsored by John Hopkins University and the University of Maryland Law School. My thanks go to all the participants in these conferences (especially to Lois Green Carr and James Henretta, who took part in both) for their useful suggestions; and also to my colleagues at Cornell who have read subsequent drafts: Margaret Washington, Clive Holmes, and I. V. Hull.

[the Bible] and swore hure & all that she said it wase thomas Brights Child."[1]

The neighborhood women—including the high-status Mistress Ann Blunt—examined Elesabeth Lockett with particular care because of widespread rumors that it was her master, Matthew Reade, who had actually fathered her child. They asked her to reveal "w[ha]t hur master Dide to hure in the husks in the tobaco house." Elesabeth responded that he "Did butt tickell hur" and assured them further that "she never knew any other mane in three quarters of a yeare [than Thomas Bright] and that she never knew hur Master but by his face and Hands." In addition to giving twentieth-century historians unusual information about seventeenth-century sexual practices, Elesabeth Lockett satisfied the court that Thomas had fathered her child after deluding her by false promise of marriage. Although she did not escape the whipping commonly imposed on women found guilty of bastardy, she did ensure that Bright would have to bear the primary financial responsibility for their child.[2]

Elesabeth Lockett's crime was the one most frequently charged against women in seventeenth-century Maryland; fifty-eight women, or nearly 38 percent of all female criminals, were accused of bearing bastard children. That only thirty men (5.5 percent of male criminals) were brought to trial for an offense that required the participation of both sexes suggests the "gendered" nature of crime and law-enforcement in the Chesapeake colony. When men and women committed the same crime of bastardy, they were treated differently by the courts. Even more important, men and women in general tended to be charged with different types of offenses. If men were relatively infrequently accused or convicted of bastardy, women were rarely charged with the offenses most common among men—a set of crimes involving challenges to the provincial authorities. Those transgressions ranged from treasonable conduct, which was punishable by death, to failure to appear for jury service, penalized by a fine. Fully 41 percent of all male criminals were called into court to answer such charges, whereas only nine females (or 6 percent of their number) were tried for a similar offense.

Just as neighbors provided crucial testimony in Elesabeth Lockett's case, so too they frequently played major roles in prosecutions of men for contempt of authority. Indeed, unless a man was as foolish (or as drunk) as Edward Erbery, who in 1666 called the lower house "a Turdy shitten assembly" in the presence of several of its members, the colony's leaders often had to learn of contemptuous words from unsolicited reports by ordinary folk. So the records of such cases occasionally begin with variants of the phrase, "the Court being informed of certaine mutinous speeches. . . ." Protestants were accused of declaring, "hang them Papists Dogs they Shall have no right here," Catholics of asserting that Protestants (in power briefly in the mid-1650s) "did not grant true Justice." One early governor learned from two informants that a local official had spoken of him "in a scoffing & scornefull manner" and that "in his common talke & discourse he revyeth the pr[ese]nt Govr." To escape a punishment that might have included whipping and certainly would have involved a heavy fine, the official "humbly" petitioned for forgiveness and admitted that his words had been "fowe," "rashly" spoken, and "alltogether false."[3]

The offending remarks would never have reached the governor's ears if the two witnesses had not voluntarily come forward. In fact, most crimes, whatever their nature, were brought to the attention of the courts by ordinary residents of the colony, not by sheriffs, constables, or other officials. In seventeenth-century Maryland, which lacked an extensive law-enforcement hierarchy, authorities depended almost exclusively on victims or bystanders to report violations of the law.[4] This necessarily involved the entire community, not just provincial legislators and justices, in defining what constituted unacceptable behavior. Actions that a law declared criminal might go unreported if neighbors regarded them as harmless; conversely, colonists could take individual or collective initiative by seeking remedies for egregious wrongs the authorities had overlooked. Precisely that happened in April 1673, when "some of the Neighbourhood" brought into the provincial court one Elizabeth Russell, whose stepfather had in their opinion "inhumanely beaten and abused" her. The judges, shown the marks of the latest beating, directed that Elizabeth be removed from that household and placed in the care of a female neighbor, the expenses to be borne by her late father's estate.[5]

Crime in the colony was thus not an objective phenomenon but rather to a large extent culturally determined. And Marylanders' culture was far from monolithic. As David Sabean has observed, culture is both a structure of shared values and "a series of arguments among people about the common things of their everyday lives."[6] By the way they defined and dealt with crime, early Marylanders revealed the basic assumptions that informed their existence and the arguments they shared about those assumptions. Deeply embedded in their lives was a gendered value system defined partly by disagreements over its application. That value structure attempted to delineate proper behaviors for men and women—and to differentiate between them. It underlay the laws the assembly adopted, the way those laws were enforced, and male and female colonists' attitudes toward both the laws and those who violated them.

The functioning of that gendered system of thought is the subject of this essay. Although the evidence is drawn from criminal records, this is not a study of crime or the criminal law as such. Rather, it takes advantage of the colony's attempts to identify and punish deviants in order to investigate the multifaceted ways in which notions of gender affected the daily lives of Anglo-Americans who lived in the seventeenth-century Chesapeake.[7]

Defining Crime

The published Maryland court records for the seventeenth century contain documents describing the prosecution of 640 criminal cases, 89 of them involving women alone, 66 involving couples or mixed sex groups, and 485 involving only men. The 155 cases with at least one female defendant represent 24 percent of the total number of prosecutions.[8] Throughout the century men constituted a large (though diminishing) majority of the colony's population, so that proportion is probably somewhat larger than might have been anticipated in the earlier part of the period and is undoubtedly smaller by its end, but is still roughly comparable overall. In other words, despite some variations among decades, neither men nor women seem to have been disproportionately prosecuted in the colony. A breakdown by status likewise fails to show a disproportionate prosecution of servants; that just 107 (or 17 percent) of defendants are explicitly identified as servants suggests that masters brought servants into court only for major infractions.[9]

The crimes these persons were accused of committing varied dramatically in nature, ranging from such minor offenses as profanity and drunkenness to theft and murder. But the vast majority of crimes shared one characteristic: they were not specifically defined in Maryland's statutes. Although in the first decade of the colony the assembly drafted temporary criminal laws on several occasions, in early 1647 it abandoned that effort and from thence until 1678 allowed the courts considerable leeway in the administration of justice. The Act Touching Judicature provided simply that the governor and other judges were to follow "the Lawes of the Province and in defect of Lawe, then according to the sound discretion of the said Governor or other Chiefe Judge and such of the Councell as shall bee present in Court."[10]

The legislators were clearly relying on the values they assumed they shared with the community when they chose such broad wording as the basis for their criminal-justice system. Since they believed everyone else in the colony—at least every other white person of English descent—

agreed on what constituted "deviant" behavior, they saw no need to define crime precisely. As shall be seen, however, their assumption was at least partially incorrect. And in any event the legislators made three significant exceptions to the general imprecision. The criminals who drew the assembly's attention with some regularity were runaway servants and those who harbored or assisted them; hog-stealers; and servant women who, like Elesabeth Lockett, bore bastard children. Specific statutes defined those crimes, indicating that these three offenses were particularly troublesome to the society at large. Several times the legislators decided that the provisions of laws concerning runaways and hog-stealers were "ineffectual" or "not sufficiently penall," and they increased both the severity of punishments and the incentives for reporting violators. They also amended the bastardy law twice, in 1662 lowering the standard of proof for identifying the father, then in 1669 raising it once again.[11]

The community's primary concern in bastardy cases was not morality, but rather ensuring that the public would not have to bear the cost of raising bastard children. For that reason, prosecutions were vigorous and comprehensive, probably encompassing most unmarried maidservants whose babies survived infancy.[12] The runaway servants brought to court by their masters, on the other hand, clearly represented only the tip of the iceberg. Such servants were almost always insubordinate repeat offenders; such phrases as "[he is] a Constant Runnaway" or "[she is] often running away from him" fill the owners' formal complaints to the authorities. More than a loss of labor was involved in these cases. Also at stake was the social order itself, for servants who refused to submit to their masters threatened the maintenance of the proper hierarchy of deference that linked the society from bottom to top.[13]

The concern with livestock theft evident in the statutes was paralleled by the occasional involvement of entire neighborhoods in the prosecution of offenders. An especially well-documented case was heard on Kent Island in January 1655/6, when the partners William Eliot and John Ringgold filed hog-stealing charges against John and Jane Salter and their co-resident tenant William Price. Eliot and Ringgold were suspicious of Price and the Salters because "many hoges beeing lost amongst the neighbors & sume of theire own hoges gone th[a]t ussed [to be] about whom [home] very strangly of a suden; & pork offten seene in theire [the Salters'] house & had no hogs of theire owne to kill." Moreover, a constable searching the house had found a piece of fat pork that could not have come from "a wild small hog," as the accused had claimed. Ironically, neighbors' suspicions had first been aroused by Jane Salter's friendly gesture in offering another woman "sum singed porcke which was a good groth" the previous October; where, everyone wanted to know, had she acquired the meat? After listening to further testimony about unexplained gunshots in the woods, the judges ordered Salter not to kill hogs unless two neighbors were present and directed that Price stand in the pillory. It further decided to break up the larcenous household, telling Price to move out.[14]

Such concerted action was unusual. More commonly, single individuals came forward with tales of injury, thereby defining what had been done to them as a crime and asking court officials to agree with that definition.[15] But men and women differed significantly in their willingness to approach the courts. Men almost always appeared on their own behalf, whereas female complainants were often represented by men. Very few women personally came to the authorities with definitions of crime; instead, masters or relatives appeared for them. Perhaps for this reason, a substantial period of time often separated an offense against a woman and the filing of formal charges. Men, by contrast, reacted quickly to real or imagined injuries.

On August 31, 1650, for example, Thomas Maidwell complained against John and Ann Dandy "for assaulting [him] in a violent manner & striking him to the ground with a Hammer and dangerously wounding him" earlier that same day. The judges responded swiftly, ordering John Dandy (a violent man who was later hanged for murdering one of his servants) to post bond for good behavior. Likewise, the servant William Tuncks, whose shirt was stolen in December 1665, submitted a deposition on the very day of the theft. Only one group of male complainants— servants charging their masters with abuse—appeared hesitant about complaining publicly, but it is clear they expected a fair hearing when they did come forward. In September 1657 one servant even boldly complained to a panel of judges that included his master that he and his fellow servants were "unhumanly beat[en]," were forced to work at night, and often lacked sufficient food. The judges ordered their colleague to correct the problems.[16]

Men therefore readily sought redress from the legal system when they had been physically harmed or suspected their property had been stolen. The willingness of male victims to look to the courts for assistance stands in sharp contrast to women's failure to take the initiative in asking the authorities to define injuries they had suffered as criminal. No legal barrier prevented a woman from going to a constable or a judge with an account of damage done to her, but daughters, wives, and especially maidservants nevertheless deferred to fathers, husbands, and masters in this regard. It is almost as though free women believed that the civil status that placed their property in men's hands affected their ability to function as independent individuals in the criminal courtroom as well.

Accustomed to being represented by men when their finances were at issue, free women also seem to have depended on men to represent their interests if they should suffer personal harm. And servant women were even less likely to take the initiative.

When Thomas Hays struck Elizabeth Thompson with a hoe and kicked her as she lay on the ground, therefore, not she but her master brought suit. When Elizabeth Gary was raped, not she but her stepfather recorded a complaint. When Mary Cole was duped by a mock marriage ceremony, it was her master who sued his own overseer for damages. And when Anne Gould was raped and infected with venereal disease by her former master, her new owner was the person who complained. Because such men acted according to their own timetables, the complaints of female victims took much longer to reach the ears of court officials than did those of males. The charges listed above were filed seven months, one year, five months, and three years, respectively, after the alleged injuries. Indeed, by the time Anne Gould's case was heard, she had already died from the effects of the disease her former master had given her.[17]

This is not to say that female victims never went to the magistrates with complaints; it is, rather, to point out that women did so less commonly than men and under somewhat different circumstances. For example, although some maidservants accused their masters or mistresses of mistreating them, few of those women initiated the prosecutions that brought them to court. Instead, they offered their stories of mistreatment during their trials for running away. So the maidservant Ann Harlow in March 1653/4 accused her master of impregnating her when he charged her with absenting herself from his plantation without permission, and the runaway servant Sarah Taylor complained of the "divers wronges & abuses" she had suffered at the hands of her master and mistress when she and two couples suspected of sheltering her were tried for those offenses in October 1659.[18]

The only complaints other than mistreatment that even a handful of female victims brought directly to court were claims against the fathers of their illegitimate children. A few bastardy cases came to light when women appeared of their own volition to name the men who had impregnated them and to request child maintenance. Since in such instances the women were subjecting themselves inevitably to whipping, they must have been in particularly desperate straits. That certainly seems to have been the case with Susan Warren, who in June 1651 accused Captain William Mitchell of having forced her into a sexual relationship, then of having compelled her to take an abortifacient.[19]

In short, what distinguished the few female victims who personally initiated prosecutions from most of the women victimized by crime was that those who took such actions were in especially difficult circumstances. Like Sarah Taylor, they were being savagely and repeatedly beaten by vicious masters and mistresses; or, like the pregnant Susan Warren, they needed financial support for themselves and their expected children. They were driven to court by sheer desperation. Unlike men, who expected magistrates to listen sympathetically to their complaints and who rarely hesitated to ask for redress of their grievances, women were reluctant to approach the authorities on their own. They waited either until male superiors would do so for them or until the conditions of their lives had deteriorated so badly that their very survival might be at stake.[20]

In the absence of definitive evidence, it is possible only to speculate about the sources of women's hesitancy to come forward with complaints. Perhaps they expected to be badly treated by the courts; perhaps they deferred to their male relatives' decisions about pursuing prosecutions. Or perhaps women, whose own social power rested primarily in gossip and other informal control mechanisms, felt alien and out of place in the formal legal institutions created by men.[21] In any case, women's failure to act reveals one facet of a shared argument with their menfolk, a disagreement about the merits of relying on the courts for the redress of grievances.

Any victim, of course, could decide not to define an injury as a crime requiring action by the legal system, and some men joined women in choosing that course of action (or, more precisely, nonaction). In adultery cases wronged spouses were especially likely to maintain silence. Surely the eleven recorded adultery prosecutions do not reflect the actual incidence of extramarital sexual relationships in seventeenth-century Maryland, especially in light of the unbalanced sex ratio.[22] Yet no wife and just one husband formally accused a spouse of infidelity in a criminal trial. In November 1657, Robert Robins charged that his wife, Elizabeth, "(who had long time lived from him . . .) was with Child," and after the baby had been born he produced witnesses who attested to her promiscuous behavior and her reluctance to swear that he had fathered the child. The court, however, refused to accept the evidence as conclusive, ordering Robins to "take the sayd Elisa: his wife againe, & provid[e] for her & her children."[23]

Each of the other adultery prosecutions in which the records are sufficiently detailed to allow analysis of its origins arose from peculiar circumstances. All but one involved unfaithful wives and single men, suggesting that spouses and witnesses simply ignored husbands' infidelities. Two complaints were filed by female neighbors, one by a midwife, and one by a husband (Robert Holt) who accused his wife and another man of plotting to kill him. Only in the course of the latter investigation did the court discover that Holt's wife, Dorothy, and her accomplice, Edward Hudson, were lovers and that the household in question had been a ménage à trois. The informer in one of the two cases involving neighbors, Mary Gillford, was an inquisitive and suspicious observer of the movements of the adulterous couple; in the other, the complainant—Bridgett Johnson—was herself an interested party, for the man in question had been her adulterous lover before he spurned her to take up with another married woman who lived nearby. Unfortunately for Goodwife Johnson, the court uncovered the truth and ordered her whipped, while her ex-lover was fined, and her rival received no punishment at all.[24]

The primary question that arises from these cases is: why did the injured husbands fail to seek assistance from the courts in ending their wives' adulterous relationships? True, Robert Holt did so eventually, but not until he feared a plot to kill him; he had consented to his wife's extramarital affair when he allowed her lover (for whom she had initially abandoned him) to join their household. The other husbands never appeared in court at all. The answer to this conundrum is suggested in yet another adultery case, that involving Mary Taylor of Patuxent.

The details of that incident, which first came to the court's attention when the midwife Ann Johnson volunteered a deposition on April 30, 1653, were simple. Mary Taylor had borne a full-term baby boy in December 1652, but nine months previously she had been in Virginia, appearing in court on her husband's behalf. Everyone—the midwife, the husband, relatives, and other women who had attended the birth—could count the months, so despite Mary Taylor's initial denials she was questioned until she revealed the identity of the baby's father: George Catchmey, a Virginia planter who she claimed had "with his Deluding Toungue deluded her." Robert Taylor's reaction to his wife's admission of infidelity was described by Ann Johnson:

> She came and fell upon her knees and Said Good husband forgive me, for Gods Sake Good husband forgive me, O! thou wicked base woman how can I forgive thee, I cannot forgive thee, the Law will take hold of thee, would I had given tenn thousand weight of Tobacco I had Saved thy Creditt, thou wicked woman couldest thou forgett me and the Children Soe Soon, I bid thee to have a Care of thy Creditt when thou wentest away . . . and he replyed that he could not forgive her, the Law would take hold of her.

When Taylor later had the opportunity to confront Catchmey directly, he continued to threaten legal action, telling the Virginian that "both their lives lay in his hands" and asking, "what will the Court do in it"?

Catchmey's response to that question, which caused Taylor to rethink the matter completely, provides the key to the husbands' behavior in all these cases: "the Court would Record him Cuckold and Catchmey Should keep the Child." The two men decided that Catchmey should pay Taylor "a Little Tobacco," Taylor should raise the boy as his son, and neither "name [should be] brought in question." So Ann Johnson, who had predicted that "Robert Taylor would put it up [*i.e.*, put up with it], if the world did not take Notice of it," was proved correct.[25]

Thus is explained the husbands' reluctance to take formal action against their adulterous wives: concern for their own sexual reputations. Like Robert Taylor, they were unwilling to be known as cuckolds and preferred to handle the situation in other ways. For some months they successfully managed to keep their names—and those of their wives—out of court until other circumstances intervened to break the silence.[26]

That these crimes came to the courts' attention even though the victim husbands did not want to see their wives prosecuted makes the cases particularly fascinating and important. Significantly, in each instance a woman was the major complainant. No information is available about why Mary Gillford acted, but the motives of both Bridgett Johnson and Ann Johnson are obvious from the case records. Bridgett was furious because her lover had abandoned her for another woman. Ann was angry because Mary Taylor had refused to pay her a bribe (a pair of gloves) to ensure her continuing silence. That both women sought revenge for these slights by taking their information to the authorities indicates that knowledge of criminal activity could offer women genuine power: the possibility of breaking with common female behavior patterns and coming to court unbidden gave a woman a potentially devastating weapon to wield against an opponent. Even though that weapon backfired on Bridgett Johnson and misfired for Ann Johnson (since Mary Taylor was never formally punished), its ultimate usefulness was undiminished.

The pattern in adultery cases is anomalous because crimes were rarely reported to the courts by persons other than the victim. In Charles County in November 1663 "the voyce of the People Crie[d] shame" at Arthur Turner's treatment of a manservant. Earlier that year in the same court Joseph Dorrosell reported that his master John Lumbrozo had raped and impregnated, then tried to induce an abortion in, his fellow servant Elizabeth Wilde. Only in a few scattered instances like these did the persons who reported crimes appear to be acting in the interests of abstract justice.[27] At other times, as in the adultery cases, the observers who brought offenses to the attention of the authorities often turned out to have their own axes to grind.[28]

In one category of crime—murder—it was by definition impossible for the victim to complain in person. In such cases the magistrates had to depend on witnesses' accounts and on coroners' juries, which were convened to view the bodies of victims and to determine the cause of death. The speed with which such crimes were reported to the authorities varied considerably, depending on the identity and status of the victim and the circumstances of the death.[29] That was especially true of infanticide, a unique form of murder in that it invariably involved an unwed mother and a newborn.

The births were usually reported by masters or male servants, who heard "something Cry like a pigg or a Child" or found "a bundle of Lynnen" with a dead baby inside. When questioned, the mothers uniformly started by denying that they had been pregnant or had had a child. Thus the Calvert County servant Elizabeth Greene first said she had not been pregnant, then that "she had a thinge Came from her like a dogg head," then admitted that "she had One but did not murder it, nor did not see what she had whether it was a Childe form'd or not." So too Jane Crisp of Talbot County "was delivered of A Child without doors in the plantation and shee would nott [have it] bee knowne that shee had A Child," but, after being examined by a midwife, "Confessed that shee had A Child and the Hoggs had Eaten it."[30]

The most unusual infanticide prosecution was initiated when Robert Joyner, a former servant of James Langworth, approached a magistrate in early January 1660/1 to reveal that in the spring of 1657—nearly four years previously—he suspected Elizabeth, a maidservant on the same plantation (now free and married to a planter, Samuel Harris), of committing infanticide. He recounted how he and another man had seen some cloth by the river. He asked Elizabeth what was hanging out of it; she replied that it was "fish gutts" and "Snatcht it up and flung it into the water." But he retrieved the cloth, found "there was a man Child within itt," and rejected Elizabeth's suggestion that they bury the body. Intending to tell Langworth, he walked to the house, but it "being full of Company thought best to lett it rest untill the next morning." The next day, the baby was gone, and he evidently did nothing further in the matter for four years. At Elizabeth Harris's trial, the other male witness confirmed his story; Elizabeth admitted that she had seen the dead child; and Margaret Marshguy, another former female servant of Langworth's, testified that she did "often lye with the abovesd Elizabeth, but did never knowe nor as much as suspected that the abovesaid Elizabeth was ever with Child." Elizabeth Harris was acquitted, and many questions remain unanswered: did she actually bear the child, or was it possibly Margaret's? Why did Joyner accuse one maidservant and not the other? Was Margaret lying about Elizabeth's condition? And most of all, why did Joyner wait so long before telling his story? Why not speak sooner, or, given that he had kept silent for so many years, why speak at all?[31]

Although the case record does not supply responses to these questions, the very act of asking them demonstrates how heavily prosecutions depended on the individual initiative of the injured party. Unless a victim came forward to complain about an injury within a reasonably short span of time, prosecution appears to have been unlikely. Certainly any crime not defined as such by the victim would probably not have been so defined by anyone else, unless it was a particularly brutal murder or perhaps a juicy sex scandal that was the subject of much neighborhood gossip. (Even so, in Mary Taylor's case depositions reveal that at least six men and four women knew her baby had been fathered by George Catchmey; not one of them took that information to the authorities until after Ann Johnson told her story.)[32]

Since women were more reluctant than men to approach the courts with definitions of crimes, it is highly likely that offenses with female victims were less often prosecuted than crimes with male victims, particularly if the woman in question was a servant. Indeed, although there is considerable evidence of the sexual abuse of maidservants, which will be discussed below, no case was ever initiated for that criminal offense. Rather, testimony about abuse was offered in support of claims by masters for damage to the servant or was elicited to buttress such other charges as adultery or attempted abortion. It is true that maidservants subjected to repeated physical abuse by masters or mistresses did receive some protection from the courts, but it hardly helped Alice Sandford, whose body was "beaten to a Jelly" by her master Pope Alvey, that he was convicted of manslaughter and branded on the thumb.[33]

Convicting and Punishing Criminals

The tables on page 135 list all categories of crimes comprising at least 2 percent of the offenses with which men and women respectively were charged. (Cases involving couples or mixed groups have been counted twice, once in each table.) Six types of crimes appear in both tables: theft, running away, bastardy, murder, assault, and mistreating servants. Just three of the six—running away, murder, and mistreatment—appear in approximately equal proportions. Men were charged with theft and assault more frequently than women, and, as already noted, women were accused of bastardy much more often than men.[34]

TABLE 1

Crimes Most Frequently Committed by Women

TYPE	NUMBER	PERCENT
Bastardy	58	37.7
Running away	16	10.4
Infanticide	11	7.1
Adultery	10	6.5
Theft	9	5.8
Fornication	8	5.2
Mistreating servants	6	3.9
Assault	5	3.2
Murder	5	3.2
Other	27	16.9
Total	155	99.9

TABLE 2

Crimes Most Frequently Committed by Men

TYPE	NUMBER	PERCENT
Contempt of authority, treason	80	14.5
Neglect of duty	70	12.8
Theft	55	10.0
Assault	41	7.5
Running away	41	7.5
Bastardy	30	5.5
Murder	29	5.3
Drunkenness	27	4.9
Killing animals	24	4.4
Aiding runaways	18	3.3
Mistreating servants	16	2.9
Profanity, blasphemy	15	2.7
Other and unknown	100	18.8
Total	546	100.1

More revealing than such proportional differences are ten types of crimes unique to one of the tables. For women, those offenses are infanticide, adultery, and fornication; for men, contempt of authority or treason, neglect of duty, drunkenness, profanity or blasphemy, aiding runaway servants, and killing animals that belonged to others (a form of theft). The crimes unique to women, in short, were all sexual offenses. Those unique to men involved minor forms of misbehavior (drunkenness, swearing), tampering with another man's property (servants or livestock), or—most often—conflict with the Maryland authorities, either through direct resistance (contempt of authority, treason) or through

neglect of an obligation, such as jury or militia service. Fifty-seven percent (89) of all female defendants in the colony were accused of sex-
related crimes, in contrast to only 11 percent (58) of men; while, as
already noted, just 9 women (6 percent) were prosecuted for all the
crimes against authority that accounted for 41 percent (226) of men's
offenses.

The divergent accusations aimed at men and women point to significant differences in their social and political roles. Only men in seventeenth-century Maryland had a sufficiently direct relationship to the
government to be prosecuted for crimes involving the polity. The Maryland authorities worried about the allegiance of male colonists but paid
little attention to the political views of women. There is scattered evidence
that female Marylanders did not always agree with the policies (or even
the identity) of the colony's current governors.[35] Yet men alone were
prosecuted for contempt of authority or treason; only members of their
sex had politically relevant opinions. Further, the colony placed just one
formal obligation on its female residents: if summoned, they had to
appear as witnesses in civil or criminal cases. Men, by contrast, were also
expected to serve on grand and petty juries, muster with the militia, fill
a variety of major and minor offices, and occasionally perform other
services such as repairing roads or bridges. As a result, men were penalized far more often than women for failing to meet the colony's
demands.[36]

If in the list of men's crimes the preponderance of conflicts with authority is notable, even more striking is the overwhelming dominance
of bastardy among women's offenses. Indeed, with the exception of
bastardy—which makes up more than one-third of the charges against
women—no other single crime accounts for more than about one-tenth
of the accusations included on either table. The explanation for the high
incidence of bastardy trials lies not in any unusually promiscuous behavior on the part of early Maryland's unmarried women, but rather in
the contrast between the selective prosecution of other offenses and the
nearly universal prosecution of bastardy cases. For two reasons, a woman
who produced a bastard child was unlikely to escape without trial and
punishment. First, her child represented a considerable potential financial liability for the province; and second, unlike most other criminals,
she could be easily identified.[37]

Maryland officials wanted to ensure that neither the colony nor the
masters of pregnant maidservants would have to pay for rearing bastards. Consequently, the province's bastardy statute, first passed in 1658
and amended only minimally thereafter, focused specifically on unmarried female servants who had become pregnant "to the Great dishonnor

of God and the apparent damage to the . . . Owners of such Servants."
It sought to impose on one or both of the parents an obligation to pay
the costs of childrearing, saying nothing explicit about other penalties.
If the mother could not prove paternity, she alone was liable for costs;
if the father was a servant, the parents shared equal responsibility; if
the father was free, he had to pay "the whole damages." If the father
had promised marriage, he was either to fulfill that promise or pay a
sum to the mother. By the 1670s local constables were vigilantly enforcing the law, bringing to the attention of the county courts the preg-
nancies of single women in their districts and occasionally naming
suspected fathers as well. What the constables missed, masters reported:
some bastardy cases originated as civil suits for damages filed by the
masters of pregnant maidservants against the babies' reputed fathers.[38]

The scarcity of prosecutions for other types of nonmarital sexual intercourse demonstrates both that the colony's judges were primarily
concerned about the financial burdens of bastardy and that sexual crimes
which did not involve births were difficult to uncover. Unlike in New
England, where premarital as well as extramarital conception led to the
punishment of offenders, in Maryland couples were not penalized for
having babies within seven or eight months of their marriage. When a
child conceived out of wedlock was subsequently legitimized and thus
guaranteed adequate financial support, the provincial authorities did
not concern themselves with the morality of its parents' conduct. Similarly, only sixteen individuals were tried for fornication, a crime that
did not involve an illegitimate birth.[39]

Not only was bastardy more likely to be prosecuted than other crimes,
the overall conviction rate was extremely high—87 percent. In the 44
cases with known outcomes, 89.5 percent of females and 90.5 percent
of couples charged with the offense were found guilty. If defendants
are defined by status, the same was also true of 96 percent of servants.
Indeed, almost everyone formally prosecuted for bastardy was convicted;
just one couple (whose defense was marriage) was acquitted of the crime.
But the authorities also withdrew formal charges against 20 parents they
had identified (11 women, 9 men), apparently because their sexual partners had already been held financially liable for the bastard child.[40]

Still, more than finances was on the minds of Maryland's judges, for
they usually went beyond simply determining who would bear the financial responsibility for illegitimate children. Although the bastardy
statute did not authorize any such punishment, they also ordered both
servant and free mothers to be publicly whipped. Fathers, by contrast,
suffered only financial penalties, regardless of whether they were servant
or free.[41]

Significantly, in almost half (thirty) of the bastardy cases the authorities seem to have made no attempt to identify the father. Since just nine male servants were charged with fathering bastards, and it is highly unlikely that servant women had sexual relationships only with free planters, many of the unknown fathers were probably servants.[42] Although the bastardy law provided that servant fathers and mothers would equally share childrearing costs, once the magistrates had identified one servant parent (the mother), they had little incentive to penalize the other, since servants did not have access to funds in the form of tobacco. Free planters, on the other hand, could be assessed full, actual damages. Thus Maryland's rulers showed little interest in punishing two servant parents.

The combination of this failure to prosecute servant fathers and the assignment of whipping penalties to free mothers suggests that court officials were focusing their attention on bastard-bearers as women, not as servants. Because conviction on bastardy charges was essentially inevitable for either partner if prosecution was pursued, the key distinctions in the treatment of men and women lay not in conviction rates but rather in the initial decision to prosecute (or not to prosecute) and in the punishments ultimately imposed.

The pattern of prosecutions and penalties in bastardy cases implies that the courts applied different standards of judgment to Maryland's men and women, at least in certain types of crimes. This tentative conclusion is borne out by the analysis of verdicts rendered and punishments assessed in the 568 criminal cases in which outcomes are known. The data demonstrate that sexual offenses committed by women were regarded with particular seriousness, for female sexual offenders of all descriptions—not just the servant mothers of bastards—were penalized differently and more severely than defendants of other descriptions. Thus the evidence suggests that seventeenth-century Maryland authorities enforced a dual standard of sexual conduct that saw sex crimes committed by women as especially threatening to the maintenance of social order.

Overall, the conviction rate varied little with respect to the sex of the defendant: approximately two-thirds of all those tried were found guilty, with women being convicted at a somewhat lower rate than men.[43] Free status carried an advantage, for 79 percent of servants but just 66 percent of free people were found guilty. When crimes are divided into two categories, sexual offenses and "other" offenses, the largest differential in conviction rates is among women: more than three-quarters of all women brought to trial for sex crimes (79 percent), but just 50 percent of women tried for other offenses, were found guilty.[44] Although servants were also more likely to be convicted of sexual crimes than other misdeeds, the difference was smaller: 86 percent to 67 percent. By contrast, the distinction between sexual offenses and other crimes had little effect on the fate of male defendants: 71 percent were convicted of sexual offenses, but so were 69 percent of those charged with other types of crimes.[45]

The differential in conviction rates for women, though proportionately smaller, is maintained even when bastardy cases are removed from consideration. In the 39 nonbastardy sex crimes with known outcomes, 62 percent of female defendants were found guilty, as opposed to the 50 percent of female defendants convicted of other crimes. No such persistent differential is found for either men or servants. Male defendants were convicted of nonbastardy sex crimes at precisely the same rate as women—62 percent—but that proportion was lower than the percentage of men's convictions for other offenses (69 percent). And four of the seven servants accused of such crimes were acquitted (for a conviction rate of just 43 percent). Therefore women's disproportionate conviction rate in sex-crime prosecutions cannot not explained by bastardy verdicts alone.

All women convicted of sexual offenses, not just maidservants found guilty of bastardy, received harsher penalties than any other category of defendant. The punishment most frequently assessed on defendants of both sexes and all statuses was a fine (defined here as including additional terms of service assigned to servants), followed by whipping, posting bond for future good behavior, and a scattering of other penalties such as public shaming or mutilation.[46] But convicted men—both servant and free—were considerably more likely than women to be fined and much less likely to be whipped.[47] These differences were magnified in all sex-crime cases, not just bastardy prosecutions. Fifty-eight percent of convicted female sexual offenders (free and servant) were whipped, as opposed to just 14 percent of those women found guilty of other crimes. Men were in fact slightly less likely to be whipped for sexual offenses than for other crimes.[48] Since only a few of Maryland's criminals were prosecuted under statutes that explicitly set forth punishments, the penalties imposed reflected the judges' preferences rather than the requirements of the law.

The pattern of differentiated penalties appears with greatest clarity in the forty-three cases in which men and women were convicted together of the same misdeeds. Although the sexes received similar treatment when found guilty of other types of crimes, they were punished differently for sexual offenses. In sex crimes, just 21 percent of defendants were assessed the same penalties as their partners, whereas in other prosecutions 73 percent were treated equally. The key distinction in the twenty-eight sex-crime verdicts was that 77 percent of women were whipped, in contrast to just 9 percent of men; conversely, 60 percent of men but only 23.5 percent of women were fined.[49]

The explanation for the contrasting penalties lies in two crucial differences between fines and whipping as forms of punishment. First, whipping required only what everyone possessed (a body), whereas the assessment of a fine presupposed a criminal's access to property—if not real or personal property, then the "property" that accrued to servants through the value of labor. Since married women did not control property in their own names, fining them actually meant fining their husbands. A court that wanted to ensure that a married woman was herself punished could not choose a fine as her penalty. (So not one of the married women convicted of adultery was fined.) Even though widows and single women, especially servants, could legitimately be assessed economic penalties, their imposition could prove to be less than satisfactory: a heavy fine could bankrupt the estate of a poor widow and her dependent children, thereby forcing them to seek public assistance; and an added term of service alone in most cases seemed inadequate punishment for a servant who had given birth to a bastard.

Second and more important, although the trial was held in public, a fine was subsequently paid in private. A fine was therefore a "hidden" penalty; a person who did not attend a trial might never learn of a neighbor's conviction and would certainly not witness the punishment. Whipping, on the other hand, was imposed in public. The whipping post was located near the site of court sessions, and punishment was usually delivered on a court day when the colonists had gathered from miles around to attend the sessions. Whipping inflicted both physical pain and humiliation, the lashes always being delivered on a man or women stripped to the waist. For women, that posture was especially shameful.

Public punishments in the seventeenth century, J. M. Beattie has observed, were "calculated to shame and to dishonor the offender, to diminish his moral worth" in the eyes of neighbors and friends. The rituals were to some extent "moral-degradation ceremonies in which the crowd that watched played an important part . . . , reaffirming the moral boundaries of the society." Beattie found that, in England, men charged with felonies were treated more harshly than women at every stage in the judicial process and were more likely to be subjected to public punishments. He accordingly concluded that English judges and juries saw women as posing "a less serious threat to lives, property, and order" than men.[50]

In Maryland, the priorities seem to have been quite different, particularly where the maintenance of sexual and moral order was concerned. Three-fifths of female sexual offenders, but fewer than 15 percent of male sex criminals, were subjected to public punishments (including shaming, mutilation, and hanging in addition to whipping). Even in other types of cases, women were more likely than men to be punished publicly, although only about one-fifth of the criminals of either sex were so penalized.[51] A culture in which many female criminals but proportionately few men had to undergo such ordeals was one that stressed proper behavior by women and feared female deviance more than male misconduct. The Maryland authorities wanted to send an unmistakable message to female colonists about the possible consequences of misbehavior, especially sexual misbehavior.

Implicit in the male judges' and juries' scale of values was the notion that women rightly bore the primary responsibility for nonmarital sexual relationships and their consequences. Only if a woman—like Elesabeth Lockett—could prove she had been misled by a false promise of marriage could she escape the full force of the law. The public punishment of deviant women was accordingly intended to prevent other women from imitating female sexual criminals. Because they did not punish men publicly as well—particularly given the compelling economic motives that underlay bastardy prosecutions—it is possible to speculate that male jurists were making the crucial assumption that women, not men, controlled (perhaps even initiated) most sexual relationships. They seem to have believed that women engaged in nonmarital sexual intercourse only through choice, and that the sight of other women being whipped or otherwise publicly punished for making such a choice would deter female viewers from following their example.

That belief, however, bore little resemblance to reality. In only one sex crime does any testimony hint that the woman might have initiated the relationship. In all the remaining cases in which there is any evidence, men appear to have pressured the women to engage in sexual intercourse. Moreover, complaints in other lawsuits indicate that women—especially maidservants—were vulnerable to sexual exploitation by planters, particularly their masters or overseers. One man boasted in 1650, for example, "that he had got the finest lye upon Williams [his servant] that ever any man had, and that if he had not taken that Course of beating of her he Should never have gained it." When another man some years later saw that his servant "woold not yeald quiatly" to him, he "plucked his hankerchif out of his pocket and stope[d] her mouth and forch [sic] her whether shee will or noe." In 1657 the naïve maidservant Mary Cole was not raped or beaten, but she was nonetheless sexually abused. After a mock marriage ceremony conducted by the married overseer whose sexual advances she had rejected, she was duped into sleeping with her new "husband," one of the overseer's confederates. Such stories lead one to suspect that the encounter with her master described in 1656 by the servant Anne Gould could well have been a common experience:

> theare was non left in the house but mr Owines & yor deponent, & prsently after the Overseer was gone hee pincht & abused her & threw her upon a bed, hee allsoe forst yor deponent & had the usse of her bodie, which was much to yor deponents greife, beeinge the Custome of weomen was upon her, ussinge often theise Expressiones, what am I the better for thee, what the plauge doe I keepe thee for, & the licke.

What made matters all the worse, Gould declared, was that during the rape Owens did "keepe her down uppon her face, th[a]t shee could noe wayes help her selfe," and that he had given her a venereal disease to boot.[52]

Significantly, men, who were rarely whipped or otherwise publicly punished for sexual offenses, were more often subjected to such penalties for crimes against persons or property. Although men were always much more likely to be fined than to be assessed another punishment, about one-fifth of the men convicted of theft or other property offenses were publicly punished, as were more than one-quarter of those found guilty of crimes against persons. Since the public or private nature of the punishment provides a guide to the level of the authorities' concern with a particular offense, Maryland's magistrates seem to have perceived men prone to theft or violence as the most dangerous male criminals, along with those who had been convicted of treason or serious crimes against the state (a few of whom were executed).

Women accused of the offenses most common among men were regarded with relative complacency. The prosecution of such women was relaxed, because judges evidently saw little reason to believe that female thieves or murderers would spawn imitators. Only half the women charged with such crimes were convicted and, of those, very few were publicly punished; notable among them were two women whose ears were mutilated for perjury and forgery, respectively. In those cases the need for deterring other potential offenders was clear, but when the criminal was seen as less dangerous (for example, a runaway female servant) the authorities believed a fine would suffice as punishment.[53]

The nature of a male criminal's offense influenced his treatment by the courts in only two ways: if he was charged with a sex crime and tried in conjunction with a female partner, he was much more likely to be convicted than in other circumstances; and, if convicted of murder or theft, he had a greater probability of being publicly punished. With these limited exceptions, the courts handled all male criminals in a similar fashion, regardless of their status or the type of offense they had committed.

Therefore neither sex *per se* nor status as servant or free significantly affected either conviction rates or types of penalties. When crimes were not sexual in nature, women and men, free people and servants, were penalized roughly comparably, especially if they had been convicted together for the same misdeeds. But if a female offender (regardless of whether she was free or servant) stood accused of a sexual offense, the nature of her crime determined her fate. She was both more likely to be found guilty and more likely to be publicly punished than were other accused persons. That the authorities thus distinguished among women charged with different sorts of crimes demonstrates that *gender*—a culturally constructed role definition—not *sex*—their biological identity—was the crucial factor in their treatment. The former, of course, depended on the latter, but the sex of the defendant by itself made little difference to the outcome of a trial. It was not all women the Maryland courts judged more harshly, but those women accused of crimes that specifically violated the standards of sexual behavior accepted by the community.

Voicing Women's Concerns

Since judges and juries were composed exclusively of men, it is impossible to know from court verdicts and penalties what women thought about the members of the community—both male and female—who committed sexual offenses. Yet because large numbers of women were called as witnesses in sex-crime prosecutions, their opinions appear in the record even if they had no direct say in the cases' outcomes. A total of ninety-seven women testified in thirty-four trials for sexual offenses. The overwhelming majority of these women were from ordinary families; just twenty were of high status, and only four were servants.[54] The court testimony of female witnesses in such cases accordingly reflected not an attempt by a social and economic elite to impose its behavioral standards on other colonist, but rather revealed values that were widely held among women in the community.

Most of the witnesses in sex-crime cases, male and female, were either eyewitnesses or gossipers. The majority told the court about events they had actually seen; for example, a husband and wife deposed that Henry Carline and Elizabeth Garnier "did Lye in Bed together and went under the Notion of man and wife." Others described what they had learned from talking to participants in a crime. Thus Ann Lambert's statement that Sarah Spurdence had told her "that shee was with Child by [William] Mullins and moreover shee said that hee had Layne with her ought enough to gett her with Child if shee was nott" was the key piece of evidence at Spurdence's bastardy trial in 1665. Likewise, when the provincial court in 1659 was attempting to decide whether Arthur Turner had fathered Lucie Stratton's child, it took testimony from a large number of witnesses (seven men and three women) who had talked to one or both of the parties about the matter.[55]

Both men and women served as eyewitnesses and gossipers, but only women appeared as the third type of witness: a person charged by the community—and occasionally by the court itself—to investigate sexual offenses. Many such witnesses can be identified as midwives, or at the very least women who had had considerable experience attending births. Women's active involvement in these prosecutions was crucial to their outcome, particularly if bastardy was at issue. That was so because of the seventeenth-century belief that at the moment of birth a woman could not lie about the identity of the father of her child.[56] The presiding midwife was expected to interrogate the mother while she was in labor and to report the results to the court. The records show that midwives took that obligation very seriously.

Thus, just as the neighborhood women closely questioned Elesabeth Lockett in 1661, so too ten years earlier Mary Clocker had interrogated Susan Warren. When she supervised at the stillbirth of Warren's fetus in August 1651, Clocker admonished her patient "to Speak the truth and to give Such an Answer as She would give an accompt of to God and man, and whether those things that She had Spoken of Concerning Capt Mitchell that he was ffather of the Child, and had given her Phisick to destroy it were true or noe, and She answered that they were all true."[57]

Midwives could also be called in at other times and in other types of cases. In Calvert County in 1664 the midwife Grace Parker, along with a number of other women, told the court about their conversations with and examination of the servant Elizabeth Greene, charged with having killed her newborn bastard. Parker testified, "That she was a stranger to the wench and did not see her above once all the time she was wth Childe and that she did search her breast and the wench deny'd she was wth Childe but there was milke in her breasts And it was a goeing away being hard and Curdled." The testimony of the women led to Greene's conviction and execution even though the child's body was never found. In a similar case five years earlier another group of Calvert County women examined the body of an infant born to the unmarried servant Anne Barbery; the point at issue was whether it had died naturally or through its mother's neglect. Here the facts were less conclusive, for there was some evidence that Barbery had cared for the baby. Accordingly, she was whipped for bastardy instead of being hanged for infanticide.[58]

The cases of Mary Taylor and Jane Palldin, both of which involved the Anne Arundel County midwife Ann Johnson, later Dorrington, demonstrated that midwives on occasion assumed an investigative role without being ordered to do so by a court. This implies that their role was based more on custom than on strict legal requirements, and that they may have seen themselves as protectors of community values. Although Johnson did not question Mary Taylor about the paternity of her son at the moment of birth—telling her assistant that Mary "had Sorrow Enough at that Instant"—she did so several days later. She described the interrogation to the court:

> Your Deponent tould her that She had both offended God and Defamed herself and wronged her husband and Children Soe whereupon her Cuzen [Margaret Broome] and I urging of her to Speake the truth of the matter whose the Child was that he might take part of the Shame as well as She, Cuz. tould Mary Taylor that her husband Said that he would turne her & the Bastard out of Doors, Soe Said Cuz: I am greived to the very heart to See how yor Husband takes on. O! Cuzen Said She doe not let your Husband worke to Maintaine another Man's Child, Soe yor Deponent replyed and Said, noe truely I would lay the Saddle upon the right horse.

That argument evidently did the trick, for Mary Taylor then broke down and identified George Catchmey as the father of her child.[59]

Ann, by then Mrs. William Dorrington, played the same role three years later when she recognized the signs of pregnancy in Jane Palldin, who belonged to her husband but was temporarily hired to another planter, John Norton. Dorrington asked the pregnant Palldin to name the father of her child. When Palldin responded that she did not know, Ann took a clever tack, inquiring "whether She was So Impudent a whore that She did not know the father of it"? For a while Jane continued to profess ignorance, but then declared that the father had been a stranger who stopped by Norton's house one day. Another woman present remarked, "this Cannot be that you would lye with a Stranger." Her attempts at dissembling thwarted, Palldin admitted that John Norton himself was the father. Thereupon Ann Dorrington told her, "Come Jane, let us go to the Court, and deliver your Self there." And so Palldin formally accused Norton.[60]

The role played by midwife witnesses was formalized when courts convened female juries to examine the bodies of accused women. On four occasions—in 1656, 1657, 1662, and 1668—such groups were constituted by the Maryland courts (twice by the provincial court, twice by the Kent County court). Two of these juries were charged with discovering whether or not a woman was pregnant and two with learning if the accused had ever borne a child. In the case of Robert Robins's estranged wife, Elizabeth, suspected of becoming pregnant in an adulterous relationship and of having taken an abortifacient, the jury found that she was pregnant but perhaps carrying a dead fetus (the child was eventually born alive). In two prosecutions for infanticide, the matrons concluded that neither woman had recently had a child. In a bastardy case—a prosecution of a man—the jury reported that it could not decide if the woman was pregnant, and, since the case records end there, she probably was not. All four juries included a mixture of high-status and ordinary women; one had six members, one nine, one eleven, and one twelve.[61]

It is notable that in three of these four cases and in most of the instances in which midwives were formally consulted by the courts, the women's decisions worked to the benefit of the accused. Such results reveal the dimensions of the shared arguments embedded in Maryland's culture. In sex-crime prosecutions, these arguments were between ordinary women, especially midwives, and the high-status men who sat as the colony's judges. The court records, in short, suggest the existence of a female value system that differed from that of the male-dominated legal structure.

In a bastardy case in Kent in 1670, for example, the clerk noted that after the female servant defendant was sentenced to the standard twenty lashes, "by the Request of her master & som women the Corporall Punishment was Remitted, And she only to pay Costs of Sute." The reason for the remission was clear: the servant complained "of her Abuses And Ill usedg as by the Marks And tokens she hath shewed, ag[ains]t her Masters Mr. William Bishop & Robert Palmer, the wch she allsoe Proved by 3 wittnesses." Since she named another man as the father of her child, it is likely that her masters had already whipped her severely for her pregnancy; that women who witnessed the beating or officiated at the birth (two of them testified about the man she named while in labor) sympathized with her plight and requested mercy; and that one of her masters realized that a court-ordered whipping would render her even more of a liability—in terms of her ability to work—than would her new baby.[62]

An even clearer indication that midwives sometimes disagreed with laws governing sexual offenses came in 1669, when Ann Johnson Dorrington, Grace Parker, and five other women petitioned the provincial court to stay the scheduled execution of the spinster Joane Colledge, who had been convicted of infanticide. The court record indicates that her offense had been "concealeing the birth of her Child" rather than clearly proven murder. Under an English law dating from the reign of James I, an unwed mother who gave birth in secret to a child that was later found dead was considered guilty of infanticide unless she could prove that the baby had been born dead, a difficult if not impossible task under the circumstances. The colony's experienced midwives (and other women as well) clearly questioned the justice of the verdict in Colledge's case and perhaps even the substance of the law itself. Their petition for a stay was accepted, but there is no indication of whether Colledge was eventually executed.[63]

An especially revealing example of women's—particularly midwives' —differences with the values embodied in the legal system occurred in 1656 during the September session of the provincial court. Three days after they had reported to the court their opinion in an infanticide case, two members of the female jury offered unsolicited depositions on an entirely different matter: a miscarriage that had been suffered by the wife of a prominent planter. One of the witnesses, Elizabeth Claxton, saw Francis Brookes beat his wife repeatedly and watched him attack her with a pair of tongs just before she miscarried. The other witness, the midwife Rose Smith, had officiated at the delivery of the fetus. Bruises on the little body aroused her suspicions, and so she confronted Brookes, having heard that "the[y] Lived discontentedly." Smith deposed that she had "told him that it Came Soe through his Misusage, and . . . [that] he would dearly Answer [for] it although he [e]Scaped in this world, yet in the world to Come he Should Answer for it before a Judge that useth no partiality." Brookes replied, Smith reported to the court, that his wife "fell out of the peach tree, And he asked her if She did not fall out of the Peach Tree and She Said yes."

It is probable that, brought together by serving on the female jury, Claxton and Smith began discussing the incident at Francis Brookes's plantation. Even though Claxton had been present at the stillbirth, she might not have told Smith previously that she had witnessed the brutal beating that caused the miscarriage. Or, if the two women had compared notes earlier, service on the matrons' jury might have given them the

opportunity or the confidence to tell their story to the magistrates. Whatever the reason, the women clearly reached a decision during that session
to present their evidence formally in court. The judges' response was
telling. They ordered Brookes to post bond to reappear in six months
to answer the charges, but when he did return they released him without
trial. Rose Smith had been correct: the "partial" male justice in Maryland
would not accept her assessment of guilt.[64]

In the attitudes of witnesses in sex-crime cases, therefore, the effects
of gender differences are as clearly revealed as they are in the fates of
male and female offenders or in the actions of victims. Midwives seemed
even more determined than magistrates to identify the fathers of
bastards—the judges, after all, let many men escape punishment altogether, whereas the women attending a birth were insistent that the
mother reveal the name of her sexual partner so that he too could be
brought to trial. Women likewise came to court unbidden to report
adulterous relationships or—like Rose Smith and Elizabeth Claxton—
to complain that another woman had been mistreated by her husband.
By contrast, women were noticeably absent from the ranks of complainants in infanticide cases; they took an active prosecutorial role in only
one trial, that of Elizabeth Greene. In all other such cases, the testimony
of midwives or female juries worked on behalf of accused women, clearing them of the charges or requesting clemency.[65] They, far more than
men, could sympathize with women accused of committing desperate
acts.

THE PATTERN of prosecutions and penalties in sex-crime cases reveals
the problematic nature of gender relationships and definitions in seventeenth-century Maryland. The imbalanced sex ratio caused numerous
difficulties for those who wanted to maintain order in the colony. They
could have focused their attention—as did their New England
counterparts—on the "excess" young men in their ranks. But perhaps
because the province had such a heavy preponderance of male youths
and a relative lack of females, the magistrates appear to have been disproportionately concerned with women who threatened to violate the
moral order. The shortage of women in the colony made it impossible
to re-create the system of family order the settlers had known in England,
a system in which most persons lived in nuclear households under the
direction of a married couple. In Maryland, households took distinctive
forms, being headed variously by individual men, by two male "mates"
(partners), or by a couple and the husband's male partner, who (as was
seen in the case of the Holts and Edward Hudson) might share the wife's

sexual favors as well as her cooking, laundering, and cleaning skills. Because seventeenth-century English men and women believed that an orderly society required orderly families, gender relationships—particularly those embodied within households—were of vital concern to their governments. That Maryland's peculiar demography appeared to threaten the very existence of orderly families may help to explain the magistrates' special sensitivity to women's sexual offenses, which threatened family order at its roots.[66]

Strikingly, though, the authorities (and most men) showed a relative lack of interest when men committed such crimes, with the partial exception of bastardy, in which the courts' concerns were economic. In sharp contrast to New England judges, who punished men comparably to women for sexual crimes,[67] Maryland's jurists showed leniency to men accused of sexual offenses but punished them more harshly for thefts and violent crimes against persons. One may therefore speculate that whereas men believed that the preeminent value for women in the colony should be expressed in premarital chastity and marital fidelity, for men themselves the equivalent virtue was respect for others' persons and possessions. Sexual continence does not appear to have been part of the male value structure in early Maryland.

Women's sexual conduct, like men's financial conduct, was viewed as a proper subject for public concern. If magistrates learned of incidents in which women had sexual intercourse with men to whom they were not married, the authorities intervened to restore order, especially if the birth of bastards had resulted. Both men and women concerned themselves with women's morality, but only women demonstrated much interest in applying similar standards of behavior to men.[68] Although women did not serve as judges or jurymen, their roles as complainants and witnesses in trials for sexual offenses allowed them to take the initiative and to press their views upon the courts.

Their influence was magnified because when female sexuality was at issue the courts relied exclusively on women's expert knowledge. Never did a court ask a male physician to examine a woman's body and report his observations, nor did the judges themselves ever presume to assess whether a woman was pregnant or had borne a child. Instead, they summoned women to fulfill those functions. Thus female sexuality, public though it was, was not a matter upon which men intruded. Women controlled it, and so midwives in particular had an important public role. In exercising that role, they frequently showed their independence by differing from the definitions of morality advanced by male judges and juries.

In one limited but extremely important area, therefore, at least some women played a powerful role in the public life of seventeenth-century Maryland. The problematic nature of gender-role definitions and relations between men and women in a society with both an unusual demographic composition and a belief that order could not be sustained in the absence of what was seen as "normal" family life placed women's traditional control of female sexuality at the heart of public affairs. The goal of maintaining order in the state led the authorities to prosecute women for moral offenses, while the identical aim prompted many trials of men for contempt or treason.

So the patterns of accusation and prosecution stressed proper political and economic behavior for men and proper sexual behavior for women. Judges and juries, men and women, free people and even servants collaborated in achieving the collective goal of maintaining order in both realms. Maryland's residents argued about details, but were fully in accord on the central point: preserving family order was as essential to the society as preserving political order, for the two were intertwined. Men placed the burden of fostering sexual order solely on women's shoulders. Women believed that men's sexual behavior should also be subjected to public scrutiny, but women could not formally implement their ideas because men controlled the colony's legal structure. They tried to persuade the courts that fathers should bear equal responsibility in bastardy cases; that at least one father should be punished for feticide while some women charged with infanticide should be freed; and that both men and women should be punished for adultery and fornication. If women rarely succeeded fully in their aims, that did not lessen the significance of their efforts.

The Committee Movement of 1779
and the Formation of Public Authority
in Revolutionary America

RICHARD BUEL, JR.

I

A LONG TRADITION celebrates the uniqueness of the American Revolution, and the recent work of Theda Skocpol on modern social revolutions has underscored a new way in which that uniqueness can be understood. Though modern revolutions have invariably involved unprecedented mass-mobilizations, the American Revolution was distinctive in shunning the creation of a centralized state autonomous to the popular aspirations that initially fueled the movement.[1] The Americans fought most of their Revolutionary War without a constitutionally established central government and with state governments that invariably gave the representatives of local interests more formal power than they vested in the executive.[2] Though the revolutionaries finally succeeded in implementing the Articles of Confederation in March 1781, the new government did not possess many powers normally associated with state sovereignty. Until the constitutional "revolution" of 1787, the central government had no choice but to depend on the individual state governments for such vital matters as the raising of money and the regulation of commerce. Nor did the framing, adoption, and eventual implementation of the new, federal constitution substantially change the balance of power between the states and the central government. The new federal government still lacked a fully developed bureaucratic structure and, in the beginning at least, could only claim what power post-Revolutionary Americans wanted to give it. History has never seen, either before or since, the emergence of a less autonomous state system, in both principle and reality, than that which issued from the American Revolution.

The persistent aversion to centralized power in America's Revolutionary culture deserves more scrutiny than it has received. Its localist orientation not only is striking by way of contrast with other revolutions, but also appears to be dramatically dysfunctional. After all, there was a war on for much of this time, and wars require centralized authority, particularly if one is confronting a powerful military adversary. A close examination of the actual conduct of the war suggests that the patriot leadership was ingenious in devising ways for decentralized institutions to perform centralized functions.[3] But while the ingenuity of the leadership cannot be questioned, the effectiveness of their expedients is another matter, as the porousness of most areas to British military incursions and the collapse of the continent's credit after 1778 made clear. American commitment to decentralization repeatedly triumphed over the requirements of efficiency.

The localist orientation of American politics had grown directly out of the colonists' experience in settling and developing the wilderness. Success had depended on the mobilization of everyone's energies in response to local problems.[4] Even tasks traditionally assumed by a central power, such as defense, fell largely to local agencies. Settlers quickly realized that their alternatives were to either abandon their property and possessions or rely on their own resources in wilderness warfare. The aid of a centralized power continued to be solicited, but there was not much it could do after diplomatic alternatives had been exhausted besides ordering the evacuation of dispersed settlements to strong points and launching retaliatory raids to destroy the enemy's food supplies.[5]

Development over a century introduced the colonists to two kinds of centralization from which they benefited, but in ways that reinforced the positive value Americans attached to localism.

The first grew out of changes in the colonial economy. Though patterns of trade so vital to colonial development remained complex, the exchange of North American surpluses for imports from overseas came increasingly to be concentrated in the larger ports due to the shipping economies they could effect.[6] But the interior retained a grievance against the emerging cities, despite the advantage country folk derived from them. Much of the local economy depended on credit, and the creditors or their representatives often lived in the trading centers. A delinquent rural debtor hauled into court by his urban creditor could not but resent the source from which his discomfort seemed to emanate, particularly as the final judicial authority of the colony was situated there as well. Ports might mean greater efficiency in the exchange of surpluses for imports that raised the general standard of living, but they also meant debt and the distress associated with it. Despite the indispensable services they provided, the urban centers were as much resented as valued.[7]

Growing imperial rivalries gave rise to another kind of centralization that evoked mixed feelings among the North American colonists. The competition between the great European powers in the New World gradually subsumed local conflicts over local resources into larger, more generalized struggles directed from overseas. The change forced the elaboration of imperial structures in the colonies capable of responding to military challenges from abroad. But the emergence of these new imperial structures further exacerbated existing tensions between central and local authority. The imperial government's representatives proved even less responsive to local needs than the more centralized elements of the colonial governments. At the same time they were a good deal less effective, due to the colonists' resourcefulness in turning their assemblies into potent barriers obstructing the implementation of policies emanating from London.[8]

Despite dramatic economic development during the late colonial period, the experience of Americans during the first half of the eighteenth century powerfully reinforced a tendency of the colonists—present from the formation of American culture—to look to themselves, to harness local energies through local initiatives, to build political coalitions across space to resist the intrusion of external threats, and to be suspicious of any centralization of power in direct proportion to its remoteness from their immediate purview. The imperial crisis that began in the early 1760s simply reinforced these tendencies.

It is hardly surprising, then, that the colonists mobilized patriot energies for revolution by resorting to local committees of inspection and correspondence in 1774–75. The committee system can be traced back to the "Sons of Liberty" that had organized resistance to the Stamp Act in 1765. But formal, standing committees first emerged when local merchants attempted to create a Nonimportation Movement during 1768–70 directed against the mother country's attempt to tax imports from Britain.[9] The Nonimportation Movement had collapsed in 1770 without achieving all of its declared objectives. But colonial leaders attached more significance to the elaborately orchestrated pressures directed against Nonimportation by British officialdom than to the failure of the movement to secure a repeal of all of the revenue laws. The struggle led them to conclude that they faced an adversary committed to doing the colonists injury, but also one acutely vulnerable to an effective commercial boycott.[10]

The Continental Association sponsored by Congress in 1774 attempted to perfect the Nonimportation Movement of 1768–70. Instead of local committees sponsoring a variety of inconsistent agreements, Congress proposed a common agreement and charged local committees with its enforcement. These committees subsequently undertook the task of maintaining surveillance over elements hostile to the patriot cause.[11] And when it became necessary to raise troops in response to the outbreak of hostilities, to counter an unexpectedly large British expeditionary force in 1776, and to form the permanent army in 1777, local committees stepped forward to supply the necessary incentives to recruits by raising bounties and applying verbal persuasion. Despite the collapse of Nonimportation in 1770, the political experience of the revolutionaries, at least through 1777, gave Americans good reason to think that popular mobilization at the local level was one of their strongest suits. Certainly the state governments continued to devolve onto local authorities the principal responsibility for implementing their policies thoughout the war.[12]

If the impulse of Americans was to turn to local power, especially when trying to mobilize revolutionary energies, how did centralization manage to make any headway at all against the preferences of the revolutionaries to keep things as local as possible? The question brings certain long-neglected aspects of the Revolutionary War into a new focus. This essay concentrates on the popular committee movement of 1779 to regulate prices, a movement that was intensely local and attracted a fair amount of attention then, but has attracted very little since.[13] It certainly was not a particularly glorious episode of the Revolution. But an understanding of it can provide insight into the processes whereby authority was made or impugned in this mass-mobilizing, popular revolution.

II

The most intractable problem that arose during the Revolutionary War involved the depreciation of the currency. Despite the recent debate about the compatibility of classical republicanism's emphasis on civic virtue with the commercial values of the marketplace, the revolutionaries behaved from the start of the war as though the two were perfectly reconcilable. Though republicanism required voluntary energies to sustain it, Revolutionary leaders assumed that appropriate compensation should be tendered in exchange. Instead of shunning the marketplace, they went into it looking for goods and services in unprecedented quantities and, in the first years of the struggle, found them at attractive prices.[14] What could be more republican than equalizing the burdens borne in the Revolutionary mobilization by an exchange of equivalents and the harnessing of private energies to public purposes through the consensual mechanisms of the marketplace? Individual colonies took the initiative in resorting to market mechanisms, but Congress quickly followed suit by issuing its own currency on the joint credit of the states.[15]

At first, both the state and continental money held its value and served its purpose. But, beginning with the defeats at Long Island and New York at the end of the summer of 1776, it progressively lost value. People started to discount it as the success of the Revolution appeared increasingly problematic.[16] Once begun, the depreciation proved difficult to halt. The currency's declining value penalized anyone holding it for very long, yet the disruption of normal peacetime commerce with the outside world made it difficult to invest the money in anything but domestic produce sought by the army. This pushed up the price of commodities needed to prosecute the war and forced Congress, given the Revolutionary leadership's hesitancy about taxing, to issue more money to procure in the marketplace.[17] By the middle of 1777 the continent was locked in a cycle of runaway inflation and depreciation, and by the beginning of 1778 it was clear that time was working against the Americans. At current rates of expenditure the revolutionaries were accumulating a debt that in short order would be unpayable and would make a mockery of their efforts to free themselves from subordination to a "bankrupt" British state.[18]

The failure of Americans to bring the war to a victorious end during 1777 made 1778 a particularly critical year. Financial prudence pointed to cutting back their effort to a level more consistent with what they could afford, but the Franco-American alliance offered the prospect of putting a quick, decisive end to the conflict. To take full advantage of the alliance, though, required Americans to exert themselves to the utmost. Congress succumbed to the temptation to "go for broke" in the campaign of 1778, maintaining the heroic levels of mobilization that had characterized the two previous campaigns, in the hope that one last push would bring the war to a quick conclusion.[19] They could only do so, though, by issuing additional currency certain to fuel the fires of depreciation. Still, if the war could be brought to a successful conclusion by the end of the ensuing campaign, there would be time enough to sort out the republic's chaotic finances in the more congenial environment of peace.

Congress's decision was undoubtedly influenced by a brief rise in the value of the currency during the spring of 1778, a product of expectations that the war was about to end, or at least that some form of transatlantic trade would resume.[20] But Congress wasn't oblivious to the risk that the patriots might exhaust themselves in the forthcoming campaign without achieving a decision. If that happened, they might find themselves unable to continue the war. The risk seemed worth taking, though, since scaling back might tempt the French to pervert the alliance to ends that were unacceptable or, even worse, to repudiate it entirely.[21]

The gamble did not work. The campaign failed either to end the war or to impel a British withdrawal from the continent. Instead, the British served notice that they intended to respond to the Franco-American alliance by changing the character of the struggle and striking at civilians along the coast.[22] For the Americans, the prospect of a prolonged war of attrition was especially unwelcome as it coincided with the collapse of the patriot economy. Not only did the winter of 1778–79 see acute shortages develop in the basic supplies needed by the army, but in many areas the civilian population suffered as well, making it all the more difficult to procure for the military.[23] Both developments had an adverse effect on the value of the currency, which had resumed its downward slide in the autumn, leaving Congress with no choice in the near term, short of abandoning the struggle, but to continue expanding the money supply, and in so doing accelerating still further the depreciation.[24]

Though by the end of 1778 Congress's options in dealing with the depreciation had been severely reduced, two possibilities remained. One was to embark on a policy of heroic taxation to reduce the money supply. The difficulty with this option was that Congress lacked power to raise revenue and needed to work through the thirteen sovereign states, each with a timetable of its own. Even if all the states acted quickly in unison, a tax could not be collected in less than nine months.[25] Yet the war had to be carried on in the interval without setting off an even more ruinous cycle of depreciation. Which led to the second option, namely the attempt to regulate prices. While price regulations were widely recognized as being self-defeating in the long run, they might momentarily halt the depreciation and protect the financial position of the continent until other remedies like taxation came into play.[26]

Both Congress and the separate states had experimented with such regulations, though never with much success.[27] Congress could only recommend such measures; implementation rested with the states. They, in turn, found that their jurisdictions did not correspond with the markets they were trying to influence. For instance, any attempt to regulate prices on the part of Pennsylvania could be frustrated if New Jersey, Delaware, and Maryland refused to join in the measure, since many producers had the option of taking their produce out of state if they were dissatisfied with the locally regulated price. From the beginning of the war regional conventions had tried to patch together interstate cooperation, but without much success.[28] Each locality had slightly different ideas about what prices should be.

Moreover, aside from the problem of comprehensive implementation, severe political tensions at the local level obstructed regulation's effectiveness. These tensions can best be understood by analyzing how farmers and town dwellers respectively viewed price controls. Urban artisans, whose dependence on the market was more or less complete, for the most part favored regulation. Indeed, they could point to the traditional assizes of bread to justify their preference.[29] By contrast farmers, angry about the shortages and high prices of imports, sought to protect their interests in two, not necessarily consistent, ways. First, they used their political control of the legislatures to maintain some parity between the price of imports and farm produce; second, they withheld supplies from the urban markets until the price bore a desired relationship to imports. In other words, they were all for regulating the price of imports but less anxious to sell their own produce on anything but advantageous terms.[30] Regulation was usually resisted by the merchants. Though occasionally favoring the fixing of agricultural prices, they viewed all restraints on the spontaneity of the marketplace with suspicion because they thought of themselves as a political minority.[31] The same ambivalence infected the commissariat, though for slightly different reasons. It feared any measures that might discourage production, but when facing an immediate shortage it often resorted to any expedient, including seizure at a specified price, to weather the emergency.[32]

Regulation had few unqualified supporters. Until the spring of 1779 the initiative for it had come principally from the state legislatures, though the idea was occasionally discussed in Congress. On May 25, 1779, however, a popular movement to regulate prices sprang up in Philadelphia without explicit sponsorship from either Congress or the Pennsylvania legislature. Its declared objective was first to halt the upward spiral of prices and then progressively to lower prices until they reached their prewar levels.[33] And it proposed to achieve its objectives through popularly elected local committees—the same means that had been used in enforcing the Continental Association of 1774–75.

Because of Philadelphia's commanding position as a market in its region, the enforcement of these regulations was felt as far away as Baltimore and Alexandria. Equally important, Philadelphia's example was followed not only in the rest of Philadelphia County, but in Chester and Lancaster counties, in towns as distant as Reading and York, as well as in Newcastle County, Delaware, and Burlington County, New Jersey, and possibly as far away as Williamsburg, Virginia.[34] What is more, a committee of Boston merchants promptly adopted Philadelphia's regulatory scheme, and its action had a comparable impact throughout New England.[35] Committees quickly sprang up in the secondary towns surrounding Boston. And the committee movement then spread to the commercial towns of Rhode Island, New Hampshire, and eventually to many of the rural towns of southern New England. These local committees sought to coordinate their activities by summoning representative conventions, often on a statewide basis. In Massachusetts 121 towns sent delegates to such a convention at Concord in mid-July.[36] In its reliance on local initiatives and merchant participation, the committee movement of 1779 resembled the Nonimportation Movement of 1768–70 more than it did the Continental Association of 1774–77. Nonetheless, its sponsors stressed the affinity between their actions and the revolutionary mobilization of the early war years.[37]

Controversy surrounded the committees of 1779 from the start. Some opposed them as a dangerous attempt to usurp the fragile authority of the state governments and Congress. They feared the "mobbish principles" of those who sought to harness popular power to the quixotic objectives of regulation.[38] The movement also had to cope with commercial jealousies, much as had Nonimportation in 1768–70. Thus Baltimore refused to follow Philadelphia's lead, though publicly invited to do so, because of the rivalry that existed between the two ports.[39] With some exceptions, most notably Maryland but to a lesser extent Connecticut, the committee movement was strongest in areas proximate to the great market centers. As one moved to the fringe of the Philadelphia and Boston markets, enthusiasm declined. Thus Hampshire and Berkshire counties in Massachusetts were less supportive of the regulatory movement than were Worcester County and Rhode Island.[40] And New York, which had become economically isolated because of the British occupation of New York City, saw only a halfhearted and unsuccessful effort at regulation in Albany County.[41] There was no movement to speak of in either Virginia or North Carolina.

While the committee movement of 1779 hardly embraced the entire continent, it nonetheless spontaneously achieved a remarkable unanimity in diverse geographical areas. All the committees seemed to endorse the initiative of the Philadelphia committee, not only in seeking to halt the relentless rise in prices but also in trying to reduce them gradually to prewar levels.[42] Though the committee movement collapsed within a few months, and certainly failed to dampen the runaway depreciation which characterized 1779, that it should have arisen at all begs for some explanation. Why did constituencies with apparently conflicting interests suddenly come together on a grassroots level to achieve an uncommonly unanimous stance on the issue of price regulation, albeit only momentarily? And what were the consequences of this attempt to appropriate the prestige that the committee movement had acquired, particularly during 1775–76, to the solution of the nation's financial ills?

III

The best way to approach these questions is to examine the origins of the committee movement in Philadelphia. Before the war, Philadelphia had been the leading market in which grain surpluses, largely in the form of superfine flour, were exchanged for foreign imports. Seventy percent of the colonies' prewar exportable grain surplus was shipped by Philadelphia merchants whose hinterland stretched from the tributaries of the Delaware in New Jersey in a great arc around to the Susquehanna and the northern Chesapeake.[43] Philadelphians, then, were not accustomed to going short of bread. But in the spring of 1779 their grain prices began to rise to unheard-of levels.[44] Much of the rise could be attributed to the delayed impact of the British invasion of the area in the summer of 1777. Wheat was normally sown in September to be harvested in the following July. Shortages arising from the disruption of the 1777 planting season would last until mid-August 1779, when the crop planted in September 1778 would finally become available.[45]

There was another dimension to Philadelphia's problem in early 1779, however. The British occupation of the city until June 1778, and its subsequent evacuation, had left the port stripped of virtually all its shipping. Its overseas trade had been reduced to a mere trickle. Though the city's merchants were scrambling furiously to rebuild their fleet, without the desired imports farmers had no incentives to bring their surpluses to the urban market. So even what grain there was in the region had ceased to flow through accustomed channels.[46]

Nothing better illustrated the dire straits to which Philadelphia had been reduced than an incident that occurred in April 1779. In late March a small fleet of merchant vessels had arrived from the West Indies, bringing with it the first substantial quantity of imports since the British evacuation. Under normal circumstances this should have led not only to a decline in the price of imports but also to a decline in the price of domestic produce as farmers sent their surpluses to the urban market. Instead, the price of both began to climb astronomically, seemingly in tandem with each other. Popular resentment focused on a French polacre, the *Victorious*, which had arrived with the fleet but had been slow in unloading its cargo because of a misunderstanding between the owners and their appointed agent, Robert Morris. An investigating committee constituted by a rump meeting of the town's populace reported that the delay in unloading had been deliberately engineered to force prices still higher.[47] The charge only made sense in the light of a series of assumptions that seemed self-evident at the time: first, that what had been imported was insufficient to meet current demand, and second, that any further supply of foreign goods was unlikely, at least in the immediate future.

Popular resentment against Morris's handling of the *Victorious*'s cargo launched the committee movement in Philadelphia. But a good deal more than resentment was involved. The dramatic rise in prices threatened the survival of artisans. If foreign commodities were necessary to procure agricultural surpluses, those lacking access to imports faced a raw prospect at best. They could either migrate back to the countryside or attempt to regulate prices. And if they chose the latter alternative, they could not settle for half-measures, since the high price of domestic produce was linked to the high price of imports. Under the circumstances the Philadelphia committee had no choice but to try to regulate all significant exchanges in the urban market.

The committee could, to be sure, have settled for simply halting the precipitous rise in prices. But instead it committed itself to lowering prices progressively until they reached prewar levels. The committee hoped to stimulate economic activity through progressive price reductions. One effect of the depreciation had been to make the possessors of commodities reluctant to sell them for currency, since goods were rising against currency. But if money could be made to rise against goods, the tables would be turned. Those who were now hoarding commodities would be induced "to exhibit to sale whatever they may have to spare, in order to avoid the loss that must necessarily attend a contrary conduct. . . . Farmers and every other order of men, will exert themselves to get something to sell, because they will expect to receive something for it of value."[48] Though proponents of a falling market argued it would stimulate market exchanges in general, it remained principally a strategy for getting farmers to release their supplies.

Is it not extraordinary, then, that the movement caught hold, not just in other port cities like Boston—which had reason enough to copy Philadelphia's example because the circumstances of each were roughly parallel—but in the hinterlands as well? The pattern of the committee movement's proliferation in Connecticut shows that the countryside's commitment to regulation often exceeded that of the more commercial centers. Regulation here found greater favor among the inhabitants of the peripheral towns than along the Connecticut River. Thus Fairfield and Windham both voted on July 1 to call county conventions long before a notice appeared in the *Connecticut Courant* advising that Hartford County's committees of inspection would meet in Hartford in the middle of August.[49] When the Fairfield County committees met in Reading on August 10, they issued a ringing endorsement of the Philadelphia plan, calling on the towns throughout the state to form individual committees for this purpose.[50] By contrast, the Hartford County meeting issued no declaration to the public and neglected to call a statewide convention as other New England states had. The call for a state convention was instead issued by a Windham County convention, with the support of some towns in adjacent New London County. While some of the river towns like Hartford and Middletown eventually agreed to send delegates to this statewide convention, others like Wethersfield continued to oppose such a meeting. And when the convention finally met in October, attendance was so light that no action was taken.[51]

The reluctance of Connecticut's principal commercial centers to take the initiative for regulation was noted as far away as Portsmouth, New Hampshire.[52] It is tempting to dismiss their behavior as reflecting the merchants' traditional distrust of regulation, but peripheral commercial towns like Danbury, Norwalk, and Stonington supported the committee movement that merchants in the larger ports had sponsored. So did essentially agricultural towns such as Canterbury, Ashford, and Lyme.[53] Why should they be so anxious to implement regulations designed to benefit urban areas, particularly when they were suspected of subverting the effective operation of price controls earlier in the war?[54] And why did so much unanimity manifest itself in both town and countryside at this time, areas that before had been at loggerheads over price controls?

The answer lies in the larger context in which the regulation was implemented. For concurrently with popular action in Philadelphia, Congress had committed itself to an heroic effort at taxation, forwarding to the states a requisition for $60 million to be withdrawn from circulation by taxation.[55] Though the tax would take time to collect, it seemed reasonable to assume that money would gradually grow scarcer and the depreciation would reverse itself.[56] Once that happened those holding what remained of the currency might flock to the loan offices to lend it at its current rate in the hope of reaping an enormous capital gain that would accompany an appreciation, as well as the nominal interest. Such a development would cumulatively reduce the money supply still further and accelerate the appreciation.[57] The scenario of appreciating continentals was even more likely to become a reality if France proved able to defeat Britain before the end of 1779. That prospect seemed real enough in light of the rumor that Spain had declared war against Great Britain, potentially making France's and Spain's combined fleets superior to the British.[58]

Superficially, an appreciating continental currency looked like an unmixed blessing. Certainly it would solve the problem of public credit that had plagued the patriot war effort until this point. But there was also a darker side to an appreciation of the currency, particularly a radical appreciation which would take the currency back to par. If the depreciation had penalized those who held the money while it lost value and protected debtors from creditors, because creditors weren't interested in being paid off in depreciated money,[59] an appreciation, in reversing the process, might benefit creditors as much as they had previously been penalized. As the currency increased in value, debtors would be forced to trade at ever more disadvantageous terms with creditors so as to acquire the money, in increasingly short supply, with which to retire their private debts and public tax obligations.[60]

Since most people were both debtors and creditors, it was not necessarily clear to them whether they would benefit or lose in a currency appreciation. But the less substantial members of society were anxious about becoming the victims of "the opulant Farmer and Trader" who would have the "power, unless restricted, to increase the price of articles they have in hand, in proportion to the increase in their Taxes," thus casting the "great burthen of the Taxes . . . on the poor & middling" sorts.[61] And rural elements remote from the commercial centers had special reason for fearing they would be at a disadvantage in scrambling for what might remain of a dwindling supply of the currency.

These circumstances help explain the rapid spread of the committee movement to the countryside during the summer of 1779 even though it was originally directed against withholding by rural elements. Regulation by popular committees seemed like a potent weapon to bring the expansion of the currency debt to an end and save some shred of the continent's credit. In this respect the interests of the towns and countryside were one.[62] But those interests diverged when it came to appreciating the currency. Farmers could accept a small rise in the currency so long as all commodity prices fell simultaneously. But they wanted to make sure that the appreciation of the currency which would depress the price of their agricultural produce depressed other prices in equal proportion. Wartime shortages of imports suggested that this might not occur, making a currency appreciation potentially disastrous for them.[63] The country committees were more interested in freezing the value of the currency in relation to commodities than in stimulating activity in the marketplace, though they were perfectly willing to ally themselves temporarily with influential elements in the towns to effect their ends.

As it turned out, rural elements had little reason to fear an appreciation. Long before the state requisitions were due, the depreciation had progressed to the point where Congress had to declare a halt to the issuance of any further bills of credit. Congress attempted to continue financing the war effort in the short term by issuing warrants on the state loan offices into which the state fiscal authorities were directed to deposit their collections of the $60 million requisition. But the warrants usually exceeded what was available in the loan offices because the states were delinquent in meeting their quotas.[64] And this way of financing the war effort subverted the objective of reducing the money supply. The currency might still have been rescued by decisive allied victories, but these failed to materialize during the remainder of 1779. Instead the autumn saw the attempt to take Savannah crumble, a development which administered a coup de grace to the last remnant of credit the old continental currency enjoyed.[65] Though it continued to circulate until well into 1781, no one could seriously propose that it be redeemed at par again after November 1779.

IV

The continued depreciation of the currency removed the principal incentive for rural areas to support the committee movement. Concurrently two other developments seriously compromised the movement's appeal.

The first was the much-publicized effort by the Philadelphia committee to restrict the transit of commodities from the urban market out to the hinterland.[66] Though stimulating economic activity may not have been the highest item on the agenda of committeemen in the interior, they could not afford to be cut off from all sources of external supply. Gouverneur Morris wrote jubilantly to Robert R. Livingston in late August 1779 that the Philadelphia committee's refusal to release any salt to agents of the town of Albany had killed the movement in New York.[67]

The second was a less-publicized confrontation that took place between the French consul in Philadelphia, John Holker, and the committees of Wilmington, Delaware, and Philadelphia. Holker had commissioned Jonathan Rumford to assemble a parcel of flour in Delaware for the French fleet in the West Indies. Rumford had a dubious reputation, and the Wilmington committee had seized the parcel upon suspicion that it was about to be exported clandestinely on private account. Inferring that local millers would not sell flour at the regulated price because Rumford was offering more, the Wilmington committee then sent the confiscated parcel on to the Philadelphia committee, which was desperately looking for provisions.[68] French ambassador Gerard protested the seizure of the flour and the publication in the *Pennsylvania Packet* of the Philadelphia committee's criticism of Holker's actions.[69] Although Gerard eventually backed away from insisting that the *Packet* be prosecuted, the incident nonetheless suggested that regulation was at odds with the smooth workings of the Franco-American alliance. In doing so it raised further general doubts about the wisdom of price fixing that helped hasten the dissolution of the committee movement outside the great ports during the autumn.[70]

The committees of Philadelphia and Boston did not pass from the scene so gracefully. For the urban artisan, regulation seemed the only strategy for survival in an economy plagued by acute agricultural shortages. But attempts to regulate the urban marketplace in the absence of a large supply of imports were bound to be self-defeating. In Philadelphia, the committee's activities continued to discourage both importers and producers from sending goods to market.[71] The city's mercantile community, still struggling to replace its lost tonnage, felt that the regulation simply compounded the difficulties they were trying to surmount in restoring the port's trade.[72] Though a minority, many merchants and some tradesmen refused to collaborate with the committeemen in provisioning the city at regulated prices, and their resistance culminated in the bloodshed of the Fort Wilson Massacre in early October 1779.

A good deal has been written about urban violence in Philadelphia during the Revolution, most of it by those anxious to exonerate the crowd from responsibility for aimless anarchy. That approach does not explain why the Fort Wilson incident led to the collapse of regulation in the town. A mounted cavalry unit led by President Reed charged the militia—composed of regulators—in the street and, after a pitched battle in which at least six lost their lives, arrested its members rather than those in Wilson's house. The violence had the effect of isolating and discrediting the regulators who had been seizing "tories" suspected of resisting the regulation. Despite the acute distress that lasted through an unusually severe winter, the committee movement withered away.[73] The Fort Wilson incident convinced the city that an inadequate market was preferable to regulation and bloodshed. But Philadelphia's poor suffered terribly before a modest revival in overseas commerce along with the new harvest began to stock the city's markets more abundantly in the summer of 1780.[74]

Boston's regulation pursued a slightly different course. Though its hinterland was a good deal poorer than Philadelphia's, it did not have to cope simultaneously with the immediate consequences of a British occupation and the acute shortages that plagued the Revolutionary economy in 1779. Boston had had three years to replace the tonnage that had been lost during the enemy occupation of 1774–76, and Massachusetts Bay was much harder to blockade than were the capes of the Delaware or the Chesapeake. As a consequence goods, particularly foreign goods, flowed more freely into the Massachusetts economy during most of the war than they did farther south.[75] The state's commercial advantage was compromised by the British seizure of the Penobscot region in June 1779. But Massachusetts immediately acted to dislodge the British. The province's merchants readily lent their private warships and transports to the venture. Provisioning the expeditionary force required reaching westward to the grain regions of the Hudson Valley and letting Boston prices rise to record levels. They could do this because the flow of imports and prizes continued unabated through the spring months, giving them something to bargain with in distant New York.[76]

The city's artisans resented the restructuring of the local economy that the Penobscot expedition entailed, so they enthusiastically supported the committee movement, initiated by the merchants and traders, in the town meeting.[77] But they enjoyed much less power in Boston than their counterparts enjoyed in Philadelphia.[78] Until the departure of the expeditionary force for Penobscot in mid-July, military requirements took precedence over the activities of committees and conventions that were called to coordinate the committees. Moreover, many artisans benefited indirectly from the mounting of the expedition, and could expect to benefit even more from its success, which would presumedly secure the town's navigation and ensure the continued arrival of both imports and domestic produce in the future.

Unfortunately the expedition ended in disaster with the loss of all the state's naval tonnage and a considerable portion of its private warships and merchant tonnage.[79] This catastrophe was to some extent counterbalanced by a lucky stroke on the part of the fledgling Continental Navy. In August 1779 three Continental frigates, the *Providence*, the *Ranger*, and the *Queen of France*, managed to fall in with the Jamaica fleet off the Grand Banks and, with the help of a heavy fog, to capture eleven large ships, eight of which finally arrived in Boston.[80] In monetary terms the windfall of West India goods probably exceeded the value of the vessels lost at Penobscot. But it was not clear who was going to benefit from the windfall. Though the prizes had been sent into Boston, Jeremiah Wadsworth, the retiring commissary general, saw in them an opportunity to solve the army's acute supply problems. He suggested to the government of New York that the Continental Congress barter the cargoes for provisions in the Hudson Valley and appealed to Congress for authority to execute this scheme.[81]

Doing so meant transferring the potential benefit of the West India goods to another locale—an idea even less popular in Boston's artisan circles than the measures taken to provision the Penobscot expedition. The Marine Committee's agent there, William Bradford, found himself subjected to considerable local pressure to continue sales.[82] Given the provision shortages that plagued the Boston market, a confrontation seemed to be shaping up very much like the one that had occurred in Philadelphia. In Boston, however, the regulation collapsed more with a whimper than a bang.

The city's merchants, clearly sobered by news of the violence in Philadelphia, joined in a scheme to form a public magazine to feed the town. They subscribed imports, principally West India goods, promising to barter them for surpluses in the countryside.[83] Arrivals from other Massachusetts ports as well as foreign vessels continued to supply the town with a steady flow of commodities and prizes seeking to take advantage of its market. But the magazine of imports at regulated prices proved to be a quixotic scheme. It never received enough subscriptions to solve Boston's provision problem. Furthermore, while magazine managers tried to maximize the quantity of country produce procured, merchants undercut them by offering higher—unregulated—barter prices for imports.[84]

The magazine did serve the useful function of reassuring the immediate countryside that they would not be cut off from all imports by schemes like Wadsworth's or limitations like those that had been imposed on the Philadelphia market.[85] It also kept attention focused on Congress's policy of attempting to withhold its prize goods, which was criticized, among other reasons, for subverting local price controls by aggravating shortages.[86] The perception that Congressional policies were at loggerheads with price regulations in turn weakened the authority of those regulations. But even more influential in this connection was the fate of a large quantity of goods imported by French merchants into the town at the end of the summer. They ended up being carted overland to markets that were not regulated.[87] By late autumn price limitations had pretty much been discarded in Boston.

V

The inspiration for the committee movement of 1779 clearly lay in the associations that had sponsored the Revolutionary mobilization between 1768 and 1777. The impending collapse of the Revolutionary economy necessitated deploying an extraordinary weapon of such proven potency.

The failure of popular committees to redeem the Revolutionary economy in turn diminished the credibility of both price regulation in particular and popular committees in general.

The committee movement's collapse at the local level triggered contradictory responses from the state and national governments. The first response of the states was to call for a congressionally sponsored price-fixing scheme on a continental scale.[88] This tactic was supported by panicked members of the commissariat who saw in regulation their only hope for making any provision for the army.[89] In the longer run, after efforts at continental cooperation had predictably come to naught, the collapse of the committee movement strengthened the hand of those who felt reliance on governmental command shouldn't supersede the market as the principal agency for directing the war effort. In March 1780 they instituted a plan to revive the marketplace by replacing the old continental currency with a "new emission" currency in a scheme designed to protect the nation equally against an appreciation and a depreciation.[90]

The collapse of the committee movement also discredited direct popular action as a remedy for extraordinary problems, at least in areas in which the regulation of 1779 had been most in evidence. Spontaneous popular mobilizations, such as those in Connecticut and Massachusetts toward the end of the war, were more easily contained than might have been the case had the prestige of popular Revolutionary action not been previously qualified. In Connecticut the state's inability to control the illicit trade with Long Island caused a political crisis in 1782 that spawned a resurgence of popular committees. It is significant that voices could then be raised against resorting to such means to check trading with the enemy without having their loyalty impugned. These voices could speak because the regulation of 1779—which seemed to underline in palpable, unmistakable terms the tendency of local initiatives to lead to an ineffectual anarchy—had armed the opponents of misguided, popular enthusiasms with a powerful weapon.[91] And this weapon again proved useful during 1783 in controlling a regional hostility to commutation throughout southern New England as well as resentment directed against tories at the conclusion of the war.[92]

Fear of spontaneous local initiatives failed to suppress all popular committees and conventions. The interior of Massachusetts Bay continued to be plagued by such irregularities throughout the early 1780s, a legacy of the long interregnum between the dissolution of royal government in 1774 and ratification of the state's Constitution of 1780.[93] And attempts by the state's leadership to invoke the fear of anarchy in 1786 to diffuse the explosive confrontation that emerged in Massachusetts between a desperate debtor majority and a creditor minority proved ineffectual. Nonetheless the New England elite were able to circumvent popular challenges after the conclusion of the war—with the exception of Shays's Rebellion—partially because the direct application of popular power had been found so wanting in 1779 as the desperately needed remedy to the nation's financial ills.[94]

On the other hand, the demonstrated impotency of popular mobilizations in solving critical economic problems did not in itself establish the authority of those who wished to replace the localist orientation of Revolutionary political culture with a centralism based on Congress's fiscal authority. Significantly, the "new emission" scheme of March 18, 1780, still depended upon the power of the states to pay the interest due on the bills and settled for simply sharing the benefits between the continent and the states, an arrangement that worked much better on paper than in practice.[95] Robert Morris's attempts to implement a more centralized fiscal alternative in 1781–83 also failed. If he had succeeded in getting Congress vested with the power to raise an impost, the outcome might have been different. Short of this, his leverage over the nation's finances remained entirely dependent on French subsidies. Not only was the source unreliable—the subsidies were withdrawn with the peace—but it was also unpopular because foreign.[96] In the wake of his resignation, the separate states went their own ways in their efforts to establish public credit. Not until Shays's Rebellion had clearly demonstrated the inability of the states to provide for the nation's credit by themselves, was a central government with powers adequate to the circumstances confronting the nation finally framed and adopted.

Not all agreed on the wisdom of the Constitution as a remedy for the problems the nation faced. But again, significantly, opponents of the convention's handiwork did not establish popular committees coordinated by counter-conventions throughout the nation to oppose the Constitution, despite the call of some disgruntled Antifederalists that they do so.[97] If they had, the outcome of the ratification process might have been different. As it was, the demoralized condition of local leaders and of the populace at large by the end of the Confederation period gave the national elite a unique chance to quell the principal source of popular insurgency by solving the problem of the war debt that had given rise to it in the first place. Had the members of the Philadelphia Convention faced a popular political culture at the local level whose authority was uncompromised by previous failures, they might, as a threatened elite, have been under greater temptation to counter with less liberal remedies than the ones actually used.

From this perspective, the failure of the committee movement in 1779 may ironically have been symptomatic of conditions in American society favorable to the establishment of liberty. So long as the Revolutionary leadership could avoid destructive confrontations with a mobilized populace, like the one they had faced in 1779, they could look beyond their own parochial problems to those of the society at large. And so long as they proved able to come up with solutions, a liberal political order— in which their authority flowed directly from their competence in solving these problems rather than from the exercise of coercive power—remained a possiblity here more than anywhere else in the world.

A Different Thermidor

THE REVOLUTION BEYOND THE
AMERICAN REVOLUTION

MICHAEL ZUCKERMAN

W E DO NOT really understand the American Revolution. We
do not have a convincing conception of its causes, its conduct,
or its consequences. And the most compelling account we do
have of its origins very nearly precludes comprehension of its outcomes.
On that account, the terms of American embarkation upon rebellion
make all but inexplicable the terms of American emergence from the
struggle.

It has always been hard for historians to see how a few puny provincial
outposts ever came to the conviction that they could defy the mightiest
military power on the planet. It has always been difficult for historians
to say how a congeries of colonies which had displayed no previous gift
for cooperation ever acted together so effectively in 1776 or stayed
together afterward.

In the nineteenth century and well into the twentieth, students of the
young republic resolved such dilemmas by positing an aboriginal and
progressively maturing love of liberty in the colonial character. Indeed,
they rearranged the first two centuries of American history so as to
sustain that unriddling of the Revolution. They celebrated the early
settlers of the South as cavaliers seeking freedom from Cromwellian
coercion. They acclaimed the founders of New England as devout Puritans planting principles of religious liberty. They took petty provincial
uprisings like Bacon's Rebellion as auguries of the greater rebellion

which would follow. They treated modest social movements like the Carolina Regulations as anticipations of the grander insurgency which would make a new nation. They exalted institutions like the town meeting as embodied expressions of an invincible folk freedom.

In our own time, however, an expansion of perspective has made such views very nearly untenable. Students of the national past with broader social sympathies began to see that the history of the American people would have to include more than the elites and their interests. Early American history would have to take on a new aspect. The first planters of the Chesapeake began to be reconceived as men who gained their estates and entitlements by appropriating the labors and abrogating the liberties of people whom they plunged into depths of bondage unknown in England and Africa. The founding faithful of New England began to be exposed as sectarians who sought freedom to persecute far more than freedom from oppression. Bacon's Rebellion began to be depicted as an instance of inveterate English antagonism to the Indians, or an illuminating moment in the consolidation of a creole elite, or a decisive development in the onset of slavery and racism, rather than as a stage in the advent of liberty. Movements such as the Carolina Regulations began to loom larger as symptomatic skirmishes in chronic class conflicts, or efforts to bring unruly frontiers under formal governance, than as expressions of irresistible frontier freedom. Institutions such as the town meeting began to be interpreted more as means to mobilize consent in the service of social conformity than as epitomes of early American democracy.[1]

I

All of these new understandings emphasized control of conduct and containment of conflict as essential impulses of colonial experience. All of them abandoned the traditional position that predicated an invincible love of liberty implanted from the first in American bosoms and an irresistible release of energy evident ever after. All of them contributed to a clearing of interpretive ground for a new conception of the course of the Revolution which has come to dominate discourse in recent years.

On this conception, the story of the Revolution is a story of ideas more than of instincts. It begins in classical antiquity, in the Italian Renaissance, and in the eighteenth-century emergence of the British Empire. It gathers force in the unprecedented financial and commercial growth of Hanoverian England and in the contemporaneous consolidation of mo-narchical authority and its adjunct, the Whig Party of Robert Walpole.

It culminates in an unlikely series of appropriations and distortions of English ideas in a colonial context for which they were never intended.

The aggrandizements of the economy and of the Crown were, to most eighteenth-century Englishmen, exhilarating aspects of the expansion of empire, and systematic political corruption seemed a small price to pay for the first political stability England had enjoyed in generations.[2] But the unsavory means by which Walpole brought Parliament to heel were, to a few Englishmen of outmoded attachment to an older intellectual tradition, too high a price to expend for men who meant to maintain their integrity. In this tradition, which Machiavelli took from the ancients and refurbished for the humanists of the Renaissance, man was made for citizenship rather than for personal advancement or private fulfillment. He attained social standing and moral stature by his participation in the process of republican government. He found freedom itself in his engagement in the common cause of the community, since liberty was a property of political entities rather than of private individuals. Republican liberty was an attribute of societies whose citizens were virtuous, and virtue lay in the willingness of individuals to subordinate their private interests to the public good. Commerce was often inimical to virtue, for it often led men to an undue infatuation with their own immediate interests in the marketplace. Such surrender to the imperious urgings of pecuniary passion was corruption.[3]

The thinkers who took up this classical republican tradition in England were an intriguing lot. They included Milton and Harrington in the seventeenth century, and they ranged from radical Whigs to Tories and from original theorists to unimaginative popularizers in the eighteenth. They had in common neither social background nor political allegiance nor even a name. They called themselves Republicans, or Old Whigs, or Commonwealthmen. They shared only their impotence to arrest the progress of Walpole's political machine and their rage at English imperial expansion. Their radical fulminations repelled most Englishmen of moderation, who approved of the status quo, as well as most Englishmen of ambition, who sought simply to rise within it.[4]

But the same shrill denunciations which were repellent to Britons appealed powerfully to American colonists of capacity, who stood still further outside Walpole's system than the "alienated intellectuals, outraged moralists, and frustrated politicians" of the English opposition. Provincial Americans adapted the arguments of the English agitators to their own purposes. Like the ideologists across the ocean, they aimed to arouse "a virtuous people against the potential aggressions of a hostile sovereign." But unlike the English dissenters, they succeeded. The accusations that rang hollow at home seemed richly resonant in the colonies, where settlers experienced few of the benefits of the new order and felt all too palpably their dependence on royal prerogative.[5]

Opposition ideology expressed a "fierce and total unwillingness to accept" the maturation of the British Empire. The incendiary aspect of the colonial appropriation of that ideology was its "strident and impassioned critique" of English dominion and of the ready reliance on corruption that attended it. Even more than their radical Whig mentors in the mother country, Americans feared the consequences of corruption for the British liberties they believed they were entitled to enjoy.[6]

It was, indeed, their apprehension of the dialectic of virtue and corruption which convinced the leaders of the colonies that they had to rebel and that they could actually succeed. And it was the diffusion of this conviction of the leaders to large numbers of other Americans that turned resistance into revolution. Colonists who came to see the salience of commonwealth conceptions did not doubt England's military strength so much as her social stamina. Her inhabitants had forsaken the plain paths of virtue for the winding ways of corruption. Their very indisposition to subordinate private desire to public design left them incapable of controlling their still-vigorous provincial offspring. "Who but a pompous blockhead," asked one American, could expect dissipated voluptuaries to conquer "a hardy, virtuous set of men" who were "strangers to that luxury which effeminates the mind and body?"[7]

The recovery of this republican understanding of experience has enabled historians to make sense as their predecessors never could of the colonists' audacious readiness for revolution. But this same insistence on the obsession of American whigs with their own virtue and with the corrosive consequences of corruption also presents interpretive problems of its own. In the end, it clouds as much as it clarifies. It irradiates our conception of the colonies that entered upon resistance, but it obscures our vision of the nation that came out of the Revolution.

The most radical impulsion of Revolutionary ideology lay in its lust for social regeneration through civic virtue. More than a few of the most fervent patriots imagined that they were at the threshold of the millennium. Many of the instigators of independence called upon their countrymen to return to their ascetic beginnings and establish a state whose virtue would be luminous in a polity without partisanship, an economy without individualism, and a society without sectarianism.

It is therefore all the more unfathomable that they were undismayed by the appearance, in the decades after the Peace of Paris, of the very symptoms of decadence they had so recently denounced. Rather than execrating postwar political faction, economic profiteering, and religious splintering, a majority of the most influential inheritors of independence accepted them with equanimity and even with élan. Ardent republicans such as George Clinton promoted political parties. Others such as Thomas Jefferson led the legislative effort that dismantled the Anglican establishment of the South and opened the way to an unprecedented proliferation of sects in the region. Everywhere, citizens of the new republic gave up their pre-Revolutionary pursuit of homogeneous community and embraced—or, at any rate, accepted—the pell-mell of pluralism. The most outspoken of them soon came to pride themselves upon their politics of self-professed interest groups, their economics of unabashed enterprise, and their religious regime of voluntarism.

A transformation so swift and sweeping would be baffling enough under any circumstances. It is quite beyond conceiving in the context of currently prevailing ideological accounts of the Revolution. For those accounts hold that the ideology they elaborate was neither an intellectual epiphenomenon nor a propagandistic rationalization of more immediate and material concerns. It was an essential "map of social reality" for its American adherents. It encapsulated and crystallized "those shifting patterns of values, attitudes, hopes, fears, and opinions through which people perceive[d] the world and by which they [were] led to impose themselves upon it." The republican reading of experience literally "made life comprehensible" for the colonists.[8]

It is this very insistence of the ideological accounts on the embeddedness of radical whig premises in colonial culture and consciousness which leaves the attenuation of those assumptions in the aftermath of independence so perplexing. And it is our inability to reconcile the Revolutionary vocabulary of virtue with the early national language of liberalism which obstructs an adequate answer to the question posed in a recent assessment of our interpretive impasse: "If the Revolution was fought in a frenzy over corruption, out of fear of tyranny, and with hopes for redemption through civic virtue, where and when are scholars to find the sources for the aggressive individualism, the optimistic materialism, and the pragmatic interest-group politics that became so salient so early in the life of the new nation?"[9]

Historians have hardly acknowledged that question, let alone addressed it. Immured in their separate specializations, they have studied the ideology of the colonial era or the ethos of the ensuing years without attending to the transition from one configuration to the other. Yet it is the transition which we must study if we would understand our origins as a nation. The liberalism which succeeded so speedily the extended ascendancy of republicanism has animated our public life ever since.[10]

It was in the transition that the ideological lineaments of modern America emerged. And it was in the retrospect of the transition that

J. G. A. Pocock called the Revolution "the last great act of the Renaissance" rather than the raising of the curtain on a recognizably American drama. That is why the assumptions of the Revolution lay so long unseen and have only so lately been retrieved by professional specialists. The discontinuity between the world which we know and the world of the men and women who broke with Britain commenced almost immediately upon their appeal to arms. The outlook which informed the battle they began in Philadelphia scarcely survived the victory they won at Yorktown and in Paris.[11]

II

Even while these perplexities were emerging in the realm of ideas, solutions were taking shape in other areas. Even while some historians were poring over pamphlets and other elite publications, piecing together the ideas of the advantaged and articulate, others were working through wills and deeds and inventories, painstakingly reconstructing the everyday life of the population at large.

These students of the mundane material ways of the colonists did not undertake their arduous explorations to dissolve the dilemmas the political and intellectual historians were creating. They aimed, before all else, to recover the routines of everyday existence. They aspired to answer the most quotidian questions, about the ages at which early Americans married and the number of children they bore, about the size of houses and the fashion of furnishings, about networks of friendship and the distances over which such relations ranged. And they have done as they intended. We are learning from them things we never even thought to ask, let alone imagined to answer.

But beyond that, we are beginning to turn a tantalizing circle. The very sense we make of the commonplace conditions of early American life intimates intriguing ties to the issues of the imperial crisis.

In studies of subjects from furniture to food, of regions from the Chesapeake to New England, and of sources from estate inventories to animal bones, scholars of everyday life have come to conceive of a consumer revolution sweeping across provincial America, especially after 1750. By patient analysis of a remarkable array of artifacts, they have shown both an astonishing indifference of the first generations of Americans to the barest essentials—as we would consider them today—of domestic comfort and personal privacy, and an extraordinary surge of concern for the creation of a convivial environment in the home which occurred around the middle of the eighteenth century. Americans of the generation before the Revolution were keen, as their ancestors had never been, to spend time and money on items of convenience, amenity, gentility, and even extravagance, and to derive personal identity and social standing from such investment.

In the seventeenth century, and into the eighteenth, few households even of the affluent had the furniture for congenial conversation, the utensils for gracious family dining, or the musical instruments or games for entertaining. In the Chesapeake, colonists other than the elite lived in crudely built dwellings of but a room or two, in which a single chamber served successively or simultaneously as eating, sleeping, sitting, and cooking space, and often as workplace as well. Poorer folk sometimes managed without a bed, cooking pots, and chests, and commonly did without chairs, tables, bedsteads, sheets, chamber pots, and indoor lighting. Middling families had such comforts more frequently but far from universally. Even the elite lived in houses quite "mean and little" by contemporary English standards and furnished those quarters with domestic props not notably different in kind from those of their more modest neighbors.[12]

In the absence of any more elevated standards, such rough sufficiency defined the domestic decency of the day. A storage trunk served interchangeably as a work surface and a dining table because few families lavished any time together on meals anyway. Implements as elemental as knives and forks, glassware, ordinary china, teapots, and teacups were unknown in most homes because eating was rarely a social occasion. In early America, most settlers were satisfied if they had enough food. Few demanded that it be varied, or tasty, or wholesome, or well cooked, or appealingly presented.[13]

But by the middle of the eighteenth century, men and women began to demand a more elaborated domestic environment. More than that, they began to spend significant amounts of money on the sorts of commodities that could sustain the sociability they now sought. The change appeared earlier among the rich than among the rest, and earlier in the southern and middle colonies than in New England, but it spread swiftly and diffused deeply. Where few had even owned a table or chairs fifty years before, fair numbers were purchasing mahogany furniture by the beginning of the bloodshed at Lexington and Concord. Where eating utensils, glassware, and china scarcely showed up at all in the probate records of the seventeenth century, they appeared with some regularity, even among the lower orders, in the records of the Revolutionary generation. Where tea-drinking and tea service had been virtually unknown beyond the upper reaches of society in the early eighteenth century, the practice and its equipage reached every social stratum after 1750.[14]

Apart from the fifth of the population which remained enslaved, a veritable consumer culture emerged in America. The avidity for commodities of comfort erupted with different force in different circumstances, but it appeared across the social spectrum. Affluent families entered upon cycles of conspicuous consumption. Lesser folk engaged in emulation, or sought respectability, or simply came to enjoy the gratifications that the goods they could afford could confer. The habits of the whole population were drawn toward what one observer called "the rising tide of extravagance." As James Habersham lamented, "the large strides which people of all ranks are making to throw off the pleasing path of virtue and goodness and to substitute in their room luxury and dissipation portend the worst consequences."[15]

The rage for articles of amenity and indulgence sparked an extraordinary boom in imports and a revealing rush to debt in the decades before the Revolution. Great southern planters grew notorious for their dependency on debt and their delinquency in discharging obligations. Smaller southern growers even in relatively remote areas became familiar with a burgeoning array of country stores whose Scots owners and operators allowed them to buy extensively on the security of the tobacco in their fields. And profligate southern planters were easily exceeded by their northern neighbors. New Englanders and middle colonists expanded their exports and international services after 1750, but not nearly as much as they increased their imports. Around the middle of the century, Americans brought in British goods worth about £1.1 million a year. A decade later, the average value of imports had doubled, to more than £2.1 million. In 1750, the colonial economy had essentially paid for the processed goods it purchased from the mother country by its own products and services. By 1760 it was £2 million in debt, and by 1772, more than £4 million in arrears. And virtually all of the imbalance accrued in New England and the Middle Atlantic, where the new craving for consumption goods was not offset by income from subtropical staples.[16]

The escalating urgency of such acquisitiveness triggered credit spirals that deranged the economies of the northern colonies, especially of their commercial capitals. Expansion, contraction, and reluctant re-extension of loans followed one another in bitter succession in Boston, reducing local debtors and creditors alike to subservience to British moneylenders and merchants. Overextension also plagued Philadelphia, where the "gloomy prospect" worried William Allen as he fretted over friends "failed, who were in no way suspected, and a probability of some others, as the whisper goes."[17]

Classical republican thought allowed no place to the pressures to achieve a rising standard of living which were driving Americans into debt. Taking limited economic horizons as axiomatic, it assumed what we would today call an inelasticity of supply and demand. Commonwealthmen did not dream that "consumers might acquire new wants and find new means to enhance their purchasing power." The notion that such alterations might in turn generate further spending and additional innovation, which would ultimately increase the wealth of nations was, for Old Whigs, "unthought of if not unthinkable." They could only imagine an immense perenniality of things, against which individual initiative could avail nothing, and they therefore strove primarily to assure the predominance of the common good over untoward assertions of personal advantage.[18]

III

The subversive implications of the consumer revolution did not emerge immediately. First there intervened a fascinating interlude which dovetails delicately with what we know of the ideology that rationalized provincial resistance to imperial pretensions. Through the third quarter of the eighteenth century, the provincial elite which led that resistance turned the anxiety engendered by its own ambitions and accumulations to involutionary ends by redoubling their rhetorical allegiance to the ideals of cohesive community.

Before the Revolution, there were assuredly Americans who put their own interests before the general welfare. The most ardent advocates of republican principles acknowledged as much. No one supposed it would be simple to uphold the common weal or still the whisperings of individual aspiration. The most conservative of peasants in the Old World were not averse to acquiring another cow or arranging an advantageous marriage for an attractive daughter, and there were few conservative peasants in early America. But there were few self-conscious or articulate exponents of a comprehensive conception of society predicated on competitive self-seeking in early America, either; and there was certainly no systematic moral sanction for such activity. To the time of the Revolution, Americans who thought explicitly about such matters were unable to envision an alternative to the imperatives of restraint and regulation because they could not see how the release of the individual from deference to the demands and expectations of his neighbors could result in anything but chaos. To the day of the Declaration, Americans could only imagine that the gains of the greedy would occur at the expense of the less fortunate and of the public welfare.

Hardly anyone had yet come to the intoxicating liberal belief that people unleashed to look out for their own interests would be guided, as if by an invisible hand, into paths of prosperity for all. The ardency for consumer comforts so evident after 1750 made most who expressed themselves on the matter acutely uncomfortable. It violated venerable notions of the natural limits on enterprise. It invited unlovely lusts and dangerous desires.

Hardly anyone had yet embraced the fond liberal faith that personal freedom would inspire unparalleled productivity. According to the only social philosophies current in the colonies, unbridled ambition presented a dark problem, not a dazzling prospect. In terms of the only economic ethics then available, debt was a mark of moral debility, not a means of stimulating commercial activity. Debt led to pathologies of personal character, not to possibilities of economic development and the democratic distribution of its benefits.

And hardly anyone had yet espoused the serene liberal conviction that the legitimation of private prerogative might be compatible with the maintenance of social harmony. To the very eve of independence, the men who dominated provincial discourse remained convinced that self-interest could only breed anarchy. Even after the outbreak of hostilities, they assumed that the republic could survive solely on a conception of the people as a homogeneous body and of the public good as a unitary entity to which the separate cares of separate citizens had steadily to be sacrificed.[19] Moreover, masses of less philosophically sophisticated colonists concurred in such Old Whig attitudes, even if those multitudes spoke more compellingly in the streets than in the newspapers and pamphlets. They gathered in great mobs to maintain the ways of the traditional moral economy and to rebuke the encroachment of market modes which put private profit before public interest in times of social stress.[20]

But even as colonists railed against extravagance and rioted against engrossment, they could hardly help acknowledging their own experience. They felt the force of the selfishness all around them. A merchant, dismayed at the periodic collapse of public credit, decided that the disappearance of specie was "a just punishment upon us for our extravagance, pride, and prodigality." A planter, distressed by the rampancy of corruption, raged that "the representatives of the people" went "out of the way of their duty instead of into it" and that the people themselves were worse. There was "hardly a man to be met with who [paid] the least regard" to "public virtue."[21]

The men who made the Revolution saw such acquisitive passions and self-indulgent sensuality as tokens of a degeneracy at home every bit as disturbing as the symptoms of decadence they discerned in England.

Indeed, their very awareness of their departure from spartan self-denial may have made them more acutely sensitive to British debauchery and more anxiously insistent on colonial virtue. England was sinking in a slough of voluptuousness, and America was in danger of being dragged into the same moral mire. But the menace was not merely external. Colonial criticism of imperial conspiracy was, ultimately, self-criticism. Provincial Americans professed apprehensiveness of English descent into enervating luxury, but they worried most about their own mounting indebtedness, indolence, and self-indulgence. Gentlemen experienced unease at their increasing accumulation of commodities. Yeomen felt resentment at the readiness of the rich to slip the old sanctions of community sentiment and the old standards of collective control. And a considerable part of the power of republican ideology lay in its capacity to crystallize the disparate concerns of the different strata of colonial society.

By the middle of the eighteenth century, Americans could see where their development was drifting, and for many of the most articulate the prospect appalled even as it allured. On just that account, the self-knowledge it implied had to be denied. Republican spokesmen would not recognize and deal directly with their own advancing affluence. Instead, they transmuted their doubts about the moral soundness of their social system into ritual reaffirmations of solidarity and shared purpose. Colonies in the throes of a consumer revolution promulgated nonconsumption resolutions. Citizens sinking steadily deeper into debt proclaimed non-importation policies. Communities in which tea ceremonies had become the epitome of display and aspiration cursed those who imbibed the brew and stood officially aside as unruly crowds refused to allow the landing of East India Company shipments or dumped them in the Atlantic. And in all these actions, the colonists addressed their messages to the mother country but spoke most significantly to themselves.

Avowals of virtuous simplicity intensified in the years after 1750. Professions of republican submission of self to society came to a crescendo in the final decades before the break with Britain. As opulence grew, Sam Adams asserted that the citizen "owes everything to the commonwealth." As men discounted the claims of the community, Benjamin Rush averred that the individual was "public property" and that "his time and talents—his youth—his manhood—his old age—nay, more, life all belong to his country."[22]

The exaggerated emphasis that such Americans put on the mobilization and maintenance of a unified enterprise afforded them a reassuring consciousness of collectivity as they entered on revolution. But in the end their affirmations of social solidarity ran counter to the direction of the country's development. In the culture which was taking shape in the second half of the eighteenth century, republican ideology represented a reactionary ethic. Even as it encapsulated colonial ideals of communitarian commitment and crystallized them so cogently that Americans found in it their fondest imaginings of their best identities, the reality in which that ideology was rooted slipped steadily away. There was a flush of finality in the overblown urgency of Old Whig rhetoric, like the bloom on the lush roses of late summer.

On just that account, at just that juncture, the rhetoric of republicanism acquired an extraordinary resonance. Had civic-humanist values not been at such variance with emerging reality, there would have been no need for their extravagant emphasis. Had the traditional structure of provincial villages and towns remained intact, there would have been no necessity for protesting too much the priority of communal good over partisan interest. But Americans adopted the ideology they did precisely in order to resist the receding of the old modes of mutual plight. They tried to cope with the corrosive tendencies of the consumer revolution by begging their countrymen to recover their civic virtue "from the latter-day stew of self-interest into which they had been falling."[23]

Americans were at once attached to their new standard of living and fearful of its consequences. Their very verbiage of virtue revealed the confusion they felt as they struggled with their diverging desires and doubts. The tenets of republicanism themselves asserted the necessity of secure possession and unencumbered enjoyment of property even as they declared the subjection of such private entitlements to the claims of the community. Commonwealthmen located "the essence of republicanism" in a "heightened concern with the moral integrity of the individual" even as they extolled the submission of the individual to the collective will.[24]

In the crucible of imperial crisis, these confusions and incoherences were energizing. The very tensions which impelled Americans to embrace the ideas of the Old Whigs redoubled resistance and galvanized rebellion. Indeed, one function of republican ideas was to enable provincial patriots to absolve themselves of responsibility for the untoward aspects of their activities and ambitions. Civic humanism permitted them precisely to project their anxiety for their spiritual safety and ethical identity onto the British, decrying as they did the sinister transoceanic design "to undermine the moral and economic independence of the colonies." So long as they concentrated on their assumptive virtue, they did not have to dwell on their eagerness for imported commodities. They could simply condemn the cabals of metropolitan merchants to entrap them in debt and of king's ministers to enslave them in taxes.[25]

As a recent observer has remarked, such rationalizations were "at once absurd and convincing, bizarre yet understandable, vague but operative." As he might have added, such dilemmas were no more daunting than the one which underlay American resistance itself. The rebellion which triggered the morning gun of the modern democratic transformation was fought in the name of ideals which resolutely repudiated that transformation, by men who sought staunchly to hold back the tides of self-seeking which were surging all around them and which they felt rising all too forcibly within themselves.[26]

IV

The tides could not be stemmed. The seas of self-interest could not be held back indefinitely by ideology alone. But the breakwaters gave way more quickly than anyone could have imagined. A country that seemed, at the commencement of the Revolutionary conflict, to possess "more than Roman virtue" came by its conclusion to "have more land and stock-jobbers than any place on earth." A people which appeared, in the righteousness of its resistance to tyranny, "incapable" of corruption was suddenly seized by "a spirit of avarice and peculation."[27]

As early as 1778, it was evident to patriots that the people were "all infatuated [and] running mad into luxury and extravagance of every kind." A year later, Alexander Hamilton confessed his despondency at the difficulty of rousing his countrymen from "the lethargy of voluptuous indolence" or dissolving their "fascinating character of self-interest." A year after that, he despaired that "the worst of evils seems to be coming upon us—*a loss of our virtue*." John Adams confided an identical dismay that "disinterested virtue is disappearing among us." And George Washington himself admitted his anguish at the "astonishing changes" that "a few years" proved "capable of producing. . . . From the high ground we stood upon, from the plain path which invited our footsteps, to be so fallen! so lost! it is really mortifying."[28]

As evidence of their "unprincipled pursuit of private speculations" and "sacrifice of the public honor and interests to the selfish objects of individuals" mounted, Americans moved toward the dark knowledge that they had "betrayed their Revolution . . . almost before it was over." The momentous moral drama of their reliance on rectitude had turned tragic. By their own republican logic, "republican liberty could not long survive."[29]

In many ways it was the Revolution itself which stimulated the cupidity and profiteering that obliterated "every other principle and spring of action." The defense of American rights ultimately required the mobilization of more than 100,000 fighting men, and the recruitment and retention of such numbers necessitated incentives more crass and material than those that committed civic humanists envisaged. Washington discovered from the first that the ranks of his army could not be filled by appeals to idealism. The yeomen farmers of America were not moved "by any other principles than those of interest." And the gentlemen of the officer corps were no better. The few who acted upon "principles of disinterestedness" were, "comparatively speaking, no more than a drop in the ocean."[30]

The supply of that fighting force released acquisitive impulses even more powerful than its enlistment. The war went on longer than any military action in American history before Vietnam, and it touched almost every sector of American society. The troops had to have bread and blankets, rifles and rum, wagons and warm clothes. The ravenous demands of the quartermasters made marketeers out of husbandmen who had never traded with anyone but their neighbors. The inflationary paper money issues of the Revolutionary governments made speculators out of artisans and yeomen who had previously operated only in a book-keeping barter economy. And such developments spurred a disenchantment with Old Whig ways among a still larger mass of Americans who saw some men make fortunes by standing aside from the fighting while others did the dirty work.

Republican rhetoric of mutuality rang hollow in the ears of enlisted men who knew too many truants who escaped the dangers and deprivations of combat by purchasing substitutes to serve in their stead. Commonwealth conceptions of self-denial sounded tinny to soldiers who cursed that their crops languished in the fields back home while wealthier men reaped the rewards of their ability to buy exemption from military duty. And civic-humanist ideals of dedication to public purpose seemed specious when some Americans, in the comfort of their counting houses, profited infamously by supplying other Americans, in the bitterness of their wintry bivouacs, with maggoty meat, watered whiskey, and shoddy shoes. Rebels who reflected upon such ill-gotten gains were unlikely to be ardent adherents of an ideology of shared sacrifices for the common cause.[31]

There were signs in every season. In Massachusetts, at the outset of the fighting, the increased demand for commodities caused by the extended British siege of Boston led merchants and farmers to run up their charges in disdain of the appeals of suffering artisans and laborers for "that harmony and unity among us which . . . is our strength." Efforts to reinstate such strength proved unfailingly futile, as "private avarice combined with a flood of continental and state currency to fuel a staggering inflation over the next four years." In Pennsylvania, a couple of years later, soldiers starved at Valley Forge while farmers in the surrounding countryside withheld their harvests from the American army because the British offered better prices in Philadelphia. Endeavors to curb windfall profits for the few by price controls for the benefit of the many collapsed in the Fort Wilson Riot of 1779. In Virginia, a few years after that, a governor pressing hard to provide Washington the supplies he "needed most urgently" at the climax of the conflict found himself reviled by his constituents. "The only recompense he earned" for his presumption upon republican principles "was the hatred of a great part of his fellow citizens."[32]

Such citizens were incensed at any demands that impinged upon their own opportunities to seize the main chance. They began to realize that classical republicanism had held them back as much as it had helped them on. Its elitist and hierarchical doctrines offered scant incentive to people who were unwilling to remain in their appointed—and inferior—places. And more than a few Americans were unwilling. Ambitious planters were disinclined to defer indefinitely to the landed gentry. Agrarian entrepreneurs refused to take seriously an ideology that condemned commercial farming. Aspiring traders disdained to distance themselves from the marketplace as republican theory required. Men like these meant to rise in the world. The Revolution inflamed their ambition and inspired them to believe that they could fulfill it.

The very openness of their aspirations grieved people who persisted in the old commonwealth convictions. Like Sam Adams, such Revolutionary radicals lamented the eagerness of their comrades for "foolish gratifications" and deplored the alacrity of their fellows in "prostituting all our glory, as a people, for new modes of pleasure." Like Benjamin Rush, they trembled at the "excess of the passion for liberty" engendered by the war and even saw in it a new "species of insanity" demanding a new clinical category, "anarchia."[33]

Of course, the alteration that sorrowed the Founding Fathers need not surprise us. With two centuries of historical hindsight, we know something of war's corrosive consequences for moral fervor. But Americans of the 1780s and 1790s experienced more than a mere collapse of morals. They experienced the collapse of a moral configuration, and the advent of a very different set of commitments and conceptions. By 1785, Noah Webster could deny that public virtue was an essential foundation for republics, since he saw that it would never overcome self-interest. By 1786, Charles Thompson insisted that most Americans had no other "object" than their own "individual happiness." By 1787, the Providence *Gazette* proclaimed that "virtue, patriotism, or love of country never was, nor never will be till men's natures are changed, a fixed, permanent principle and support of government." By 1788, Enos Hitchcock said, as if it were self-evident, that "society is composed of individuals" and nothing else.[34]

After the Revolution, Americans came to an acceptance of qualities in themselves that had previously caused them discomfort. Indeed, they came to aspire to a character they had previously scorned, as free individuals rather than as virtuous communards. After decades of devotion to the self-denying norms of republicanism, they moved with remarkable rapidity toward the ideology that the nineteenth century would know as liberalism.

Some moved in disillusionment with the possibilities of popular virtue. In 1779, for example, Thomas Paine made an anguished switch to the new economic views in the course of the controversy over price controls in Pennsylvania. In despairing resignation to the impossibility of subordinating partisan desires and demands to a common endeavor, he gave up the Old Whig effort to connect morality and government. A year later, Alexander Hamilton bewailed the decay of public spirit in his adopted land and then erupted, "I hate Congress—I hate the army—I hate the world—I hate myself." He came to his rejection of social purpose only upon the defeat of his republican idealism. He subsided into self-hatred and approval of self-seeking only after his abandonment of all hope for virtuous and vivifying community.[35]

Others ensconced themselves eagerly in new moral milieu that could countenance the release of enterprise. So far from settling for the mechanisms and mentality of the market after the defeat of dearer dreams, they caught excitedly at the opportunities which the emerging ethos promised to provide. They saw in them a spur to their imaginations and an invitation to their energies. In a very few years they would make the new nation the bastion of an ethic of unfettered individual entitlement unparalleled in human history.

Just as the revolutionaries extolled extravagantly the precepts of the republican past, their successors idealized extravagantly the prospects of the liberal future. A rhythm of excess ruled the country in the last half of the eighteenth century. An oscillation of ideological exaggerations shaped the establishment first of American independence and then of American identity. In the years of imperial crisis, people unable to moralize the appetites that the consumer revolution aroused in them embraced immoderately the doctrines of classical republicanism: the very vigor of their denunciation of the self and of their demand for its abasement betrayed their attentiveness to its importunate call. In the era after the Revolution, people unwilling to face the implications of their failure to live up to their republican ideals asserted immoderately the propriety of the pursuit of private happiness; the very ardor of their insistence on the legitimacy of individualistic ambition exposed their unease at consecrating the conduct they had criticized a few brief years before.

On the new view, self-interest and self-sufficient isolation seemed natural rather than ignoble, right rather than regrettable. And on this notion of nature and natural ethics, a multitude of other inversions of the old outlook developed as well. William Findley caught the character of these alterations when he pronounced the payment of a personal debt a moral obligation but dismissed the payment of taxes as an amoral affair which men might evade as prudence suggested. To partisans of the new persuasion, virtue "lost its public character and attached itself instead to the private rectitude essential to a system of individual bargains."[36]

Much as virtue came to pertain to private rather than public relations, liberty came to be an attribute of individuals rather than of the social order. In republican theory, the constituent units of society were corporate bodies, not persons. When the patriots who promoted the Revolution referred to self-determination, they referred to the rights of communities to decide their own destinies. When they spoke of sacrificing their lives for liberty, they meant "the liberty of the group to have local control." When they thought of a free man, they had in mind a person who could participate in the public life of his time. In their view, independence implied "civic attachment, not detachment of private interests." So when Americans of the early national era arrived at a conception of "public and private liberty as antagonistic rather than complementary," they were departing sharply from the assumptions of 1776.[37]

The impact of these new notions was felt most profoundly among men of the commercial classes. Mercantile operators of the early national age simply did not accept the restrictions on individual initiative that their ancestors had. They did not look askance at commerce, and they did not presume the public good a product of deliberate design. They advanced toward a view of business as benign and a conception of the common welfare as simply the sum of individual interests.[38]

Without even reading Adam Smith, they naturalized a notion of the economy as an aggregation of profit-seeking producers and satisfaction-searching consumers. They accepted "an idea of man as a consuming animal with boundless appetites, capable of driving the economy to new levels of prosperity." They counted on commercial freedom to release the economic energies of the country and to sustain an endless material expansion.

Where their parents supposed a certain perenniality in the collective economic prospect, they projected a vision of progress. Where their parents worried about the effects of prosperity on the cohesion of their communities, they reconciled themselves to a social order that was scarcely more than the resultant of diverging personal goals. By the end of the eighteenth century, they had convinced themselves that such striving for separate ends was actually of public utility. As the *Farmer's Register* wrote, "it is only by competition that a town or city can flourish. The united efforts of rival artisans give energy to trade."[39]

In the political practices of the young state, a similar complacency about competition and interest emerged. Where republicans denounced political divisions among the people, liberals appreciated the place of legitimate difference in public life. Just as they accepted divergent ends and means in economics, so they admitted diversity and dissidence in politics. Just as they believed that contest could promote progress and advance prosperity, so they trusted that conflict could protect rights and enhance prerogatives.

Through the first three-quarters of the eighteenth century, Americans censured every semblance of partisanship. On a republican view of governance, parties necessarily represented illegitimate lusts for power or schemes of self-aggrandizement. Commonwealthmen sought "a collective consciousness of belonging to a virtuous community, unanimously roused in support of its dearest rights." They therefore execrated all deviance from the common course. In their Old Whig discourse, they could only construe factiousness as corruption and dissent as disloyalty.[40]

But patriots who predicated their resistance to the mother country on an unwavering aspiration to solidarity required only a few years of independence to discover that distinctions in their society were "various and unavoidable." During the decade of the 1780s, "parties and factions without number" arose in the infant nation. So far from supposing these new formations precursors of a dismaying decadence, observers insisted that they would "contribute to preserve the liberties of America." So far from rueing these unprecedented alignments as pollutions of the body politic, contemporaries considered them "a basic and necessary prop" for the new order. By 1787, James Madison called the regulation of the "various and interfering interests" in society "the principal task of modern legislation," and one which inevitably involved "the spirit of party and faction in the ordinary operations of government." Rather than marking a new departure, his Tenth *Federalist* codified emergent experience in many places.[41]

The transition that was in train at the time of the adoption of the Constitution was essentially complete by the turn of the century. Jeffersonians not only accepted the logic of voluntary participation but also built their grassroots organizations by mobilizing private passions and interests that designedly did not comprehend the entire population. Indeed, in the face of Federalist power that culminated in the Alien and Sedition Acts of 1798, they concluded that "party, not government, defended America's independence." The "honest party," to Jeffersonians, ceased to seem a contradiction in terms and appeared instead "the primary protection against . . . corruption." The government ceased to seem the antithesis of party and appeared instead "a mere tool for the corrupt party." And upon the triumph of the Jeffersonians, Federalists came around to the same conviction. Like those they had reviled through the 1790s, they themselves then withheld legitimacy from the administration in office. Like them, they then located rightful rule with their own essentially private association. As Fisher Ames put it, "party is an association of honest men for honest purposes." Both sides accepted "the inevitability of competitive parties" in the political arena, in much the way many accepted the efficacy of competitive production in the marketplace. The people could no longer be understood as an organic entity with an underlying identity of interest. They were only "an agglomeration of hostile individuals coming together for their mutual benefit to construct a society."[42]

In the religious life of the new society, a similar dismissal of the claims of the community and a comparable passion for personal freedom prevailed. During the decades after the Revolution, New Englanders curtailed almost all of the legal privileges of the Congregationalists, and southerners dismantled the Anglican establishment. Regimes of religious pluralism were created or confirmed everywhere. Rights of free association were recognized. Emergent evangelical sects competed on terms of approximate parity with erstwhile orthodox churches. And since the sectarians insisted on setting the conscience of the individual before the convenience of the community, gathering adherents in essential disregard of formal parochial boundaries, they inevitably destroyed the traditional identity of the territorial church with its secular surroundings.[43]

Baptists, Methodists, and other evangelicals led this ravaging of republican hopes for communal unity. But even communions such as the Presbyterians, which clung for a while to the old aspirations to Christian commonwealth, gave way soon enough to disillusionment and renunciation of their millennial anticipations. Before the eighteenth century was out, they too accepted an ethic of competitive denominationalism.[44]

Church people in the days of the Great Awakening, half a century earlier, had taken the deterioration of religious consensus and communal cohesion as an omen of God's anger. Denominational adherents in the decades after independence took the collapse of religious conformity as a token of man's opportunity. The proliferating sects would become "a mutual balance upon one another." Their "collisions" would avert "mutual oppression" and stimulate evangelical exertion. And such suppositions were not simply fanciful. Partisans of the new pluralism found satisfaction in statistics that showed rising rates of religious participation everywhere in the open environment of post-Revolutionary America.[45]

And in the intimate life of the raw republic, ripples of the encomia to independence also spread. Wives ceased to be so submerged in their husbands, and children in their parents. A focus on friendship and complementarity between husbands and wives appeared in the final decades of the eighteenth century, where once a patriarchal hegemony of husbands had been idealized.[46] A degree of parity for women developed in divorce proceedings in the Revolutionary age, where before neither adultery nor abuse by men had been a basis for legal recourse for matrons immured in obligations of obedience and submission.[47] An enlargement of the economic competence of wives and widows emerged after independence, where previously men had been more mistrustful of their spouses' economic acumen and more inclined to confine them to their traditional dowers.[48]

Young people also evaded the control of their elders. Sons and daughters alike declined to seek parental approval of their nuptial partners or even to await parental permission to commence courtship. As indicated by the explosive increase in rates of premarital pregnancy at the end of the eighteenth century, males and females were meeting and mating on their own; the young woman's pregnancy simply precluded parental objection to the match. And, as the steady surge in marriages out of sibling sequence suggested, adolescents and early adults were increasingly acting for themselves in a competitive marriage market; younger sons and daughters refused to wait patiently each for their own turn, in age order, as their ancestors had done for generations. In these most personal preferences and passions as in more public matters of getting and governing, Americans of freedom's first generation were simply unwilling to submit their own desires to the countermanding claims of the group. As they explored the implications of autonomy, they remade their society and their culture on a new model.[49]

V

The lineaments of modern America became legible in the years after independence as they had never been before. Indeed, it may well be that one reason we have had so little sense, as Gordon Wood has said, "of the irretrievability and differentness of the eighteenth-century world," is that it was succeeded so swiftly by one so recognizably like our own. The ideas and ideals of American culture, as the country entered upon rebellion in 1776, were those of republican communalism. The norms of the nation as it entered upon the nineteenth century were very different.[50]

Liberalism disallowed the corporate conception of society and economy which the patriots had prized. It invited the atomization of every relation, novel as well as venerable, private as well as public. It undermined old republican rationales for the discipline of the underclasses and the authority of the elites. It unleashed struggles for status throughout the community, and it intimated egalitarianism in principle even if it achieved no such leveling in practice. Liberalism promoted democratization because it released the energies of ordinary people and, more, because it accorded such commoners the capacity for virtuous conduct. Unlike republicanism, it did not reserve its accolades and entitlements to men of sufficient means to stand above the pell-mell of passion and the entrapments of dependence. Emphasizing opportunity as it did, liberalism offered masses of Americans "an escape from the self-denying virtue of their superiors" and the social control that attended it.[51]

The social control that the emergent culture of the new era did permit was a residuum of "autonomous individuals freely exerting themselves to take care of their own interests" and, more, of "the voluntary cooperation of private persons." Such cooperation, in self-constituted companies bound together solely to serve the convergent interests and ambitions of the individuals who entered them, disturbed those Americans still convinced that social cohesion could be achieved only by the conscious construction of consensus. George Washington spoke for that obsolescent orthodoxy when he stigmatized the Democratic-Republican clubs of the Jeffersonians as "self-created societies." But the Jeffersonians knew that there could be nothing wrong with self-created societies in a self-created nation, and they insisted that private associations were "sanctioned by the first principles of social life" among a liberal people.

By the time the dust settled on the dispute, at the dawn of the nineteenth century, it was evident to all that such societies would proliferate limitlessly. They were, as Tocqueville would one day explain, almost the only institutions in America which could collect the isolated atoms of liberal society to any effect at all, creating coalitions capable of pursuing social purposes amid the kaleidoscopically shifting interests of mobile individuals in unstable communities.[52]

Just as it was the era after the Revolution that saw the development of democracy and the evolution of the voluntary association, so it was the same years that witnessed the beginning of the ethical acceptance of consumption in America. Republican culture came to its culmination in a wariness of worldliness. Liberal culture, on the contrary, expended little effort in praise of frugality or in celebration of self-denial. Liberal spokesmen sought a democratic diffusion of amenities. Their insistence on "comfort," a term they brought into currency, contrasted tellingly with the Old Whig emphasis on necessities and its implication that virtuous citizens would not attempt to exceed traditional confines of conduct and consumption. Their ambitions for "refinement and opulence" set at naught civic-humanist certainty that such aspirations demonstrated the nation's decadence and presaged its declension.[53]

The break with republican presumptions could hardly have been more explicit. The new norms of the new nation allowed people to admit their craving for commodities far more frankly than they had half a century before. Age-old assumptions of limited good were yielding, at least in moral imagination, to a vision of progress and prosperity. Consumption could be acknowledged as an American way of life.

VI

The story was more complicated, of course. Concepts such as republicanism and liberalism are willful simplifications, constructed by historians to afford us an orientation amid dense thickets of incomplete and ambiguous evidence. They make it possible for us to trace a tale in forests of facts that do not speak for themselves. But they also impose an order which was never obvious to the participants themselves. The men and women of the late eighteenth century acted in the same dark we all do.

Their liberalism was therefore always more tangled in the traditional outlook than philosophical consistency could accommodate. They never abandoned entirely the values by which they won their independence or the ethos in which they had evoked their ideal image of themselves during that struggle. In pulpit preachments and Fourth of July orations, in school texts and stump speeches, the sentiments which republican ideology had consolidated and crystallized remained a powerful presence in American consciousness.

Indeed, most Americans continued to live daily lives too dependent on the assistance of others to jettison entirely the old habits of mutuality. Even as people reveled in the pleasures of private consumption, they continued to need one another. In the absence of tractors and other such labor-saving technology, they had to have help at harvests. In the absence of a specialized construction industry, they had to have the aid of their neighbors in house-raisings. In the absence of hospitals and efficacious medical expertise, they had to have the attendance of friends in the recurrent emergencies of illness and childbirth. In the absence of savings banks and insurance plans, they had to have comrades they could count on to tide them over times of unemployment and sustain them through seasons of disability and old age. And in the presence of causes for celebration—the christening of a son, say, or the wedding of a daughter—they had to have others to share in their joy and pride. In the endless crises of rural life, few men or women outside the elite really wanted—or could afford—the splendid independence prescribed by liberal ideology.

However restive people may have been under the restraints of the consensual ethos, few of them really wished to live under a liberal regime. Most sought some sort of community to fill the void that liberalism never could, because it was precisely liberalism which created that void, in its exposure of the individual to the buffets of fate, uncushioned by any claims that he or she might legitimately levy on kinfolk or neighbors. People persisted in prior patterns of mutual attachment because the same liberal creed that offered them the opportunity to rise also inflicted upon them the necessity of suffering their falls alone and unaided. And their persistence opened ever-widening rifts between the rich who had the resources to weather most storms and the poor who did not, between the cosmopolitans whose connections and concerns reached far beyond the locality in which they lived and the parochialists whose allegiance and alliances extended no further than their neighborhood.

American society was coming apart, morally as well as socially, and it would never quite be whole again. The fissures of the era after the Revolution forecast not only the increasing social distances that would characterize the nineteenth-century nation but also the deepening cultural cleavage that would separate those who held to old habits of mutuality from those enamored of more freewheeling possibilities of enterprise.

In the ongoing contest for the soul of the nation, the liberal individualists had obvious advantages. They commanded assets and controlled channels of communication which enabled them to impart a profoundly liberal tilt to the country's laws and its economic institutions.[54] But beneath the institutional surface, other principles endured. On city stoops and street corners, on the stump and in the smoke-filled rooms, around the hot stove and in the ladies' auxiliaries, at camp meetings and in parish halls, in all the settings in which the great majority of Americans came together, the old aspiration to close, consensual community survived.

The ideals which gave birth to the nation were invincibly if obscurely republican. They bequeathed to generations ever after an ineradicable urge to make moral meaning of their lives in ways which liberalism could neither allow nor even fathom. They put an abiding premium on social harmony and created a continuing discomfort with conflict—values that constitute tacit conditions of American sociability to this day. They instilled a hunger for the ethical order of the unified community which persists despite the dismantling of almost every institution which might satisfy it.

For two hundred years, Americans have had to confront, catch-as-catch-can, the tension between the claims of neighbors and the prospects that presented themselves if they forsook their fellows and pursued their own personal advantage. The continuity of the values of virtuous community in the teeth of the triumph of liberalism was already the defining dilemma of American life in the years after the Revolution.

And that dilemma continues to inform the developments and disputes of our own time. It is implicit in everything from our uncertainties about suburbanization to our distress at de-industrialization to our controversies over the women's movement. It keeps us from ever deciding how much we wish for ourselves and how much we owe to others. It underlies our endless efforts at liberation and our haunting anxiety that we are already far too free. It is, in many ways, the defining dilemma of American life still.

The Transforming Impact
of Independence, Reaffirmed

1776 AND THE DEFINITION OF
AMERICAN SOCIAL STRUCTURE

PAULINE MAIER

S EVERAL PATHBREAKING arguments in *The Ideological Ori-gins of the American Revolution* (1967) evolved through an intense intellectual effort that engaged both Bernard Bailyn and his graduate students.* Those students went on to publish books and articles that sometimes took exception to Bailyn's arguments or assumptions (and to those of each other), but also extended his work, demonstrating the logic of the independence movement, comparing anew the thought of Loyalists and Revolutionaries, and showing how "the commanding structures of the first state constitutions and of the Federal Constitution" were built upon "new territories of thought" first opened before 1776, in the debate over imperial relationships.[1]

Not all agenda items in *Ideological Origins* have, however, been brought to equally satisfactory resolutions. Consider particularly Bailyn's assertion in the book's final pages that "changes in the realm of belief and attitude" during the decade before independence "in time would help permanently to transform" the "essentials of [American] social organization."[2] Despite an enormous outpouring of historical literature on the Revolution and on American society, the preeminent effort to connect those subjects remains J. Franklin Jameson's *The American Revolution*

*This essay was written under a grant from the National Endowment for the Humanities.

Considered as a Social Movement (1925), which overstated the social change caused by the departure of Loyalists, expansion of the franchise, redistribution of Loyalist lands, and testamentary reforms of the Revolutionary era. Clearly society was not recast between 1776 and 1789 as immediately and dramatically as were the institutions of American government.[3]

Many scholars go further and deny that the Revolution had a formative impact on American society. One interpretation, old but still influential, traces the distinctive traits of American society back to the earliest English settlements in the "New World." Another more recent interpretation associates independence with a socially reactionary "civic humanist" tradition that had to be abandoned before a modern "liberal" society could emerge. Still another set of historical writings implicitly denies that the Revolution significantly altered the trajectory of American social development by suggesting that, despite the Revolution, the structure of American society in the early nineteenth century was essentially like that of other capitalist societies. Often taking E. P. Thompson's *The Making of the English Working Class* (1966) as a model, such studies have sought to trace the development of "class" or "class formation" in the postrevolutionary United States.

The last of these efforts is particularly interesting for both the problems and the possibilities it raises. As David Brody noted in 1979, no "The Making of the American Working Class" has emerged from a wealth of careful, sensitive studies of American workers in the early industrial era.[1] The obstacle to class development was not economic; inequality of wealth among Americans might have reached an historic high at about 1860.[5] But for Thompson class was never a simple economic phenomenon: it was a cultural bond among persons whose places in the productive system shaped shared traditions, ideas, values, and institutions.[6] And American workers' culture seems to have been determinedly different from that of English workers. It was marked, as the "new labor historians" have discovered, by persistent invocations of the American Revolution, from which workers derived their concept of American society and of their places within it. Just as the Revolution separated the United States from England, so workers (and many employers) insisted that the divisions of English society not be replicated here. Perhaps, then, a Thompsonian process of social formation had un-Thompsonian results in the American context, producing not just different cultural expressions but different forms of group identities and locating structural social conflict at different places than in England.

The place to begin sorting out this maze of historical issues is, as Bailyn suggested, with the Revolution itself and those "changes in the realm of belief and attitude" of the late eighteenth century relevant to the organization of society. Were those changes simply outgrowths of the colonial past, or were they a new beginning? What impact did they have on later times?

I

The American Revolution was above all a political event. Its significance lay primarily in the decision of 1776 to link independence with the founding of a republican government.[7] From the beginning, however, the establishment of a republic had far-reaching social implications. To reject government by king, lords, and commons was to reject at once the political and the social structure of England, which gave authority and rank to persons by virtue of birth. The reasons were stated in Thomas Paine's *Common Sense* (1776), above all in his memorable assertion that nature disapproved of hereditary right "otherwise she would not so frequently turn it into ridicule, by giving mankind an *ass for a lion*."[8]

From that rejection of hereditary rule followed the first and fundamental meaning of equality, the most prominent social doctrine to emerge from the Revolution. The assertion of 1776 that "all men are created equal" meant that "no one can exercise any authority by virtue of birth. All start equal in the race of life." This elementary meaning of the natural equality of men persisted into the nineteenth century along with a second definition, "that no man comes into the world with a mark on him, to designate him as possessing superior rights to any other man."[9] The tradition of equal rights, like the rejection of hereditary rule, took hold, as Bailyn argued in *Ideological Origins*, during the early years of the American Revolution. At first colonists contended for their equal rights as a people: they were entitled collectively to the rights of Englishmen no less than the King's subjects at home. By the 1780s, however, the doctrine was cited to support the equal rights of persons within American society.[10]

Equality in these senses was not necessarily antihierarchical: it remained compatible with political or social rank which was founded upon criteria other than birth or legal privilege and which did not violate the equal rights of the people. Even "radicals" such as Samuel Adams, who favored "that constitution of civil government which admits equality in the most extensive degree," understood that there had to be some rank, some acceptance of authority and subordination, for the republic to survive. What he and other Americans of the Revolutionary era emphatically rejected was a particular form of hierarchy that they described as English, European, or, sometimes, "feudal." It consisted essentially of "unnatural" and ascriptive rankings, like England's king, lords, and commons. They further associated such a "European" system with societies composed, as Hector St. John de Crevecoeur said, "of great lords who possess everything and of a herd of people who have nothing." The result was not just widespread poverty and powerlessness, but degradation. "Even in the freest country in Europe," wrote "Philadelphiensis" in the course of debates on the federal constitution, "a lady's lap-dog is more esteemed than the child of a poor man." A Europe so defined provided a powerful negative reference. It stood for all that American society was not and what it must diligently avoid becoming.[11]

To define American society in positive terms was more difficult. That challenge became urgent with the Revolution because, according to established political wisdom, stable governments had to fit the people they governed. The citizens of a republic needed to share a modest level of wealth and an "independency," that is, a freedom from economic dependence on others. Such a people was likely to be frugal, industrious, resistant to corruption, and public-minded or "virtuous." Societies that retained great inequalities of privilege and wealth, and the self-indulgent habits they encouraged, were better suited for monarchy.[12]

The need to differentiate America from "Europe" meant that descriptions of American society were characteristically comparative. That tendency was reinforced by the European origins of many late-eighteenth-century Americans, the firsthand contact with Europe of some others, and the writings of European intellectuals, who often constructed "an image of the New World that contrasted sharply with the Old" to describe their own "dreamed-of new order." Crevecoeur's eulogy of America as "the most perfect society now existing in the world" and of the American as a "new man" verged on caricature. His description of the American people as distinguished by "a pleasing uniformity of decent competence" was, however, widely endorsed.[13] American observers of their society stressed the broad diffusion and what Benjamin Franklin charmingly called the "happy mediocrity" of wealth, along with the "independent temper" it fostered. They also noted the high incidence of working people in this "land of labor" and the paucity of men so wealthy that they could "live idly upon their rents or incomes." There were, Charles Pinckney insisted, "fewer distinctions of fortune & less of rank" in America "than among the inhabitants of any other nation."[14]

Important distinctions nonetheless remained, differences that were, as Melancthon Smith of New York said in 1788, unavoidable because they came from nature. Natural distinctions could provide a legitimate basis for an American social order: John Adams opened his *Defence of the Constitutions* (1787) with Alexander Pope's verse, "All Nature's difference keeps all Nature's peace."[15] On the other hand, manmade institutions might rigidify social differences that were accidental or temporary, reproducing a "European" social system and undermining the republic. Americans of the late eighteenth century tried persistently to distinguish "natural" differences among men from those that were manmade, but their efforts to define, in effect, the components of an American social structure were constrained by the overwhelmingly political context of their debates. Indeed, the very concept of a social structure apart from political structure remained problematic. For that reason, the social differences they described usually distinguished members of the political community, all of whom were adult white males.

Americans often described society as divided into two or three "orders" or "classes," a word which signified little more than a category within a general classification system. Twofold divisions generally emphasized power relationships, real or intended, as between "wolves and sheep," "*Great Folk*" and "*Little Folk*," or simply the "Few and the Many."[16] References to three strata—the upper, "middling," and lower orders—more often designated distinctions of wealth and labor. Even those threefold divisions were, however, frequently compressed into two, essentially the familiar "few" and "many." For example, the "Federal Farmer" divided "the people of this country" into a "natural aristocracy" composed of those "few men of wealth and abilities" and "the great body of the people," or "the democracy," which in turn comprised "the middle and lower classes."[17]

After 1776, self-styled spokesmen for the "many" assumed the mantle of "democracy" and associated their enemies, the "few," with "aristocracy." As Richard Bushman has observed, "the entry of the word *aristocrat* into political discourse . . . as a new term of opprobrium" testified to the social significance of the Revolution, which "discredited the entire ethic on which traditional society was based."[18] The new language of politics was, however, less a description of social reality than an adaptation to republican circumstances of an older rhetoric of opposition. Since the early eighteenth century, both English and American opposition groups had claimed to speak for the interests of the people against factions of men who sought power for their private benefit. To accuse opponents of seeking to usurp power in the interest of the "few" over that of the community was to accuse them, in effect, of sedition, since the legitimacy of the state was founded in theory upon its service to the commonweal. After 1776, to describe the "few" as "aristocrats" was to accuse them of undermining the Revolution and the republican regime it founded. That charge became common in part from fears over the fate of the republic, but also because of a continuing need to justify partisan politics. The language of "aristocracy" and "democracy" therefore persisted so long as the legitimacy of parties remained at issue.[19]

With increasing frequency, however, those who reflected upon the structure of political society designated a large number of social "orders" or "classes." Thus James Madison's effort of October 1787 to specify the "various and unavoidable" distinctions within "all civilized societies," which began with differences founded upon individuals' "unequal faculties" for acquiring property. "There will be rich and poor," he said, "creditors and debtors; a landed interest, a monied interest, a mercantile interest, a manufacturing interest." Such "classes" could be further subdivided to reflect different "situations & soils" or branches of trade and manufacturing. All these were for Madison "natural distinctions," unlike those "artificial" distinctions that depended upon "accidental differences in political, religious or other opinions, or an attachment to the persons of leading individuals."[20]

The new emphasis on interest groups indicated, as Bailyn noted, a significant shift in focus from the "formal orders of society derived from the assumptions of classical antiquity" toward those "transitory competitive groupings into which men of the eighteenth century actually organized themselves in the search for wealth, prestige, and power." But since power as well as wealth and prestige was at issue, lists of "classes" often mixed interest or occupational groups with categories that were essentially political, including, for example, among the "several orders" or "natural classes in . . . society" those "which we call aristocratical, democratical, merchantile, mechanic, &c."[21]

Such classifications reveal not just the politicization of social conceptions and a pervasive concern with separating "natural" from "artificial" social distinctions. They also indicate that not all Americans were, as their celebrators often suggested, of "middling fortune." On other occasions both foreign travelers and Americans testified more directly to the existence of striking disparities in wealth and condition, particularly within the southern colonies and the "large towns" farther north. By the 1790s a newspaper essayist complained that even in the small towns of New Jersey "scarce a day passes in which beggars do not accost us, bewailing their misfortunes, and imploring charity. . . ."[22]

Attitudes toward the poor and the rich, both aberrations from the celebrated "middling" character of the American people, reveal much of the social vision that emerged from the Revolution. Observers of the poor drew careful distinctions between the "idle and abandoned" who were able but unwilling to work, and those who had been "reduced to poverty by the frowns of Heaven without any willful fault or negligence of theirs." The latter category might include the "industrious and honest poor" who, due to "calamities" which "no prudence can prevent or elude" such as accidents, disease, or unemployment, suddenly found themselves "objects of charity," and were entitled to relief. But the "idle and vicious poor" (who supposedly comprised the great mass of beggars) won at best a grudging pity.[23]

The reason lay in a widespread assumption that this "land of labor" would amply reward those who worked. Land on the frontier was the key: "hearty young laboring men" could undertake wage labor for a few years, then buy land and achieve a sufficiency, that is, wealth enough to support a family and provide for old age without working for others. Not great riches but a "mediocrity of circumstances," that "middle state between the savage and the refined," gave "the greatest facility," and that goal was, writers agreed, within reach for those men who would make the effort.[24]

The distant future, when the lands were all claimed, might be different; but for the time, abject poverty was frequently ascribed to the character of the poor, and the reformist impulse of the Revolution suggested few solutions that would satisfy the humane inclinations of later times. "Now is the season for the country to attend to every reform that shall make her citizens better men, and relieve her of those burdens which have had their influence in sinking older nations," argued a writer in Boston's *Independent Chronicle* of 1784. No longer should public funds drawn from the "*virtuous* and *industrious*" be used to support ever-increasing numbers of "the *vicious* and *idle*." Only "*fear of starving*" could provide an "incentive to industry or frugality" in those who had "lost all sense of honour and shame." They should therefore be fed only bread and water in a public "*bettering house*" and taught that "it was in their power" to improve their condition "if they were only willing to work." Nor were such attitudes confined to the "upper order." Walter Brewster, a Connecticut artisan and essayist of the 1790s, defended the cause of the "poor and illiterate," but only those willing "to obtain a living . . . by industry." Government, he said, should devise "such measures as will eventually cause idle and dishonest persons to suffer in consequence of their idleness."[25]

Great wealth caused more widespread concern. If the poverty of the "idle poor" depended upon character defects that could be changed, the wealth of the rich had a less mutable, natural basis in their greater "faculty" for acquiring property and also in a commendable industriousness. During the Revolutionary era, moreover, a selfish "desire of making money" was said to motivate "Americans of every class and description" and "in all parts of the country." Since the American constitutions ruled out titles of nobility, it seemed by the 1780s that "the possession of wealth will in a short time be the only distinction in this young country," and "the spirit of avarice . . . the single road to superiority."[26]

But wealth was dangerous. "As riches increase and accumulate in a few hands, . . . the tendency of things" would be, as Alexander Hamilton noted, "to depart from the republican standard." The existence of the rich detracted from America's republican equality; the very rich were also prey to the vice of idleness, since they could live on the labor of others, and to luxury, the bane of republics.[27] More than any other element of American society, moreover, the world of the rich seemed a throwback to the "feudal," European past. The rich constituted, in short, an omen of aristocracy. Indeed, an essayist in the *Maryland Gazette* insisted that wealth everywhere constituted the essence of aristocracy, its "true definition," not the possession of titles, which was of little or no consequence.[28]

What was an appropriate basis of rank in a republic? "We often see men who, though destitute of property, are superior in knowledge and rectitude," Rufus King told the Massachusetts ratifying convention of 1788. Men should be valued, others argued, not by "wealth, titles, or connections," but for their "true characters," their "real worth"; they should be esteemed for their "talents, integrity, and virtue," for "abilities and knowledge," "sense and discernment." Those deserving influence were the "wise and worthy" or "wise and good," the "men of sense," those with "virtue and talents," the "ablest & best men."[29]

The claim of wealth to status had supporters, but by the late 1780s they were on the defensive. More important, their arguments affirmed common ascriptions of republican rank to personal merit. The rich deserved respect not for their property but because they were more likely better people than the poor: Hamilton, for example, argued that "the advantage of character belongs to the wealthy," whose vices were "probably more favorable to the prosperity of the state than those of the indigent, and partake less of moral depravity."[30] But if, as Franklin said in the Constitutional Convention, honesty and wealth went together, and poverty "was exposed to peculiar temptation," the possession of property also fed a desire to acquire more, such that "some of the greatest rogues he was ever acquainted with, were the richest rogues."[31]

If "virtue & abilities" were the criteria of respect and power, it was difficult to deny access even to the highest offices in the land to men who had those qualities but were "not worth a shilling."[32] Moreover, if the wealthy had an independence that was a classic accompaniment of virtue,[33] a chorus of commentators found sufficient independence for that purpose among the possessors of more modest property. The virtue of the country would therefore logically be sustained more effectively if great accumulations of wealth were divided among a greater number of people.

A redistribution of property was, however, difficult to accomplish. Agrarian laws like those by which the Romans redistributed property or a socialistic "community of goods" would violate the rights of property which Americans firmly supported. Even defenders of the "lower orders" such as William Manning and Pennsylvania's William Findley defended property rights, which, like other equal rights, sustained their dignity as citizens. "The poor man's shilling," Manning said, "aught to be as much the care of the government as the rich man's pound."[34] Moreover, laws that transferred property from the rich to the poor undermined the motivation for work. New Jersey's Governor William Livingston made that point when he drafted a mock petition for a "community of goods" so the "poorer sort" could live "upon the industry of the richer" until there was a "perfect equality," and appended to it names such as Amos Spendthrift, Josiah Workless, John Tippler, Peter Holiday, and Simon Dreadwork. Livingston's opponents might dispute his arguments, but not his values. Abraham Clark, who favored legislation that would undercut "that inequality of property . . . detrimental in a republican government," and other "democratic" spokesmen for the poor were second to none in their appreciation for work.[35]

In the course of the 1780s, a growing number of writers came to question prevalent assumptions about the debilitating effects of luxury and economic inequality. The model of ancient republics, they noted, was not wholly appropriate for the United States. Certainly Americans were unwilling to adopt "the Spartan community of goods and wives, . . . their iron coin, their long beards, or their black broth": Americans were "too full a taste of the comforts furnished by the arts and manufactures to be debarred the use of them." Nor should they be. The possession of "comforts" and "luxuries" that commercial development afforded were, like liberty itself, attributes of a civilized society; moreover, a desire for material betterment encouraged industriousness and undermined sloth. Even "the very great inequality of property" produced by commerce would pose no danger to the republic, Noah Webster argued in 1785, so long as that wealth circulated freely through the community, "revolving from person to person," and brought no political privileges.[36]

There remained nonetheless broad agreement on the importance of widespread property-holding in a republic, and, in the end, Americans settled upon a device for its promotion that neither threatened property rights nor discouraged labor while facilitating the free circulation of wealth. They abolished the remnants of primogeniture and entail, by which landed estates were held intact and descended to the oldest son, and sang the praises of partible inheritances. By 1776, primogeniture, which affected only landed property and only the estates of persons who died intestate, remained legally binding only in the southern states.[37] Americans of the Revolutionary generation nonetheless expected the change to have a powerful long-run effect. By this reform in the law of descents, a diffusion of landed property would be encouraged, "poverty and extreme riches" avoided, and "a republican spirit would be given to our laws, not only without a violation of private rights, but consistent with the principles of justice and sound policy."[38] To the extent that it served those ends, the abolition of primogeniture and entail perhaps did so indirectly, for example, by encouraging a more equal division of property in wills. The reform retained a powerful significance among Jacksonian critics of business corporations, who saw in the Revolutionary abolition of primogeniture and entail an injunction against legal devices that allowed the accumulation and perpetuation across generations of large concentrations of capital.[39]

Many Americans of the late eighteenth century sought to shape American society in a similar way through education. Tracts, proposed legislation, and provisions in the first state constitutions called for a broad dissemination of knowledge and learning as "essential to the preservation of a free government." Widespread education would further distinguish the United States from Europe, where the monopolization of knowledge by "the sons of fortune and affluence, the expecting brood of despotical succession," allowed them to tyrannize over "the despised, enslaved, and stupid multitude."[40]

Education was not the work of schools alone: the press was also enlisted in that cause. Schools, however, particularly attracted the attention of reformers obsessed with institutional design and the challenge of developing "natural genius" wherever it occurred. Soon writers from all segments of the post-1776 political spectrum called for the establishment of paternalistic state school systems so "every class of citizens" and "every child" could be educated.[41]

Those educational proposals sought to prepare for positions of leadership talented boys regardless of their parents' circumstances and to create an informed electorate. Schools would, moreover, help young men "support themselves when they come of age" and "manage their private concerns properly," and so facilitate their acquisition of property and the personal independence it allowed. For that reason writers as politically different as Noah Webster and Robert Coram linked the establishment of an appropriate system of education with adjustments in the laws of inheritance. Both would allow "every citizen a power of acquiring what his industry merits," and were therefore "*sine qua non* of the existence of the American republics."[42]

Schools would also foster virtue, that is, a commitment to the common good. For educational reformers (and many others), virtue implied not selflessness but an enlightened self-interest. An educated man would understand his rights and those of others, and, "discerning the connection of his interest with the preservation of these rights, he will as firmly support those of his fellow man as his own." Young people would also be taught "proper subordination—for they, who never learned to obey," Jonathan Jackson said, "must govern but very badly." Such lessons were essential in a republic, where order and obedience to authority had to come from the voluntary and informed decisions of the people, not from the servile dependencies of the "feudal" past. Schools would, however, emphasize that "personal merit," not the rank and antiquity of ancestors, commanded respect. The press, which took its educational mission seriously, similarly cautioned men of "lower rank" against craving offices for which they were not "fit" because they lacked the necessary "stock of learning and parts," but insisted that subordination be ceded "without descending to servile complaisances."[43]

Ambitious proposals for comprehensive systems of education came to nothing. The most striking changes in American educational institutions after independence occurred on the secondary level, with a flowering of academies, and in higher education: more colleges and universities were founded during the 1780s and 1790s than through the entire colonial period.[44] Knowledge was diffused still more powerfully by a spectacular increase in magazines and newspapers. On the eve of independence, Isaiah Thomas calculated, 37 weekly newspapers were published in what became the United States; by June 1810, the number had grown to 360, some of which were published daily. Newspapers' content also changed from an earlier emphasis on news toward informative essays on topics from politics through literature, science, and art, such that the press became "the means of conveying, to every class in society, innumerable scraps of knowledge." Never, wrote the Reverend Samuel Miller, "was the number of political journals so great in proportion to the population of a country as at present in ours. Never were they . . . so cheap, so universally diffused, and so easy of access."[45] That development was, moreover, not paternalistic, but market-driven, supported by a thirst in the people for information and self-improvement. Nothing promoted more powerfully the egalitarian tendencies of the Revolution.

Here, then, were the essential elements of the new American social order: property was to be widely distributed through a population of respectable, "independent" men; people of all ranks would be literate and informed, and a man's status would be determined by not wealth or parentage but individual merit. In retrospect, the social aspirations of the Revolutionary era and the measures taken for their realization might seem modest. But within a world still ruled by kings and nobles, where radicals in both England and France dreamed of establishing meritocracies, the social message of the Revolution was one of liberation. Over time it had a powerful impact, not just abroad but at home.

II

Was the social vision of late-eighteenth-century Americans a product of the Revolution? Or were their "egalitarian" convictions founded long before 1776 in the original social conditions of American life?

"The decisive moment in American history," Louis Hartz wrote a generation ago, was "the time of the great migration of the seventeenth century"; that was "our real 'revolution,' and what happened in 1776" was only an "aftermath, an experience determined by the earlier era." The determinative power of migration lay in what colonists left behind—"the whole of the historic feudal culture"—and in the "magnificent material setting" they found. There "the spirit which repudiated peasantry and tenantry flourished with remarkable ease," and "social fluidity was peculiarly fortified by the riches of a new land."[46]

Some recent historians, particularly Gordon S. Wood and Joyce Appleby, have drawn upon the work of J. G. A. Pocock to define more careful distinctions among the European contributors to American political and social thought than did Hartz, for whom Americans were all Lockean liberals. Upon that basis they, too, question the long-term significance of 1776. Independence, they argue, was the product of a "civic-humanist" or "classical republican" tradition that constituted a "reactionary effort to bring under control the selfish and individualistic impulses of an emergent capitalistic society." Englishmen within that tradition in the time of Walpole condemned as "engines of corruption" the bank, stock speculation, and other "instruments of the new capitalist economy," and saw in agrarian America a refuge from English decadence. Under their influence, the argument goes, Americans adopted independence to ward off further English corruption and to reform their country so it would fit classical republican ideals more exactly.[47]

The leaders of the American Revolution hoped to establish, in Wood's words, an organic, hierarchical social system "led by natural aristocrats who would resemble not the luxury-loving, money-mongering lackeys of British officialdom but the stoical and disinterested heroes of antiquity." They therefore stressed the importance of "virtuous" behavior, which supposedly demanded that the mass of men lay aside personal ambitions for wealth or advancement, accept a spartan style of life, and defer to the authority of their betters. This "sacrifice of individual interests to the greater good of the whole" was for Wood "the essence of republicanism" and "the idealistic goal" of the Revolution, which was "socially radical" mainly in its attempt to alter popular behavior.[48]

The Federalists of 1787–88 and the Federalist Party of the 1790s allegedly remained faithful to this archaic vision. They sought to establish "a patrician-led classical democracy" in which the people would defer to gentlemen of wealth, education, and leisure, who alone were capable of disinterested leadership. But independence, according to this interpretation, released "pent-up forces" that imperiled the Federalists' social vision. It brought into politics "new men" whose attitudes were founded, Appleby argues, in a "period of striking economic growth" during the half century before independence. These "tradesmen, mechanics, and newly launched merchants" developed an appreciation for self-interest and a "liberal vision of society" totally incompatible with classical republicanism and its injunctions to selfless deference. Such people, Appleby asserts, "turned the resistance movement into a revolution." Wood stresses instead the economic impact of the Revolutionary War, which accelerated capitalistic development, extending the market economy, stimulating consumerism, and expanding the ranks of the upwardly mobile. Auguries of "the liberal, interest-ridden democracy 'of nineteenth-century America" appeared for him among certain Antifederalist "new men," such as Pennsylvania's William Findley.[49]

A Hartzian "encompassing liberal tradition" took hold for Wood only after 1787–88, when the Federalists refused to acknowledge their "aristocratic conception of politics" and in a "disingenuous" way appropriated democratic arguments that "more rightfully" belonged to their opponents. The triumph of liberalism, Wood says, "shattered the classical Whig world of 1776" and brought "the end of classical politics." The "vast transformation" from the controlled, austere, eighteenth-century world of classical republicanism to the "sprawling, materialistic, and licentious popular democracy" of the next century is for him "the real American revolution."[50]

While Wood indicts the Federalists for denying their class-based values, Appleby stresses the uniquely Jeffersonian character of the triumphant American liberal tradition. Its intellectual roots, she argues, lay in the work of certain English seventeenth-century writers, including Locke, who are for her wholly outside the classical republican tradition.

But liberalism's long-term impact on American political culture stems, she argues, from Jefferson's triumph in 1800 over those "conservative elements that had survived the Independence movement" and defended rule by "the rich, the well-born, and the able."[51]

The discovery of classical republicanism appealed strongly to Appleby in part because it showed "that liberalism did not sprawl unimpeded across the flat intellectual landscape of American abundance, as Louis Hartz maintained."[52] Despite Appleby's and a series of earlier scholarly objections, however, Hartz's views have proven remarkably resilient, in part because many of his assertions about colonial society were well founded. Recent pioneering work in colonial labor history, for example, confirms that Americans' search for independence and the freehold land that supported it went back to the early seventeenth century, when settlers brought from England a conception of wage labor and other forms of dependency as base and demeaning. Immigrants were drawn to America by promises of social mobility and material betterment as well as by the hope of political freedom. And by the 1760s and 1770s, the proportion of independent families of middling status within the free population of British North America was "substantially more numerous than in any other contemporary Western society."[53]

Hartz's interpretation had, moreover, deep historiographical roots. Some of the first historians of the Revolution, such as Mercy Warren and David Ramsay, cited the lack of feudal traditions, widespread incidence of property-holding, and general "mediocrity" of wealth in colonial America to explain why Americans founded a nation without an acute and demeaning "distinction of ranks." Even William Findley, who wrote a history of the Whiskey Rebellion, traced the unique character of the American people to the process of settlement: those who migrated to America were, he said, "generally of same class in society. . . . Privileged orders never made a part of the mass in the colonial settlements."[54] Warren, Ramsay, and Findley affirmed the revolutionary character of 1776, but understood its significance as more global and political than domestic and social. For them, the Americans had "enlightened mankind in the art of government," but changed their own political institutions "without the effects of those changes operating any sensible alteration in the circumstances of the people." Their histories therefore sustained Hartz's position that the Revolution of 1776 was meant to conserve or secure a free and equal America that already existed.[55] That "conservative" understanding of the Revolution could be politically useful for those who first embraced it: Warren, for example, having described colonial Americans as "born under no feudal tenure, nurtured in the bosom of mediocrity, educated in the schools of freedom," could accuse her "elitist" political enemies of attempting to establish an aristocracy where "it had never before been tasted."[56]

Alexis de Tocqueville's *Democracy in America* (1835–40) again emphasized the early settlers' selective transplantation of European traditions to the New World, the similar social status of immigrants, and the pervasiveness of small landholdings, as well as the local base of authority in colonial America. Americans had the great advantage, he said, of having "arrived at a state of democracy without having to endure a democratic revolution"; they were "born equal instead of becoming so." Hartz seized on this "series of deep insights," endorsing Tocqueville's "famous notion of equality" and chiding scholars who preferred "Beardian notions of social conflict."[57]

Tocqueville, however, had recognized anti-equalitarian tendencies in colonial America, which he labeled "English" rather than "Puritan." For him, moreover, American society was "shaken to its center" by the testamentary reforms of the Revolution, which he erroneously thought had made partible inheritances mandatory and so destroyed the colonial remnants of English aristocracy. Hartz was no less conscious that the Revolution brought "an attack on the vestiges of corporate society in America," but considered that attack of little significance because for him the landed gentry of the Hudson Valley and the South were a frustrated aristocracy under duress, forced "to rely for survival upon shrewd activity in the capitalist race."[58]

The error in Hartz's vision of late colonial America lies, then, less in what he observed than in his sense of the direction of historical change. What was for him—as for Tocqueville—the isolated, embattled remnants of an alien aristocratic tradition were, it seems, the results of a relatively recent process of Anglicization that affected all Anglo-American colonies in the eighteenth century. English institutions, customs, and styles that had no place in the more primitive America of the previous century were adopted and welcomed, particularly by colonial elites who modeled themselves upon the English upper classes. The emergent social hierarchies of late colonial America were "less finely developed and more open than in metropolitan Britain"; colonial merchant "princes" were less English aristocrats than middle-class, self-made men, and even in Virginia the status of planters was to a considerable extent meritocratic, founded upon their ability to produce high-quality tobacco. But pre-Revolutionary America had at least "tasted" aristocracy; and its development was clearly and self-consciously set toward an ever greater approximation of England.[59]

With independence, Americans assumed a starkly different model for their future. What had often been embarrassing signs of the colonies' "provincial" backwardness—the "mediocrity" of American wealth, the fluidity of social ranks, the meritocratic basis of status—were confirmed and celebrated. Seymour Martin Lipset understood, unlike Hartz, that the association of "equalitarian, anti-class" values with American national identity had a powerful impact on American society. It changed the trajectory of American development, which in time made it strikingly different not just from Britain, but also from Canada, a country that shared with the United States many "ecological conditions" including an abundance of land, but lacked the American Revolutionary tradition. Canadian history and society were shaped instead by Loyalists, dissenters from the American Revolution who consciously rejected the novel social doctrines of the United States and continued to emulate England. As a result, Lipset argued, Canada remained "a more conservative and rigidly stratified society."[60]

Americans caught in the turmoil of the mid-1770s understood that independence implied not stasis but social change. Those colonists who needed the carefully calibrated scale of a traditional social order often became Loyalists. The partisans of independence—even those customarily described as "conservative" in later political divisions—were able to accept the more fluid and egalitarian social order that the Revolution affirmed.[61]

Consider, for example, Gouverneur Morris, who is generally viewed as one of the most "aristocratic" revolutionaries. Morris initially regarded with horror the prospect of social leveling, which he identified in a Manhattan public meeting of May 1774. "The mob begin to think and reason," he wrote in one of the most extreme antidemocratic statements of the Revolutionary period: "Poor Reptiles! . . . they are struggling to cast off their winter's slough, . . . and ere noon they will bite, depend upon it." Only reconciliation with Britain could save the gentry. Two years later, however, Morris had broken with the politics of his mother and wealthy neighbors in the Hudson Valley and became an outspoken advocate of independence who understood and defended its social implications. Independence meant, he suggested in a speech to the New York Provincial Congress, "living in a country where all are on an equal footing." And he assured those "gentlemen . . . apprehensive of losing a little consequence, and importance" that "virtue in such a country will always be esteemed, and that alone should be respected in any country." An independent, equalitarian future promised peace, liberty, security, as well as a flourishing commerce, greater wealth, population growth, and a diffusion of knowledge such as would make America an asylum for the oppressed of all nations. Instead to indulge "a few in luxurious ease," a practice Morris clearly associated with the traditional society being left behind, served "to thin the ranks of mankind" and encourage a "general profligacy of manners," which he condemned as "criminal in the highest degree."[62]

There was no hint of a "backward-looking," socially and economically regressive "classical republicanism" in Morris's speech, nor in the early republican creed of Timothy Pickering, who would later become a staunch Federalist. "Having from my earliest remembrance . . . looked on all mankind as possessing equal rights," he wrote in 1780, "I am wont not to make those distinctions between the high and the low which gave birth to the term *politeness*" or, again, "I think too highly of the dignity of human nature, of the equal rights of all mankind . . . to worship at the shrine of any individual, or collection, of my fellow mortals."[63]

Some Federalists did hold conceptions of society that conformed closely to the "classical republican" model, though it seems inaccurate and unfair to label them as men who "survived" the Revolution, given their roles in its success. George Washington, for example, harbored no conception of the United States as a nation of "Jeffersonian" freeholders. He continued to support a hierarchical social system that entrusted power to members of the landed gentry like himself, and proposed that the children of the poor be given a distinctly different education from that appropriate for "young Gentlemen of good families" with a "high sense of honour." In making military appointments and promotions, however, even Washington felt the transforming hand of the Revolution: according to a recent study, he moved away "from an ideology of deference, 'interest,' and honor, toward an ideology espousing reward of individual talent and service according to supposedly objective criteria." Within the "governing classes," he came to believe, "men should rise on the basis of their personal merits."[64]

The original republican faith of such men was sometimes sorely tested during the 1780s and 1790s. Their early commitment to a world where all were on an "equal footing" or where rank would come from personal merit—which necessarily shifted attention from social categories such as "gentlemen" to the attributes of individuals—is nonetheless important. It suggests that the critical divisions with respect to ideas of American social structure were more chronological, between the dominating conceptions of colonial and early national America, than factional, between groups within the politics of the early republic. That chronological division was founded upon the pervasiveness of "new men" in American politics after 1776. Though some Federalists such as Morris were born into the colonial upper order, many others, including John Adams, William Paterson, and Alexander Hamilton, were not. They could readily endorse meritocracy and an impermanence of social statuses because they themselves had risen by virtue of their talents and contributions to the public. Even that "High Federalist" Fisher Ames was, as his political opponents noted, merely the son of an almanac writer.[65]

The argument that two ideologically opposed conceptions of society lay behind American political divisions of the late eighteenth century, and that the "liberal" vision of a classless nation of free, enterprising individuals emerged triumphant only after 1789 is, in fact, undercut by a mass of evidence that the vision emerged earlier, took on power and coherence with independence, and was affirmed in the 1780s by persons across the political spectrum.[66] Opposition to wealth as a basis for rank linked "democrats" such as John Smilie or Benjamin Franklin with "conservatives" such as Rufus King; respect for work over leisure and idleness bound Governor William Livingston with "radicals" such as Abraham Clark or Walter Brewster; and a commitment to the broad diffusion of knowledge that would undercut aristocracy, enhance mobility, and promote personal independence bound future Federalists and future Republicans.

Even those upwardly mobile members of the Revolutionary movement cited by Appleby and Wood for their "liberal" ideas harbored "classical republican" values. During critical debates in the Pennsylvania assembly over the Bank of North America, William Findley and his colleagues insisted that they were more "disinterested" than their opponents, justified the possession of property by the "independence" it brought, and, moreover, effectively used "virtue" in the cause of equalitarianism. "A virtuous man," John Smilie said, "be his situation what it may, is respectable."[67] If "classical republican" values such as independence and virtue had been incapable of sustaining such "democratic" arguments, then Samuel Adams—a republican who adhered to the creed of virtue so exactly that he was called "one of Plutarch's men," but also held extreme egalitarian convictions—would remain an unresolvable paradox.[68] So would the persistence of those values into the "democratic" nineteenth century, when "classical republican" ideas shaped the arguments of both Whigs and Jacksonians.[69]

Those who stress the socially regressive implications of "classical republicanism" err in their interpretation of those writers within the English dissenting tradition that shaped eighteenth-century American thought. More important, they misconstrue how and why those writings were received in the colonies. *Cato's Letters*, a series of newspaper essays by John Trenchard and Thomas Gordon that were widely cited and reprinted in the colonies, has been described as socially reactionary largely on the basis of one letter against charity schools, which has been misread, and in any case had little relevance for Americans. Such an

interpretation ignores other letters that support commerce, individual
enterprise, and the natural equality of men, defend the definition of
rank on the basis of merit alone, and assert the right and ability of the
people to judge their rulers. Such arguments fit the needs and experience
of eighteenth-century Americans; without such a fit, their impact would
be inexplicable.[70]

The arguments of what was once called the English "Commonwealth"
tradition that had the most powerful impact in the colonies went back
less to the opponents of Walpole than to English revolutionaries of the
seventeenth century, and were received less for their social and economic
than their political utility. English "revolution principles" asserted the
fiduciary nature of power and the right of the people to judge, resist,
and ultimately displace their rulers. They provided the ideological foundation for eighteenth-century American politics, and, ultimately, for the
independence movement. On those principles there were no critical
distinctions between the "liberal" Locke and anti-Walpolean "classical
republicans" such as John Trenchard and Thomas Gordon: they were
of a piece.[71] Moreover, a tradition received for its insistence upon the
right and duty of the people to judge legally constituted authority was
intrinsically at odds with old-style hierarchy and deference. As Bailyn
noted, the ideology of the Revolution reversed ancient lines of power
and authority, making rulers the servants of the people, implicitly undermining the traditional social order. Powerful evidence supports his
position. Gouverneur Morris, for example, first recognized a threat to
the gentry in a popular assembly whose justification depended upon
"revolution principles." Similar meetings of the "body of the people" in
Boston gave "the lower part of the people such a sense of their importance," Thomas Hutchinson complained in 1770, "that a gentleman does
not meet with what used to be common civility, and we are sinking into
perfect barbarism."[72] The road toward Jackson's rowdy inaugural, it
seems, came clearly into view during the years immediately preceeding
independence.

There remained ample room for division within the bounds of an
American "republican" vision that celebrated equality without rejecting
hierarchy, and that argued for a meritocracy based on "ability and virtue"
without defining just what those words implied. Conflict and consensus
are not necessarily functional opposites: shared values, assumptions, and
the language that expressed them sustained and supported the violent
political strife of the early republic.

In the nineteenth century, moreover, those same shared values and
assumptions helped undercut the development of class consciousness,
which characteristically occurs, as Lipset observed, when new economic

groups emerge in traditionally hierarchical societies and find their values at odds with "dominant cultural norms" that support "the political and social positions of old elites."[73] In the United States, dominant cultural norms did not sustain rule by an established elite, nor was there a ruling class with values vastly different from those of an emergent nineteenth-century bourgeoisie or working class.

In short, both Hartz and his critics underestimated the transforming impact of independence. American partisans of 1776 were not bound to a regressive, "civic-humanist" social agenda, nor did independence simply confirm a liberal America already firmly in place. The dominant social and cultural norms of the early republic had roots in the colonial past, but they were powerfully affirmed, and countervailing tendencies checked, with the Revolution. They were not therefore the givens of American life, but part, as Jonathan Jackson said in 1788, of the "national character we . . . assumed" at the time of independence.[74]

III

The conception of American society professed in the first decades after independence continued into the next century, shaping actions as well as words. European stratification remained a negative reference for Francis Cabot Lowell, who designed Lowell, Massachusetts, according to John Kasson, to avoid the development of an oppressed and self-perpetuating working class like that in Manchester, England. Lowell turned for his work force to local farm girls who, he thought, would serve as operatives for a few years, then return to traditional lives as wives and mothers. The amenities that made Lowell a showcase of the industrial world—the lectures and neat boarding houses, even the potted geraniums—were meant to assure that time spent there would be uplifting and so appropriate to a republic. American "industrial pioneers" in Pennsylvania and the South were moved, according to Charles L. Sanford, by a similar "moralizing impulse." They "shared with poets, painters, reformers, professional men, and pioneer farmers the pervasive American hope of redeeming men and society from the sins of a supposedly corrupt Old World" and so sought to avoid "the ill consequences of European manufacturing."[75]

Workers also shared those objectives. Paul Faler noted that shoemakers in nineteenth-century Lynn, Massachusetts, "frequently pointed to the countries of Europe with their arrogant nobility and a mass of workers in 'utter misery and wretchedness.' " Citing the precedent of 1776, they resisted changes that would reduce them " 'to the misery and degradation of our unfortunate brethren of other countries.' " In *Chants Democratic*, Sean Wilentz told the story of a British immigrant of 1830 who urged a New York drugmaker to divide labor and so increase productivity. "This, sir," he was told, "is a free country. We want no one person over another which would be the case if you divided labor." Everywhere the proposal got the same response, sometimes with an addition that explicitly linked hostility toward having "one person over another" with the American Revolution: "Tories may be very well in England but we want none here."[76]

Clearly nineteenth-century Americans, like their ancestors, dreamed of being their "own men," working for themselves under no one, and still saw in the reserves of western land a way their society could avoid the rigid tiers of power and dependency that they continued to associate with Europe. The political advocates of "Free Soil," Eric Foner observed, considered land a means of preserving "Free Labor," which implied for them freedom to leave the working class after acquiring "enough money to start one's own farm or business."[77]

To grasp the full significance of Revolutionary ideals for American society—to explain where social conflict emerged as well as where it failed to emerge—demands extending the conceptual limits of most eighteenth-century discussions of American society. Because in the 1780s and 1790s "society" generally referred to the community of persons who participated in the *polis*, writers could speak of "the people" or even "the inhabitants of America" as if only white men were present.[78] Occasionally, however, essayists referred to the "constitution of society" in its broader dimensions. Then the critical divisions of American society in a larger and, to us, familiar sense, and the relationships they bore to each other in the "ordering" of that society, began to become clear.

The components of an American social order had to be "natural." For that reason, Americans debated passionately whether the observable differences among men served to define a "natural aristocracy," and, if so, what its role should be in a republic. Both the character and the meaning of those differences were open to dispute. Robert Coram, a radical egalitarian who thought all differences among men were "purely artificial," argued that the very difficulty of distinguishing superior from inferior men proved his point. If there were a need for "two distinct hereditary orders of men in a society," he asserted, those "created subordinate . . . would at their birth be possessed of certain characteristic marks by which each class would be distinguished."[79]

White adult males were not so distinguished from one another. Other human beings were, however, marked at birth with "certain characteristic marks" that allowed a definition of "classes" or categories of persons to which were assigned distinctive social roles. Men and women occupied separate "departments" or "spheres." Men were "formed" for the "hardy" work of government, the field, and the marketplace, women for "domestic concerns, and for diffusing bliss into social life." If a woman "quits her own department" and "obtrudes herself" upon her husband's business, "she departs from that sphere which is assigned *her* in the order of society"; and the imperative of order made it necessary "to consider man as the superior in authority." For John Adams, another example of "natural authority," where again biological differences connoted a power relationship, was that of parents over children. Only when women and children were left "out of the question," he said, could individuals in the state of nature be described as "equal, free, and independent of each other."[80]

Except that men of different races were on different planes. Thomas Jefferson's painful discussion of the "real distinctions which nature has made" between blacks and whites in his *Notes on the State of Virginia* was distinctive mainly for its open confrontation with the issue. Others were less cautious than he in drawing conclusions. "We may sincerely advocate the freedom of the black man," wrote the Democratic-Republican Tunis Worthman in 1800, "and yet assert their moral and physical inferiority." Even "enlightened" foreign visitors who celebrated American equality observed, with no apparent sense of contradiction, that blacks' "unfortunate" color would "always make them a separate caste." It was not therefore "only the slave who is beneath his master; it is the Negro who is beneath the white man."[81]

Thus "natural" biological differences—those of sex, age, and race—identified categories of people for whom dependency seemed right and natural, and so defined the components of an American social structure in which white men ruled white women, who helped govern white children, all of whom were superior to blacks. That was the hierarchical social order described in George Fitzhugh's *Sociology for the South* (1854), the first American book with a title that included the new word "sociology." Its currency went beyond the South, however. In the North, early advocates for industrialization and machine technology frequently argued that factory labor could be performed by women and children.[82] Objections to divisions of labor that put "one person over another" as un-American were operative only for adult white men; for others, different rules applied.

The Revolution inspired efforts to ameliorate the conditions of the nation's subordinate peoples—so long as those efforts did not disrupt the social order. The emancipation of slaves in the northern states was perhaps the single most powerful social change that the Revolution brought. But early advocates of emancipation like Worthman or those Federalists who were ardent opponents of the slave system had no intention of making free blacks equal to whites. Similarly, eighteenth-century supporters of women's education often hoped to uplift women without changing their social position: "a weak and ignorant woman," Benjamin Rush argued, "will always be governed with the greatest difficulty," by which he meant that educated women, who understood the laws of nature, would accept their subordinate place without resistance. "That education is always *wrong*," Noah Webster said, "which raises a woman above the duties of her station."[83]

In a society so publicly averse to positions of dependency, in which other ascriptive social ranks were considered "European" and illegitimate, "natural" social distinctions founded on physical differences became invidious, and so more demeaning than in less self-consciously egalitarian nations. Meanwhile, equalitarian principles and substantive changes in the post-Revolutionary situation of women, children, and blacks encouraged them to make new claims for status and respect. Sex, age, and race therefore defined the critical fault lines of American society, where conflict could and did develop, and thereby determined the character of powerful group identities. "Natural" distinctions also served to divide those who held similar positions in the American productive system. Thus an American woman worker who wrote in 1847 of the "class to which it is my lot to belong" referred, as Nancy F. Cott observed, not to the working class, but to women.[84]

The language of the Revolution, which served to legitimize and so reinforced "natural" social divisions, also helped make sense of disturbing changes in American life during the first century after independence. The extension of commerce, development of manufacturing, and growth of cities had, by the mid-nineteenth century, produced distinctions of wealth and welfare that recalled the invidious European model. In Lowell, for example, as the pressures of an increasingly competitive market undercut the benign working conditions of earlier days, jobs once filled by New England girls were increasingly taken by families of Irish immigrants who seemed firmly and enduringly proletarian. Rather than acknowledge the emergence of an industrial working class as a result of economic development, native observers frequently attributed the depressed state of many American workers to their "racial" identity. By the 1850s, references to the Anglo-Saxon and Celtic "races" and the "innate and ineradicable characteristics of each permeated the columns of newspapers, political monthlies, and literary magazines and were even filtering into schoolbooks and . . . government publications."[85] Meanwhile, southern slaveholders invoked racism to realize "the liberal ideal of a classless society," attempting to heal divisions between themselves and an aggrieved yeomanry through the common cause of white supremacy.[86]

In time, of course, the burden of American racism rested most enduringly on blacks. Their fate effectively undercuts celebrations of American classlessness. In other New World countries such as Cuba, where a modern class system had begun to develop before emancipation, socioeconomic distinctions among individuals of African descent were more readily recognized, according to Herbert Klein, and the possibility of social mobility was far greater than in the United States. Here the "natural" classification of race remained a confining and demeaning ascriptive designation, far more restrictive than the "artificial" horizontal social categories it replaced.[87]

White Americans often continue to use race as a rough approximation of class, a phenomenon that J. Anthony Lukas observed in *Common Ground: A Turbulent Decade in the Lives of Three American Families* (1985). In other ways, too, hints of eighteenth-century social sentiments remain—in attitudes toward the "idle poor" that have outlived the economic context that first sustained them, in the demand that persons of wealth and high standing contribute to charitable and other causes for the public good. In short, an examination of historic conceptions of American society might help explain far more than the resistance of Americans to think of themselves and their society in modern class terms. Habits of mind formed in an eighteenth-century revolution that set the United States on a course consciously different from that of England and took nature as the arbiter of the acceptable have persisted long after their beginnings were forgotten, with results that were seldom anticipated, much less intended. In those origins lie a key to the course of American social history, and to a complex dynamic that continues to shape American life.

The Transition to Capitalism
in America

JAMES A. HENRETTA

T HOUSANDS OF MEN and women—most of them unknown
to posterity—were active agents in the American transition
to a full-fledged capitalist economic system between 1770
and 1800.*

In 1773, Sylvanus Hussey, the owner of a dry goods store and twelve-
acre farm in Lynn, Massachusetts, entered into a barter agreement with
Nicholas Brown, a prominent merchant of Providence, Rhode Island.
Hussey exchanged 100 pairs of shoes, accumulated from local artisans
in return for store goods, for 100 pounds of imported tea. Such transactions were not new; for decades shopkeepers had run a complex system
of barter linking local producers with transatlantic merchants. But Hussey was less a sedentary storekeeper than an enterprising entrepreneur.
He—and dozens of other Massachusetts traders—were actively mobilizing labor, advancing credit and raw materials to induce their customers
to make hand-sewn shoes during slack times in the agricultural cycle.
The success of these creative architects of the first major American put-

*I presented earlier versions of this paper to the History Department at The Johns
Hopkins University, the Philadelphia Center for Early American History, and as the
Burke Inaugural Lecture at the University of Maryland. I am grateful for the crit-
icisms and suggestions offered by those audiences, graduate students in History 668,
and the following individuals: Philip Morgan, Lorena Walsh, Daniel Vickers, Lois
Green Carr, Paul Clemens, Stephen Innes, Laurel Thatcher Ulrich, and Lucy Simler.

ting-out system was phenomenal. By 1800, the male journeymen and female outworkers employed by merchants and manufacturers in the town of Lynn produced nearly half a million pairs of shoes each year.[1]

Agricultural entrepreneurs near Philadelphia were equally assiduous in directing labor, rationalizing production, and expanding markets. In 1781, Caleb Brinton, an established farmer in Chester County, Pennsylvania, proposed a contract to George Henthorn. Brinton offered to rent Henthorn a small house and garden plot for £4.15s. In return, Henthorn had to assist "with all the hay and wheat harvest" at "three shillings Per day without Liquor . . . the whole to go towards the rent," and to do all Brinton's weaving at "the same price . . . James Rolins did."[2]

Once again, this contractual relation was not new. Henthorn and Rolins were cotters, landless men who bartered their skills as weavers and husbandmen for a house and garden. They were familiar figures in the social landscape of eighteenth-century England and, increasingly, in the American Middle Colonies. By the 1780s cotters and other landless workers accounted for half the population in many districts of southeastern Pennsylvania. Enterprising, improving farmers like Caleb Brinton now used their labor in an ever more efficient manner—producing a variety of goods, grain, butter, and textiles, for sale or exchange in the market economy.

The market-driven use of dependent labor grew more pervasive in the Tidewater Chesapeake region as well. In 1784, Mary Mallory, an affluent widow in Elizabeth City County, Virginia, used thirteen adult slaves and nine slave children to farm her property of 250 acres. She also hired out, for the term of a year, five male slaves, four females, and four children—receiving approximately £65 in labor rent for their services.[3]

Hiring-out was not new in the 1780s, but its extent was. For the first time, many Chesapeake slaveowners had more laborers than they needed to farm their plantations in a traditional manner. Some proprietors became agricultural improvers, using Enlightenment knowledge to raise productivity and diversify output. Others emulated major English landowners, becoming agricultural capitalists by leasing their plantations to prosperous tenant-middlemen. Still others, like Mallory, hired out their slaves in a capitalist labor market.

These quotidian business deals—by Hussey, Brinton and Henthorn, and Malloy—took place in widely separated locales, yet formed a common pattern. Each transaction was not merely an *event*, the exchange of goods in a market "place." Rather, it was part of an increasingly prevalent *process* that involved the conscious and active mobilization of labor "time."[4] Northern merchants and traders no longer derived profits only

from control of market exchange; as capitalist entrepreneurs they organized the productive process itself. Similarily, Scotch merchant houses
subsidized the rapid expansion of the Piedmont tobacco economy, advancing credit in "futures" contracts for subsequent crop harvests. In
the Tidewater, enterprising planters raised profits by devising new forms
of plantation management and work discipline. Even the Indian trade
changed in character. Before 1750, native Americans carried pelts and
skins directly to merchants in Albany or Montreal and returned with
manufactures. Thereafter, European and American merchant houses
dispatched their own agents into the forests. These white traders negotiated price bargains and exchanged goods directly with Indian producers, bypassing tribal intermediaries or chiefs. Like Lynn shoemakers
and Piedmont planters, native American hunters and trappers were
becoming, as Eric Wolf has argued, "specialized laborers in a putting-
out system, in which the entrepreneurs advanced both production goods
and consumption goods against commodities to be delivered in the
future."[5]

The dimensions of economic existence had changed. Thousands of
farm families and artisan households were now more deeply embedded
in profit-oriented exchange relationships. Thinking in causal terms, calculating financial outcomes, they were not merely "in" the market but
"of" it. Many thousands more, a full tenth of the free labor force, worked
for wages; they had to engage the market simply to earn their daily
bread. Finally, thousands of enslaved southern blacks experienced new
capitalist intrusions into their lives—through hiring-out, a task system
of production, and sale to new owners. The intensity and diversity of
market relationships in the domestic economy were everywhere on the
rise.[6] Partly in consequence, American foreign trade changed in character and declined in relative importance. As early as 1770, American
merchants earned more from the "invisible" export of shipping services
than from the sale of any single commodity export. Moreover, foreign
trade amounted to 15–20 percent of total output in 1770, but only 10
–15 percent in 1800, and less than 10 percent by 1820.[7] The creation
of a "national" American economy was part of the process of capitalist
transformation.

This transition to a more intensive system of domestic capitalism was
the product of four interrelated developments. First, a buoyant transatlantic demand for agricultural products encouraged thousands of ordinary Americans to sell more goods in the market. Second, rapid
population growth—from natural increase and in-migration—created a
surplus of workers, facilitating the emergence of wage labor. Third,
many American merchants, landowners, and artisans became aggressive

entrepreneurs, reorganizing production to exploit the new market opportunities and labor supply. Finally, as a result of American independence, the political state became increasingly responsive to the needs
and interests of these "monied men." At the same time, newly politically
conscious farmers, artisans, and planters advanced an alternative set of
economic policies. The struggle for home rule had pushed forward the
transition to capitalism. And, to paraphrase Carl Becker, the American
Revolution also set in motion a fifty-year battle between monied men
and rural smallholders over which group—and which system of political
economy—would rule at home.[8]

I

The legacy of the past was particularly apparent in mid-eighteenth-
century New England. The original migrants to New England came from
a society in the midst of a capitalist agricultural revolution. As early as
1700, owner-occupiers cultivated less than 30 percent of the arable land
in England and propertyless cotters or wage laborers formed a majority
of the rural population. Aristocratic and gentry landlords benefited most
from the enclosures that dispossessed tens of thousands of peasants from
their common-field use-rights, but less affluent property owners profited
as well. Nearly three-fourths of the yeomen families in seventeenth-
century England and one-half of the husbandmen hired the labor of
one or more servants-in-husbandry. By contrast most early settlers in
New England, while not averse to large holdings and servant labor,
favored widespread landownership. The land-distribution policies of
general courts and town meetings provided farms for most families,
inhibiting the development of the English system of agricultural capitalism based on wage labor. Servants numbered only 5 percent of the
population during most of the seventeenth century, and worked in fewer
than 20 percent of rural households. Daily hired labor was equally scarce
and expensive. Day laborers received 20–30 pence per day, nearly twice
the English rate of 12–15 pence.[9]

Settlers in Essex County, Massachusetts, adapted to the abundance of
land and the shortage of labor in three ways. First, middling farmers
relied on their own labor—and that of their sons and daughters—as
they set farm tasks and production goals. Second, wealthier farmers
called upon poorer property owners to assist them with the spring planting and the hay and grain harvests. They paid for their neighbors' labor
with money, produce, or access to pasture land. Third, land-rich settlers
used attractive "developmental" leases to attract tenants to their holdings.

Most leases were short, ten years or less, and permitted tenants to sell their capital improvements—houses, barns, fences—to the next occupant. Low annual rents also assisted tenant families, who numbered no more than 10 percent of the population, to accumulate movable goods and capital and eventually to acquire landed property.[10]

This system of family-run farms, labor exchange, and life-cycle tenancy shaped the character of rural New England well into the nineteenth century. Even rapid population growth did not undermine the "household mode of production" (as Michael Merrill has termed it). In Andover, Massachusetts, for example, there were 435 people in 1680, but 1,425 in 1730, and over 2,900 in 1780. Despite a growing surplus of workers, most middling farmers continued to rely primarily on family (rather than hired) labor. Deacon John Abbot of Andover, who died in 1754, indentured two of his eight children; the other six worked full-time on the family property from the age of sixteen to the time of their marriages. Four sons provided Abbot with sixty-eight years of labor, while two daughters contributed twenty-seven years of labor to his wife.[11]

The ethic of economic cooperation likewise remained vital, in part because of the historic pattern of property ownership. One-half of the 19,000 farms listed on the Massachusetts valuation list for 1772 did not have plows or oxen; 40 percent lacked enough cultivated acres to be self-sufficient in grain; and two-thirds did not have enough pasture for their livestock. Interdependence was an economic necessity and created a productive system (and cultural values) based primarily on local barter, not commercial markets. "Many farmers undoubtedly entered into exchange, not for profit or to raise their standard of living," Bettye Pruitt has argued, "but simply to be able to feed their families." As in the seventeenth century, poorer farmers (or their sons) worked regularly for their more affluent neighbors, the 5,000 farmers on the valuation list who owned more than twenty acres of tillage and hay land.[12]

As in the past, land-poor families sought low-cost "developmental" leases. Beginning in the 1730s they migrated in large numbers to newly founded communities in central and western Massachusetts, eastern Connecticut, and, eventually, southern Maine. To accumulate the cash to purchase frontier farmsteads from land speculators, young men sought military bounties in the Seven Years' and Revolutionary wars, lived at home while working as day laborers, or went to sea as sailors or fishermen.[13]

The pressure of population growth thus pushed some men and women into capitalist markets for land and labor. By the late colonial period, one-half of the ordinary hands in the Nantucket whaling fleet were the sons of mainland farmers. Enterprising merchants induced these young men to become whalers by advancing cash and goods to them or their families; in return, traders received a written labor contract obligating the recruit to turn over his "lay" (his proportionate share of the profits). These contracts then circulated as bills of exchange; and, as Daniel Vickers has argued, the whaler's "labor now belonged to his creditor."[14]

Many New England families sought to avoid such dependence. Their goal was neither self-sufficiency nor profit maximization, but autonomy. They wanted to preserve the traditional system of local political power and economic interdependence that inhibited control over their lives by outside agents—be they merchants, creditors, or government officials. Consequently, Pruitt has concluded, farmers participated in the market but would not accept "specialization and large-scale investment." Storekeepers and merchants had to accumulate goods for export "through innumerable small-scale purchases and exchanges." "The farmers have the game in their hands," an exasperated Alexander Hamilton complained in 1781 while trying to amass food for the Continental Army. Living in virtually self-sufficient communities, rural producers "are not obliged to sell because they have almost every necessary within themselves." Patriotic residents of New England equated this economic and political autonomy with republicanism itself. As the Northampton town meeting put it during a debate on the Massachusetts Constitution of 1780, no man should have "any degree or spark of . . . a right of dominion, government, and jurisdiction over [an]other."[15]

Autonomy required increasing ingenuity, as land in coastal New England grew scarce and expensive. The economic strategies of the land-poor family of Caleb Jackson, Jr., a fifteen-year-old farm boy in Rowley, Massachusetts, provide a case in point. Every August and September, the family picked cherries for, as Caleb noted in his journal, "cherries . . . are ready cash." In October and November, the family gathered apples from their own and their neighbors' orchards and pressed them into cider for sale in Ipswich, Salem, or Newburyport. In addition, Caleb, Sr., had his sons cultivate "Mr. Jonathan Woods Planting land . . . and have half the crop for our labour," plant "our field of potatoes at Capt. D," and pasture their cattle on other families' meadows.

This creative expedient, of using the family's ample supply of labor on neighboring farms, was only partially successful. To ensure a comfortable subsistence for his family, Mr. Jackson "made a bargain with Captain Perley to make shoes for him" in 1802. Every winter thereafter, he dispatched his two sons to an outbuilding to make one hundred pairs of shoes for a variety of local traders. Unlike husbandry, shoemaking was an unpleasant obligation, a task "we have got to [do]," Caleb, Jr., complained. While such outwork "was better than regular day labor,"

Daniel Vickers has argued, the Jackson family had compromised its cherished "independence" and began "to cross the frontier of what rural New Englanders considered a satisfactory way of life." Other young men considered even more drastic alternatives. Far off in western Massachusetts, an advertisement in the Hampshire County *Gazette* promised "good wages in CASH" to "able bodied . . . industrious, sober men . . . to labor at the town of *Patterson*, in the state of *New Jersey* . . . in the greatest manufacture going on in America."[16]

As young men worked more for employers outside the household, women and young girls labored harder within it. The life of Martha Ballard—a midwife who migrated with her family from densely settled eastern Massachusetts to Hallowell, Maine, in 1777—was typical. Ballard's husband operated saw- and grist mills with his sons and worked as a land surveyor. In 1790 he earned £38 for three months' survey work for the Kennebec Proprietors, one of the many groups of speculators who claimed much of the best land in southern Maine. In the same year Martha Ballard's cash income was £20, the return for her labor as a midwife (at 6 shillings a delivery) and as the manager of a household textile manufactory. At first, the work force consisted of her two daughters, ages seventeen and twenty-one. The Ballard girls spun flax and wool for neighboring women weavers. Mrs. Ballard acquired a loom in 1787, and her daughters quickly learned to weave a wide variety of textiles. The family kept most of the cloth for its own use, but exchanged some textiles for goods, labor services, and cash. When her daughters married in the early 1790s, Ballard replaced them with servant girls who received room, board, and £6 per year.[17]

Ballard's textile manufactory was not unique. In the 1790s 50 percent of the probate inventories in Hallowell listed looms. Weaving had become a normal female household responsibility and one with a significant impact on the local economy. Ballard and other women traded with blacksmiths for iron parts and repairs for their looms, with timbermen for potash to process flax, and with shopkeepers for goods from Boston. Their activities, and those of thousands of other women and girls, expanded the productive base of the American economy, in part by increasing the domestic supply of cheap cloth. "Among the country people in Mass. Bay," the British consul in Philadelphia reported in 1789, "coarse linens of their own making are in such general use as to lessen the importation of checks and even of coarse Irish linens nearly ⅔rds. . . . 40,000 yards of coarse New England linen have been sold in Phila within the last year."[18] Yet the Ballard women also used large quantities of imported cloth, making dresses from English chintz and quilting imported calico. The expansion of the market economy simultaneously increased domestic production and foreign imports.

This system of cloth production was not organized directly by merchants. Nor was the increasingly prevalent by-employment of nail-making. Few men and women in New England worked within the rigid confines of the *Verlagsystem*, the form of cottage industry in which capitalist merchants owned all the raw materials and held rural workers in a position of nearly complete economic dependence. However, these American farmer-artisans were now part of a *Kaufsystem* of artisan production. To remain as members of the "yeoman" class of rural property owners, they sold not only their surplus crops, but also their labor and domestic manufactures.[19] They owned most of the means of production and, like the Jackson family, enjoyed considerable economic freedom. Even hired workers maintained some autonomy. In July 1799, Sally Fletcher abruptly left her servant's position in Martha Ballard's modest household textile manufactory. Her parting threat to Ballard and her husband, to "sue us in a weak from this time if we did not pay her what was her due," echoed the traditional cultural value of independence.[20]

As in European regions with a *Kaufsystem* of proto-industrialization, the family income of many rural workers rose. They lived better as a result of new work opportunities outside the household or more systematic exploitation of labor within it. Yet their economic lives were increasingly intertwined in a market system that altered their behavior and values. Some farmers fell into debt to commercial middlemen, who often extracted excess profits through their knowledge of the market system. Other farmers beat traders at their own game by careful calculation and astute bargaining. Ultimately, both groups became more conscious of profits and of costs. Traditionally, merchants had used high markups to defray inventory costs and to offset delinquent accounts. Beginning in the 1780s they reduced profit margins but charged interest on overdue bills. Farmers likewise began to levy interest on personal loans to friends and neighbors. Only 5 percent of a sample of rural estates probated in Middlesex County, Massachusetts, before 1780 contained charges for interest. The proportion jumped to 20 percent between 1780 and 1800 and to 33 percent in the first decade of the nineteenth century. Simultaneously, affluent farmers and investors formed an array of profit-seeking voluntary associations (banks or canal, bridge, and turnpike companies), some of which issued securities that paid more than the "lawful rate" of interest.[21]

The transition to a robust capitalist economy had begun in New England by 1800, but was far from complete. Merchants and entrepreneurs had expanded their activities and devised new capitalist institutional structures. But as yet they lacked more than a modicum of control over the production of rural farmer-artisans. In economic affairs as in political life, the yeoman legacy remained strong, personifying the Democratic-

Republican vision of the ideal American future. "The class of citizens who provide at once their own food and their own raiment," James Madison argued, "may be viewed as the most truely independent and happy . . . [and] the best basis of public liberty. . . ."[22]

<h1 style="text-align:center">II</h1>

Both merchants and landlords controlled the productive system with far greater success in the Midatlantic region. From the outset, large property owners in New York, Pennsylvania, and New Jersey relied less on family members and yeomen neighbors than did their counterparts in New England and more on "bound" labor. They regularly used slaves, indentured servants, convicts, and tenants to work their businesses and farms. The arrival of tens of thousands of Scotch-Irish and German migrants in the mideighteenth century created new opportunities for established property owners and for ambitious entrepreneurs. Peter January was a case in point. In 1767, January appeared on the Philadelphia tax list as a propertyless master cordwainer. Over the next eight years he used his craft skills and managerial energies to organize a shoe manufactory. By 1775 January was the master of seven servants (mostly Scotch-Irish) and two apprentices. By renting a building, directing servant labor, and selling shoes, he made the jump from artisan to entrepreneur. January called himself a "merchant" on the 1780 tax list.[23]

The continuing influx of migrants prompted the transition to a capitalist system of work discipline in Philadelphia. The ample supply of workers pushed down wage rates, thereby encouraging employers to replace bound men and women with free wage laborers. Servants and slaves accounted for 38 percent of the Philadephia work force in 1751, but only 13 percent in 1775; simultaneously, the proportion of "laborers" on the tax lists rose from 5 to 14 percent. By 1800, the proportion of bound workers had fallen to less than 2 percent and more than a quarter of the work force labored for wages. As employees came to be paid by the day or week (or on a piecework basis), their lives became less secure. No fewer than forty-nine journeymen woodworkers passed through the five positions in Samuel Ashton's cabinet shop between 1795 and 1803; they averaged only 145 days of work. The paternalistic labor system of the early eighteenth century, when even free workers boarded with their employers on year-long contracts, had given way to a more flexible and transient pattern of work relations. The new system of wage labor aided entrepreneurs, who could now respond more quickly and efficiently to changing market conditions.[24]

The surplus of labor, in combination with the booming transatlantic market for grain, had an equally dramatic impact on productive relations in the countryside. The population of Europe rose steadily after 1750, bringing a sharp increase in cereal prices and land values throughout the Atlantic world. Wheat prices on the Amsterdam and Philadelphia markets jumped 30 percent between 1740 and 1760, and then rose even more dramatically after 1790.[25] Philadelphia merchants responded to the opportunity for windfall profits in the cereal trade with "a vigorous spirit of enterprise." One firm dispatched ships to Quebec to buy surplus wheat; many others hired factors in Maryland and Virginia to purchase huge quantities of wheat and corn. Still other merchants specialized in the procurement of agricultural goods from the countryside. Indeed, by 1785 there were no fewer than fifteen "flour merchants" in Philadelphia. These firms stimulated production for market by contracting with hundreds of large-scale farmers; Levi Hollingsworth, the most successful, drew from a network of four hundred producers that spanned the Midatlantic region. Enterprising merchants also created a reliable and efficient land and water transportation system to handle bulky grains and encouraged the construction of mills to grind them into flour. As early as the 1770s the Brandywine River in Delaware was dotted with mills, "8 of them in a quarter of a mile," noted one traveler, "so convenient that they can take the grain out of the Vessels into the Mills."[26]

The aggressive pursuit of profits by Philadelphia merchants played a major role in the transition to a capitalist agricultural system. They stimulated increased production and created the infrastructure to carry it to market. British merchant houses likewise encouraged trade by extending liberal terms of credit. Beginning in the 1750s, they allowed colonial merchants a year (rather than six months) to remit payment for the flood of goods—dry goods, ceramics, ironware—pouring out of workshops and factories of England's increasingly industrialized economy. American merchants now had greater financial incentives to penetrate the rural market, where 90 percent of sales were on credit and payments waited until the harvest. Many rural producers responded with enthusiasm to the new market opportunities. They increased their output of wheat, flaxseed, and meat, and used the returns to purchase imported manufactures. The per-capita consumption of British goods in the Middle Colonies nearly doubled between the 1720s and the 1770s (from £0.80 to £1.50 sterling). Equally significant, per-capita exports from the region increased during the disruptions of the Revolutionary era, rising from £1.01 sterling in 1768–72 to £1.11 in 1791–92.[27]

The life histories of George Henthorn and Caleb Brinton reveal the spectrum of opportunities in this expansive rural environment. In 1781, Henthorn was a recently married man. Over the previous four years he had moved from one farm job to another in search of advancement. He declined to sign the contract for housing and labor-service drawn up by Brinton. Instead, Henthorn negotiated a better deal for himself with a landholder in a nearby township, beginning a slow climb up the agricultural ladder. In 1799, after two decades as a cotter and tenant, he purchased a six-acre property for £165. At his death in 1815, Henthorn left personal possessions valued at $426.25: sundry clothes and household furnishings; a few farm implements; a mare, two cows, and four pigs; and two spinning wheels and three looms. Through hard work and careful calculation, Henthorn had achieved his goal of a "competence." He ended his life as a relatively autonomous property owner. His small farmstead provided shelter, pasture, and land for a truck garden and a small orchard, while the sale of his labor as a weaver provided a modest and respectable standard of living.[28]

Caleb Brinton did not suffer greatly when Henthorn refused to enter his service. The supply of labor for hire was ample in Chester County, and Brinton had the resources and the enterprise to employ it advantageously. Brinton was the fourth-generation descendant of two of the first Quaker migrants to Pennsylvania. In 1783 he owned at least two farms (of 190 and 260 acres) and sizable herds of cattle and sheep. At his death in 1826, at the age of ninety-eight, Brinton's probate inventory listed his personal financial assets at a spectacular $303,000 in cash, bank balances, mortgages, and bonds at interest. If Brinton began his working life as a land-rich, market-oriented farmer, then he ended it as a capitalist landlord.

The account books and journals of George Brinton, Caleb's son, reveal the capitalist agricultural practices that accounted, in part, for this impressive accumulation of wealth. In 1788, George and his bride, Elizabeth Yeatman, received a 282-acre farm from Caleb Brinton. By 1793 the young couple had three children. They hired one full-time and one part-time female worker to assist with house- and dairy work. George Brinton himself employed two propertyless male fieldhands, renting them cottages at £4 per year and paying them for farm labor. To keep his hired fieldhands busy, he planned an intensive year-round agricultural regime. His workers planted nitrogen-rich clover in the early spring and, to improve productivity further, carted dung and lime to newly plowed fields. Then Brinton sheared his sheep, selling the wool or sending it out to be woven into cloth, and sowed flax, spring wheat, and corn in succession. In June, the workers harvested hay, since Brinton's large dairy herd needed winter fodder. Meanwhile, Brinton engaged in a variety of market transactions, selling some of his sheep and the first batch of the 700 pounds of cheese that he would produce in 1794. His workers then planted buckwheat, pulled flax, and harvested the spring wheat. Brinton saved 26 bushels of wheat for seed, reserved 20 bushels for family use, and sent 100 bushels to the mill to be ground and sold as flour. In October, he directed the planting of winter wheat, the harvest of potatoes and apples, and the making of cider. As the days grew cooler and shorter, he mobilized his workers to break and dress flax and to spin tow yarn.[29]

The extent of Brinton's commitment to the market marked him out as a capitalist- rather than as a yeoman-farmer. He invested heavily in the labor, livestock, and capital equipment needed to produce cheese, cider, and yarn, as well as wheat and meat. And he used these resources in a calculating and risk-taking manner. Unlike Caleb Jackson, Brinton sought to maximize profits, regardless of his consequent "dependence" on others—recalcitrant workers, hard-bargaining merchants, or fickle consumers. He relied on his managerial skills and his well-placed confidence in continuing agricultural prosperity to see him through.[30]

Many of Brinton's propertied neighbors likewise moved toward a capitalist productive system based on wage labor and market sales. In 1799, fifty-one property-owning farmer and artisan families resided in East Caln township in Chester County. They employed the labor of twenty-four married inmates or cotters and forty-eight propertyless freemen. The money wages—and goods—paid to these landless laborers enabled some of them to become small property holders, like George Henthorn. Yet their labor also provided substantial profits for their employers; and their need for clothing, land, mortgages, and other services augmented the wealth of other merchants and landowners.

Like Caleb Brinton, the property owners of southeastern Pennsylvania were becoming not only a privileged economic class, but also the capitalist managers of hired labor and substantial financial assets. By the 1780s, bonds, mortgages, and other paper instruments accounted for nearly 50 percent of the value of all probated estates in Chester County and nearly 30 percent in nearby Bucks County. As Winifred Rothenberg has argued with regard to the increasing importance of financial assets in Massachusetts after 1780: "The enhanced liquidity of rural portfolios *is* the transformation of the rural economy . . . [and] must loom large in whatever is meant by the coming of capitalism to the . . . village economy."[31] In the Midatlantic region, this transition was the product of aggressive merchants exploiting a buoyant transatlantic market for grain and entrepreneurial landowners mobilizing European migrants for market production.

III

Planters in the southern colonies had long used coerced labor to produce staple crops for the capitalist world economy. During the seventeenth century Chesapeake planters ruthlessly exploited tens of thousands of English indentured servants. Subsequently, they (and the low-country planters of South Carolina) used physical violence to extract labor from hundreds of thousands of African slaves, expropriating the crops, goods, and children that they produced. Social oppression yielded economic prosperity. Per-capita exports from the tobacco colonies of Virginia and Maryland averaged about £3 sterling per free resident around 1770, while exports of rice brought £9 to each white in South Carolina. These systems of coerced-labor, staple-crop production underlay the political power of the Virginia gentry and the fabulous wealth of low-country planters. Of the ten wealthiest men who died in the mainland colonies in 1774, nine made their fortunes in South Carolina.[32]

The traditional rice economy of South Carolina persisted until the 1820s, but the productive system of the Chesapeake region changed in fundamental ways beginning around 1750. To take advantage of the boom in cereal prices, large-scale planters in Maryland and the Northern Neck of Virginia grew wheat and corn for export to Europe and the West Indies. Like Caleb and George Brinton and "improving" landlords in England, they became "vigilant managers." Many planters introduced new technology and a more intensive year-round work routine. They boosted production by using plows (rather than less-efficient hoes). To feed the greater number of draft animals required by plow-agriculture, they expanded the acreage devoted to hay, oats, and other fodder crops. Planters rotated crops and introduced clover and other "English grasses" to increase yields. These "gentlemen farmers" likewise made more efficient use of their labor force, training male slaves as plowmen and women as spinners and weavers. By adopting a different crop mix, new technology, and a sexual division of labor, many planters increased productivity and profits.[33]

Other Chesapeake planters emulated the estate-management practices of English aristocratic landlords. They leased their lands to middling tenants, who then managed the property and its work force. In the early 1790s Robert Carter personally supervised only two of his eighteen plantations. He leased the rest to tenants, fully stocked with slaves, livestock, and equipment. The tenant-managers of Carter's six plantations in eastern Frederick County paid their absentee landlord £490 in rent annually.

Finding the direct exploitation of his 500 slaves to be distasteful, Carter became an urban capitalist. He moved to Baltimore, buying and renting out urban properties and investing in banks and stock.[34]

Other wealthy planters pursued somewhat similar strategies, renting out some of their slaves and land to middling planters and tenant farmers. In Elizabeth City County, Virginia, the top 10 percent of white property owners owned 40 percent of the county's slaves, and hired them out with increasing frequency. Rates varied according to sex and age, with male adults fetching about £10 per year, adult females about £4, and young boys and girls from ten shillings to £1. Hiring-out was profitable for owners, for the average rental was one-fifth of the assessed value of the slave. Ambitious smallholders benefited as well from the ample supply of labor and land; by 1810, tenants cultivated at least the 30 percent of the land in the county that was owned by absentee landlords.[35]

Blacks gained little from the new management practices. In fact, their lives may have become harder and less secure. Hiring-out freed some slaves from close patriarchal control by their masters and gave them somewhat more autonomy in their work lives. But it did not usually result in emancipation through self-purchase. Hiring-out also separated parents from one another and probably resulted in an earlier and more systematic exploitation of the labor of their children. Likewise, vigilant management by profit-minded owners or tenants meant harder year-round labor for many slaves. Most important of all, the labor surplus prompted the sale or forced migration of thousands of slaves. Between 1755 and 1780, over 17,000 Tidewater slaves were moved to newly opened Piedmont plantations. Most of these forced migrants were young and unmarried; a majority were female, purchased either for their tobacco- and corn-planting skills or as capital goods whose offspring would increase the size of the plantation work force. Thus, the Tayloe family sold fifty slaves from its Mount Airy, Virginia, plantation in 1792, and John Tayloe III sold as many more, mostly young girls, between 1809 and 1828. In subsequent decades, Tayloe's sons forcibly moved another 364 slaves from Mount Airy to a brutal life on cotton plantations in Alabama.[36]

The increased emphasis on efficiency and profitability in the late-eighteenth-century Chesapeake may also account for the expansion of the "task system." By the eve of the American Revolution, many slaves in South Carolina already worked under this system of work discipline. Philip Morgan has suggested that tasking represented a partial victory for slaves in the struggle with their masters over the conditions of work. As a contemporary observer noted,

Their work is performed by a daily task, allotted by their master or overseer, which they have generally done by one or two o'clock in the afternoon, and have the rest of the day for themselves, which they spend in working in their own private fields, consisting of 5 or 6 acres of ground, allowed them by their masters, for planting of rice, corn, potatoes, tobacco, &c. for their own use and profit, of which the industrious among them make a great deal.[37]

By creating work incentives for slaves, the task system may have increased planters' profits. The annual rate of return on a 200-acre South Carolina rice plantation with forty slaves was about 25 percent. Alternatively, the high profit margin may simply have reflected the expanding demand and high prices for rice on the transatlantic market. In any event, slaveowners in other regions gradually introduced the task system, using it to increase the output of their labor force. Around 1800, some sugar-plantation managers in the British Caribbean formed their workers into "jobbing or task gangs." They hired them out to planters who paid a fixed amount per acre of ground cleared, holed, or cut. This piecework system made these laborers the hardest-worked of any West Indian slaves.[38]

Chesapeake planters likewise adopted the task system. By the 1770s many masters regularly assigned nightly tasks to their slaves. After dusk, Thomas Anbury reported in 1789, each slave "has a task of [tobacco] stripping allotted which takes them up some hours, or else they have such a quantity of Indian corn to husk, and if they neglect it, are tied up in the morning, and receive a number of lashes."[39] Trapped by their racism and their privileged position in society, Chesapeake planters refused to abolish the relatively inefficient system of coerced labor. Some became rentier-capitalists, leasing their plantations to tenant middlemen and living from their rents. Others remained personally involved with their estates. They became "vigilant managers" who used the market and incentives of hiring-out, tasking, and crop-diversification to enhance their profits. Longtime participants in the capitalist world markets, buying slaves and selling staple crops, they now applied capitalist methods to the productive process itself.

This use of "capitalist" incentives within a coerced-labor system underscored the changing character of the slave regime. Like employers in late-colonial Philadelphia, planters were exploring indirect means of coercion to extract work from laborers. Upland cotton planters established individual tasks for plowing, hoeing, and picking the crop. West Indian planters eventually introduced individual tasking into the cane-holing operation, a job traditionally performed by labor "gangs" under the close supervision of a "driver." Indeed, planter Jonathan Steele of Barbados offered financial inducements to slaves to perform a variety of tasks in a given day. As a British journal, *The Quarterly Review*, noted in 1823, these Caribbean labor experiments were a "means of paving the way for the introduction of voluntary labor on the part of the negroes." In the antebellum southern United States, commentators placed less emphasis on the "ameliorative" aspects of the task system than on its superior economic efficiency. "The advantages of this system," the editor of *Southern Agriculture* suggested, are "the avoidance of watchful superintendence and incessant driving." Whatever the reason, the task system became ever more widespread. "By the 1830's," Morgan has concluded, "a majority of slaves in the Anglo-American world were working by the task."[40]

Despite these changes, slavery remained a coerced system of labor. Masters continued to own property rights in their workers and their offspring and, ultimately, they used physical force (rather than wage incentives or dismissal) to extract labor. The task system worked to the advantage of slaves only in a few regions. The overwhelming numerical dominance of blacks in the South Carolina low country, combined with absentee ownership and a lucrative crop, gave slaves enviable and unusual opportunities. By the late eighteenth century, they were able not only to regulate their work lives but also to acquire property rights—in garden plots, in cash or goods exchanged for vegetables and chickens, and in mules and horses—and to pass them to their offspring. They lived both as coerced laborers and as proto-peasants, producing food for market sale.[41] In other areas the task system served the masters' interests, maintaining output while reducing the supervision costs of "gang" labor. Even so, the transition to tasking gave slaves the chance to bargain over workloads and, like dependent peasants elsewhere, to win privileges or to establish "customs" limiting exploitation.

By the early nineteenth century, tens of thousands of rural white workers in the northern states were also doing task-work. Like the Jackson boys, they worked for storekeepers or merchant entrepreneurs on a piecework basis, fabricating shoes, or brooms, or straw hats, or cloth. As the rising corporation lawyer and politician Daniel Webster noted perceptively in 1814, these men and women lacked autonomy. Although formally free, a worker employed in a factory or an elaborately subdivided putting-out system was "necessarily at the mercy of the capitalist for the support of himself and his family . . . [for he was] utterly incapable of making and carrying to market in his own account the smallest entire article."[42]

Slave hiring-out or tasking, handicraft piecework, and agricultural or factory wage labor were hardly identical forms of work-discipline. Yet they may be viewed as regional versions of an emergent capitalist system of social relations. The specific character of each regional labor system was determined, in large measure, by local traditions and social conventions. As Robert Brenner has argued with respect to the transition from feudalism to capitalism in early modern Europe, the impact of new causal forces—demographic, commercial, or political—in a given region depended upon "certain *historically specific* patterns of the development of the contending agrarian classes and their relative strength, . . . their relationship to the non agricultural classes, . . . and to the state."[43]

IV

The American War of Independence accelerated the transition to a regionally diverse capitalist society in various ways. The war disrupted the import trade, prompting the expansion of traditional home manufactures and the appearance of new rural enterprises. Wartime opportunities likewise sharpened the acquisitive instincts of thousands of farmers, both capitalist and yeoman. "The raised price of grain," the Assistant Foragemaster of the Continental Army complained in 1779, had created an "unwillingness of the Farmers to part with it while there is a prospect of a still greater advance in the Price." Merchants invested in both speculative ventures, such as privateering and government bonds, and new productive enterprises—banks, textile factories, wagons, ships, equipment, grist- and sawmills. The new American republics came out of the war with more household producers, more domestic traders, and a more highly developed market economy.[44]

Nonetheless, the results of the war also inhibited the expansion of domestic capitalism. By opening western lands for settlement, the Paris Treaty of 1783 drained off part of the surplus agricultural population, retarding the expansion of rural industry. By providing American merchants with the status of neutral carriers, independence also diverted capital into maritime investments during the wars of the French Revolution. Finally, as Michael Merrill has argued, the war increased the political influence of a "self-conscious class of small property holders" who demanded government policies "designed to enrich 'producers' rather than 'moneyed men.' "[45]

Tensions between yeomen farmers and capitalist entrepreneurs were not new in the 1790s, but the context was. Independence revealed the potential power of the state legislatures to advance American economic development and, in the process, to favor one social group over others.

A comparison of the dynamics of economic change in North Carolina in the 1760s and Rhode Island in the 1790s suggests the dimensions of this transition to a locally controlled system of political economy.

The North Carolina backcountry initially stood at the periphery of the transatlantic capitalist economy. Most settlers in Anson, Granville, and Orange counties were subsistence-plus farmers. They grew enough food to feed their families and bartered the surplus for imported salt, sugar, cloth, and farm implements. Beginning in the 1750s, enterprising planters invested heavily in slaves to take advantage of the rising market prices for wheat and tobacco. The number of slaves in Anson County multiplied by a factor of 14.5 between 1754 and 1767. To buy slaves, land, and equipment, planters went into debt to newly resident Scotch traders. When tobacco prices collapsed between 1759 and 1763, the less able planters, or the less lucky, found themselves in court. Merchants brought an average of ninety suits per year in Orange County between 1763 and 1765, as opposed to only seven per year during the previous decade.[46]

Legal confrontation prompted political upheaval. Led by Herman Husband, a migrant from Maryland with investments in milling, land speculation, and iron production, local planters formed a Regulation Movement. Regulators attacked "Scotch merchants" with verbal abuse and physical force, threatening "to kill all the Clerks and Lawyers" who were their political allies. Between 1768 and 1771, Regulators closed courts, harassed lawyers and judges, and destroyed the stores of merchants. Finally, in 1771, Royal Governor Tryon mobilized the eastern militia and suppressed the Regulation with armed force.[47]

The North Carolina Regulation illustrated the difficulty of capitalist agricultural transformation in a labor-scarce region by dramatizing the links among cultural values, political conflict, and economic change. Market production required the purchase of imported slaves with British mercantile credit.[48] Some capitalist planters in Orange County joined the Regulation because they resented the economic and political ascendancy of the new creditor class of merchants and lawyers, who filled one of the county's two assembly seats from 1762 to 1776. Yeomen farmers were equally hostile. Depicting themselves as "poor families" and "industrious peasants," they used the Regulation to protest against the new structure of credit. Like smallholders in New England, they expected flexible debt relationships; local creditors usually carried unpaid debts for two or three years and rarely charged interest. Yeomen therefore allied with their entrepreneurial neighbors to oppose the demands of "foreign" merchants.[49] Finally, the Regulation pointed to the ultimate importance of government power in upholding bargains made in the marketplace. Governor Tryon's intervention decisively upheld the authority of the court system and the legally sanctioned system of capitalist credit.

Tryon acted to protect the interests of Scottish merchants and the British mercantile system. For similar reasons Parliament passed the Currency Act of 1764, which protected British merchants from currency-depreciation schemes in Virginia and other colonies. Parliament likewise considered a ban on British migration to America in the 1770s, a measure that would have undermined the labor supply of Caleb Brinton and other Midatlantic farmers. And a long series of Parliamentary statutes sought to prevent the fabrication and sale of American manufactures. The entrepreneurial activities of Sylvanus Hussey and Martha Ballard could not expect encouragement from the home government. Within the British mercantile system, Americans were doomed to positions of inferiority and exploitation. "Every shilling gained by America" through the tobacco trade, Daniel Dulany noted bitterly in 1764, "hath entered in Britain and fallen into the pockets of the British merchants, traders, manufacturers and land holders, and it may therefore be justly called the British commerce." The rapid maturation of the American economy after 1775 proceeded in part from the demise of British mercantilism.[50]

The speed and character of economic development now depended on the balance of social and political power between yeomen farmers and capitalist entrepreneurs in the new American states. In 1734, the Rhode Island assembly had passed a Mill Act that allowed millowners to flood upstream agricultural land in return for court-assessed "rent" payments. This measure prevented farmers from using the traditional common-law remedies of trespass or public nuisance to protect their property. As Gary Kulik has argued, the act "was a form of eminent domain, sanctioning the enforced loan of privately-held land." Most farmers accepted this loss of property rights because the dams usually powered much-needed saw- or grist mills. Moreover, Fish Acts explicitly directed millowners to provide fish-runs around the dams, so that upstream farmers and their neighbors would continue to have a free supply of protein-rich food.[51]

Beginning in 1765, entrepreneurial ironmasters waged a fifty-year struggle for complete control of Rhode Island's rivers and streams. To make the most efficient year-round use of their blast furnaces and iron forges, they successfully sought exemptions from the Fish Acts. Farmers fought back. In 1773, their representatives secured passage of "An act making it lawful to break down and blow up Rocks at Pawtucket Falls to let fish pass up." The statute affirmed the common-law right of the populace to remove "public nuisances"—in this case a mill dam built of "Rocks"—by public action.[52]

The balance of power within Rhode Island shifted in the aftermath of the American Revolution. To encourage domestic manufactures, the Assembly sacrificed the interests of farmers and grist-mill operators to those of cotton-mill owners. In 1793, for example, the assembly specifically exempted the cotton mill constructed by Samuel Slater on the Pawtucket River from the Fish Act. In neighboring Massachusetts, a development-minded General Court chartered the Massachusetts Bank in 1784, lending the prestigious name of the Commonwealth to a private, capitalist institution. The Court granted an exclusive franchise to the Charles River Bridge Company in 1785; allowed millowners to rent (rather than have to purchase) flooded agricultural lands in 1796; and granted millions of acres of land in the District of Maine to well-connected capitalist speculators.[53] In nearly every state, enterprising capitalist merchants, manufacturers, and speculators won government support for their projects.

The success of these "projectors" was never assured and always difficult, for yeomen farmers and planters were now a formidable political force. Responding to smallholder demands, the New York legislature issued £250,000 in paper currency in 1786, earmarking it to buy soldiers' warrants and pay interest on war bonds previously issued by the state loan office. This measure ignored the demands of "stockjobbers" who wanted the state to pay off Loan Office certificates at face value. In Pennsylvania, farmers condemned the "amazing desire to accumulate wealth" of Robert Morris and other merchant backers of the Bank of North America. Arguing that "the commercial interest is already too powerful, and an overbalance to the landed interest," rural assemblymen repealed the bank's charter in 1785, only to see it restored two years later.[54]

For the next generation, state and national legislators continued to divide over two rival systems of political economy. One set of policies, favored by Alexander Hamilton and the Federalist Party, would use the power of the state to assist "monied men," merchants and financiers, and to pursue a "capitalist" path of commercial development. Some state legislatures actively embraced this approach, enacting hard-money laws and liberally granting economic privileges to aspiring entrepreneurs. Such measures often brought public as well as private benefits. "Our monied capital has so much increased from the Introduction of Banks, & the Circulation of the Funds," Philadelphia merchant William Bingham noted in 1791, "that the Necessity of Soliciting Credits [from England] will no longer exist, & the Means will be provided for putting in Motion every Species of Industry."[55]

Other state governments pursued the public good by spreading political favors more broadly. Their policies, advocated by Thomas Jefferson, James Madison, and the Democratic-Republican Party, favored "producers," yeomen farmers and artisans, and embodied an "agrarian" model of commercial society. To assist land-hungry tenant farmers and credit-hungry yeomen families, legislatures created state land banks, gave legal rights to "squatters," and divided frontier districts into small, affordable tracts. This legislation was the product, in many cases, of dozens of petitions from scores, even hundreds, of ordinary Americans. The "true Policy of a Republic," argued ninety Virginians who wanted land "in moderate Quantities, by Way of Head Rights," consisted in laws that assisted "the Poor and Needy to raise their Families to be reputable and useful Members of Society."[56]

Whatever their differences, these two systems of political economy assumed the existence of a vibrant market system. The newfound centrality of the "market" in American ideology and society foreshadowed the eventual triumph of the monied interest. For the market, along with private property, wage labor, and sophisticated financial instruments, constituted the institutional core of early modern "capitalism." In the short space of the fifty years between 1750 and 1800, these ingredients of a capitalist order had risen in prominence as the traditional limitations on economic development in America—the shortage of labor, of extensive markets, of entrepreneurs, and of political purpose—had been overcome. For better or for worse, perhaps a little of each, the United States would confront the nineteenth century as an increasingly capitalist commercial society.

Opening the American Countryside

RICHARD L. BUSHMAN

THE RECENT WORK on agriculture in early America has moved the study of farm life more fully into the mainstream of social history, where it certainly belongs. For years agricultural history was the work of specialists who understood the technological intricacies of farming and interpreted them for more general historians. It was a subject for people who understood farming from the inside, and the generality of historians gratefully accepted the conclusions of the specialists without delving into the details of plow design and animal breeds. Larger synthetic works paid scant attention to farm work, tools, crop and animal distributions, household production, and soil rejuvenation, and instead dealt only with the most general aspects of agricultural labor systems, lines of trade, and landownership. More recently, however, scholars who would not define themselves as agricultural historians have turned their attention to agriculture, and, building on the older studies, have incorporated elaborate investigations of farm life into more general analyses of social development. These recent works have gone a long way toward integrating agriculture into social history, and have given activities on the farm and in the farmhouse the central position they deserve.[1]

One peculiar disjunction in the emerging picture of American agriculture, however, has not yet been confronted. American agriculture does not conform to the well-established phases of agricultural development in Europe and more particularly England. In our historiography, American agriculture is strangely out of step in that it does not undergo the first stages of improvement that are called, somewhat dramatically, the "first agricultural revolution." In the broadest sense, the term "agricultural revolution" refers to the improvements in agricultural productivity that have taken place virtually all around the globe in modern times. In their classic form, the improvements came along in three phases. The first phase, which began in England and Holland in the seventeenth and eighteenth centuries and carried over into the nineteenth, saw the spread of root crops like turnips, of nitrogen-fixing legumes such as clover, improved breeds of livestock, the practice of alternating tillage and pasture and of continuous cropping—in short an array of piecemeal improvements aimed at enhancing productivity. In the second phase, which began in the midnineteenth century, agriculture was mechanized. The third phase, the biochemical revolution of the last forty years, is still in progress.[2] America clearly participated in the second and third. phases, but its role in the first is ambiguous.

For many years, the first agricultural revolution was the subject of an intensive debate among English agricultural historians. The question was when did it occur—in the sixteenth century, when signs of improvement were seen in many places, or in the eighteenth century, when reforms became widespread. The debate served to focus scholarly attention on scores of specific practices: penning animals to collect their manure, the construction of water meadows, the development of new strains of cattle, and so on. A hundred specific details could be linked to the general notion of the improvement of production, enabling researchers to comb the records with a host of specific questions in mind. Nearly everything had meaning in terms of this one question: were farmers improving or not?[3]

With all this activity in English scholarship, it would seem that American agricultural historians would have borrowed the idea of agricultural improvement from the English for the analysis of colonial farms. The first agricultural revolution was taking place in the very years when the colonies were being settled; why not organize the study of American farm practices by describing the agricultural revolution in America as English historians were tracing the changes in Britain? The problem for American historians was that America appeared to have departed from the three-phase sequence of agricultural improvement by skipping the first phase. In our histories, American farms pass through the last two phases, mechanization and the biological revolution, but not the first, the period of turnips, clover, and improved breeds. Wayne Rasmussen calls the years from 1840 to 1870, when mechanization began in earnest, "The First American Agricultural Revolution." In Clarence Danhof's

Change in Agriculture, the first phase is combined with the second. As Danhof sees it, improvements in plant varieties, manuring, and livestock breeds blended with the adoption of mechanical devices, notably the hay rake, the thresher, and the harvester, in a single period of rapid change. While acknowledging a few pioneering efforts at reform before 1800, Danhof believes that the significant changes leading to the modern system of agriculture were concentrated after 1820, when America caught up with all the preceding improvements in English agriculture at the same time as farm operations were mechanized. For these historians, there was no first phase contemporaneous with England's piecemeal adoption of agricultural improvements from the sixteenth century on.[4]

If this is true, agriculture, among all aspects of American culture, was most *retardataire*. While the colonists rapidly assimilated fashions in costume, furniture design, and architecture, they lagged behind English advances in farming, the essential business of most Americans, by more than a century. Observers at the time in many ways confirm this judgment. They did note signs of change in the late colonial period. When the agricultural craze came over England in the latter half of the eighteenth century, a few well-placed Americans began to emulate their English counterparts. They corresponded on agricultural subjects, wrote books, and organized societies.[5] But for quite some time, the efforts of the agricultural avant garde had little effect on American farming as a whole. The slovenly practices of American farmers appalled William Strickland, the emissary of the English Board of Agriculture who traveled in America in 1794 and 1795. In his journey from New England to Virginia, Strickland saw slight evidence of modern rational farming that the first agricultural revolution had brought to England.[6]

The reason for American lack of interest in agricultural reform is not hard to find. With so much land available, there were easier ways to increase production than by improving fertility. Many of the so-called improvements made no sense for land-rich, labor-poor American farmers, and they wisely held back.[7] That is probably why we appear to have had no agricultural revolution in the colonial period. But perhaps we have been premature in this conclusion. The absence of one kind of change did not mean the absence of all change. Behind the improvements in English agriculture was the booming market for foodstuffs. American farmers responded to the market just as their European counterparts did, but in distinctively American ways. Following a pattern of their own, American farmers began to change their practices well before 1820, with accompanying changes in rural culture. Looking at these peculiarly American alterations in farm practices between 1750 and 1850, we can discern the outlines of a major change that was our version of the first agricultural revolution.

I

The reason the agricultural revolution took a different form in England is that the starting point for English agriculture was so different from what it was in America. When it came to improvements, the central problem for English farmers was the maintenance of soil fertility. The yields of new lands dropped over the years as more nutriments were taken from the soil than man or nature replaced. In the arable regions of England, where the bulk of the grains were grown, farmers mitigated soil depletion by rotating their crops. In the conventional three-year rotation, farmers planted a winter grain the first year, such as wheat or rye, followed it the next with a spring grain, barley, oats, or pulses, and left the land to rest the third. That rest period, plus what dung the farmers had to spread, probably kept yields at around ten or twelve bushels an acre. The most important improvements of the first agricultural revolution simply enhanced this system. In the fallow years, the farmers planted clover, or one of the other leguminous herbs which took nitrogen from the air and fixed it in the soil. Farmers learned to feed their sheep by day on one location, and pen them on fallow lands by night, so that the animals gave more to the soil in their dung than they took through feeding. These enriched pastures and clover-planted fallows, when converted back to tillage, yielded nearly twice as much grain as before.[8]

The reasons the colonists failed to adopt these improvements when word of them spread was that American farmers did not practice rotational agriculture in the English manner. They had other methods for keeping up yields and reviving the soil. From the beginning, the settlers had reverted to the shifting agriculture practiced in jungle areas of the globe and in other places with an abundance of land. After clearing the trees, the colonists planted continuously for six or seven years until yields dropped, and then cleared new fields. The old fields grew up in bushes and saplings while gradually recovering their strength. Later reformers, who thought the practice primitive and reprehensible, said farmers entirely abandoned the soil "to such weeds, or plants, as are useless, or nearly so to man and animals, for a greater or less period, under some vague notion, that the land will recruit itself, in a few years, and be fit again for cultivation."[9] Probably animals grazed the fallow lands lightly in the summer, just as they grazed in virgin wooded areas. After twenty years of this long fallow, the land recuperated and was ready for reclaiming and replanting.[10]

We associate shifting agriculture most closely with tobacco culture because of the notorious demands tobacco made on the soil. But corn, a front-runner among the soil-exhausting crops, wore out the land in New England and the Middle Colonies just as tobacco depleted the Chesapeake. In New England the concentration on cattle for market production extended the cycle a little. Pasture required less from the land than cropping. When the corn patch was moved to a new clearing, the old field could be used for grazing. But without supplemental feed for the animals, they would eventually deplete the land until not even grass would grow.[11] To the critical eye of the reformer, New England was no more enlightened than the other regions. William Logan, Jared Eliot's correspondent, was disappointed at what he found on his visit to Connecticut in 1755. "I Can't say I met With anything Instructive relating to Farming in your Parts," he wrote, "I think the contrary, and that the Slovenlyness too generally prevails and that Nature does more for your People in general than they do by any Industry." Rather than refurbishing the soil, the New Englanders, like everyone else, let it go to rubbish fallow to work itself back on its own.[12]

The long-fallow method of land management had two interesting effects worthy of mention. The most noticeable was the appearance of the countryside. Long fallow gave the land a scruffy, unkempt look, since most of the land at any given time was uncultivated or uncleared. In the early years of settlement, probably no more than 10 percent was open for crops, pasture, and meadow. By 1760 about 40 percent was cleared in the highly developed farming areas of Chester County, Pennsylvania. In Massachusetts somewhat less than that was opened in the majority of Massachusetts towns. In 1784 in the state's most urbanized area, Suffolk County circling west and south of Boston, 49 percent of the land was cleared, but in Berkshire Country in the west only 24 percent.[13] The rest was in uncut woodland or in rubbish fallow growing up in bushes and saplings. With the useful life of the land on the average about ten years, and ten to twenty years of fallow required to bring it back, at least half of the once-cleared land at any given time would be reverting to undergrowth, with the exception of places where pasture extended the land's use. Another substantial portion was kept in woods to meet the ravenous demands of the fireplace and to supply construction timbers. Altogether the landscape appeared more closed than open. Gloria Main's description of seventeenth-century Maryland applied generally to the colonies: "The thick stands of trees alternated with abandoned and overgrown fields, all interspersed with small clearings and occasional wooden buildings, many of them quite ramshackle."[14] The landscape appeared as patches of smooth space amidst an enclosing roughness.

There was a second interesting effect of long-fallow agriculture: it made a difference in fencing. In England, hedges most commonly divided fields and contained the animals. Hedges were permanent, they harbored small game animals, and their cuttings were a source of fuel —all significant advantages. And yet hedges were virtually unknown in America until late in the eighteenth century. A French visitor of refined sensibilities complained of the American countryside's ceaseless "fences or dry hedges, of which one never ceases to have a boring view."[15] There were practical reasons for the absence of hedges. Many hedge plants could not hold up through cold winters, wood fences were relatively cheap in a land with ample timber, and they were easy to build. The worm-rail, zigzag, or Virginia fence, as it was variously called, could be thrown up very quickly once the rails were split. But there was also an advantage to rail fences that was related to long-fallow agriculture. They were portable. Under long fallow, the fields were constantly shifting about, and rail fences could be moved with the field, thus saving most of the labor that went into fence construction. It was a comparatively small matter that worm-rail fences used up space and looked sloppy compared to a stone fence or a well-kept hedge. They were clearly the best suited to the overall system of land management. Phillip Fithian noted that in Virginia in 1774, "they plant large Quantities of Land without any Manure, and work it very hard to make the best of the Crop, and when the crop comes off they take away the Fences to inclose another Piece of Land for the next years tillage. . . ."[16] In fact, because the worm-rail fence was so well suited to shifting agriculture, changes in fencing serve as indicators of changes in other practices. Hedges and stone fences marked the passing of long-fallow agriculture and the establishment of permanent, continuously cropped fields.

By 1750 changes were occurring. The general direction was away from long fallow toward continuous cropping and permanent fields, in short a change from extensive to intensive agriculture. The changes proceeded gradually, perhaps imperceptibly to the participants themselves. The new practices in American husbandry emerged gradually out of the old, just as the first phase of the English agricultural revolution was essentially a series of small improvements in the traditional rotational system. A year or two was added to the life of a field through extra dunging; a decision was made to keep a field in permanent use and a longer-lasting fence was built to enclose it; grass was sown on a worn-out cornfield to make a better pasture; or fruit trees were planted to start an orchard. By such small steps affecting only a field here and there, American farmers moved toward a new agricultural system.[17]

The pressures to change came from many directions, but I wish to emphasize two. The first was the long-term improvement in agricultural markets as the curve of European population turned upward in the latter half of the eighteenth century.[18] Continuous cropping was an aspect of commercialization, a sign of market influence. As prices improved, it was natural to try to extract one more harvest from a field before throwing it into fallow, even though the farmer knew the land would suffer. The improvement in prices made marginal lands profitable. Even a small harvest was better than none at all when prices were up. Or he cleared an old field of rubbish to make it more suitable for sheep pasture as wool prices rose. In 1838 a critic of this rash course, looking back on the change, attributed continual cropping to "the haste to be rich."[19]

The second influence was cultural rather than commercial. After the middle of the eighteenth century, agricultural reformers began to admonish farmers to give up extensive agriculture in favor of intensive use of the land. The reformers, most often intellectuals who had found a cause rather than practicing farmers, so badgered the rural population that no one who aspired to any degree of respectability could disregard their instructions with impunity. The holdouts were castigated as indolent and ignorant. Culture and commerce thus worked together against long fallow and in favor of continuous cropping.

By the middle of the eighteenth century, travelers were noticing the difference. They commented that in some places the countryside was open, clear, and pleasant, quite different from the heavy woodlands and unkempt rubbish fallow noted earlier. Especially near towns, where farmlands benefited from the stimulus of the market, the countryside opened out. Alexander Hamilton, the Annapolis physician who rode through New England in 1744, found the lands between Boston and Cambridge "inclosed with fine stone fences," and noted that "the country all around is open and pleasant. . . ."[20] Those were the towns surrounding Boston that showed 70 to 80 percent cleared land in the 1784 tax valuations. Town markets had the effect of clearing the nearby land for more intensive use, and the opening of the countryside proceeded outward from such places along the best transportation routes.

Robert Honyman, a Scots physician traveling north from Virginia in 1775, noted in his journal upon reaching the Eastern Shore of Maryland that the planters there "begin to go upon the plan that begins to be followed as in Virginia." The plan he had in mind was "of having several large fields, and putting them in grain of several kinds and letting them rest alternatively and in rotation," the English rotation system as contrasted to the American method of long fallow. Honyman made no mention of clover or grasses needed to complete the rotation and maintain fertility under a system of convertible husbandry, but he did observe that in Maryland "they . . . Dung from their Cow houses and not by penning as in Virginia," both acceptable methods of improved agriculture.[21] Honyman identified those local farmers who, along with contemporaries in Virginia, had made the transition to continuous agriculture with appropriate manuring in a rotational system.

The spotty progress of the new methods revealed itself a few miles farther east on the Delmarva Peninsula beyond Middletown, where Honyman said the roads were good, "but the country is not so well-cleared as on the other side, only near the Towns. . . ."[22] The closing in of woods and scrub as he traveled along was not a sign of poor land. Honyman thought the soil good, and that particular stretch was in fact the best land in the state. The pressures for continuous cropping simply had not reached farms that far from the waterways. Near the towns, where urban markets worked their influence, Honyman again found open countryside.

Fencing began to change along with the alteration in the overall system. The stone fences near Boston which Hamilton saw were a good sign of permanent fields. They cost two or three times more labor than rail fences and were only practical where fields were to stay put. The transition to continuous cropping, along with the disappearance of woodlands, made consideration of alternatives to rail fencing worthwhile. Stone fences came into their own in New England at the end of the eighteenth century, and in the Middle Colonies hedges enjoyed a season of popularity about the same time. John Beal Bordley, a gentleman farmer and lawyer of the Eastern Shore, wrote in 1799 that the shortage of timber would necessitate attention to better fencing, but apart from the timber supply, "whether we have large or small portions of rail timber on our estates, it is advisable that a beginning be immediately made towards acquiring permanent live fences."[23] The French visitor to Delaware happily reported that "what gives the eye the greatest pleasure in the eight or nine miles before reaching Newcastle are the living hedges peculiar to this section." Hedging became a subject of propagandizing and debate in Delaware after the turn of the century. "Good fences of durable material," even if not up to the standards of English hedges, were indicators of "finished husbandry" in the approved modern style.[24] As late as 1850, 79 percent of all rural fencing, it is estimated, was still worm-rail, but after 1800 the new agriculture, coupled with the shortage of timber, made consideration of more substantial and more respectable fences interesting to American farmers for the first time.[25]

By the beginning of the nineteenth century, travelers' accounts and other kinds of evidence suggest that improving farmers in all the more settled portions of the United States were beginning to crop continuously on permanent fields, building more stable fences. Less and less land was left in rubbish fallow. To the observer the countryside appeared to open up. We are not left to surmise the appearance of the nineteenth-century landscape as the changes came over it; the Massachusetts tax-valuation lists record the growing amount of cleared land. In Worcester County in central Massachusetts, the amount of cleared land—tillage, meadow, and pasture—compared to closed land—woodland, unimproved, and unimprovable—increased 76 percent between 1801 and 1850. By the middle of the century the median of cleared land in fifty-eight Worcester County towns was 62 to 63 percent. Judging from land usage in urban areas along the coast, 80 to 85 percent was maximum usage, suggesting that the Worcester County towns were approaching full utilization of workable land by 1850.[26]

The naive painters, who began to make their own records of the countryside in the first half of the century, tell much the same story. The pictures show large stretches of open space, broken with fence and tree lines, and graced with well-kept, painted farmhouses. The countryside had become an extended field, interrupted by patches of trees, rather than a tangle of trees and bushes interspersed with occasional cultivated lands and pastures as before. The pictures do not represent conditions everywhere.[27] Long-fallow agriculture was still practiced in the nineteenth century, particularly on newly opened western land. Even in settled areas in the East, the old style must have continued. In five of fifty-eight Worcester County towns, cleared land hovered around 40 percent in 1850.[28] The paintings do not tell the whole story for a reason. Among their other advantages, permanently cleared fields were fashionable, the sign of a progressive farmer. It was the people who practiced the stylish new methods who wished to show off their holdings, cleared of trees and brush, cultivated, fenced, and well under control. The old-style farmer had less to show off and may even have suffered embarrassment at the appearance of his fields. Paintings, often commissioned by the proud farmer himself, exaggerate the extent of the change to continuous cropping, but they surely record the fact that in many regions, the countryside was steadily opening in the first half of the nineteenth century.[29] The clearing of the land represents one palpable measure of agricultural change.

II

What did more cleared land mean for farmers? The technical innovations in farm practices are interesting in themselves, but we really want to know how individual farmers were affected. Were their lives improved along with their farms? In some respects the transition to continuous cropping after 1750 appears to have added to their difficulties. For one thing, it brought American farmers face to face with the old nemesis of European agriculture: soil depletion. Farmers who had avoided the problem through most of the colonial period by clearing new fields and letting the old ones rest for long stretches now had most of their farms in active use and little uncleared land to turn to. The old fields yielded less and less, and there was no reserve of uncleared land to replace them. Farmers who were still committed to older methods worked the land continuously without doing much to maintain its strength, steadily draining the soil of nutriments. The first phase of the agricultural revolution in America, instead of improving fertility as in England, actually decreased yields per acre, precipitating what contemporaries thought of as an agricultural crisis. "Continual cropping will destroy the best soils," one agricultural writer commented. "There must be change or rest; it is preposterous to talk of not understanding the reason of land growing poorer, while the suicidal course adopted by many of our farmers is persisted in."[30]

But it took one backward step to prepare for two forward. Continuous cropping brought American farmers to the starting line where English improvements began—an acknowledged need for better methods of soil management. As the soil wore down, and the need became obvious, the new methods were put into practice, and the soil was built up again. In the decades after 1800, farming moved in two directions at once: while continuous cropping depleted the soil, agricultural improvements restored it. There were many reports of a crisis in agriculture in all the cultivated regions along the Atlantic coast, but also of efforts to restore fertility. Strickland, looking on the dark side as always, said farmers did introduce a fallow year into their rotation, "but the fallow is stated to be so very imperfect, as to be little better than the rubbish pasture. . . ." But he admitted that in the Middle Colonies "clover is in some places just beginning to be introduced, and is said to increase the produce of wheat at least five bushels to the acre. . . ."[31] Timothy Dwight, a New England booster, reported in 1796 that "the cultivation of clover has become a considerable object, and the use of gypsum been widely extended." The entire aspect of the farm was improving. "Fences are in many instances better made. The quantity of labor is frequently confined to a smaller extent of ground, and farms in many places are assuming a neater and more thrifty aspect."[32] In the village of Riverhead on Long Island, after yields declined markedly at the end of the eighteenth century, farmers began changing their ways. By 1820 they were carting and plowing in dung, spreading fish on the soil, and alternating clover and grass pastures with corn and potatoes.[33] The charges of ignorance and stubbornness that filled the agricultural handbooks and the correspondence between gentlemen farmers seem now to have been beside the point. Apparently as farmers felt the need and developed confidence in the new methods, they were put into effect.[34]

With agriculture moving in two directions simultaneously, it would be hard to guess the overall direction of productivity. Did declining yields under continuous cropping lower overall productivity, or did the adoption of improved methods raise it? Either seems possible. In 1969 Clarence Danhof surmised that before 1840, when improvements were just being adopted, "early gains in productivity were offset by continuing declines in the fertility of soils that had long been cultivated. . . . Net gains in productivity did not become substantial until after 1840."[35] Although a plausible surmise, it proved to be wrong. A subsequent analysis of production figures showed the reverse to be true. Working with the series prepared by Marvin Towne and Wayne Rasmussen, Robert Gallman concluded that output per worker and output per dollar investment in land in constant dollars (roughly equivalent to output per acre) were both increasing between 1800 and 1840. In fact the rate of growth in the 1820s and 1830s was much higher than in any other decade in the nineteenth century, including the period after 1840 when mechanization spread.[36] The exact reasons for the startling increase have yet to be determined, but it seems safe to say that a combination of all the factors that went into the first phase of the agricultural revolution in America had more of an effect than we had thought. The efficiencies of continuous cropping, better manuring, better-balanced rotations, and improvements in tool design must have made the difference.[37] Perhaps most important was the effect of increased individual exertions under the stimulus of the market. The same influences that led farmers to work their land harder made them work themselves and their families harder too.[38]

Individual farmers seem then to have benefited from these increases in productivity, but it was not inevitable that they would. Farmers' income would not have gone up if they had not made an important decision about their families. They could have divided their lands into smaller and smaller parcels to give each child a farm. There had always been a problem in providing for all the offspring in a large family. Some had been forced to migrate or take up trades from early in the eighteenth century. Judging from the high demand for western lands, however, young people in the nineteenth century still wanted to farm.[39] About 2.3 million new farms were opened up between 1820 and 1870.[40] With the improvements in production, farm parents might have concluded that a smaller amount of land could support a family, and broken up

their holdings to give each child a portion. In that case improved productivity would not have meant increased income for each farm family.
More children would have received land, but they would have stayed at
about the same income level. Parents, however, did not make that decision. Both studies of individual communities and a large sampling of
northern farms show that farm size remained at a respectable level. In
Concord between 1749 and 1850, the average number of landowners
oscillated narrowly between 194 and 213, and the average size of landholding between 56 and 61 acres per owner.[41] In the Bateman-Faust
sample of farm households in 102 townships from Kansas to New Hampshire in 1860, the average number of acres per farm was 126, and in
the oldest areas, the average farm size was 109 acres. The older-area
farms were smaller, but the number of improved acres on each was
larger, 78 acres per farm, as contrasted to 67 acres on the average in
the newer regions. Farm size remained up everywhere through 1860,
not just in newly opened territory. In his study of farm-family fertility
in the midnineteenth century, Richard Easterlin concluded that "it appears that farm households in older areas were having fewer children,
despite a greater capacity to support them."[42]

The consequences of the decision not to divide farms surely had significant implications for farm life. Combining greater productivity with
maintenance of farm size can only mean an increase of income per farm
on the average. If anything, that was more true in crowded older areas
than in new regions. The overall value of farms in older areas was 50
percent greater than in new areas, a measure of the old farms' superior
earning power.[43] Falling prices for farm products did not weaken farm
income, either. Farm prices oscillated, it is true, but in close synchronization with the price index for all commodities, so that a drop in farm
prices did not mean a drop in purchasing power. All told it seems clear
that as productivity rose, so did real farm income.[44]

III

The changes in farm practices and the resulting increase in real income
bring us to the question of rural culture. For the increase in productivity
and farm income is only half of the story of agricultural development.
There was a cultural side to the first agricultural revolution as palpable
and far-reaching as the transition to continuous cropping. Culturally
speaking, the farmer was not in as advantageous a position as we sometimes think in our fascination with agrarianism. He was, it is true, the
beneficiary of the classical tradition of agrarian writing that exalted the

simple virtues of rural life over the corruptions of the city, an attitude expressed in Jefferson's *Notes on Virginia*. But the agricultural reformers, who monopolized the literature for and about farmers, were not full of praise for plain farmers. They credited only the improving farmers with the rural virtues. Plain farmers practicing traditional agriculture were thought to be improvident and wasteful. American reformers, like their English counterparts, often as not spoke of the ordinary farmer as lazy and slow-witted. Strickland, as I have said, thought of the mass of the farmers as "ignorant, uneducated, poor, and indolent." John Beal Bordley, an American, was equally critical. "In many parts of America," he wrote in 1799, "are idle improvident people, masters of farms, who spend their time in taverns or other places of wasteful amusement: any where rather than at *home*. These haunts are at the expense of their *domestic* happiness." "*Such a people* can never be brought to soil cattle, or at all improve their farms." "The meanness, the selfishness and the folly of these *husbands, fathers* or *masters*, are conspicuous, degrading and shameful. . . ." "They mount their horses and hurry to the tavern, the race, nine-pins, billiards, excess upon excess of toddy, and the most nonsensical and idle chat, accompanied with exclamations and roarings, brutal and foreign to common sense and manners as the mind of wisdom can conceive of depraved man."[45]

The vast agricultural press that came into being after 1819, ostensibly to aid the farmer, was not much more complimentary. The editors' efforts to defend farm life began with the assumption that it was under attack. "There is a belief in this country," one of them said, "that agriculture is a vulgar occupation." A farmer writing from Batavia, Illinois, said that the farmer's boasted independence consisted of "an absolute denial of most of the comforts and refinements of life, indispensably necessary to maintain a creditable station in society."[46] Silas Deane at the turn of the century thought it unfortunate that agriculture was commonly considered "below the attention of any persons, excepting those who are in the lowest walks of life; or, that persons of a liberal or polite education should think it intolerably degrading to them, to attend to practical agriculture for their support." Writer after writer spoke of farm life as coarse, intellectually debilitating, and lacking in desirable refinement. Judging from comments in the press, the loss of children to the city made the cultural deprivation of farm life most painful. The editors rebuked the sons and daughters who left "in pursuit of some genteel mode of living," and who preferred "some more easy sedentary occupation with the fallacious idea of appearing genteel in the eyes of the world."[47]

At the same time that the editors deplored the lure of genteel living, their pages instructed farmers in good manners, how to set a proper table with napkins and glasses, and how to eat with a fork rather than a knife, in an effort to introduce refinement into rural households. Farm journals offered recipes for such staples of elegant life as Beef Soup à la Française and an "excellent polish for mahogany." An essay entitled "Make Farm Life Attractive" acknowledged that children found farm work dull, monotonous, and totally lacking in mental stimulation and so left for the city to achieve a "certain means of refinement." The trouble was that "on the farm, very frequently are rooms without books, walls without pictures, manners without grace, clothes without fitness and grounds without shaping and decoration." To hold their children, farmers had to introduce curtains, swept floors, carpets, and of course a parlor, plus creating a front yard with lawn, shrubs, and a picket fence. There had to be a realm, in many ways a feminine realm, set off from the animals, dirt, and sweat that were the farm's natural environment.[48]

As those cultural pressures built up, we can readily see the uses for the enhanced income resulting from improved agriculture. Again the painters give us a useful visual impression. Genre painters reveal interiors filled with items we would not find in an ordinary colonial household: a wide array of ceramics—vases, figurines, and pots—a lot of fabric, some of it quite luxurious, even occasional rugs. The boots and shoes worn in the pictures appear to be stylish improvements on the work of the village cobbler. All in all, farmers do not appear to have limited their purchases to the bare necessities of life. Instead of going to the store to replace homemade with purchased goods, rural families in actuality added new things to their household inventories to adorn themselves and their houses. They did not give up subsistence production as purchases increased, but enhanced their lives with things they had not enjoyed before. A sample of estate inventories from Kent County, Delaware, a rural area in the middle of the state, provides one clear measure of the change. In the 1770s, not a single inventory listed a carpet. In the 1840s all of the inventories from the topmost quartile showed a carpet, and, what is more telling, 31 percent of the inventories in the bottom quartile. The same holds true for looking glasses, mahogany, walnut, and cherry furniture, and ceramics. Where there was none or very little in the 1770s, a third to a half of the inventories in the bottom half listed such amenities by the 1840s. In the upper half, two-thirds to all of the inventories showed such items. Along with the transition to improved farming practices, marked by opening land and continuous cropping, came the adoption of rural consumerism.[49]

The material in the houses—the figurines, the curtains, the chairs, the brooms, the hats, the dresses, the clocks—were as much a part of the American agricultural revolution as rotation systems and improved fences. For by the early nineteenth century, farmers were subject to cultural pressures as demanding and unrelenting as the depletion of the soil. Purchases of the things in the pictures were as necessary to alleviate the strains in their cultural position as manure and clover were to halt the decline in fertility of the land. Farmers were actually fighting two battles in these decades: one for the productivity of the soil, and the other for dignity and cultural self-respect.

The smoothing, softening, and decorating of the farmhouse can be seen as a rural rejoinder to the aspersions of boorishness, vulgarity, and coarseness that haunted the nineteenth-century American farmer. William Sidney Mount depicted the issue graphically in his 1835 painting *The Sportsman's Last Visit*. In a relatively plain farmhouse room sits a lovely young lady gorgeously attired in a fashionable dress with leg-of-mutton sleeves, her feet in delicate slippers, sewing a fine seam. Apparently the young woman has a choice between two suitors, a well-off but rustic country sportsman and a refined and fashionable gentleman, probably of city breeding. The title suggests whom she will choose. Perhaps her father would not have objected if she married the country man, but doubtless he wanted her to have the choice. The simplicity of the room furnishings, suggesting a lack of polish in the father, was not to repel suitors for the daughter's hand. She was never to be scorned or pitied because she lacked the apparel to adorn her beauty. However plain the father, she was to have the clothes that made her appear stylishly genteel. At least he must provide her with the means to enter the circle of refinement and to be eligible for the respect and love of a cultivated gentleman. The variations on the plot were endless, but the underlying theme was the same. In buying fabrics, ceramics, and furniture with his improved income, the farmer purchased dignity for himself, happiness for his offspring, and membership for his family in the respectable middle class.

IV

All of these changes in rural life in the first half of the nineteenth century can be thought of as the outgrowth of commercialization. The abandonment of long-fallow agriculture, it seems fair to assume, resulted from the stimulus of market opportunities, and so the opening of the countryside into broad vistas of tilled fields and grassy pastures can be thought of as an indicator of commercialization. Along with specialization in crops, the increased percentage of actively worked land implies the existence of intensified production for the market.[50]

But the word "commercialization," if narrowly conceived, fails to do

The Sportsman's Last Visit, 1835. Oil on canvas by William Sidney Mount.
THE MUSEUMS AT STONY BROOK; GIFT OF MR. AND MRS. WARD MELVILLE, 1958.

justice to the transformation that has been described. It does not take into account the cultural plight of farmers, their fears of envelopment in vulgar rusticity, and their yearning for redeeming tokens of refinement. The changes in farm practices between 1750 and 1850 grew out of cultural circumstances as much as from a raw desire for profit. The opening of the countryside meant clearing the land of woods and bushes and engaging in continuous cultivation; it also meant the opening of the country to influences from the city—to urbanity, refinement, and middle-class values. In the absence of those cultural aspirations, farmers might have divided their lands into much smaller parcels simply to provide a subsistence existence for their children. Surely they would not have denied younger sons land in order to preserve substantial farm acreages unless a compelling cultural priority made a higher standard of living a necessity. The transformation of middle-class values in the nineteenth century exerted pressures that aspiring farmers could not resist. To achieve respectability by the spreading standards of vernacular gentility, they had to to reach a level of buying power that enabled them to furnish parlors, dress their daughters in fashionable gowns, and send their children to school.[51] It was that kind of necessity—really a cultural and not a subsistence need—that kept up farm size and made farmers intensify production. The changes in farm life were as much cultural as economic. Market production and cultural aspiration were inextricably intermixed. Only if commercialization is broadly conceived to encompass this intricate interplay of culture, agriculture, and the market does it accurately describe the changes in farm life.

Because of the interplay of culture and commerce in this transformation, we must look for indicators of agricultural change in farmhouses as well as in barns and fields. In the parlors, bedrooms, and kitchens we will find the fruits of intensified commercial agriculture as much as in the orchards. Wallpaper, carpets, matched sets of dishes, and upholstered furniture marked the improving farmer as surely as permanent fences and clover cover crops. The county histories of the 1880s from virtually every section of the country advertise in their engraved illustrations the kind of life farmers hoped to achieve. The pictured farms were given names like Belle View, Mansion Farm, and Pleasant Park. In imagination anyway, carriages drove up the drives, and gentlemen escorting ladies with parasols strolled toward the houses. These were doubtless exaggerations, and in any case far beyond the reach of most farmers, but they represented an ideal. It may have been the ideal that more than any other directed the toil of adult Americans in the nineteenth century: an independent farm capable of sustaining the rudiments of a refined existence for the farmer and his family.[52]

We must heed the contents of the houses for another reason. Those objects direct our attention to the other side of agricultural improvement. The very gentility of the successful farmers, along with their permanent fences and neat barns, clearly distinguished them from those who failed to prosper. Agricultural improvement etched deep lines across American rural society. The arrival on the landscape of painted frame houses in Greek Revival or Italianate styles made the gray, weathered, hewn log houses of the majority of farmers appear more dingy and degraded than ever. In shedding their rusticity, middle-class farmers dumped the burden of rural shame on those who were unable to improve their dwellings, educate their children, stylishly adorn themselves, and adopt the latest farming methods. Some struggled bravely to rise above their condition and acquired a semblance of gentility with a tea set, a small parlor, or a front yard. Others fled to the cities, to factories, or to the west to make another try. Still others retreated into backward pockets of rural poverty and created sub- and countercultures of farmers who chose not to improve or were unable to do so. An account of the losers would be a much less cheerful story than the one depicted in Mount's painting, but one of momentous importance in the history of early American agriculture.[53]

BIBLIOGRAPHY

OF PUBLISHED WORKS

BY BERNARD BAILYN

The following bibliography of Bernard Bailyn's published writings includes books, essays, and major reviews (in that order) by year through 1990. From 1962 until 1970 he served as editor-in-chief of the John Harvard Library; and from 1967 until 1976 and 1984 until 1986 he served as co-editor of *Perspectives in American History*, an annual published by the Charles Warren Center for Studies in American History, Harvard University. Specific reprints and foreign-language editions are not included.

ABBREVIATIONS

AHR   *American Historical Review*
JEH   *Journal of Economic History*
MVHR *Mississippi Valley Historical Review*
NEQ   *New England Quarterly*
WMQ   *William and Mary Quarterly* (3rd series)

1950

"The Apologia of Robert Keayne," WMQ, 7 (1950), 568–87. Reprinted in several collections.

1951

"Braudel's Geohistory—A Reconsideration," JEH, 11 (1951), 277–82.

1952

"Hedges' Browns: Some Thoughts on the New England Merchants in the Colonial Period," *Explorations in Entrepreneurial History*, 4 (1952), 229–33.

1953

"Communications and Trade: The Atlantic in the Seventeenth Century," JEH, 13 (1953), 378–87. Reprinted in five collections.

1954

(With John Clive), "England's Cultural Provinces: Scotland and America," WMQ, 11 (1954), 200–13.

"The Blount Papers: Notes on the Merchant 'Class' in the Revolutionary Period," WMQ, 11 (1954), 98–104.

"Kinship and Trade in Seventeenth Century New England," *Explorations in Entrepreneurial History*, 6 (1954), 197–205.

Review of Perry Miller, *The New England Mind from Colony to Province* (1953), in NEQ, 27 (1954), 112–18.

1955

The New England Merchants in the Seventeenth Century (Harvard University Press, 1955). Two paperback editions: Harper Torchbooks, 1964; Harvard University Press, 1979.

1956

"Becker, Andrews, and the Image of Colonial Origins," NEQ, 29 (1956), 522–34.

Review of Carl Bridenbaugh, *Cities in Revolt: Urban Life in America, 1743–1776* (1955), in WMQ, 13 (1956), 258–61.

Review of Patrick McGrath, ed., *Merchants and Merchandise in Seventeenth-Century Bristol* (1955), in AHR, 61 (1956), 1011.

1957

"The Beekmans of New York: Trade, Politics, and Families," WMQ, 14 (1957), 598–608.

Review of E. N. Hartley, *Ironworks on the Saugus: The Lynn and Braintree Ventures of the Company of Undertakers in New England* (1957), in MVHR, 44 (1957), 339–40.

1958

"History and the Distrust of Knowledge," *The New Republic*, 139 (December 15, 1958), 17–18. An essay review of Daniel J. Boorstin, *The Americans: The Colonial Experience* (1958).

Review of Clifford K. Shipton, *Biographical Sketches of Those Who Attended Harvard College . . . X, 1736–1740* (1958), in NEQ, 31 (1958), 531–35.

1959

(With Lotte Bailyn), *Massachusetts Shipping, 1697–1714: A Statistical Study* (Harvard University Press, 1959).

"Politics and Social Structure in Virginia," in James M. Smith, ed., *Seventeenth-Century America: Essays in Colonial History* (University of North Carolina Press, 1959), 90–115. Reprinted in seventeen collections of essays.

Review of W. W. Abbot, *The Royal Governors of Georgia, 1754–1775*, in WMQ, 16 (1959), 597–99.

1960

Education in the Forming of American Society: Needs and Opportunities for Study (University of North Carolina Press, 1960). Three paperback editions: Vintage, 1962; University of North Carolina Press, 1970; and W. W. Norton, 1972.

"Boyd's Jefferson: Notes for a Sketch," NEQ, 33 (1960), 380–400.

Review of Richard Pares, *Merchants and Planters* (1960), in WMQ, 17 (1960), 536–38.

1961

"A Whig Interpretation," *Yale Review*, 50 (1961), 438–41. An essay review of Richard L. Morton, *Colonial Virginia* (1960), 2 vols.

1962

"Political Experience and Enlightenment Ideas in Eighteenth-Century America," AHR, 67 (1962), 339–51. Reprinted in twenty-three collections of essays, including four in translation.

"Butterfield's Adams: Notes for a Sketch," WMQ, 19 (1962), 238–56.

1963

"The Problems of the Working Historian: A Comment," in Sidney Hook, ed., *Philosophy and History: A Symposium* (New York University Press, 1963), 92–101.

"Education as a Discipline: Some Historical Notes," in John Walton and James L. Kuethe, eds., *The Discipline of Education* (The University of Wisconsin Press, 1963), 125–44.

Review of Mack Thompson, *Moses Brown: Reluctant Reformer* (1962), in MVHR, 50 (1963), 117–19.

Review of Richard S. Dunn, *Puritans and Yankees: The Winthrop Dynasty of New England* (1962), in AHR, 68 (1963), 1082–84.

1964

Ed., *The Apologia of Robert Keayne: The Self-Portrait of a Puritan Merchant*, in Colonial Society of Massachusetts *Transactions, 1952–56* (1964), 243–341. Reprinted as a Harper Torchbook (1965) and by Peter Smith (1970). Excerpts have appeared in various collections and readers.

Review of Emery Battis, *Saints and Sectaries: Anne Hutchinson and the Antinomian Controversy in the Massachusetts Bay Colony* (1962), in WMQ, 21 (1964), 123–27.

1965

(With the assistance of Jane N. Garrett), ed., *Pamphlets of the American Revolution, 1750–1776*, I (Harvard University Press, 1965). Awarded the Faculty Prize of the Harvard University Press.

"The Man Himself Still Eludes Us," *The New York Times Book Review*, November 21, 1965. Review of Alfred Owen Aldridge, *Benjamin Franklin: Philosopher and Man* (1965).

1966

"The Years Before the Fourth," *The New York Times Book Review*, July 3, 1966. Essay Review of Lawrence Henry Gipson, *The British Empire Before the American Revolution*.

Review of Jackson Turner Main, *The Social Structure of Revolutionary America* (1965), in AHR, 71 (1966), 1431–33.

1967

The Ideological Origins of the American Revolution (Harvard University Press, 1967). Reprinted as a Harvard Press paperback, 1971, and in Calcutta by the Scientific Book Agency in 1969. Translated into Spanish; French translation in progress. Awarded the Pulitzer Prize for History and the Bancroft Prize.

1968

The Origins of American Politics (Alfred A. Knopf, 1968). Reprinted as a Vintage paperback (1969) and translated into Japanese (1975).

1969

(With Donald Fleming), eds., *The Intellectual Migration: Europe and America, 1930–1960* (Harvard University Press, 1969).

"A Comment" on Jack P. Greene, "Political Mimesis: A Consideration of the Historical and Cultural Roots of Legislative Behavior in the British Colonies in the Eighteenth Century," AHR, 75 (1969), 361–63.

1970

"Religion and Revolution: Three Biographical Studies," *Perspectives in American History*, 4 (1970), 85–139. The third biography, of The Reverend Stephen Johnson, is reprinted in George J. Willauer, Jr., ed., *A Lyme Miscellany, 1776–1976* (Wesleyan University Press, 1977).

"The American Revolution," in John A. Garraty, ed., *Interpreting American History: Conversations with Historians* (Macmillan, 1970), I, 63–91.

1971

"L'ideologia politica nel periodo della Rivoluzione," in *Terzoprogramma*, 4 (1971), 15–22.

1972

(With Donald Fleming), eds., *Law in American History* (Little, Brown, 1972).

1973

"The Index and Commentaries of Harbottle Dorr," *Proceedings* of the Massachusetts Historical Society, 85 (1973), 21–35.

"Common Sense," in *Fundamental Testaments of the American Revolution* (Library of Congress, 1973), 7–22. Reprinted in four collections.

"The Central Themes of the American Revolution: An Interpretation," in Stephen G. Kurtz and James H. Hutson, eds., *Essays on the American Revolution* (University of North Carolina Press, 1973), 3–31. German and French translations.

1974

The Ordeal of Thomas Hutchinson (Harvard University Press, 1974). Reprinted as a Harvard University Press paperback, 1976 and 1988. British edition, 1974. Awarded the National Book Award in History.

1975

"Lines of Force in Recent Writings on the American Revolution," XIV International Congress of Historical Sciences (San Francisco, 1975), 50 pages.

Ed., "A Dialogue Between an American and a European Englishman by Thomas Hutchinson, [1768]," *Perspectives in American History*, 9 (1975), 341–410.

1976

"1776: A Year of Challenge—A World Transformed," *Journal of Law & Economics*, 19 (1976), 437–66. Reprinted, in revised form, in *Notes and Records of the Royal Society*, 31 (1977), 179–99.

1977

"Shaping the Republic," Part I of *The Great Republic* (D. C. Heath, 1977; 3d ed. 1985); Italian translation in *Le origini degli Stati Uniti* (Bologna, 1987).

"Review Article: *French Historical Method, the Annales Paradigm*, by Traian Stoianovich," JEH, 37 (1977), 1028–1034.

"Morison: An Appreciation," *Proceedings* of the Massachusetts Historical Society, 89 (1977), 112–23. Reprinted in *More Lives of Harvard Scholars*, William Bentinck-Smith and Elizabeth Stouffer, eds. (Harvard University, 1986), 33–43.

1979

"Recollections of PFL," in Robert K. Merton *et al.*, eds., *Qualitative and Quantitative Social Research: Papers in Honor of Paul F. Lazarsfeld* (The Free Press, 1979), 16–18.

1980

(With John B. Hench), eds., *The Press and the American Revolution* (American Antiquarian Society, 1980).

1982

"The Challenge of Modern Historiography," AHR, 87 (1982), 1–24. Spanish translation, 1990.

1985

"New England and a Wider World: Notes on Some Central Themes of Modern Historiography," in David D. Hall and David Grayson Allen, eds., *Seventeenth-Century New England: Publications* of the Colonial Society of Massachusetts, 63 (1985), 323–28.

"History and the Creative Imagination" (Washington University, St. Louis, 1985).

1986

"Foundations" and "Why Kirkland Failed," in *Glimpses of the Harvard Past* (Harvard University Press, 1986), chapters 1, 2.

The Peopling of British North America (Alfred A. Knopf, 1986). British edition, 1987; Vintage paperback edition, 1988.

(With the assistance of Barbara DeWolfe), *Voyagers to the West: A Passage in the Peopling of America on the Eve of the Revolution* (Alfred A. Knopf, 1986). British edition, 1987; Vintage paperback edition, 1988. Awarded the Pulitzer Prize for History, the Saloutos Prize of the Immigration History Society, the Distinguished Book Award of the Society of Colonial Wars, and the Society of the Cincinnati Triennial Prize for 1986–88.

1988

"From Protestant Peasants to Jewish Intellectuals: The Germans in the Peopling of America," *German Historical Institute, Washington Annual Lecture No. 1* (Berg, 1988).

"The Peopling of the British Peripheries in the Eighteenth Century" (Australian Academy of Science, Canberra, 1988).

Review of R. C. Harris, ed., *Historical Atlas of Canada: From the Beginnings to 1800*, vol. I (1987), in *Canadian Historical Review*, 69 (1988), 531–34.

1990

Faces of Revolution: Personalities and Themes in the Struggle for American Independence (Alfred A. Knopf, 1990).

1991

(With Philip D. Morgan), eds., *Strangers Within the Realm: Cultural Margins of the First British Empire* (University of North Carolina Press, 1991).

1992

Ed., *The Debate on the Constitution* (Library of America, 1992), 2 vols.

PH.D. DISSERTATIONS
DIRECTED BY BERNARD BAILYN
AT HARVARD UNIVERSITY

YEAR	NAME	TITLE OF DISSERTATION
1958	Jurgen Herbst	"Nineteenth century German scholarship in America: A study of five German-trained social scientists"
1958	S. Alexander Rippa	"Organized business and public education; the educational policies and activities of the Chamber of Commerce and the National Association of Manufacturers, 1933–1956"
1958	David B. Tyack	"Gentleman of letters; a study of George Ticknor"
1959	Richard M. Brown	"The South Carolina Regulators"
1960	Jerome W. Jones	"The Anglican Church in colonial Virginia, 1690–1760"
1961	Thomas C. Barrow	"The Colonial Customs Service, 1660–1775"
1961	Richard L. Bushman	"Government and society in Connecticut, 1690–1760"
1961	Stanley N. Katz	"An easie access: Anglo-American politics in New York, 1732–1753"
1961	Theodore R. Sizer	"The Committee of Ten"
1962	Richard V. Buel	"Studies in the political ideas of the American Revolution, 1760–1776"
1962	Thomas J. Condon	"The commercial origins of New Netherland"
1963	Mary A. Connolly	"The Boston schools in the new republic, 1776–1840"

1963	Jonathan C. Messerli	"Horace Mann: the early years, 1796–1837"
1964	Jere R. Daniell	"New Hampshire politics in the American Revolution, 1741–1790"
1964	Craig R. Hanyan	"DeWitt Clinton, years of molding, 1769–1807"
1964	Michael G. Kammen	"The colonial agents, English politics, and the American Revolution"
1964	Gordon S. Wood	"The creation of an American polity in the Revolutionary era"
1965	Philip J. Greven	"Four generations: a study of family structure, inheritance, and mobility in Andover, Massachusetts, 1630–1750"
1965	Arthur D. Kaledin	"The mind of John Leverett"
1965	Nathan C. Shiverick	"Virginia and the western land problems, 1776–1800"
1966	Richard D. Brown	"The Boston Committee of Correspondence in the Revolution 1772–1774"
1967	Miles L. Bradbury	"Adventure in persuasion: John Witherspoon, Samuel Stanhope Smith, and Ashbel Green"
1967	David B. Potts	"Baptist colleges in the development of American society, 1812–1861"
1967	Michael W. Zuckerman	"The Massachusetts town in the eighteenth century"
1968	Lois G. Carr	"County government in Maryland, 1689–1709"
1968	James A. Henretta	"The Duke of Newcastle, English politics, and the administration of the American colonies, 1724–1754"
1968	Pauline R. Maier	"From resistance to revolution: American radicals and the development of intercolonial opposition to Britain, 1765–1776"
1969	Mary Beth Norton	"The British-Americans: the loyalist exiles in England, 1774–1789"
1970	James E. Bland	"The Oliver Wolcotts of Connecticut: the national experience, 1775–1800"
1970	Peter C. Hoffer	"Liberty or Order: two views of American history from the revolutionary crisis to the early works of George Bancroft and Wendell Phillips"
1971	Stephen W. Botein	"Reluctant partisans: the role of printers in eighteenth-century American politics"
1971	Carl F. Kaestle	"The origins of an urban school system: New York City, 1750–1850"
1971	Joel D. Meyerson	"A Quaker commonwealth: society and the public order in Pennsylvania, 1681–1765"
1971	William E. Nelson	"The Americanization of the common law during the Revolutionary era: a study of legal change in Massachusetts, 1760–1830"

1972	John M. Hoffmann	"Commonwealth College: the governance of Harvard in the Puritan period"
1972	Peter H. Wood	"Black Majority: Negroes in colonial South Carolina from 1670 through the Stono rebellion"
1973	James H. Kettner	"The development of American citizenship 1608–1870"
1973	David T. Konig	"Social conflict and community tensions in Essex County, Massachusetts, 1672–1692"
1975	Ann G. Condon	"The envy of the American states: the settlement of the loyalists in New Brunswick, goals and achievements"
1975	Jack N. Rakove	"The Continental Congress and the beginnings of national politics, 1774–1789"
1975	Maris A. Vinovskis	"Demographic changes in America from the Revolution to the Civil War: an analysis of the socioeconomic determinants of fertility differentials and trends in Massachusetts from 1765–1860"
1976	Allan B. Judson	"Some characteristics of the Bay Colony founders' early thinking about their dealings with the physical environment in New England"
1976	George D. Smith	"Religion and the development of American culture: western Pennsylvania, 1760–1820"
1977	James C. Hippen	"Government contracting, 1745–1760. Christopher Kilby and his associates"
1977	Christopher M. Jedrey	"The world of John Cleaveland: family and community in eighteenth-century Massachusetts"
1978	Michael R. Yogg	"'The best place for health and wealth': a demographic and economic analysis of the Quakers of preindustrial Bucks County, Pennsylvania"
1980	Thomas M. Doerflinger	"Enterprise on the Delaware: merchants and economic development in Philadelphia, 1750–1791"
1981	Fred W. Anderson	"War and the Bay Colony: soldiers and society in Massachusetts during the Seven Years' War, 1754–1763"
1981	Kent A. Coit	"The diffusion of democracy: politics and constitutionalism in the States, 1790–1840"
1981	Sally Schwartz	"'A mixed multitude': religion and ethnicity in colonial Pennsylvania"
1982	David P. Jaffee	"The people of the Wachusett: town founding and village culture in New England, 1630–1764"
1983	Helena M. Wall	"Private Lives: the transformation of family and community in early America"
1984	Virginia DeJohn Anderson	"To pass beyond the seas: the Great Mi-

		gration and the settlement of New England, 1630–1670"
1985	John Frederick Martin	"Entrepreneurship and the founding of New England towns: the seventeenth century"
1986	Peter C. Mancall	"Environment and Economy: the upper Susquehanna Valley in the age of the American Revolution"
1988	James Russell Snapp	"Exploitation and control: the Southern frontier in Anglo-American politics in the era of the American Revolution"
1990	Marilyn C. Baseler	"Immigration patterns and policies in eighteenth-century America"
1990	William A. Braverman	"The ascent of Boston's Jews, 1630–1918"
1990	David J. Hancock	"'Citizen of the World': commercial success, social development, and the experience of London merchants trading overseas"
1990	Thomas J. Siegel	"Governance and curriculum at Harvard College in the eighteenth century"
1991	Thelma W. Foote	"Black life in colonial Manhattan, 1664–1786"

Ph.D. CANDIDATES

Robert J. Allison	Rebecca D. Larson
Frederick A. B. Dalzell	Jeffrey P. Moran
Sally E. Hadden	Jeffrey L. Pasley
Eric A. Hinderaker	Mark Peterson
Gretchen Z. Koning	Michael J. Prokopow

NOTES

Bernard Bailyn, Historian and Teacher

MICHAEL KAMMEN *and* STANLEY N. KATZ

1. J. Anthony Lukas, "After the Pentagon Papers—A Month in the New Life of Daniel Ellsberg," *The New York Times Sunday Magazine* (December 12, 1971), 98–99.
2. Bailyn to Michael Kammen, May 11, 1988.
3. See Michael Zuckerman, "Fiction and Fission: Twentieth-Century Writing on the Founding Fathers," in M. Zimmerman *et al.*, eds., *Religion, Ideology, and Nationalism in Europe and America*: *Essays Presented in Honor of Yehoshua Arieli* (Jerusalem, 1986), 227–42, esp. 235–39; Thomas J. Archdeacon (not a student of Bailyn's) and Maris A. Vinovskis, "Ideology and Social Structure in the Coming of the American Revolution: A Critique of the Bailyn Thesis," unpublished paper presented at the annual meeting of the Organization of American Historians, Denver, Colorado, April 18, 1974.
4. Bailyn to Michael Kammen, September 25, 1980.
5. Bailyn to A. Roger Ekirch, April 16, 1981; remarks made by Bailyn following the conference banquet in Cambridge, Massachusetts, October 30, 1987.
6. Bailyn to Ekirch, April 16, 1981.
7. See, especially, his review article concerning the *Annales* school, in *Journal of Economic History*, 37 (1977), 1028–34; Bailyn and Donald Fleming, eds., *The Intellectual Migration: Europe and America, 1930–1960* (Cambridge, Mass., 1969); Bailyn, "The Problems of the Working Historian: A Comment," in Sidney Hook, ed., *Philosophy and History: A Symposium* (New York, 1963), 92–101; and Bailyn, "History and the Creative Imagination," a pamphlet (Saint Louis, 1985).
8. *The Origins of American Politics* (New York, 1968), 124.
9. In addition to Bailyn and Bailyn, *Massachusetts Shipping, 1697–1714: A Statistical Study* (Cambridge, Mass., 1959), see Lotte Bailyn, *Mass Media and Children: A Study of Exposure Habits and Cognitive Effects* (Washington, D.C., 1959); Lotte Bailyn, *Experiencing Technical Work: A Comparison of Male and Female Engineers* (Cambridge, Mass., 1986).

10. See Bailyn, "Recollections of PFL," in Robert K. Merton *et al.*, eds., *Qualitative and Quantitative Social Research: Papers in Honor of Paul F. Lazarsfeld* (New York, 1979), 16–18.

11. Robert K. Merton, *On the Shoulders of Giants: A Shandean Postscript* (New York, 1965).

12. Bailyn to Michael Kammen, September 1, 1979.

13. For highly concentrated illustrations of these emphases, see Bailyn's two essays in Bailyn *et al.*, eds., *Glimpses of the Harvard Past* (Cambridge, Mass., 1986), 10, 13–16, 22, 27, 43.

14. Bailyn, *The Peopling of British North America: An Introduction* (New York, 1986), 4–5.

15. *Ibid.*, 60, 68, 85, 112, and the quotation at 114.

16. See Daniel Blake Smith, "The Study of the Family in Early America: Trends, Problems, and Prospects," *William and Mary Quarterly*, 39 (1982), 6; and Bailyn's unpublished address to the American Academy of Arts and Sciences meeting in Boston on May 21, 1980. For additional examples of distinctiveness in American higher education, see Bailyn, ed., *Glimpses of the Harvard Past*, 10, 13, 18.

17. Bailyn, *Voyagers to the West: A Passage in the Peopling of America on the Eve of the Revolution* (New York, 1986), 4.

18. Bailyn, "Foundations," in *Glimpses of the Harvard Past*, 9. For additional examples of "anomaly," see *ibid.*, 27, 43.

19. Review of Jackson Turner Main, *The Social Structure of Revolutionary America* (1965), in the *American Historical Review*, 71 (1966), 1433.

20. Bailyn, "Becker, Andrews, and the Image of Colonial Origins," *New England Quarterly*, 29 (1956), 522–34; Bailyn, "French Historical Method, the Annales Paradigm, by Traian Stoianovich," *Journal of Economic History*, 37 (1977), 1028–34; review of R. C. Harris, ed., *Historical Atlas of Canada: From the Beginnings to 1800*, vol. I, in *Canadian Historical Review*, 69 (1988), 531–34.

21. See A. Roger Ekirch, "Bernard Bailyn," *Dictionary of Literary Biography*: vol. 17, *Twentieth-Century American Historians*, ed. Clyde N. Wilson (Detroit, 1983), 19–26; J. C. A. Stagg, "The New British World of Bernard Bailyn," *Virginia Quarterly Review*, 64 (1988), 361–73.

22. See Jesse Lemisch, "Bailyn Besieged in His Bunker," *Radical History Review*, 4 (Winter 1977), 72–83; Kenneth S. Lynn, "The Regressive Historians," *The American Scholar*, 47 (Autumn 1978), 471–500; the double review of *Peopling of British North America* and *Voyagers to the West* by Joyce O. Appleby and Allan Kulikoff in *William and Mary Quarterly*, 44 (1987), 791–99; another review of both books by W. J. Eccles in *The Historian*, 51 (1988), 126–28.

23. Israel Shenker, "Historians Collide on a Slippery Subject: Revolution," *The New York Times* (August 28, 1975), 34. An equable response has ordinarily been the case. Bailyn almost never replies in print to critical reviews. For interesting exceptions, see his responses to T. H. Breen, concerning *The Peopling of British North America* and *Voyagers to the West* in the *New York Review of Books* for April 9, 1987 (Breen's review appeared there on January 29, 1987); and to Gary Nash concerning "The Central Themes of the American Revolution, An Interpretation," in *William and Mary Quarterly*, 32 (1975), 182–85.

24. According to Bailyn, Lazarsfeld loved the nonpedantic use of "*Look!*" See Bailyn, "Recollections of PFL," 18.

25. Bailyn to Michael Kammen, March 15, 1968, and October 19, 1970.

26. Thomas Reed Powell (1880–1955) taught constitutional law at the Harvard University Law School from 1925 until 1949. The quotation is from Jacob Zeitlin and Homer Woodbridge, *Life and Letters of Stuart Pratt Sherman* (New York, 1929), II, 730.

The Creative Imagination of Bernard Bailyn
GORDON S. WOOD

1. Bailyn, *History and the Creative Imagination* (St. Louis, 1985), 4.
2. *Ibid.*, 3, 4, 13, 10, 13.
3. Bailyn, "The Challenge of Modern Historiography," *American Historical Review*, 87 (1982), 2.
4. Bailyn, "New England and a Wider World: Notes on Some Central Themes of Modern Historiography," in David D. Hall and David Grayson Allen, eds., *Seventeenth-Century New England* (Boston, 1985), 323.
5. Bailyn, *The Peopling of British North America: An Introduction* (New York, 1986), 8.
6. The textbook was T. Harry Williams, Richard N. Current, and Frank Friedel, *A History of the United States* (New York, 1959), I, 95–96.
7. According to an index of over a thousand scholarly journals for the year 1980 compiled by the Institute for Scientific Information, The *William and Mary Quarterly* was judged to be the most frequently cited journal of historical scholarship in the world, during that one year at least. See *A News Letter from The Institute of Early American History & Culture*, 73 (March 1, 1983), 73.
8. Bailyn, "Review Article," *Journal of Economic History*, 37 (1977), 1033.
9. Bailyn, "The Problems of the Working Historian: A Comment," in Sidney Hook, ed., *Philosophy and History: A Symposium* (New York, 1963), 94.
10. Bernard Bailyn and Lotte Bailyn, *Massachusetts Shipping 1697–1714: A Statistical Study* (Cambridge, Mass., 1959).
11. Bailyn, "Lines of Force in Recent Writings on the American Revolution," unpublished paper presented at the XIV International Congress of Historical Sciences (San Francisco, 1975).
12. For some of the personal sources of Bailyn's desire "to transcend the limits of our naturally parochial perspective," see Bailyn, *From Protestant Peasants to Jewish Intellectuals: The Germans in the Peopling of America*, German Historical Institute, Annual Lecture Series No. 1 (Oxford, 1988), 11–12.
13. Indeed, so thorough going, so scrupulous, is the standard of editing that Bailyn set for himself in the first *Pamphlets* volume that it is unlikely, given his absorption in the Peopling project, that he will have the time to finish the three remaining volumes.
14. As if to prove that, like any of his four creative historians, he can both conceive of an entire past world and at the same time "locate, control and absorb very large quantities of hitherto unused or underused data," for his most recent book, *Voyagers to the West* (New York, 1986) Bailyn immersed himself in the manuscripts of dozens of archives, ranging from locations in Orkney, Scotland, to Charlottesville, Virginia. At the same time, in this longest of his histories, he carried his preoccupation with "individuality, concreteness, detail" to astonishing lengths, particularity in the micro-narratives in the latter part of the book. At first glance "these separate small-scale histories" seem excessively detailed, profusely meticulous, and altogether too much of a good thing; but the reader's continued immersion in their particularity eventually conveys, as no summary statements ever could, the huge separation that commonly exists between the smooth, determinate generalizations of historians and the chaotic reality of the contingencies that constituted people's daily lives (xxi).
15. Bailyn, "Review Article," *Journal of Economic History*, 37 (1977), 1033.
16. Bailyn, "Braudel's Geohistory—A Reconsideration," *Journal of Economic History*, 11 (1951), 282.
17. *Ibid.*

18. Bailyn, "Essay Review: Becker, Andrews, and the Image of Colonial Origins," *New England Quarterly*, 29 (1956), 532–33.
19. Bailyn to A. Roger Ekrich, April 16, 1981.
20. Bailyn, *Peopling of America*, 6.
21. Bailyn, "Essay Review," *New England Quarterly*, 29 (1956), 531, 532.
22. When the *Journal of American History* in its March 1965 issue chose not to review Stephan Thernstrom's *Progress and Poverty: Social Mobility in a Nineteenth Century City* but merely to list it in the *Journal's* "Book Notes," along with such throwaways as *The Secret Loves of the Founding Fathers*, I wrote the editor of the *Journal* to express my astonishment. He replied that he had originally decided not to review Thernstrom's book, which was one of the pioneering studies of the new social history of the 1960s, because he and his colleagues considered it to be sociology, and not "squarely in the field of American history." Editor, *Journal of American History*, to author, April 28, 1965.
23. Bailyn, "Essay Review," *New England Quarterly*, 29 (1956), 532.
24. Bailyn, "Challenge of Modern Historiography," 3.
25. Bailyn, "Communications and Trade: The Atlantic in the Seventeenth Century," *Journal of Economic History*, 13 (1953), 380.
26. John Murrin said in 1972 that "much (perhaps most) of the current interest in colonial demography derives in one way or another from the highly suggestive introductory essay to [Bailyn's] *Education in the Forming of American Society. . . .*" Murrin, "Review Essay," *History and Theory*, 11 (1972), 228.
27. Bailyn, "Politics and Social Structure in Virginia," in James Morton Smith, ed., *Seventeenth-Century America: Essays in Colonial History* (Chapel Hill, N.C., 1959), 91.
28. When the distinguished colonial historian Frank Craven first heard Bailyn's paper at the April 1957 symposium on seventeenth-century America, he at once declared to W. W. Abbot, "That's the colonial historian of the next generation."
29. Bailyn, *The Origins of American Politics* (New York, 1968), vii–viii.
30. *Ibid.*, 96, 98–99, 101.
31. Namier, "Human Nature in Politics," *Personalities and Powers* (London, 1955), 4; Namier, *England in the Age of the American Revolution*, 2d ed. (London, 1963), 129.
32. Herbert Butterfield, *George III and the Historians* (London, 1957), 219.
33. Bailyn, ed., *Pamphlets of the American Revolution, 1750–1776, Volume I: 1750–1765.* (Cambridge, Mass., 1965).
34. Namier, "History," in *Avenues of History* (London, 1952), 2, 3.
35. Bailyn, review of Perry Miller, *New England Mind: Colony to Province*, in *New England Quarterly*, 27 (1954), 112–18.
36. Bailyn, "Political Experience and Enlightenment Ideas in Eighteenth-Century America," *American Historical Review*, 67 (1961–62), 339–51, quotations on 345, 346, 349, 351.
37. *Ibid.*, 351.
38. Bailyn, *Origins of American Politics*, ix.
39. Bailyn, ed., *Pamphlets of the Revolution*, I, vii.
40. Bailyn, "General Introduction: The Transforming Radicalism of the American Revolution," *Ibid.*, I, 190.
41. Bailyn, *The Ideological Origins of the American Revolution* (Cambridge, Mass., 1967), 283; Bailyn, "The Central Themes of the American Revolution: An Interpretation," in Stephen G. Kurtz and James H. Hutson, eds., *Essays on the American Revolution* (Chapel Hill, N.C., 1973), 12; Bailyn, "Lines of Force," 13.
42. Bailyn, "Lines of Force," 4.

43. Pocock, "Machiavelli, Harrington, and English Political Ideologies in the Eighteenth Century, *William and Mary Quarterly*, 3d ser., 22 (1956), 550.

44. Bailyn, *Origins of American Politics*, 41, 26, 13, 52, 53; *Ideological Origins*, 174, 307; Bailyn, "Religion and Revolution: Three Biographical Studies," *Perspectives in American History*, 4 (1970), 97; Bailyn, "Central Themes," 7, 10.

45. Bailyn, "Central Themes," 11–12.

46. Bailyn, *The New England Merchants in the Seventeenth Century* (Cambridge, Mass., 1955), 40; Bailyn, "Communications and Trade," *Journal of Economic History*, 13 (1953), 386; Bailyn, "Politics and Social Structure," 102.

47. Bailyn, "Central Themes," 14.

48. Bailyn, *Ideological Origins*, 232, 302.

49. Bailyn, "Central Themes," 18–19.

50. Jack N. Rakove, "The Great Compromise: Ideas, Interests, and Politics of Constitution Making," *William and Mary Quarterly*, 3d ser., 44 (1987), 426.

51. Jeffery C. Alexander, *Twenty Lectures: Sociological Theory Since World War II* (New York, 1987), 302–29.

52. For an elaboration of this point about the inseparability of ideas from circumstances, culture from society, see Gordon S. Wood, "Intellectual History and the Social Sciences," in John Higham and Paul Conkin, eds., *New Directions in American Intellectual History* (Baltimore, 1979), 27–41. I must confess that earlier I helped contribute to this mistaken separation of ideas from society in the wrongheaded title, if nothing else, of my article, "Rhetoric and Reality in the American Revolution," *William and Mary Quarterly*, 3d ser., 23 (1966), 3–32.

53. Bloch, quoted in Namier, "The Profession of Historian," *Personalities and Powers*, 11.

54. Bailyn, "Lines of Force," 8, 16, 20, 25, 20. It may be that the results of the remarkable anti-Marxist revisionism going on in the historiography of the French Revolution will eventually compel us to change our generic conception of a revolution and thereby free social historians of the American Revolution from their stultifying fixation on oppression and class abuse as the primary sources of social protest and social change.

55. For a recent discussion of "whig history," which the authors describe as a special case of "present-centredness," see Adrian Wilson and T. G. Ashplant, "Whig History and Present-Centered History," and "Present-Centered History and the Problem of Historical Knowledge," *The Historical Journal*, 31 (1988), 1–16, 253–74.

56. Bailyn, *Origins of American Politics*, ix.

57. Bailyn, *Education in the Forming of American Society: Needs and Opportunities for Study* (Chapel Hill, N.C., 1960), 9–10.

58. Michael Zuckerman, "Fiction and Fission: Twentieth-Century Writing on the Founding Fathers," in H. Ben-Israel *et al.*, eds., *Religion, Ideology and Nationalism in Europe and America: Essays Presented in Honor of Yehoshua Arieli* (Jerusalem, 1986), 241.

59. Bailyn, "New England and a Wider World," in Hall and Allen, eds., *Seventeenth-Century New England*, 328.

60. Bailyn, "Lines of Force," 21.

61. Bailyn, "The Ideological Fulfillment of the American Revolution: A Commentary on the Constitution," *Faces of Revolution: Personalities and Themes in the Struggle for American Independence* (New York, 1990), 246.

62. Bailyn, "Lines of Force," 21.

63. Zuckerman, "Fiction and Fission," Ben-Israel *et al.*, eds., *Religion, Ideology and Nationalism*, 241; James A. Henretta, review of *Voyagers* and *Peopling* in *Journal*

of Interdisciplinary History, 19 (1988), 141. For an indictment of the present-centeredness of recent historical writing see David Lowenthal, "The Timeless Past: Some Anglo-American Historical Preconceptions," *Journal of American History*, 75 (1989), 1263–80.

64. Bailyn, *History and the Creative Imagination*, 13; Bailyn, "Lines of Force," 21.

65. Bailyn, "Central Themes," 15.

66. Bailyn, *The Ordeal of Thomas Hutchinson* (Cambridge, Mass., 1974), xii, vii–viii, xi.

67. *Ibid.*, 106, 107.

68. Bailyn, *Hutchinson*, ix. Carried too far, such a tragic view of the past, like neo-antiquarian or contextualist history in general, can make the past appear irrelevant. If the "distance" between the present and the past becomes sufficiently "great," if the "connections" between present and past become "finely" enough "attenuated," and if people in the present actually come to believe that they have "no stake in the outcome" of the events of the past, then that different, distant past might tend to drift away from us and be really lost. "The death of the past," in J. H. Plumb's sense of cleansing "the story of mankind from those deceiving visions of a purposeful past," of killing off "mythical, religious and political interpretations of the past," of eliminating all whiggish and other kinds of instrumental history, unfortunately tends to make people indifferent to the past that is left after all the cleansing and killing are done. If the American people do indeed reach the point where they believe that the American Revolution is so far away from them that they have "no stake in its outcome," then they may have about as much historical interest in it, as much concern with arguing and reading about it, as they now do with the Peloponnesian War. Is there one American in ten thousand today who could tell us who fought the Peloponnesian War, never mind who won it? J. H. Plumb, *The Death of the Past* (Boston, 1970), 17, 15.

69. To have too much historical consciousness is to have the temperament of someone like Andrew Eliot, whom Bailyn has written sensitively about. Eliot was the reasonable, tolerant, cautious, and indecisive Boston minister who knew too much to commit himself to the revolutionary movement. He was one of Nietzsche's historically minded men who could not "shake himself free from the delicate network of his truth and righteousness for a downright act of will or desire." Which is why Nietzsche believed that "forgetfulness is a property of all action." Too much "rumination," too much "historical sense," he wrote, "injures and finally destroys the living thing, be it a man or a people or a system of culture." Eliot was injured if not destroyed by his temperament. He could not accept absolute conclusions, intellectual or political; he insisted on seeing both sides of every major issue; and he always refused to decide anything unequivocally. He was sympathetic to the American cause, but he knew too that the break from England would bring terrible and unanticipated consequences; and thus he hesitated, and the Revolution passed him by. "It is possible we may be mistaken," he wrote: "things may appear very differently to others as upright as ourselves, and the same desirable effect may be produced by sentiments not in every respect consonant to ours." Bailyn ends his brief but penetrating sketch by underlining these "decent, reasonable, tolerant, and fatal words" of Eliot and by suggesting that these words are what the minister ought to be remembered by. He could have said the same about himself, or about any of his four creative historians. For the capacity to see things as Eliot did—to enter sympathetically into the minds of others, to grasp events in all their wholeness and without partisanship—is at the heart of the historical imagination. Bailyn, "Religion and Rev-

olution," *Perspectives in American History*, 4 (1970), 110. Friedrich Nietzsche, *The Use and Abuse of History*, trans. by Adrian Collins (New York, 1957), 6–8.

70. Bailyn, "Challenge of Modern Historiography," *American Historical Review*, 87 (1982), 6.

71. Bailyn has recently suggested that while the social history of the early American population as broadly conceived in the Peopling of America project is a new subject for him, the problem of blending analytical and narrative history is not new. "Structurally, I found some of the same problems of technical analysis and progressive narrative in *The New England Merchants*." Bailyn to Ekrich, April 16, 1981.

72. Bailyn, "Challenge of Modern Historiography," *American Historical Review*, 87 (1982), 10, 3, 13, 17.

73. Fernand Braudel, *The Mediterranean and Mediterranean World in the Age of Phillip II* (New York, 1973), II, 1244.

74. Bailyn, *Peopling of America*, 8.

75. Bailyn, "Challenge of Modern Historiography," 9.

76. Bailyn to Ekrich, April 16, 1981.

77. Bailyn, "Challenge of Modern Historiography," 5.

78. Nietzsche, *Use and Abuse of History*, 10.

79. "What one misses [in America]," writes the perceptive English historian J. R. Pole, "is that sense, inescapable in Europe, of the total, crumbled irrecoverability of the past, of its differentness, of the fact that it is dead." Pole, *Paths to the American Past* (New York, 1979), 251.

80. Bailyn, *Voyagers to the West: A Passage in the Peopling of America on the Eve of the Revolution* (New York, 1986), 4. Here in particular Bailyn seems to be drawing on the cosmopolitan perspective of the Jewish intellectual exiles he has known. From their intellectual core, which, said Bailyn, remained based in German-speaking Central Europe, the Jewish exiles of the 1930s always regarded the far outer American periphery as curious and "slightly exotic." Bailyn, *From Protestant Peasants to Jewish Intellectuals*, 11–12.

81. Bailyn, *Voyagers*, 5; Bailyn, *From Protestant Peasants to Jewish Intellectuals*, 2.

82. Bailyn, *Voyagers*, 506, 427, 502, 637.

83. See the reviews by Joyce Appleby in the *William and Mary Quarterly*, 3d ser., 44 (1987), 791–96; and by James A. Henretta in the *Journal of Interdisciplinary History*, 19 (1988), 138–42.

84. The radicalism of this eighteenth-century rise in the condition and aspirations of ordinary people can only be appreciated in the context of the scorn or indifference in which elites traditionally held the masses of common people. See Harry C. Payne, *The Philosophes and the People* (New Haven, Conn., 1976); and his "Elite Versus Popular Mentality in the Eighteenth Century," *Historical Reflections*, 2 (1976), 183–207.

85. Bailyn, *Voyagers*, 515–19.

86. Douglass Adair and John A. Schutz, eds. *Peter Oliver's Origin and Progress of the American Rebellion: A Tory View* (San Marino, Cal., 1963), 159.

87. Bailyn made an early attempt to connect his social history of the American population with politics in his essay "1776: A Year of Challenge—A World Transformed," *Journal of Law and Economics*, 19 (1976), 437–66.

"How Else Could It End?"

JACK N. RAKOVE

1. Bernard Bailyn, "The Problems of the Working Historian: A Comment," in Sidney Hook, ed., *Philosophy and History: A Symposium* (New York, 1963), 96. By

"anomalies in the data," Bailyn simply means evidence of change over time or, as the classic formulation for his seminar would have it, getting from point A to point B.

2. Subtitled, *A Passage in the Peopling of America on the Eve of the Revolution* (New York, 1986).

3. The same message was conveyed, implicitly and otherwise, to his students. As they learned only too well during their visits to Widener J, Bailyn could express this imperative in unnervingly direct terms. A typical discussion of the progress of one's research might go like this:

> BB: Well, have you been doing any work recently?
> STUDENT: [Long summary of research, findings, hypotheses, and the like.]
> BB: All this is very interesting. [Short restatement, perhaps a few sentences or so, of student's disquisition.] But . . . so what?

4. Cambridge, Mass., 1955.

5. Cambridge, Mass., 1974.

6. Subtitled, *Needs and Opportunities for Further Study* (Chapel Hill, N.C., 1960).

7. First printed in James M. Smith, *Seventeenth-Century America: Essays in Colonial America* (Chapel Hill, N.C., 1959), 90–115; on its republication, see A. Roger Ekirch, "Bernard Bailyn," *Dictionary of Literary Biography*, XVII, 21.

8. Cambridge, Mass., 1959.

9. Cambridge, Mass., 1967.

10. Bailyn, "The Central Themes of the American Revolution: An Interpretation," in Stephen G. Kurtz and James H. Hutson, eds., *Essays on the American Revolution* (Chapel Hill, N.C., 1972), 10–11, reprinted in *Faces of Revolution: Personalities and Themes in the Struggle for American Independence* (New York, 1990), 206.

11. Bernard Bailyn, *The Origins of American Politics* (New York, 1968), ix.

12. Thus in Linda Kerber's recent and quite thorough survey of "The Republican Ideology of the Revolutionary Generation," *American Quarterly*, 37 (1985), 474–95, Bailyn appears only in a passing reference in the introductory paragraph, while *The Ideological Origins* goes unmentioned.

13. Bailyn, "Central Themes," 22, 10, 14–15, 3; "Political Experience and Enlightenment Ideas in Eighteenth-Century America," *American Historical Review*, 67 (1961–62)," 351, reprinted in *Faces of Revolution*, 199.

14. Bailyn, *The Ideological Origins*, 319.

15. "Politics and Social Structure in Virginia," 91; "Political Experience," 350; *Education in the Forming of American Society*, 15–18; and see *Origins of American Politics*, 26–27, 96–97, and *The Ideological Origins*, 301–304.

16. Bailyn, "Central Themes," 24; Oscar Handlin and Mary Handlin, *Commonwealth: A Study of the Role of Government in the American Economy: Massachusetts, 1774–1861*, rev. ed. (Cambridge, Mass., 1969).

17. Oscar Handlin and Mary Handlin, *The Dimensions of Liberty* (Cambridge, Mass., 1961); and see the approving reference to this work in Bailyn, "The Challenge of Modern Historiography," *American Historical Review*, 87 (1982), 8.

18. One might note that the metaphor of territorial exploration that Bailyn used in earlier writings (*The Ideological Origins*, 21, 161, 231–32; and see below) has recently given way to a literally spatial metaphor that invites readers to view the great population movement of the colonial era from a satellite circling above the earth; "Challenge of Modern Historiography," 17, and *The Peopling of British North America: An Introduction* (New York, 1986), 3–5, 47–49.

19. Bailyn, *The Ideological Origins*, 319.

20. Nor have I forgotten Bailyn's assessment (*ibid.*, 9, 15) of the extended metaphor

that flows through Ebenezer Chaplin, *The State Compared to Rivers.* . . . (Boston, 1773).

21. Bailyn, "Politics and Social Structure," 114–15.
22. *Ibid.*, 96–104, 24–27. One is reminded of Bailyn's partiality for the opening chapter of David Cecil's *Melbourne*.
23. Bailyn, *Origins of American Politics*, 96–105.
24. *Ibid.*, 128–29.
25. Bailyn, "Common Sense," in *Fundamental Testaments of the American Revolution* (Washington, D.C., 1973 and reprinted in *Faces of Revolution*), 20, echoing "Central Themes," 24. The dig against the concept of "dysfunctionality"–a term I well recall being enjoined never to use–seems directed against Jack P. Greene.
26. Bailyn, *New England Merchants*, 88.
27. On this point, see especially *Ordeal of Hutchinson*, 199–208; and Bailyn, ed., "A Dialogue between an American and a European Englishman by Thomas Hutchinson [1768]," *Perspectives in American History*, 9 (1975), 341–410.
28. Bailyn, "Central Themes," 16.
29. Bailyn, "Butterfield's Adams: Notes for a Sketch," *William and Mary Quarterly*, 3d ser., 19 (1962), 253–54, 244–45 and reprinted in *Faces of Revolution*; *Ordeal of Hutchinson*, 2, 25–26, 371, 377.
30. Bailyn, *Ordeal of Hutchinson*, 25, 378–80; this concluding analysis is repeated nearly verbatim in "Central Themes," 16–17.
31. Bailyn, *Ordeal of Hutchinson*, 75, 380, 106–107.
32. Bailyn, *The Ideological Origins*, 75, 161, 232, 298; *Ordeal of Hutchinson*, 75; *Origins of American Politics*, 125, 130. By comparison, the throwaway metaphor of ideology as "intellectual switchboard" that Bailyn used in *The Ideological Origins* (22–23) does not merit the fussy commentary it has received. Bailyn replaced it with the image of ideology as "map" in "Central Themes," 7, 10–11.
33. Bailyn, *The Ideological Origins*, 302; *Ordeal of Hutchinson*, 106.
34. Bailyn, *Ordeal of Hutchinson*, 380; "Butterfield's Adams," 253; "Common Sense," 22; "1776: A Year of Challenge—A World Transformed," *Journal of Law and Economics*, 19 (1976), 465, reprinted in *Faces of Revolution*.
35. Bailyn, *New England Merchants*, 194.
36. Bailyn, "Political Experience," 348–49.
37. Handlin and Handlin, *Commonwealth*, 242.
38. Bailyn, *The Ideological Origins*, 246–72.
39. As quoted (without further attribution, but the "bar none" has an authentic ring to it) in Walter Berns, "The New Pursuit of Happiness," *Public Interest*, 86 (1987), 67. If memory serves me correctly, Bailyn accompanied his distribution of the text of the Statute to his students with the injunction to memorize it.
40. Bailyn, "Political Experience," 345–46.
41. For Bailyn's characterization of Madison, see "Boyd's Jefferson: Notes for a Sketch," *New England Quarterly*, 33 (1960), 388–90, reprinted in *Faces of Revolution*, 30–31; for Madison's ideas, see his letter to Jefferson, October 24, 1787, and *Federalist* 10, in Robert Rutland *et al.*, eds., *The Papers of James Madison* (Chicago and Charlottesville, Va., 1962–), X, 209–14, 266.
42. Andrew Delbanco, "Movers and Shapers," *The New Republic*, 195 (December 8, 1986), 32–38.
43. One cannot avoid being struck, too, by the extent to which *Voyagers to the West* answers Handlin's complaint that so little has been done to study either the actual transportation of immigrants to America or the role of the European exit ports in emigration; see Handlin, *The Uprooted*, 2d ed. enlarged (Boston, 1973), 310–11.
44. Bailyn, "1776—A Year of Challenge," 456.

45. *Ibid.*, 460–61.
46. Bailyn, "Challenge of Modern Historiography," 10–11.
47. One proviso bears mention, however. Among the positions that Thomas Hutchinson occupied when he halted at the outer boundaries of accepted political thought was "the need to understand allegiance as perpetual and total"; to move beyond that point—as we know best from the work of James Kettner—the Americans had "to move to a new conception altogether, in which allegiance would arise from desire, free migration and alienation, and the legalization of a mere commitment to a way of life." *Ordeal of Hutchinson*, 107.
48. Bailyn, "Challenge of Modern Historiography," 10–11.

Colonization and the Common Law
in Ireland and Virginia, 1569–1634
DAVID THOMAS KONIG

1. Ninety *English Reports* 1089; Thomas Jefferson, *Notes on the State of Virginia* [1785], ed. William Peden (New York, 1954), 132.
2. For the application of this system with regard to suppressing crime and disorder first in the English marchlands and then in Ireland and Virginia, see David Thomas Konig, " 'Dale's Laws' and the Non-Common Law Origins of Criminal Justice in Virginia," *American Journal of Legal History*, 26 (1982), 354–75.
3. Sir Edward Coke, *The Fourth Part of the Institutes of the Laws of England* [1628] (London, 1797), 244–45.
4. *Ibid.*, 229–30.
5. See, generally, J. G. Bellamy, *Bastard Feudalism and the Law* (London, 1989), esp. 128–40.
6. Irish historiography has benefited enormously from an outpouring of excellent scholarship since the 1960s. See, in this regard, the many works of David Beers Quinn, listed in a career bibliography in K. R. Andrews, N. P. Canny, and P. E. H. Hair, eds., *The Westward Enterprise: English Activities in Ireland, the Atlantic, and America, 1480–1650* (Detroit, 1979). Among more recent contributions, see Ciaran Brady and Raymond Gillespie, eds., *Natives and Newcomers: Essays on the Making of Irish Colonial Society, 1534–1642* (Dublin, 1986); Nicholas P. Canny, *The Elizabethan Conquest of Ireland: A Pattern Established, 1565–1576* (Hassocks, 1976); Stephen G. Ellis, *Tudor Ireland: Crown, Community and Conflict of Cultures, 1470–1603* (New York, 1985); Raymond Gillespie, *Colonial Ulster: The Settlement of East Ulster, 1600–1641* (Cork, 1985); Michael MacCarthy-Morrogh, *The Munster Plantation: English Migration to Southern Ireland, 1583–1641* (New York, 1985); Hans S. Pawlisch, *Sir John Davies and the Conquest of Ireland: A Study in Legal Imperialism* (Cambridge, England, 1985); Michael Perceval-Maxwell, *The Scottish Migration to Ulster in the Reign of James I* (London, 1973); Philip S. Robinson, *The Plantation of Ulster: British Settlement in an Irish Landscape, 1600–1670* (Dublin, 1984).
7. Terence O. Ranger, "Richard Boyle and the Making of an Irish Fortune, 1588–1614," *Irish Historical Studies*, 10 (1957), 259.
8. Canny, *Conquest*, 92–95. Other Anglo-Norman leaders, on the other hand, had their own plan of reform, which relied instead upon an extension of the common law. On this, see Brendan Bradshaw, *The Irish Constitutional Revolution of the Sixteenth Century* (Cambridge, England, 1979), 32–48.
9. Michael de L. Landon, *Erin and Britannia: The Historical Background to a Modern Tragedy* (Chicago, 1981), 63–100.
10. *Ibid.*, 160–61.

11. Canny, *Conquest*, 22.
12. Ellis, *Tudor Ireland*, 164.
13. These forms and practices were most notable in those areas farthest from London, notably Munster and Connaught. *Ibid.*, 161–62.
14. Canny, *Conquest*, 118.
15. *Ibid.*, 53.
16. Ciaran Brady, "Court, Castle and Country: The Framework of Government in Tudor Ireland," in Brady and Gillespie, *Natives and Newcomers*, 39–40.
17. Ellis, *Tudor Ireland*, 291; Brady, "Court, Castle and Country," 36–37; Canny, *Conquest*, 49, 116.
18. *Ibid.*, 36–37.
19. J. S. Brewer and William Bullen, eds., *Calendar of the Carew Manuscripts, Preserved in the Archepiscopal Library at Lambeth, 1515–1574* (London, 1867), 367 [hereafter, *Carew Mss.*].
20. *Ibid.*, 258. The reference was to feudal exactions of military service and forced contributions of food and supplies to their lords.
21. Liam Irwin, "The Irish Presidency Courts, 1569–1672," in *The Irish Jurist*, new ser., 12 (1977), 110–11.
22. *Carew Mss.*, xcix–c.
23. *Ibid.*
24. Sir Edward Coke, *First Institutes of the Laws of England* (Philadelphia, 1836), 9.
25. Pawlisch, *Sir John Davies*, 76.
26. Coke, *Fourth Institute*, 242; see also Sir William Blackstone, *Commentaries on the Laws of England* (London, 1765), III, 113.
27. Coke, *Fourth Institute*, 245–46.
28. *Calendar of State Papers, Ireland, 1600*, 403 [hereafter, *CSPI*].
29. Sir Edmund Spenser, "A View of the State of Irelande, discoursed by way of a dialogue between Eudoxus and Irenius" (1608), in Rudolf Gottfried, ed., *Spenser's Prose Works* (Baltimore, 1949), 147–48. On this point I am indebted to the work and communication of Nicholas Canny. See, in particular, his "Edmund Spenser and the Development of an Anglo-Irish Identity," *Yearbook of English Studies*, 13 (1983), 1–19. For a contrary interpretation of Spenser, see Ciaran Brady, "Spenser's Irish Crisis: Humanism and Expansion in the 1590s," *Past and Present*, 111 (1986), 17–49, with Canny's "Comment," *ibid.*, 120 (1988), 201–209.
30. Sir John Davies, "A Discovery of the True Causes Why Ireland was Never Entirely Subdued nor Brought under Obedience of the Crown of England until the Beginning of His Majesty's Happy Reign" [1612], in Henry Morley, ed., *Ireland Under Elizabeth and James the First*, (London, 1890), 280–85, 290–91. Davies's career and his role in promoting the common law as an instrument of "legal imperialism" are the subject of Pawlisch, *Sir John Davies*.
31. On Ley's influence, see Robinson, *Ulster*, 60–62.
32. Perceval-Maxwell, *Scottish Migration*, 211.
33. *Carew Mss.*, 399–400.
34. Spenser, "View of Ireland," 54–55, 67.
35. *Calendar of State Papers, Domestic Series, of the Reign of James I, 1623–1625*, ed. Mary Anne Everett Green (London, 1859), 134. Coke expected to die in Ireland, and Prince Charles argued against the obviously punitive purpose of sending the seventy-four-year-old justice there, pointing out that "other constructions will be put on this employment." *Ibid.*, 144, 150. See also Stephen D. White, *Sir Edward Coke and "The Grievances of the Commonwealth," 1621–1628* (Chapel Hill, N.C., 1979), 9.
36. Davies, "True Causes," 291.

37. Landon, *Erin and Britannia*, 102.
38. James H. Kettner, *The Development of American Citizenship 1608–1870* (Chapel Hill, N.C., 1978), 5–7, 31–32.
39. For the accomplishments of "the most successful of a crowd of young men" who exploited this system, see Ranger, "Richard Boyle."
40. MacCarthy-Morrogh, *Munster*, 96–97.
41. On this class, see Ranger, "Richard Boyle," 296–97, and Perceval-Maxwell, *Scottish Migration*, 210.
42. Landon, *Erin and Britannia*, 108.
43. White, *Coke*, 59, 105, 113, 136.
44. Robinson, *Ulster*, 80–82.
45. *Ibid.*, 209.
46. "The Copie of Samuell Pidgeons Petition against George Canning in Ireland with the Company," in Worshipful Company of Ironmongers Company Clerk's Outletter Books, 1620–1899, Microform (London, 1989). I am indebted to Mr. James Robinson for referring me to these materials.
47. *Ibid.*
48. *Ibid.* Compare Canning's efforts with those typical of bastard feudalism as described in Bellamy, *Bastard Feudalism*, 50.
49. On Strafford, see Hugh F. Kearney, *Strafford in Ireland 1633–1641: A Study in Absolutism* (New York, 1961), esp. 69–84.
50. On these similarities, see Brooke S. Blades, "English Villages in the Londonderry Plantation," *Post-Medieval Archaeology*, 20 (1986), 257–70, esp. 259–60, and compare with Ivor Noel Hume, *Martin's Hundred* (New York, 1982).
51. Nicholas P. Canny, "The Ideology of English Colonization: From Ireland to America," *William and Mary Quarterly*, 3d ser., 30 (1973), 575–98.
52. For a list of these men, see Howard Mumford Jones, "Origins of the Colonial Idea in England," *Proceedings of the American Philosophical Society*, 85 (1942), 463. On their concept of the two enterprises as part of a single effort, see Robinson, *Ulster*, 58–60.
53. Samuel M. Bemiss, ed., *The Three Charters of the Virginia Company of London, with Seven Related Documents, 1606–1621* (Williamsburg, Va., 1957), 14.
54. Sir Edward Coke, *The Second Part of the Institutes of the Laws of England* (London, 1797), 496. Charters were to "have no strict or narrow interpretation," but "to have a liberall and favourable construction." *Ibid.*
55. Bemiss, *Three Charters*, 9.
56. John Smith, "A True Relation of such occurrences and accidents of note, as hath happened in Virginia . . ." (1608), in Philip L. Barbour, ed., *The Complete Works of Captain John Smith (1580–1631) in Three Volumes* (Chapel Hill, N.C., 1986), I, 41. Smith, "The Generall Historie of Virginia, New-England, and the Summer Isles . . ." (1624), in *ibid.*, II, 152. Smith boasted that after his rescue by Newport "he quickly took such order with such Lawyers, that he layd them by the heeles till he sent some of them prisoners for England." *Ibid.*
57. Susan M. Kingsbury, ed., *The Records of the Virginia Company of London* (Washington, D.C., 1906–1935), III, 12–24 [hereafter, *RVC*].
58. Samuel Purchas, *Hakluytus posthumus, or, Purchas his Pilgrimes: containing a history of the world in sea voyages and lande travells by Englishmen and others* [1625] (Glasgow, 1905–1907), XIX, 56–57.
59. Smith, *Generall Historie*, II, 241–42.
60. Irene W. D. Hecht, "The Virginia Colony, 1607–1640: A Study in Frontier Growth" (unpublished Ph.D. dissertation, University of Washington, 1969), 75.
61. Helen M. Cam, *Liberties and Communities in Medieval England* (New York, 1963), xiii.

62. The governor was Edward Maria Wingfield, the councilor George Kendall. Samuel M. Bemiss, "John Martin, Ancient Adventurer," *Virginia Magazine of History and Biography*, 65 (1957), 219–20. James P. C. Southall, "Captain John Martin of Brandon on the James," *ibid.*, 54 (1946), 25–28, 31, 36–37. Lyon G. Tyler, ed., *Encyclopedia of Virginia Biography* (New York, 1915), I, 77–78. Charles E. Hatch, Jr., *The First Seventeen Years: Virginia, 1607–1624* (Williamsburg, Va., 1957), 3, 75.

63. *Ibid.*, 75; Southall, "John Martin," 41.

64. Hatch, *First Seventeen Years*, 76.

65. Conway Robinson and R. A. Brock, "Abstract of the Proceedings of the Virginia Company of London, 1619–1624," Virginia Historical Society *Collections*, new ser., VII–VIII, (Richmond, Va., 1888–89), VII, 187–88. Compare Martin's action here with that in Donegal in 1625, described by Gillespie, *Colonial Ulster*, 208.

66. Konig, " 'Dale's Laws,' " *passim*.

67. Bemiss, *Three Charters*, 98, 102.

68. *RVC*, III, 333.

69. On the emergence of this group, which rose to power on the basis of its Virginia accomplishments, regardless of transplanted social status imported from England, see Bernard Bailyn, "Politics and Social Structure in Virginia," in James Morton Smith, ed., *Seventeenth-Century America: Essays in Colonial History* (Chapel Hill, N.C., 1957), 90–115, esp. 94–97.

70. H. R. McIlwaine and John Pendleton Kennedy, eds., *Journals of the House of Burgesses of Virginia* (Richmond, Va., 1905–15), I, 4, 6–7; "Proceedings of the Virginia Assembly, 1619," in Lyon G. Tyler, ed., *Narratives of Early Virginia, 1606–1625* (New York, 1907), 262.

71. *RVC*, I, 333.

72. "Instructions to the Governor and Council of State in Virginia," in Bemiss., ed., *Three Charters*, 109–10. In a separate "ordinance and Constitution for Council and Assembly in Virginia" issued on that same date, the Company ordered those bodies "to imitate and followe the policy of the forme of government, lawes, custome, manners of loyall and other administracion of justice used in the realme of England. . . ." *Ibid.*, 128.

73. *RVC*, I, 610, 614.

74. Richard L. Morton, *Colonial Virginia* (Chapel Hill, N.C., 1960), I, 49–50.

75. *RVC*, II, 54.

76. "Proceedings of the Virginia Assembly, 1619," in Tyler, ed., *Narratives*, 262; Craven, *Dissolution*, 65.

77. Alexander Brown, *The First Republic in America* (Boston, 1898), 292–95.

78. Robinson and Brock, "Abstracts," I, 190–91.

79. *Ibid.*, I, 191.

80. Gillespie, *Colonial Ulster*, 94–101. The process accelerated under Charles I.

81. Robinson and Brock, "Abstract," I, 186–87; *RVC*, II, 40–41. Coke argued that the law of the forest was "bounded by the common laws of the realm," in *Fourth Institute*, 289–90, but others disagreed. No eyre had been held in England since the fourteenth century, owing to the resentment caused by its great powers and virtually limitless jurisdiction, but the recent publication of John Manwood's *A Treatise of the Lawes of the Forest* (London, 1615) may have supplied as much inspiration as instruction on forest privileges. For vestiges of forest law in Caroline England, see P. A. J. Pettit, *The Royal Forests of Northamptonshire: A Study in Their Economy, 1558–1714* (Northampton, England, 1968), 83–95.

82. On this turnover in leadership, see Bailyn, "Politics and Social Structure," 95–96.

83. Craven, *Dissolution*, 310–18. Appropriately, the chief justice of King's Bench was Sir James Ley, proponent of the common law of Ireland.
84. Coke, *Second Institute*, 495–96.
85. Craven, *Dissolution*, 330–31.
86. H. R. McIlwaine, ed., *Minutes of the Council and General Court of Colonial Virginia, 1622–1632, 1670–1676* (Richmond, Va., 1924), 57.
87. *RVC*, IV, 565.
88. William Waller Hening, comp., *The Statutes at Large, Being a Collection of All the Laws of Virginia (1619–1792)* (Richmond, Va., 1809–23), I, 125. It might be noted that these same "old planters" also exempted themselves from war taxes and declared that only the General Assembly could levy any taxes on land or goods. *Ibid.*, 124.
89. *Ibid.*, 127, 132–33.
90. *Ibid.*, 131.
91. H. R. McIlwaine, ed., *Minutes of the Council and General Court*, 16, 130, 484; *Virginia Magazine of History and Biography*, 27 (1919), 34.
92. Hening, *Statutes*, I, 168–69.
93. *Ibid.*, 224.

"Some Root of Bitterness"
PHILIP GREVEN

1. Among the most important studies of apocalypticism in England and America in the seventeenth and eighteenth centuries, see: J. F. Maclear, "New England and the Fifth Monarchy: The Quest for the Millennium in Early American Puritanism," *William and Mary Quarterly*, 3d ser., 32 (1975), 223–60; B. S. Capp, *The Fifth Monarchy Men: A Study in Seventeenth-Century English Millennarianism* (London, 1972); Frank E. Manuel, *A Portrait of Isaac Newton* (Cambridge, Mass., 1968), the most illuminating psychological analysis of a seventeenth-century apocalyptic yet written, although he fails to connect Newton's apocalypticism to the smoldering rage within; Robert Middlekauff, *The Mathers: Three Generations of Puritan Intellectuals, 1596–1728* (New York, 1971), the most probing study of early American apocalyptics, a rich and and sensitive set of portraits; Kenneth Silverman, *The Life and Times of Cotton Mather* (New York, 1984), an essential analysis; James West Davidson, *The Logic of Millennial Thought: Eighteenth-Century New England* (New Haven, Conn., 1977); Nathan O. Hatch, *The Sacred Cause of Liberty: Republican Thought and the Millennium in Revolutionary New England* (New Haven, Conn., 1977); Ruth H. Bloch, *Visionary Republic: Millennial Themes in American Thought, 1756–1800* (Cambridge, England, 1985). Two of the most notable studies of nineteenth-century apocalypticism are: J. F. C. Harrison, *The Second Coming: Popular Millenarianism 1780–1850* (New Brunswick, N.J., 1979), and Robert Mapes Anderson, *Vision of the Disinherited: The Making of American Pentecostalism* (New York, 1979), the most brilliant study written on this subject so far.
2. Historians have yet to explore the roots, experiences, and consequences of child abuse over the past centuries to the extent that this complex subject warrants. A beginning has been made, however; see, among others: Lloyd deMause, ed., *The History of Childhood* (New York, 1974); Elizabeth Pleck, *Domestic Tyranny: The Making of Social Policy Against Family Violence from Colonial Times to the Present* (New York, 1987); Linda Gordon, *Heroes of Their Own Lives: The Politics and History of Family Violence, Boston 1880–1960* (New York, 1988).
3. For evidence of the role of suppressed anger in apocalyptics, see: Middlekauff,

The Mathers, esp. chapter 18; Silverman, *Cotton Mather*, 228–29, 235, 254–57, 328, 433n, and *passim*; Manuel, *Portrait*, 343–48 and *passim*. Also see Philip Greven, *The Protestant Temperament: Patterns of Child-Rearing, Religious Experience, and the Self in Early America* (New York, 1977; Chicago, 1988), 109–24 and *passim*, for a discussion of anger among evangelicals.

4. The theme of punishment is central to Jonathan Edwards's theology also. See Norman Fiering's analysis of "Hell and the Humanitarians," *Jonathan Edwards's Moral Thought and Its British Context* (Chapel Hill, N.C., 1981), chapter 5. Fiering is intensely uncomfortable with psychology, and goes to great lengths to avoid dealing with Edwards's psyche. Yet even he cannot avoid the obvious fact that Edwards's obsession with punishment must have had personal roots. He acknowledges (page 201) that "Edwards's personal involvement with the idea of hell is woven into all of his discussions of the subject," yet he asks how such "a man as deeply sensitive and tender as he appears to have been" could "dwell so unflinchingly upon the most excruciating and unimaginable horrors," without providing his readers with a satisfactory answer. The question is critically important, and perhaps someone someday will try to answer it with the psychological analysis that it would require. But any such analysis will necessitate taking corporal punishments seriously, and reckoning with the long-term impact that such physical pain had upon such "sensitive and tender" souls as Jonathan Edwards's. It should not be forgotten that Edwards's daughter, Esther Edwards Burr, began to whip her daughter at the age of nine months. See Greven, *The Protestant Temperament*, 35–36.

5. The subject of corporal punishment has been ignored by most historians. The only substantive analysis in the American context so far is Myra C. Glenn, *Campaigns Against Corporal Punishment: Prisoners, Sailors, Women, and Children in Antebellum America* (Albany, N.Y., 1984). For England, see Ian Gibson, *The English Vice: Beating, Sex and Shame in Victorian England and After* (London, 1978). Otherwise, we must find partial commentaries in various scholarly studies of child-rearing and family life. See, for example: Linda A. Pollock, *Forgotten Children: Parent-Child Relations from 1500 to 1900* (Cambridge, England, 1983); Lawrence Stone, *The Family, Sex and Marriage in England, 1500–1800* (New York, 1977); Edmund S. Morgan, *The Puritan Family: Religion & Domestic Relations in Seventeenth-Century New England* (rev. ed; New York, 1966).

Even I underestimated the pervasiveness and importance of corporal punishments among evangelicals in *The Protestant Temperament* (see 49–50). Subsequent research on the nineteenth and twentieth centuries among evangelicals, fundamentalists, and pentecostals, however, has convinced me of the enduring centrality of corporal punishment for the shaping of apocalyptics and apocalypticism. See my study of corporal punishment for further discussion and analysis: Philip Greven, *Spare the Child: The Religious Roots of Punishment and the Psychological Impact of Physical Abuse* (New York, 1990). The most remarkable analysis of corporal punishment, from a psychological perspective, is Alice Miller's *For Your Own Good: Hidden Cruelty in Child-Rearing and the Roots of Violence*, Hildegarde and Hunter Hannum, trans. (New York, 1983). Her work is essential for historians concerned with this subject in both America and Europe.

6. Michael Wigglesworth, *The Day of Doom or a Poetical Description of the Great and Last Judgment with other poems*, ed. Kenneth B. Murdock (New York, 1966), 10, 57. For his memories of fire in early childhood in England, see Michael Wigglesworth, "Autobiography," in John Ward Dean, *Memoir of Rev. Michael Wigglesworth, Author of the Day of Doom* (2d ed.; Albany, N.Y., 1871), Appendix I, 136.

7. Wigglesworth, *Day of Doom*, 15, 19, 20.
8. *Ibid.*, 41–42, 44, 54, 56.
9. *Ibid.*, 58–59.
10. Edward, who was born about 1693, was the only child of Wigglesworth's third marriage, and the last of eight born, including six daughters and two sons. Edward Wigglesworth's journal is in Michael Wigglesworth, Ms. Diary (Old Ms.), S-6 I. Series W (5) 5 W 3A-3, Box 15, New England Historic Genealogical Society, Boston, Mass. (The contractions have been expanded and italics added to this text.)
11. Wigglesworth, *Day of Doom*, 60–63. The sadism of Edwards's vision of Hell is evident from the footnote on the Marquis de Sade in Fiering's *Jonathan Edwards's Moral Thought*, 254, n. 143. But Fiering himself evades the implications of his own association of Edwards and de Sade. Anyone who doubts the sadistic quality of Edwards's vision needs only to read his sermons to confront the sadism of his god. See, for instance, "The Future Punishment of the Wicked Unavoidable and Intolerable" in Clarence H. Faust and Thomas H. Johnson, eds., *Jonathan Edwards: Representative Selections* (New York, 1935), 144–54.

   For the connections between rigid character and sadomasochism, see David Shapiro, *Autonomy and Rigid Character* (New York, 1981), chapters 5, 6. His analysis provides a valuable paradigm for the psychological analysis of both Puritans and evangelicals for those able and willing to make use of it. Also see Elaine Scarry, *The Body in Pain: The Making and Unmaking of the World* (New York, 1985), for an exploration of pain and torture.
12. Wigglesworth, *Day of Doom*, 64.
13. Michael Wigglesworth, "God's Controversy With New-England," in Perry Miller and Thomas H. Johnson, eds., *The Puritans* (New York, 1938), 614, 616. For jeremiads, see: Perry Miller, *The New England Mind from Colony to Province* (Cambridge, Mass., 1953); Sacvan Bercovitch, *The American Jeremiad* (Madison, Wis., 1978); Harry S. Stout, *The New England Soul: Preaching and Religious Culture in Colonial New England* (New York, 1986).
14. Wigglesworth, "God's Controversy," 612–14, 616.
15. Michael Wigglesworth, "Meditation II," and "Meditation III" in *Meat Out of the Eater: or, Meditations Concerning the Necessity, End, and Usefulness of Afflictions unto God's Children. All tending to Prepare Them for, and Comfort Them Under the Cross.* (5th ed.; Boston, 1717), 6–7.
16. Wigglesworth, "Light in Darkness," Songs II and III, in *Meat Out of the Eater*, 41–42.
17. For other odes to flagellation, see Gibson, *The English Vice.* Also see William B. Ober, "Bottoms Up! The Fine Arts and Flagellation," in *Bottoms Up: A Pathologist's Essays on Medicine and the Humanities* (Carbondale, Ill., 1987), 3–39.
18. Michael Wigglesworth, "Meditation IX, The Carriage of a Child of God/ Under his Fathers smarting Rod," in *Meat Out of the Eater*, and in Miller and Johnson, *The Puritans*, 620–21. For contemporary examples associating parental and divine punishments, see: J. Richard Fugate, *What the Bible Says About . . . Child Training* (Garland, Texas, 1980); Larry Christenson, *The Christian Family* (Minneapolis, Minn., 1970); Paul D. Meier, *Christian Child-Rearing and Personality Development* (Grand Rapids, Mich., 1977); Larry Tomczak, *God, the Rod, and Your Child's Bod: The Art of Loving Correction for Christian Parents* (Old Tappan, N.J., 1981).
19. For dissociation and identification with an aggressor, see: Sándor Ferenczi, "Confusion of Tongues Between Adults and the Child," in Jeffrey Moussaieff Masson, *The Assault on Truth: Freud's Suppression of the Seduction Theory* (New York, 1982), Appendix C, esp. 300–302. Also see Judith Dupont, ed., *The Clinical Diary of*

Sándor Ferenczi (Cambridge, Mass., 1988), *passim*, and Miller, *For Your Own Good, passim*.

The most dramatic form dissociation takes is in the formation of multiple personalities, which always emerge from intense and violent abuse, both physical and sexual, in childhood. See, for instance: Eugene L. Bliss, "Multiple Personalities: A Report of 14 Cases With Implications for Schizophrenia and Hysteria," *Archives of General Psychiatry*, 37 (1980), 1388–97, and *Multiple Personality, Allied Disorders, and Hypnosis* (New York, 1986); Bessel A. van der Kolk, "The Psychological Consequences of Overwhelming Life Experiences," in Bessel A. van der Kolk, *Psychological Trauma* (Washington, D.C., 1987), 6–7 and *passim*. See Frank W. Putnam, Jr., "Dissociation as a Response to Extreme Trauma," in Richard P. Kluft, ed., *Childhood Antecedents of Multiple Personality* (Washington, D.C., 1985), 65–97. For personal experiences, see: Chris Costner Sizemore and Elen Sain Pittillo, *I'm Eve* (New York, 1983); Flora Rheta Schreiber, *Sybil* (New York, 1973); Daniel Keyes, *The Minds of Billy Milligan* (New York, 1981).

For a remarkable example of dissociation under the blows of God, see Cotton Mather's account of his own experience, in Greven, *The Protestant Temperament*, 79.

20. Wigglesworth, "Carriage of a Child," 621. Also see Miller, *For Your Own Good, passim*, and Greven, *The Protestant Temperament*, 77–86, 111–14.

21. Wigglesworth, "Carriage of a Child," 621–22 (italics added).

22. Edmund S. Morgan, ed., *The Diary of Michael Wigglesworth, 1653–1657: The Conscience of a Puritan* (rev. ed.; New York, 1965), 101 (italics omitted). I am deeply indebted to Professor Morgan for his meticulous edition of this diary. The Reverend Samuel Hopkins, a devoted student of Jonathan Edwards, was to make a willingness to be damned central to his theology in the late eighteenth century. For an acute analysis of this phenomenon, see Miller, *For Your Own Good*, 61, 65, 145, 192–93, and *passim*.

23. See, for example, R. E. Helfer and C. H. Kempe, eds., *The Battered Child* (2nd ed.; Chicago, 1974), and Ruth S. and C. Henry Kempe, *Child Abuse* (Cambridge, Mass., 1978). Also see Murray A. Straus, Richard J. Gelles, and Suzanne K. Steinmetz, *Behind Closed Doors: Violence in the American Family* (Garden City, N.Y., 1981), esp. 14–16.

24. For an excellent account of his life, see Richard Crowder, *No Featherbed to Heaven: A Biography of Michael Wigglesworth, 1631–1705* (n.p., 1962). Dean's *Memoir* remains invaluable as a source of information and texts concerning Wigglesworth. Other useful information is to be found in Deloraine Pendre Corey, *The History of Malden, Massachusetts, 1633–1785* (Malden, Mass., 1899).

25. Wigglesworth, *Diary*, 45, 67, 10, 21.

26. Michael Wigglesworth, "Autobiography," in Dean, *Memoir*, 137–39. For Edward Wigglesworth's account of his illness, see his letter to John Winthrop, Massachusetts Historical Society, *Collections*, 3d ser., IX (1846), 296–97. For other details, see Crowder, *No Featherbed to Heaven*, 15–17. Crowder also notes (13–14) the use of the "birch rod" by Ezekiel Cheever, Michael Wigglesworth's first teacher, observing that he was "An excellent and in-the-long-run beloved teacher despite the physical violence of his discipline. . . ."

27. For an analysis of attitudes toward the body, see Greven, *The Protestant Temperament*, especially 65–73. For a discussion of the persistent connections between hypochondria and melancholy, see Stanley W. Jackson, *Melancholia and Depression: From Hippocratic Times to Modern Times* (New Haven, Conn., 1986), chapter 11 and *passim*.

28. Wigglesworth, *Diary*, 6, 14. For a strikingly similar experience, see Allen Wheelis's

memoir of being forced to cut grass with a straight-razor for an entire summer by his invalid father, and the sudden eruption of rage and the immediate terror of reprisal by whippings that he feared from his rebellious outburst: Alan Wheelis, *How People Change* (New York, 1975), chapters 5–6.

29. Wigglesworth, *Diary*, 29, 17. All italicized entries in his diary were written in shorthand and were transcribed by Edmund Morgan. See also the notes from his Commonplace book in Dean, *Memoir*, 58–60. The "Commonplace" book is actually an erratic continuation of his previous diary, beginning with an entry dated March 1658 and continuing to 1670, with his own son Edward's journal included in the back of the volume.

Wigglesworth's relationship with his mother, Esther Wigglesworth, is frustratingly obscure. There are only seven explicit references to her in his published diary, none in the subsequent manuscript diary; and there are only three references in the published diary even to his "parents," which would include his mother. He is concerned about not being dutiful to her, not honoring her, and not loving her ("my want of love and dutifulness to my parents," Wigglesworth, *Diary*, 50). Although he notes that she moved into his household and presumably continued to live with him after his first wife's death, there is no mention of her in his later diary entries. Her death is unrecorded, and I have not been able to discover the date even after a diligent search of probate and other records. My assumption, however, is that she probably lived at least until 1670, when the Ms. diary ceases, and probably died sometime between 1670 and 1679. She would probably have been in her midsixties in 1670, assuming that she and her husband were born about the same time. Crowder assumes that she was alive in 1663, when Wigglesworth went to Bermuda, and that she had died by 1672, when his daughter Mercy married. Crowder, *No Featherbed to Heaven*, 126, 149.

30. Wigglesworth, *Diary*, 49–51.
31. *Ibid.*, 54–55.
32. *Ibid.*, 56–57. The spleen was considered to be the source of anger, spite, and malice and, according to humoral medical theories, was believed to be the primary physical cause of melancholy. See Jackson, *Melancholia and Depression, passim*.
33. Wigglesworth, *Diary*, 3–6, 9, 31. Ian Gibson explores the relationship of shame and corporal punishment in *The English Vice*, chapter 8. See also Greven, *The Protestant Temperament*, 124–40, for a discussion of sexuality among evangelicals, including Wigglesworth.
34. Wigglesworth, *Diary*, 70, 71, 75.
35. *Ibid.*, 79.
36. *Ibid.*, 79–80. He worried about "the lawfulness of marrying with a Kinswoman, because the mothers sister is forbidden" (87), but proceeded with his marriage nonetheless.
37. *Ibid.*, 85–87.
38. *Ibid.*, 87–88.
39. *Ibid.*, 88–89.
40. *Ibid.*, 91–93; Crowder, *No Featherbed to Heaven*, 90.
41. *Ibid.*, 94.
42. *Ibid.*, 96.
43. Crowder, *No Featherbed to Heaven*, 98–100, 102, 121. For diary entries after May 1657, when Morgan's edition ends, see the Ms. Diary, New England Historical Genealogical Society, Boston, Mass.
44. Wigglesworth, *The Day of Doom*, 2–3. For his own sense of being melancholy, see Wigglesworth, *Diary*, 81, 84, and *passim*.
45. See Greven, *The Protestant Temperament*, 111–13, and *Spare the Child*. Also see

Miller, *For Your Own Good*. In my review essay on John Demos's *Entertaining Satan: Witchcraft and the Culture of Early New England* (New York, 1982) in *History and Theory*, 23 (1984), 250–51, I noted the connections of witchcraft and child abuse evident in his text, and drew out some of the larger and longer-term implications of abuse for our understanding of early American culture.

46. John Owen King III, *The Iron of Melancholy: Structures of Spiritual Conversion in America from the Puritan Conscience to Victorian Neurosis* (Middletown, Conn., 1983), 28. King's analysis is illuminating, particularly in terms of tracking these patterns of melancholy and obsessive-compulsive neuroses over the course of two and a half centuries. The connections between physical violence against children in the form of discipline and punishment and melancholy and depression are rarely noted, even by sophisticated psychological studies. See, for instance, the fascinating and important analysis done by Jackson in *Melancholia and Depression*. The topics of discipline and punishment are not even mentioned in the index.

47. Alice James, whose life made her feel "in-valid," as Jean Strouse notes, was strikingly similar to Wigglesworth in her neurasthenia. Strouse observes that one of the central sources of Alice James's illness was the murderous impulse that she felt toward her beloved father, and the "towering rage" that is visible in her writings could not be expressed directly or openly toward her father, with the result that "she turned the full force of her fury on herself, making herself literally ill." Jean Strouse, *Alice James: A Biography* (Boston, 1980), 266, 120. For an excellent discussion of neurasthenia, see 102–106.

48. See David Shapiro, *Neurotic Styles* (New York, 1965), and particularly the remarkable analysis of obsessive-compulsive neurosis in *Autonomy and Rigid Character*. Also see David Leverentz's *The Language of Puritan Feelings: An Exploration in Literature, Psychology, and Social History* (New Brunswick, N.J., 1980), which focuses upon the centrality of obsessiveness for an understanding of Puritan character. He argues (page 117) that "Puritanism was not the product of strong patriarchs breaking the child's will, at least not at the start," but he fails to take into account the experiences so many people had with corporal punishments and abuse that shaped their characters from an early age.

   For an important analysis of the role of sexual abuse in the origins of hysteria, a reality that Sigmund Freud once recognized but later minimized, see: Masson, *The Assault on Truth*. For further discussion of obsessive-compulsiveness and sadomasochism, see my book on corporal punishment, *Spare the Child*.

49. For an exploration of issues around the breaking of children's wills, and the subsequent consequences for the characters and beliefs of adults, see Greven, *The Protestant Temperament* and *Spare the Child*. For a remarkably acute analysis of the feelings of children who are being beaten and abused, see Ferenczi's "Confusion of Tongues." Also see Miller, *For Your Own Good*.

50. In a rare observation, Samuel Sewall captured one of those moments when Michael Wigglesworth actually spoke out against a group of some of the most distinguished men in Massachusetts. His colleague, young Thomas Cheever, son of his former teacher Ezekiel Cheever, had been charged with using foul language in a tavern, and a council met to consider the evidence, concluding that he was guilty, and recommending that he be suspended from the church and denied communion for six months. After the meeting, attended by luminaries such as Sewall, Increase and Cotton Mather, Samuel Willard, and others, Sewall noted that " 'Mr. Wigglesworth spake, thank'd him and the Council; said [they] had cause to condemn themselves, as for other sins, so their sudden laying hands on Mr. Cheever; and now God was whipping them with a Rod of their own making.' " (Crowder, *No Featherbed to Heaven*, 226–28.) Spontaneously, there was the voice,

no longer silenced, and there was the rod again, verbally lashing some of the great men of the religious establishment of the Bay Colony.

Subsequently, Sewall heard Wigglesworth declare on May 12, 1686, that God had brought "forth him as 'twere a dead Man,—had been reckoned among the dead,—to preach." M. Halsey Thomas, ed., *The Diary of Samuel Sewall 1674–1729* (New York, 1973), I, 110. See also Corey, *History of Malden*, 266.

51. Crowder, *No Featherbed to Heaven*, 212–17, 221, 224, 228, 237, 239, 265, and *passim*. Dean, *Memoir*, 86. For transcripts of Increase Mather's letters to Wigglesworth, see: Massachusetts Historical Society, *Collections*, 4th ser., VIII (1868), 94–96. In a letter to Mrs. Avery, he wrote that "As my Late wife was a means under God of my recovering a better state of Health," he thought she also might help "Preserve & Prolong my health & life" to do God "service." See "Letters to Mrs. Avery," *New England Historical Genealogical Register*, 17 (1863), 141. For a discussion of Martha Mudge and her family, see James Mudge, "The Mudges of Malden," *The Register of the Malden Historical Society*, 5 (1917–1918), 39–54.

52. Dean, *Memoir*, 114. Also see Crowder, *No Featherbed to Heaven*, who observed (230) that:

> At this distance no adequate explanation can be made for Michael's miraculous recovery and return to public life. To what degree his ailments had been psychosomatic has never been determined. Whatever the causes of recovery, one thing seems certain: he had re-entered reality from a hysteria that had silenced him nearly thirty years before.

It seems very probable that there was an hysterical component of Wigglesworth's personality, associated with the more obvious obsessive character that was evident throughout his life. The dissociation is congruent with that diagnosis. See, for instance, Sigmund Freud's "The Aetiology of Hysteria," in Masson, *Assault on Truth*, Appendix B. Also, see Dean's comments on the nature of his illness: *Memoir*, 61–62.

Gender, Crime, and Community in Seventeenth-Century Maryland
MARY BETH NORTON

1. William Hand Browne *et al.*, eds., *Archives of Maryland* (Baltimore, 1883–1972), LIV, 205, 211. (Hereafter cited as *Md. Archs.*) It was widely believed in the seventeenth century that a woman in labor would tell the truth about the identity of the father of her child; in 1662 the Maryland assembly formally amended its bastardy law to give special weight to a mother's declaration "in the Extremity of her paynes and Throwes of Travail" (*Md. Archs.*, I, 441–42). See also notes 11, 56, below.

2. *Ibid.*, 211–12. She was ordered to pay the costs of child care already incurred by the court date, but Bright was directed to pay all subsequent charges. The following year he married another woman; what happened to Elesabeth Lockett is unknown. The law that allowed Elesabeth Lockett to use a false promise of marriage as a defense was adopted in April 1658 (*ibid.*, I, 373–74). Under its provisions Bright was supposed either to marry her or to pay her a fine "for her abuse." Neither penalty appears to have been imposed on him.

3. *Ibid.*, II, 55; X, 229, 434; IV, 439–40, 459. Erbery was given thirty-nine lashes. For the standard phraseology that opens such cases, see, *e.g.*, *ibid.*, IV, 308, 321; X, 94.

4. J. M. Beattie, *Crime and the Courts in England, 1660–1800* (Princeton, N.J., 1986), 73, and Cynthia Herrup, *The Common Peace: Participation and the Criminal Law in*

Seventeenth-Century England (Cambridge, England, 1987), chapter 4, note the crucial role of victims in initiating prosecutions. Of the 640 cases discussed here, 106 (16 percent) are identified in the records as having been filed as civil suits by a victim-plaintiff against a criminal-civil defendant. The range of charges brought to court in this manner was wide, including assault, rape, harboring runaways, and killing another man's livestock. In other instances, dated depositions reveal that the magistrates first learned of offenses when a victim or witness made a formal complaint, thereby initiating an investigation.

5. *Md. Archs.*, LXV, 90. For a discussion of the importance of the community in defining behavioral standards as revealed in defamation cases, see Mary Beth Norton, "Gender and Defamation in Seventeenth-Century Maryland," *William and Mary Quarterly*, 3d ser., 44 (1987), 5–7.

6. David Warren Sabean, *Power in the Blood: Popular Culture & Village Discourse in Early Modern Germany* (New York, 1987), 95.

7. Thus this study differs from the work of other scholars whose primary interest is criminal law or women and crime. For examples, see Beattie, *Crime and the Courts*; Herrup, *The Common Peace*; Martin J. Ingram, *Church Courts, Sex and Marriage in England 1570–1640* (Cambridge, England, 1988); Bradley Chapin, *Criminal Justice in Colonial America, 1606–1660* (Athens, Ga., 1983); N. E. H. Hull, *Female Felons: Women and Serious Crime in Colonial Massachusetts* (Urbana, Ill., 1987); G. S. Rowe, "Women's Crime and Criminal Administration in Pennsylvania, 1763–1790," *Pennsylvania Magazine of History and Biography*, 109 (1985), 335–68. Although my questions and frequently my conclusions differ from theirs, my work more nearly resembles that of Lyle Koehler, *A Search for Power: The "Weaker Sex" in Seventeenth-Century New England* (Urbana, Ill., 1980); and Roger Thompson, *Sex in Middlesex: Popular Mores in a Massachusetts County, 1649–1699* (Amherst, Mass., 1986), in that both authors also use criminal records to study social interactions. On the concept of gender, see Joan W. Scott, "Gender: A Useful Category of Historical Analysis," *American Historical Review*, 91 (1986), 1053–75.

8. The data for this article are drawn from the fifteen volumes of the "court series" of *Md. Archs.*, and from Joseph H. Smith and Phillip A. Crowl, eds., *Court Records of Prince Georges County, Maryland, 1696–1699* (*American Legal Records*, IX [Washington, D.C. 1964]). (Hereafter cited as *Am. Legal Recs.*, IX.) All extant provincial court records for the period 1638–83 have been published in *Md. Archs.*, but the later records in particular are incomplete (see an editors' note on this problem, *Md. Archs.*, LX, xxii). The cases have been analyzed using the augmented version of the Statistical Package for the Social Sciences (SPSS-X), as described in *SPSS-X User's Guide* (New York, 1983). Of the 640 prosecutions, 376 (59 percent) were pursued in the provincial court, 80 (12 percent) in Prince Georges County, 63 (10 percent) in Charles County, 56 (9 percent) in Talbot County, 55 (9 percent) in Kent County, and 10 (2 percent) in Somerset County.

9. By decades, the prosecutions break down as follows: 31 (5 percent), 1630s and 1640s; 135 (21 percent), 1650s; 183 (29 percent), 1660s; 187 (29 percent), 1670s; 105 (16 percent), 1680s and 1690s. Women comprised just 6 percent of the defendants tried before 1650; at other times, cases involving women usually made up about 20 percent of prosecutions. The only exceptional decade was the 1660s, when women were charged in one-third of the cases. An additional 28 women and 62 men participated in crimes but were not prosecuted. I have used the court clerk's notations as an admittedly crude indicator of status. In addition to the 107 servant defendants, 407 (64 percent) had no title assigned; 100 (15 percent) had high status (being termed "Mr.," "Mrs.," or "Gent." by the clerk);

and 22 (3 percent) were of mixed or other status. On the sex ratio of the Maryland population, see Russell R. Menard, "Immigrants and Their Increase: The Process of Population Growth in Early Colonial Maryland," in Aubrey C. Land *et al.*, eds., *Law, Society, and Politics in Early Maryland* (Baltimore, 1977), 88–110.

10. *Md. Archs.*, I, 210. At the first session for which records have survived, that of March 1637/8, the assembly adopted criminal laws, but these lapsed the following year (*ibid.*, I, 14–23). The assembly tried again to define crimes in 1642 (*ibid.*, I, 147–48), but those laws were in effect for only three years.

11. The first statutes against hog-stealing and running away were adopted in 1650 (*ibid.*, I, 249–51). For later modifications of these laws, see *ibid.*, I, 451, 455, 489; II, 140, 146, 277, 298, 523. On the problematic nature of hog-stealing: Norton, "Gender and Defamation," 15–16, 36–37. The bastardy law, adopted in 1658 (*Md. Archs.*, I, 373–74), was amended in 1662, as noted above, to accept the word of a woman in labor (*ibid.*, I, 441–42) but in 1669 was further amended to provide that she also had to swear to her accusation before a magistrate (*ibid.*, II, 216). In that form the law was regularly renewed.

12. See below, n. 37. Lorena Walsh concluded that all maidservants who bore bastards in Charles County, Md., were probably prosecuted (personal communication).

13. *Md. Archs.*, LIV, 184, 692–93. Approximately half of all servants accused of crimes were charged with running away, occasionally in conjunction with other offenses like theft. The judges' emphasis on deference was made especially clear in cases that involved resistance to a master's authority; see, *e.g.*, *ibid.*, XLIX, 8–10.

14. *Ibid.*, LIV, 42–43, 49–51, 60. Jane Salter was not punished. For other hog-stealing prosecutions, see *ibid.*, LIII, 544–48, 551–52; LIV, 88–89, 111, 399, 404.

15. In 232 of the 640 Maryland criminal prosecutions there are identifiable victims (many crimes, like bastardy and contempt of authority, were victimless). Of those victims, 44 were females, 181 were males, and 7 were couples. Most of the victims (135) were ordinary folk not identified by titles in the records. Forty-three were of high status, 35 were servants, and 8 were of mixed or other status.

16. *Ibid.*, X, 31–32; XLIX, 538–39, 541–43; X, 521. For some other cases—admittedly a minority—in which the courts decided in favor of complaining male servants, see *ibid.*, X, 474, 484–85, 505.

17. *Ibid.*, LX, 432–33; X, 499–500, 549–51; LIV, 270–75. See also *ibid.*, X, 400–401, LIV, 466, for husbands' complaints on behalf of wives who had been assaulted by other men. Beattie points out that in England rape prosecutions were usually initiated by a woman's male relatives (*Crime and the Courts*, 130).

18. *Md. Archs.*, X, 322; LIV, 167–69, 171, 176 (quotation on 167). Sarah Taylor subsequently returned to the county court with other stories of abuse, and the court eventually freed her from service (see *ibid.*, LIV, 178–79, 181, 224–25). She also accused her owners of causing the death of a fellow servant (*ibid.*, XLI, 500–505). In June 1662, her mistress (by then a widow) won a provincial court order declaring that the county court had acted incorrectly in freeing Taylor and directing the magistrates to compensate her for the loss (*ibid.*, XLI, 525; LIV, 234). For other mistreatment complaints offered during trials for running away: *ibid.*, X, 416–17; *Am. Legal Recs.*, IX, 227. For servants bringing such complaints directly to court: *Md. Archs.*, XLI, 68; XLIX, 318–19; LXVI, 474.

19. *Md. Archs.*, X, 80–81, 148–49, 161, 170–85, recounts the Warren-Mitchell case, which John Barth incorporated in his novel *The Sot-Weed Factor* (New York, 1960). See also *Md. Archs.*, LIII, 78, LX, 141, for other unwed mothers as complainants. For a servant woman with a rare complaint of theft, *ibid.*, LX, 100–102.

20. Sarah Taylor was not the only female servant freed by the courts after com-

plaining of mistreatment (see *ibid.*, X, 191, 416–17; XLIX, 318–19), so if women did perceive the courts as unsympathetic to their plight, they perhaps were in error.

21. On women as gossipers, see Norton, "Gender and Defamation," 5–7.

22. *Ibid.*, 13, for evidence of an adulterous relationship revealed during the hearing of countersuits for debt and defamation. In England, wronged spouses were similarly reluctant to come to court; see Ingram, *Church Courts*, 253–57.

23. *Md. Archs.*, X, 555; XLI, 20, 50–51, 79, 85; LIII, 4. In June 1659 the Robinses asked the court clerk to note their formal separation agreement in the Charles County records (*ibid.*, LIII, 33–34).

24. *Ibid.*, X, 109–12 (the Holts' ménage à trois); X, 506–509, 558, 560 (Mary Gillford, the nosy neighbor); LIV, 534–38 (Bridgett Johnson).

25. *Ibid.*, X, 272, 276, 279–90, 339, 366 (quotations from 283, 282, 286). Peter Johnson, Ann's husband, told Robert that "any man of understanding would not blame him for it [287]" but Robert obviously did not believe him. Because Robert never appeared to prosecute his wife, the charges were dropped. No tobacco ever changed hands. When Robert Taylor died in early 1661, he left less property to his son "George" than to his other two sons; see Testamentary Proceedings, I, 1661, ff. 28–29. Maryland Hall of Records, Annapolis.

26. In "Gender and Defamation," 9–10, 15–16, I argued that Maryland men were less concerned about their sexual reputations than were women. This evidence demonstrates that even so no man would voluntarily expose himself as a cuckold unless matters had taken an extreme turn—*e.g.*, Holt fearing for his life or Robins learning his estranged wife was pregnant by another man.

27. *Md. Archs.*, LIII, 407, 410–11, 387–91. A similar motive is hinted in *ibid.*, LIV, 9, 10, 125–26, but the records are too incomplete to allow certainty.

28. For example, in several cases ex-servants accused their former masters of theft, either to seek revenge for ill treatment or perhaps to deflect suspicion away from themselves. See *ibid.*, LI, 211; LIV, 508–10, 582–87.

29. As might be imagined, the deaths of servants or slaves at the hands of their masters were not always reported or investigated with dispatch; see, *e.g.*, *ibid.*, X, 522, 524–25, 534–45; XLI, 190–91, 204–206. Most such prosecutions did not end in conviction or, if they did, the accused was allowed to plead benefit of clergy and was branded on the thumb instead of being executed.

30. Elizabeth Greene: *ibid.*, XLIX, 212, 217–18, 231–36 (quotations on 218, 232); Jane Crisp: *ibid.*, LIV, 394–95, LVII, 123–24 (quotation on 395). The brief quotations: *ibid.*, XLIX, 218; XLI, 431. See also *ibid.*, XLI, 329–31. For useful discussions: Beattie, *Crime and the Courts*, 113–24; and Peter Hoffer and N.E.H. Hull, *Murdering Mothers: Infanticide in England and New England 1588–1803* (New York, 1981), *passim*.

31. *Md. Archs.*, XLI, 430–32.

32. *Ibid.*, X, 272, 276, 279–90. The women were Ann Johnson's assistant, Catchmey's sister-in-law, and two relatives of the Taylors (Robert's sister and a woman called "cousin"); the men were Johnson's husband, two male servants in the Taylor household, two men who had overheard the request for a bribe, and a man who had talked with Catchmey.

33. See *ibid.*, XLIX, 166–67, 230, 233–35, for Alvey's trial and conviction; he was allowed benefit of clergy. See n. 52, below, for the instances of sexual abuse that came to court in other guises. Women made up just 22 percent of the victims in Maryland criminal cases, less than their proportion of the population in all but the colony's earliest years.

34. Men and women were occasionally accused of the crimes most common among

the opposite sex. One woman, for example, was charged with contempt of authority in conjunction with her husband. Likewise, one man was accused of infanticide. Somewhat higher proportions of male criminals were charged with fornication and adultery (1.5 percent and 1 percent respectively), but the figures are considerably lower than those for female defendants.

35. For contemptuous statements by women that did not result in prosecution, see *Md. Archs.*, X, 229.

36. Examples of some contempt prosecutions: *ibid.*, IV, 544–46; X, 413–14, 423–29, 441, 463; XLI, 427–29, 447–50; LIV, 574–75.

37. Of course, demographic and legal circumstances also played a role in producing the bastardy prosecutions. As Carr and Walsh have pointed out, since most migrants, especially the servants who composed the bulk of the population, traveled to Maryland as individuals in young adulthood, they were free to follow their own inclinations in sexual matters without supervision by older family members. Moreover, the skewed sex ratio must have placed women under great pressure to enter sexual relationships outside of marriage. Finally, since servants were forbidden to marry without their masters' permission—which was rarely given—it was difficult to legitimize illicit conceptions retroactively. The result was not just the high proportion of prosecutions for bastardy but also a high rate of premarital pregnancy, particularly in the migrant generation. See Lois Green Carr and Lorena Walsh, "The Planter's Wife: The Experience of White Women in Seventeenth-Century Maryland," *William and Mary Quarterly*, 3d ser., 34 (1977), 542–77; and Robert V. Wells, "Illegitimacy and Bridal Pregnancy in Colonial America," in Peter Laslett *et al.*, eds., *Bastardy and Its Comparative History* (London, 1980), 349–61.

38. The statute and major amendments are in *Md. Archs.*, I, 373–74, 441–42; II, 216. For examples of bastardy presentments, see, *e.g.*, *ibid.*, LIV, 486, 495, 513, 514. For civil suits: *ibid.*, X, 332–37, 365–66, 525–26; LIV, 233, 486, 488. Significantly, when the crime had few economic repercussions because the bastards died soon after birth, prosecutions were less vigorous; either no charges were ever filed (*e.g.*, *ibid.*, LX, 115; LIV, 324, 325, 329) or the penalties were light (*e.g.*, *ibid.*, LX, 518–19).

39. For the only case involving premarital conception, see *ibid.*, LIV, 78, 84–85, 113, 121. Examples of fornication prosecutions are *ibid.*, X, 494; LIV, 366, 371, 386, 407, 429–30. Although few people were tried for fornication, the conviction rate in the eight cases with known outcomes was essentially the same as in bastardy cases: 87.5 percent. The very different attitude of New England judges is explored in Thompson, *Sex in Middlesex*, chapters 1, 3; and Koehler, *Search for Power*, chapter 7. In English ecclesiastical courts, premarital pregnancy frequently led to prosecution, especially after 1600 (Ingram, *Church Courts*, 219–37). For a general discussion, see John D'Emilio and Estelle Freedman, *Intimate Matters: A History of Sexuality in America* (New York, 1988), chapters 1–2.

40. In these 44 cases, 19 (43 percent) of the defendants were women prosecuted alone, 21 (48 percent) were couples, and 4 (9 percent) were males; 15 (34 percent) were free, 21 (48 percent) were servants, and 8 (18 percent) were mixed (free man, servant woman in all but one case, which involved a high-status woman and a man with no title). The lowest conviction rates were for the four men prosecuted alone (50 percent) and free people of either sex (10, or 42 percent).

41. The contrast in penalties is striking: of 32 convicted women, just 14 (44 percent) escaped with only financial penalties, while 18 (56 percent) were whipped; of 21 convicted men, the only one whipped was a servant. (The five other servant men were fined or required to post bond.) Although the vast majority of women convicted of bastardy and subsequently whipped were servants, two free women

were sentenced to be whipped, as were four women whose status is unknown. Another woman of unknown status had a sentence of whipping remitted to a fine, as did four servant women. For examples of bastardy prosecutions, see *Md. Archs.*, LIV, 391, 495, 513, 519.

42. Other explanations might be that the fathers had died or absconded or that the mothers had refused to name them. If any of these things had happened, however, one would expect at least some indication thereof in the court records. Instead, in these thirty cases the magistrates appear not to have inquired about the identity of the fathers at all. For a discussion of bastardy prosecutions in English ecclesiastical courts, see Ingram, *Church Courts*, 260–81. He argues that most female bastard-bearers were prosecuted and convicted, but that—as in Maryland—fathers were less likely to be charged with the crime.

43. The exact proportions are 69 percent of men and 66 percent of women. Data on English felony prosecutions in the seventeenth- and eighteenth centuries show that roughly similar proportions of the accused were convicted, with women more likely to be acquitted than men; see Beattie, *Crime and the Courts*, 436–39; and Herrup, *Common Peace*, 150. Unfortunately, Ingram does not give comparable data on conviction rates by sex in ecclesiastical courts. Unlike Beattie, I do not differentiate between "full" and "partial" guilty verdicts. Figures for conviction rates by sex in serious crimes in Massachusetts are discussed in Hull, *Female Felons*, 100–102; in the seventeenth century, women were found guilty more frequently than men. Rowe, "Women's Crime," 335–68, only incidentally mentions crime and conviction rates for men, and so no comparisons to eighteenth-century Pennsylvania are possible.

44. As used in this paragraph and elsewhere, the description "sex crime" includes the following categories of offenses: fornication, bastardy, rape, adultery, bigamy, abortion, infanticide, offenses involving one's spouse (mistreatment, assault, murder), and prostitution. I included spousal abuse because of its implicit sexual component and infanticide because in the seventeenth century it was quintessentially a crime committed by unwed mothers. (See Hoffer and Hull, *Murdering Mothers, passim.*) There were 110 prosecutions for sexual offenses; of these, 91 (83 percent) had a female defendant, and 61 percent of all defendants in such cases were women.

45. Verdicts are known in 83 of 110 sex crimes; the cases involved 37 female defendants tried alone, 14 males, and 32 couples (a total of 69 women and 46 men); of these 72 were free and 43 servants. Of the 83 trials, 44 were bastardy cases, in which the conviction rate for women was 89.5 percent and for men was 84 percent. Couples tried together were the most likely of all to be found guilty; more than 90 percent of couples were convicted in both bastardy and nonbastardy sexual-offense prosecutions. Verdicts are known in 485 "other" crimes, involving 30 women tried alone, 432 men, and 23 couples. Only 52 percent of these couples were convicted, along with 50 percent of women tried alone and 69 percent of men tried alone.

46. The categories of punishment other than fines, posting bond, and whipping account for only very small proportions of penalties levied on defendants; for example, 6 percent of women and men were subjected to shaming punishments, 3 percent of women and 2 percent of men to mutilation, and so forth. Only 16 defendants (4 women and 12 men) were sentenced to death, and fewer were actually executed. At least five death sentences (1 woman, 4 men) were commuted to lesser penalties. Just 14 percent of the penalties imposed were wholly or partially remitted by the courts; 17 of 115 convicted female criminals and 54 of 400 men had their punishments reduced or completely remitted.

47. Sixty-six percent of all males convicted of crimes were fined, as opposed to just

44 percent of women; only 10 percent of men, but 41 percent of women, were whipped. The distinction between types of penalties holds for both free and servant men and women, so whipping was not a penalty applied regularly to servants of both sexes, and was rarely given to free people of either sex. Fifty-two percent of female servants convicted of sexual offenses were whipped (40 percent of all guilty female servants received that penalty), but only one man-servant was whipped for a sexual offense (of six men whose fates are known), while 24 percent of all guilty male servants were so punished.

48. Although female bastardy defendants were more likely to be convicted than were female defendants in other types of sex crimes, a smaller proportion of them was whipped: 56 percent (18) of the 32 women convicted of bastardy and 62.5 percent (10) of the 16 women convicted of other sex crimes were sentenced to that punishment. Of the latter group, only two were servants; the other eight were free women. The percentages of male criminals whipped were 8.5 percent of sex offenders and 9.1 percent of other offenders.

49. The divergent treatment is not attributable to the differing status of these men and women; fewer than half (13) of the sex-crime prosecutions involved couples of unequal status, and of those, again, fewer than half (6) resulted in the woman being sentenced to whipping, the man to a fine.

50. Beattie, *Crime and the Courts*, 463, 468–69, 439. Michel Foucault, *Discipline and Punish: The Birth of the Prison* (New York, 1979), part 1, analyzes the implications of public penalties. Sexual offenders brought before English ecclesiastical courts were assessed both public and private punishments. Penalties included heavy fines, shaming rituals during church services or in other public places, and excommunication; see Ingram, *Church Courts*, 236–37, 257, 279–81. Again, though, Ingram does not differentiate between punishments assigned to male and female offenders, so no explicit comparison to Maryland can be made.

51. The relationship of the sex of the criminal and the nature of the penalty (private or public) in sex-crime cases produced a chi-square significance of .0000. In "other" cases, 22 percent of women and 20 percent of men were publicly punished; a chi-square test did not produce significant results. Analysis by status rather than sex shows that servants were somewhat more likely to be publicly punished for both categories of offenses than were free people (48 percent to 39 percent in sex crimes, 27 percent to 19 percent in "other" cases). The former differences are smaller than those resulting from the sex of the offender, and neither relationship proved significant in a chi-square test. In fact, of all groups defined by both sex and status, free women were the most likely to be publicly punished in sex-crime cases (71 percent of them were so penalized, as opposed to 52 percent of servant women, 14 percent of free men, and 17 percent of servant men). Almost all such cases involved the whipping or shaming of free women convicted of fornication or adultery.

52. The quotations are from *Md. Archs.*, X, 181; LIII, 388; LIV, 69; XLI, 272. The mock marriage is described in *ibid.*, X, 549–51. The sex crime with a hint that the woman initiated the relationship was the case of Mary Taylor described above, n. 25, in which George Catchmey claimed she had seduced him, though she asserted the opposite.

53. The perjury case: *ibid.*, IV, 422, 427, 429, 435–36, 445; forgery: *ibid.*, XLIX, 44–45, 53, 76–77, 86–87. Beattie, *Crime and the Courts*, 421, comments on the importance of selective prosecutions of those criminals believed to be more dangerous than others.

54. Coincidentally, 97 men also testified in 34 sex-crime trials, although the total number of such trials in which witnesses appeared was 42. Twelve men were high-status, 3 were servants, and the rest were ordinary planters. Overall, wit-

nesses testified in 219 of the 640 criminal prosecutions; 163 women appeared in 77 cases, and 540 men in 202 cases. In other words, 59.5 percent of female witnesses testified in sex crimes, whereas only 18 percent of male witnesses did likewise. Just as female defendants were concentrated in sex-crime cases, therefore, so too were female witnesses, who composed half of all witnesses in such trials.

55. *Ibid.*, X, 494; LIV, 385; LIII, 2, 6–7, 28, 30–33, 37–38; XLI, 291–94.

56. Thus in March 1653/4 a man told the provincial court that his servant woman "being with Child fathers it on John Hambleton . . . although the matter cannot be Determined until the time of Delivery" (*ibid.*, X, 337). Roger Thompson notes that this belief was enacted into law in Massachusetts in 1668 (*Sex in Middlesex*, 22–24), as it was in Maryland in 1662; see notes 1 and 11, above. In only one sex-crime prosecution, that of William Mitchell and Susan Warren, was there even a passing mention of a male doctor—and he was never called as a witness (*Md. Archs.*, X, 171).

57. *Md. Archs.*, X, 177. For Lockett, see n. 1 above.

58. *Ibid.*, XLIX, 212, 217–18, 231–36 (quotation 233); XLI, 329–31. Although midwives were not explicitly mentioned as witnesses in the prosecution of Anthony Purss and Ann Mungommory in 1665, their participation seems highly likely, for the determination of Purss's guilt or innocence turned on the question of whether her baby had been born prematurely (*ibid.*, LIV, 383, 386–87).

59. *Ibid.*, X, 280–81. Johnson's deposition is on 280–82.

60. *Ibid.*, XLI, 16. This account was given not by Dorrington but by a second woman present, Mary Hebborne.

61. For Elizabeth Robins, see n. 23, above. Infanticide: *ibid.*, X, 456–58; LIV, 250. bastardy: LIV, 233.

62. *Ibid.*, LIV, 291–92. In another sex-crime prosecution, a group of men persuaded the court to remit the punishment of a convicted male adulterer from whipping to a fine. The men made no mention of his female partner, who was whipped as originally ordered. See *ibid.*, X, 560.

63. *Ibid.*, LVII, 598–99. See the editors' note on this case, xxix. Perhaps the same sort of issue was involved when a key female witness repeatedly refused to appear at an infanticide prosecution in 1665–66; see *ibid.*, XLIX, 476, 505, 536, 566, 617, LVII, 16, 36, 74–75, 99, 111, 114, 119, 124. On the effects of the law of James I, see Hoffer and Hull, *Murdering Mothers, passim*; Beattie, *Crime and the Courts*, 113–24. Beattie speculates that stays of execution for women on grounds of pregnancy eventually became pardons (430–31); perhaps that happened in this instance as well.

64. *Md. Archs.*, X, 464–65, 488. The court record gives no indication of when the miscarriage described by Smith and Claxton occurred. Since Brookes married twice during this period, it is impossible to identify with certainty the woman who was beaten, though it was probably his second wife. His first, Ann Boulton, a former servant, married him by June 1651 and died in late 1653 or early 1654. His second, Mary, survived him at his death in 1659; she bore him at least two living children and subsequently remarried twice. On Ann, see *ibid.*, X, 79, 215, 377, and *passim*; on Mary, *ibid.*, XLIX, 297–98, 302–303, and *passim*.

65. In the case of Jane Crisp (in n. 30, above), the examining midwife did not testify at the trial, and Crisp was acquitted. The fragmentary record of another prosecution not discussed in the text hints at female witnesses' sympathy for the accused: in 1668, after two women were apparently examined about Susan Hunt, suspected of having committed infanticide, she was cleared without a trial (*ibid.*, LVII, 251, 318).

66. For discussions of English families in the seventeenth century, see Keith Wright-

son, *English Society, 1580–1680* (London, 1982), chapter 4; Lawrence Stone, *The Family, Sex and Marriage in England, 1500–1800* (New York, 1977), part 4; Margaret J. M. Ezell, *The Patriarch's Wife: Literary Evidence and the History of the Family* (Chapel Hill, N.C., 1987); and the essays by David Underdown and Susan Amussen in Anthony Fletcher and John Stevenson, eds., *Order & Disorder in Early Modern England* (Cambridge, England, 1985). The connections between state and family are examined in Gordon Schochet, *Patriarchalism in Political Thought* (New York, 1975), chapter 4; Linda Nicholson, *Gender and History: The Limits of Social Theory in the Age of the Family* (New York, 1986), part 2; and Melvin Yazawa, *From Colonies to Commonwealth: Familial Ideology and the Beginnings of the American Republic* (Baltimore, 1985), parts 1 and 2.

67. For New England conviction data, see Hull, *Female Felons*, 100–102, and Thompson, *Sex in Middlesex*, 7–8.

68. These conclusions about the varying gender values of men and women coincide with those reported in Norton, "Gender and Defamation," 35–39.

The Committee Movement of 1779 and the Formation of Public Authority in Revolutionary America
RICHARD BUEL, JR.

1. Theda Skocpol, *States and Social Revolutions* (Cambridge, England, 1979).

2. The result was that as popular enthusiasm for the cause waned, so too did the capacity of the Revolutionary state governments to mobilize and direct the energies of the people. See Richard Buel, Jr., *Dear Liberty: Connecticut's Mobilization for the Revolutionary War* (Middletown, Conn. 1980).

3. Though the state governors usually lacked the formal constitutional powers they thought they needed in military emergencies, none failed to cope when the occasion required because of a constitutional insufficiency in the executive power. Their problems stemmed more from insufficient resources. Thus, though Jefferson blamed his inability to defend Virginia against British invasion in 1781 on the constitutional structure of the state government, his difficulties had more to do with the problems associated with concentrating force in so thinly settled an area. See Julian P. Boyd, ed., *The Papers of Thomas Jefferson* (Princeton, N.J., 1950–), vols. II–III, *passim*. The governor of Connecticut was as constitutionally impotent as Virginia's, but proved more effective in organizing the state's resources through the instrumentality of a council of safety, largely because he was dealing with a smaller jurisdiction. See C. J. Hoadley *et al.*, eds., *The Public Records of the State of Connecticut* (Hartford, Conn., 1894–), vols. I–IV, *passim*. And Congress, though only a representative committee of the states through much of the war, succeeded in performing functions such as the issuance of bills of credit without a centralized revenue power. See E. James Ferguson, *The Power of the Purse* (Chapel Hill, N.C., 1961), 26.

4. Kenneth Lockridge, *A New England Town: The First Hundred Years* (New York, 1970), is still one of the best accounts of the early process of settlement.

5. D. E. Leach, *Flintlock and Tomahawk: New England in King Philip's War* (New York, 1958), still is one of the better accounts of frontier warfare before the Indians became the instruments of European rivalries. See also his *Arms for Empire: A Military History of the British Colonies in North America 1607–1763* (New York, 1973), especially chapters 1–3.

6. See Jacob M. Price, "Economic Function and the Growth of American Port Towns in the Eighteenth Century," *Perspectives in American History*, VIII (1974), 123–

86. Price's argument has the advantage of being able to explain why entrepôts did not develop around the Chesapeake tobacco trade.

7. This is a point Carl Bridenbaugh makes surprisingly little of in his *Cities in Revolt* (New York, 1955), 7, 10. The tension between town and country surfaced indirectly in controversies over such matters as taxation; see, for instance, the *Connecticut Gazette*, April 5, 1782–May 10, 1782, *passim*.

8. Bernard Bailyn, *The Origins of American Politics* (New York, 1968); Jack P. Greene, *The Quest for Power: The Lower Houses of Assembly in the Southern Royal Colonies, 1689–1776* (Chapel Hill, N.C., 1963).

9. The origins of the final revolutionary mobilization are best traced in Richard D. Brown, *Revolutionary Politics in Massachusetts: The Boston Committee of Correspondence and the Towns, 1772–1774* (Cambridge, Mass., 1970). For the "Sons of Liberty," see Pauline Maier, *From Resistance to Revolution: Colonial Radicals and the Development of Opposition to Britain, 1765–1776* (New York, 1972). The standard work on the Nonimportation of 1768–70 is Charles M. Andrews, "The Boston Merchants and the Non-Importation Movement," *Colonial Society of Massachusetts Transactions*, XIX (1916–17), 159–259. See also relevant portions of Arthur Schlesinger, *The Colonial Merchants and the American Revolution, 1763–1776* (New York, 1918), and John W. Tyler, *Smugglers and Patriots: Boston Merchants and the Advent of the American Revolution* (Boston, 1986).

10. The pressures included a resolution in Parliament reactivating a statute passed in the reign of Henry VIII for the trying of treasons committed outside the realm and the printing and circulation throughout the continent of manifests from vessels entering the port of Boston purporting to show that patriot merchants were violating their own agreement, see Buel, *Dear Liberty*, 19–20, and "Freedom of the Press in Revolutionary America," in Bernard Bailyn and John B. Hench, eds., *The Press & the American Revolution* (Worcester, Mass., 1980), 76–81.

11. Worthington C. Ford, ed., *Journals of the Continental Congress, 1774–1789* (Washington, D.C., 1904–37), I, 75–81. Barbara Clark Smith, "The Politics of Price Control in Revolutionary Massachusetts 1774–1780" (Yale Ph.D. Thesis, 1983), stresses this point; see 185ff.

12. Buel, *Dear Liberty*, 59, 117–18, 247 ff.

13. The committee movement has been written about in two studies: Stephen J. Rosswurm, *Arms, Country, and Class: The Philadelphia Militia and the "Lower Sort" During the American Revolution* (New Brunswick, N.J., 1987); and Barbara Clark Smith's thesis cited in note 11.

14. See Lance Banning, "Jeffersonian Ideology Revisited: Liberal and Classical Ideas in the New American Republic," *William and Mary Quarterly* 3d ser., 43 (1986), 3–19, and Joyce Appleby's reply, "Republicanism in Old and New Contexts," in *ibid.*, 20–34, for the historiographical controversy. The behavior of one typical state in this respect is analyzed in Buel, *Dear Liberty*, chapter 2, especially 39.

15. Ford, ed., *Journals of the Continental Congress, 1774–1789*, II, 103. See also Ralph V. Harlow, "Aspects of Revolutionary Finance, 1775–1783," *American Historical Review*, 35 (1929–30), 50–51 and insert.

16. See Ferguson, *The Power of the Purse*, 26–27. Charles W. Calomiris, "Institutional Failure, Monetary Scarcity, and the Depreciation of the Continental," *Journal of Economic History*, 48 (1988), 56.

17. John Adams's assessment of the situation is revealing, see Adams to Thomas Jefferson, May 26, 1777, in *Papers of Jefferson*, II, 21–22; also Richard Buel, Jr., "Time: Friend or Foe of the Revolution?", in Don Higginbotham, ed., *Reconsiderations on the Revolutionary War* (Westport, Conn., 1978), 130; and *Dear Liberty*,

84–85. The depreciation of the continental currency has recently attracted the attention of two economic historians, whose accounts differ from the one given above. Charles Calomiris, "Institutional Failure, Monetary Scarcity, and the Depreciation of the Continental," questions, as I do, the sufficiency of a quantity theory of money to explain the depreciation, and emphasizes instead the failure of the Revolutionary governments to back up their credit instruments with sufficient taxation. Ron Michener, "Backing Theories and the Currencies of Eighteenth-Century America: A Comment," *Journal of Economic History*, 48 (1988), 682–92, has challenged Calomiris's interpretation in an effort to defend the sufficiency of a quantity explanation of the depreciation. Calomiris has replied in "The Depreciation of the Continental: A Reply," in *ibid.*, 693–98.

18. See *Journals of the Continental Congress*, XI, 479.

19. Buel, "Time: Friend or Foe?", 133; *Dear Liberty*, 151; and "Samson Shorn: The Impact of the Revolutionary War on Estimates of the Republic's Strength," in Ronald Hoffman and Peter J. Albert, *Arms and Independence: The Military Character of the American Revolution* (Charlottesville, Va., 1984), 154.

20. Ferguson, *Power of the Purse*, 32. The rising real value of continental currency outstanding was even more dramatic than the rising exchange rate: see Calomiris, "Institutional Failure," 56.

21. Buel, "Time: Friend or Foe?", 133.

22. "Manifesto and Proclamation of the Carlisle Commissioners," October 3, 1778, listed in Charles Evans, *American Bibliography: A Chronological Dictionary of All Books, Pamphlets and Periodical Publications Printed in the United States of America, 1639–1800* (Chicago and Worcester, Mass., 1903–1959), 15832.

23. Contrary to the folklore that has surrounded the winter of 1778 at Valley Forge, the winter of 1779 was a much harder one for the army to survive; see the Jeremiah Wadsworth Papers for this period, Connecticut Historical Society. The distresses of the civilian population during the winter of 1779 are noted in Buel, *Dear Liberty*, 159–65.

24. Ferguson, *Power of the Purse*, 32; Calomiris, "Institutional Failure," 56.

25. See "A Customer," in *Pennsylvania Packet*, March 27, 1779; and "Address of the Philadelphia Committee to Fellow Citizens, July 8," in *Pennsylvania Gazette*, July 14, 1779.

26. See William Whipple to Josiah Bartlett, July 12, 1779, in Paul H. Smith, ed., *Letters of Delegates to Congress* (Washington, D.C., 1976–), XIII, 199.

27. Kenneth Scott, "Price Control in New England During the Revolution," *New England Quarterly* 19 (1946), 453–73, is the most elaborate study of the subject. See also Buel, *Dear Liberty*, 85, 86, 148–49; and Smith, "The Politics of Price Control," *passim*.

28. The difficulties encountered by the states in attempting to regulate markets that did not correspond to their jurisdictions were noted in John Ricketts to Levi Hollingsworth, August 1, 1780, in Hollingsworth Papers, Historical Society of Pennsylvania. See also Scott, "Price Controls in New England," 468; and "Petition of the City of Philadelphia to the General Assembly of Pennsylvania, September 17" in *Pennsylvania Gazette*, September 22, 1779. The proceedings of some of the New England regional conventions are printed in Hoadly, ed., *Public Records of the State of Connecticut*, 585–620; see also Scott, "Price Controls," 453, 458, 459, 460–61.

29. See Oscar and Mary Flugg Handlin, *Commonwealth: A Study of the Role of Government in the American Economy: Massachusetts, 1774–1861* (New York, 1947), 8–9.

30. See Henry Hollingsworth to Levi Hollingsworth, October 29, 1778, in Hollingsworth Papers, Historical Society of Pennsylvania.

31. Isaac Sears, a merchant resident in Boston, for instance, favored the regulation of 1779; see his letter to Horatio Gates, September ?, 1779, in The Horatio Gates Papers, 1726–1828 (Sanford, N.C.; Microfilm Corporation of America, 1978). But some of his colleagues thought him mad, see James Swan to James Hunter, Jr., and to James Price, September 30, 1779, in Hunter Garnett Papers, Alderman Library, University of Virginia.

32. Thus Wadsworth opposed them initially upon becoming commissary general, but the next year accepted them as a temporary expedient, see Buel, *Dear Liberty*, 151, 168. See also Royal Flint to Jere. Wadsworth, June 28, 1779, in Jeremiah Wadsworth Papers, Connecticut Historical Society.

33. See John Armstrong to George Washington, June 25, 1779, in Smith, ed., *Letters of Delegates to Congress*, XIII, 108; *Boston Gazette*, August 2, 1779. The committee movement had its opponents, see Robert Honeyman Diary, 354–55, in Library of Congress.

34. Fitzgerald and Peers to James Hunter, Jr., June 7, and Robert R. Randall to James Hunter, Jr., July 22, 1779, in Hunter Garnett Papers, Alderman Library, University of Virginia. Robert Honeyman Diary, July 3 entry, 355, in Library of Congress. See *Pennsylvania Gazette*, June 2, 14, July 7, and September 8, 1779; *Pennsylvania Packet*, June 17, July 3, 20, 22, and August 3, 1779.

35. *Boston Gazette*, June 21, 1779.

36. *Boston Gazette*, August 2, 1779. *Pennsylvania Gazette*, August 11, 1779. See also Evans 10228–29 and *Public Records of the State of Connecticut*, II, 568; *Norwich Packet*, June 22, 1779; *Connecticut Journal*, August 25 and September 22; *Connecticut Gazette*, August 4 and September 8; *Providence Gazette*, July 31, August 14 supplement; *New Hampshire Gazette*, August 10, September 28, October 5, November 16; see also Peter Colt to Jere. Wadsworth, September 23, 1779, in Jeremiah Wadsworth Papers, Connecticut Historical Society.

37. See "The Address of the Committee of the City and Liberties of Philadelphia, to their Fellow-Citizens throughout the United States" in *Pennsylvania Gazette*, July 7, 1779. Cf. also Thomas McKean to Sara McKean, July 26, 1779, in Smith, ed., *Letters of the Delegates*, XIII, 294.

38. See "Leonidas" in *Connecticut Courant*, July 27, 1779. Sponsors of the committee movement could claim that their actions were congruent with Congress's Address to the People of May 26, 1779, which had exhorted the virtuous citizenry to exert themselves to secure the value of the currency. See *Journals of the Continental Congress*, XIV, 649–57; and Providence Town Meeting resolves, in *Providence Gazette*, August 2, 1779. See also James Swan to James Hunter, Jr., and to James Price, September 30, 1779, in Hunter Garnett Papers, Alderman Library, University of Virginia. Also Cyrus Griffin to Thomas Jefferson, July 13, 1779, in Smith, ed., *Letters of the Delegates*, XIII, 205.

39. *Pennsylvania Gazette*, July 7, 1779; Honeyman Diary, July 3, 1779, 354, Library of Congress.

40. John L. Brooke, "To the Quiet of the People: Revolutionary Settlements and the Civil Unrest in Western Massachusetts," *William and Mary Quarterly*, 3d ser., 46 (1989), 444–45.

41. See excerpt from Robert R. Livingston to Gouverneur Morris, August 8, 1779, quoted in Smith, ed., *Letters of the Delegates*, XIII, 412n. An attempt to call a statewide convention at Claverack failed prior to Albany's action, see Barbara Smith, "Politics of Price Regulation," 473.

42. Massachusetts's Concord convention stressed that the reduction of prices would flow automatically from the states' compliance with Congress's requisitions and loans, see *Boston Gazette*, August 2, 1779.

43. Cf. Arthur L. Jensen, *The Maritime Commerce of Philadelphia* (Madison, Wis., 1963), 292, with the statistics in Timothy Pitkin, *A Statistical View of the Commerce of the United States of America* (New York, 1817), 20–21.

44. Anne Bezanson, *Prices and Inflation During the American Revolution: Pennsylvania, 1770–1790* (Philadelphia, 1951), 336.

45. Benjamin Hawley's diary, 1769–82, a copy of which is available in the Chester County Historical Society in Westchester, Pa., gives an excellent account of agricultural cycles in the region.

46. On the decline of the city's tonnage see Chaloner and White to Gouverneur Morris, July ?, 1779, in Chaloner and White Letter Book (March 15–September 18, 1779) in Historical Society of Pennsylvania. Also Juan de Miralles to Diego José Navarro, October 24, 1778, in Juan de Miralles transcripts, trans. Aileen Moore Topping, Letters of the Delegates Project, Library of Congress. For the disruption of normal trade entailed, see, for instance, the report of Thomas Lowry to Nathaniel Greene, January 17, 1780, in Nathaniel Greene Papers, William L. Clements Library, University of Michigan.

47. The whole affair can be traced in *Pennsylvania Packet*, March 6, 1779 ff. Chaloner and White to Ephraim Blaine, and to Jere. Wadsworth, both April 18, 1779, in Chaloner and White Letter Books (March 15–September 18, 1779) in Historical Society of Pennsylvania. Also Daniel Roberdeau's speech in *Pennsylvania Packet*, May 27, 1779. See also Hubertus Cummings, "Robert Morris and the Episode of the Polacre 'Victorious,'" *Pennsylvania Magazine of History and Biography*, 70 (1946), 241–42; Flemming to Thos. Jefferson, May 22, 1779, in Boyd, ed., *The Papers of Thomas Jefferson*, II, 267.

48. See unsigned article in *Boston Gazette*, February 2, 1778. Quotes are from the memorial of New Jersey General Assembly to the Continental Congress, October 7, 1779, in Papers of the Continental Congress, reel 82, item 68, 467ff. The memorial was sent to Congress immediately after the collapse of the Philadelphia movement by men anxious to preserve the feature of progressive price reductions in a Congressionally sponsored alternative regulation.

49. Extract from the town meeting records of Fairfield, July 1, 1779, in Connecticut State Library; *Connecticut Gazette*, August 4, 1779; *Connecticut Courant*, July 27, 1779.

50. *Connecticut Journal*, August 25, 1779.

51. The complex story can be traced in *Connecticut Courant*, September 28 and October 12, 1779. *Connecticut Gazette*, September 8 and 15, 1779. See also extracts from the town records of Lyme, September 21, 1779, in Connecticut State Library; Hartford Town Votes, II, 272; Middletown Town Votes and Proprietors Records, II, 378. See also Peter Colt to Jere. Wadsworth, September 23, 1779, in Jeremiah Wadsworth Papers, Connecticut Historical Society.

52. A writer in the *New Hampshire Gazette*, September 21, 1779, attributed it to the large purchases of West India goods that leading Connecticut merchants had recently made in Boston. There may have been some basis for this suspicion, see the report of a meeting of Boston Merchants and Traders, August 20, in *Boston Gazette*, August 30, 1779.

53. See Extracts from the Town Records Series, Connecticut State Library, from the town records of Fairfield, July 1; from the town records of Danbury, August 9, 1779; from the town records of Norwalk, August 16; from the town records of Ashford, September 14; from the town records of Canterbury, August 12; and from the town records of Lyme, September 21 and 28. See also Royal Flint to Jere. Wadsworth, July 6, 1779, in Jeremiah Wadsworth Papers, Connecticut Historical Society; Honeyman Diary, 354, Library of Congress. The movement

did appear to have an endorsement of sorts from Congress, see Ford, ed., *Journals of the Continental Congress, 1774–1789*, XIV, 655.

54. This point was made by "A Hartford County Man" in *Connecticut Courant*, August 3, 1779. Smith, "Politics of Price Regulation," discusses this problem in some detail and, following the work of Winifred Rothenburg, concludes that middle-men farmers near the market took advantage of the urban consumer more effectively than did rural farmers, see 428–29.

55. *Journals of the Continental Congress*, XIV, 561.

56. Such at least was Congress's assumption; see *Journals of the Continental Congress*, XIV, 653.

57. Cf. "T.S.," in *Pennsylvania Packet*, June 22, 1779; also "Resolves of the Concord Convention," in *Boston Gazette*, August 2, 1779; "Address of the Concord Convention convened October 6th," in *ibid.*, October 25, 1779; and Buel, *Dear Liberty*, 147, 201.

58. See *Pennsylvania Packet*, February 27, 1779. Also Honeyman Diary, 329–30, in Library of Congress; Juan de Miralles to José de Galvez, May 14, 1779, in Juan de Miralles transcripts, trans. Aileen Moore Topping, Letters of the Delegates Project, Library of Congress.

59. See Walter Livingston to Abraham Livingston, August 8, 1779, in Walter Livingston Letter Book, New York Historical Society.

60. See "T.S.," in *Pennsylvania Packet*, June 22, 1779. Also the "7th Resolve of the Concord Convention" in *Boston Gazette*, August 2, 1779; Belchertown and Billerica Remonstrances, Massachusetts Archives, CLXXXIII, 292ff., 307, as quoted in Handlin and Handlin, *Commonwealth*, 14. See also Henry Marchant to William Greene, October 2, 1779, in Smith, ed., *Letters of Delegates to Congress*, XIV, 63.

61. Quote from Scott, "Price Controls," 468. The danger of appreciation could have been alleviated by the legislature's issuing new bills to compensate for the withdrawal of the old, but the trauma associated with the depreciation had reduced popular confidence that such reasonable remedies might be relied on.

62. This theme was emphasized in the Philadelphia committee's address of July 8, 1779, in *Pennsylvania Gazette*, July 14. The same point is made by Smith, "Politics of Price Regulation," 429.

63. Royal Flint to Jere. Wadsworth, July 30, 1779, and John Trumbull to Wadsworth, September 16, in Jeremiah Wadsworth Papers, boxes 128, 129 in Connecticut Historical Society.

64. Ferguson, *Power of the Purse*, 52, gives a flattering account of the states' compliance with Congressional warrants. A different estimate of the situation is supplied by Buel, *Dear Liberty*, 201, 205–206. For the long term, Congress attempted to finance the war effort by requisitioning the states for supplies.

65. *Ibid.*, 205–206.

66. See *Pennsylvania Gazette*, June 30, August 11, and September 1, 1779; *Pennsylvania Packet*, July 8, 1779; *Boston Gazette*, September 20, 1779.

67. In *Letters of the Delegates*, XIII, 411. See also Chaloner and White to Jere. Wadsworth, September 13, 1779, in Chaloner and White Letter Book (March 15–September 18, 1779), Historical Society of Pennsylvania.

68. See *Pennsylvania Packet*, July 24, 1779. The full documentation surrounding the affair can be found in the Papers of the Continental Congress, reel 124, item 96, 51ff.

69. The report of the Wilmington committee's actions appeared in the *Pennsylvania Packet*, July 24, 1779. For Gerard's protest see Papers of the Continental Congress, July 26, 1779, reel 123, item 94, 335–38.

70. Initially Gerard and Holker had tried to pressure Congress and the executive

council of Pennsylvania into condemning the *Packet* and the committee movement. Congress obliged only to the extent of passing the matter on to the government of Pennsylvania, and Gerard had the discretion to drop the matter once
he realized how reluctant the executive council was to act. See *Journals of the
Continental Congress*, XIV, 898, 913–15, 919; see also Joseph Reed to John Holker,
August 9, 1779, in Papers of the Continental Congress, reel 124, item 96, 190.
For the effects of the incident see Rosswurm, *Arms, Country, and Class*, 189. Among
other things, it seems to have helped convince the Pennsylvania legislature of
the advisability of abandoning regulation, see Chaloner and White to Jere. Wadsworth, September 17, 1779, in Jeremiah Wadsworth Papers, Connecticut Historical Society.

71. John and Thomas Ricketts to Levi Hollingsworth, June 12, 1779, in Hollingsworth Papers, Historical Society of Pennsylvania.

72. See "Report of the Committee of 17 on a Memorial of the Merchants of Phila-
delphia," in *Pennsylvania Packet*, September 10, 1779; also Thomas Doerflinger,
*A Vigorous Spirit of Enterprise: Merchants and Economic Development in Revolutionary
Philadelphia* (Chapel Hill, N.C., 1986), chapter 5.

73. The standard accounts of the massacre are John K. Alexander, "The Fort Wilson
Incident of 1779: A Case Study of the Revolutionary Crowd," *William and Mary
Quarterly*, 3d ser., 31 (1974), 602–606; and Rosswurm, *Arms, Country, and Class*,
222–27. See *ibid.*, 228ff., and Nathaniel Peabody to Meshech Weare, October
26, 1779, in Smith, ed., *Letters of Delegates*, XIV, 125, for the collapse of the
movement.

74. The commercial arrivals can best be traced in published notices appearing in the
Pennsylvania Packet and the *Pennsylvania Journal* for these years. See also Levi
Hollingsworth's Flour Ledger B, no. 598, in Hollingsworth Papers, Historical
Society of Pennsylvania.

75. See Alexander Hamilton to Robert Morris, April 30, 1781, in E. James Ferguson,
ed., *The Papers of Robert Morris* (Pittsburgh, 1973–), I, 38, n. 58.

76. See Jere. Wadsworth to Philip Schuyler, April 8, 1779; Samuel Leonard to Wadsworth, May 1; Peter Colt to Wadsworth, May 2, June 6, and July 2, in Jeremiah
Wadsworth Papers, Connecticut Historical Society.

77. See *Boston Gazette*, August 2, 1779.

78. Largely because there were not so many of them, see Price, "American Port
Towns," 176–83.

79. See Massachusetts Archives, vol. 145, 168. Most of the losses occurred when the
leaders of the expedition ordered the scuttling of the fleet at Bagaduce after the
arrival of a large British naval reinforcement.

80. See Peter Colt to Jere. Wadsworth, August 15, 1779, and August 28; John Jeffrey
to Wadsworth, August 28, all in Jeremiah Wadsworth Papers. Also William Bradford to the Marine Committee, August 12, 1779, in William Bradford Letterbook,
II, Library of Congress. Also William M. Fowler, *Rebels under Sail: The American
Navy during the Revolution* (New York, 1976), 101–102.

81. For the value of the seizures, see William Bradford to William Whipple, September 23, 1779, in Bradford Letterbook, II, Library of Congress. Wadsworth's
scheme is outlined in Jere. Wadsworth to George Clinton, ?, *Public Papers of
George Clinton, First Governor of New York . . .* (Albany, N.Y., 1901), V, 265; Wadsworth to the Committee of Congress, September 5, 1779, in Papers of the Continental Congress, reel 104, item 78, vol. 24, 79ff.

82. Bradford to Whipple, September 23, 1779, and to Francis Lewis, October 1, in
Bradford Letterbook, II, Library of Congress; also *Journals of the Continental
Congress*, XV, 1031.

83. "Boston Town Records 1778–1783," *Twenty-sixth Report of the Record Com-*

missioners (Boston, 1895), 94. See also Smith, "Politics of Price Regulation," 488–89.

84. "Boston Town Records," 101.
85. Cf. *ibid.*, 89. Withholding by farmers of country produce was a major anxiety in Boston, to judge from the attention the problem received in the newspapers, see *Boston Gazette*, September 6, 20, and 27, 1779.
86. William Bradford to William Whipple, September 23, 1779, in Bradford Letterbook, II, Library of Congress. Congress subsequently censured Bradford for selling the prize goods at the regulated price when he knew that they could fetch a much higher price elsewhere; see *Journals of the Continental Congress*, XV, 1342.
87. George Benson to Nicholas Brown, September 30, 1779, in Brown Papers, John Carter Brown Library, Brown University.
88. The proposal originated from the legislature of New Jersey immediately after the Fort Wilson incident: see New Jersey General Assembly to Congress, October 7, 1779, in Papers of the Continental Congress, reel 82, item 68, 467ff.
89. See Azariah Dunham to Ephraim Blaine, December 20, 1779, in E. Blaine Papers, Library of Congress.
90. Buel, *Dear Liberty*, 218–20.
91. The incident is discussed in *ibid.*, 287–88. See also "Pacificus" in *Connecticut Courant*, July 30 and September 3, 1782.
92. Buel, *Dear Liberty*, 304–15.
93. See John L. Brooke, "To the Quiet of the People," 429–57.
94. *Ibid.*, 429–31, 445–46, gives a good sense of how extensive these were.
95. See Ferguson, *Power of the Purse*, 51–52.
96. *Ibid.*, 126ff.
97. See "Letters of Centinel," in Herbert J. Storing, ed., *The Complete Antifederalist* (Chicago, 1981), II, 192; Steven R. Boyd, *The Politics of Opposition: Antifederalists and the Acceptance of the Constitution* (Millwood, N.Y., 1979), 98. Though Centinel's call met with some response in Pennsylvania, it did so largely after the Federalist success in that state and had little impact. The only state where local Antifederalist organizations had a significant effect on the ratification process was New York. There they ensured that the New York ratifying convention would have an Antifederalist majority. See *ibid.*, 73–82, 96.

A Different Thermidor
MICHAEL ZUCKERMAN

1. See, *e.g.*, Edmund Morgan, *American Slavery—American Freedom: The Ordeal of Colonial Virginia* (New York, 1975); Ann Kibbey, *Rhetoric, Prejudice, and Violence: The Interpretation of Material Shapes in Puritanism* (Cambridge, England, 1985); Wilcomb Washburn, *The Governor and the Rebel: A History of Bacon's Rebellion in Virginia* (Chapel Hill, N.C., 1957); Richard M. Brown, *The South Carolina Regulators* (Cambridge, Mass., 1963); Marvin L. Michael Kay, "The North Carolina Regulation, 1766–1776: A Class Conflict," in Alfred Young, ed., *The American Revolution: Explorations in the History of American Radicalism* (DeKalb, Ill., 1976); Michael Zuckerman, *Peaceable Kingdoms: New England Towns in the Eighteenth Century* (New York, 1970).
2. J. H. Plumb, *The Growth of Political Stability in England 1675–1725* (London, 1967).
3. J. G. A. Pocock, *The Machiavellian Moment: Florentine Political Thought and the Atlantic Republican Tradition* (Princeton, N.J., 1975).
4. Caroline Robbins, *The Eighteenth-Century Commonwealthman* (Cambridge, Mass., 1959).
5. Bernard Bailyn, "The Central Themes of the American Revolution: An Inter-

pretation," in Stephen Kurtz and James Hutson, eds., *Essays on the American Revolution* (Chapel Hill, N.C., 1973), 9; Richard Buel, "Democracy and the American Revolution: A Frame of Reference," *William and Mary Quarterly*, 3d ser., 21 (1964), 167. See, more generally, Bernard Bailyn, *The Ideological Origins of the American Revolution* (Cambridge, Mass., 1967), and Gordon Wood, *The Creation of the American Republic, 1776–1787* (Chapel Hill, N.C., 1969).

6. Wood, *Creation of the Republic*, 15; see also Michael Zuckerman, "The Irrelevant Revolution: 1776 and Since," *American Quarterly*, 30 (1978), 224–42.

7. Wood, *Creation of the Republic*, 100.

8. Clifford Geertz, "Ideology as a Cultural System," in David Apter, ed., *Ideology and Discontent* (Glencoe, Ill., 1964), 64; Bailyn, "Central Themes," 11.

9. Joyce Appleby, "The Social Origins of American Revolutionary Ideology," *Journal of American History*, 64 (1977–78), 937.

10. One of the few historians who has recognized the salience of the question in a sustained fashion is Gordon Wood. See, *e.g.*, "Interests and Disinterestedness in the Making of the Constitution," in Richard Beeman, Stephen Botein, and Edward Carter, eds., *Beyond Confederation: Origins of the Constitution and American National Identity* (Chapel Hill, N.C., 1987), 69–109, and "The Significance of the Early Republic," *Journal of the Early Republic*, 8 (1988), 1–20.

11. J. G. A. Pocock, "Virtue and Commerce in the Eighteenth Century," *Journal of Interdisciplinary History*, 3 (1972), 120.

12. Lorena Walsh, "Urban Amenities and Rural Sufficiency: Living Standards and Consumer Behavior in the Colonial Chesapeake, 1643–1777," *Journal of Economic History*, 43 (1983), 109–10. Such standards were not confined to the early Chesapeake. The mean value of consumption goods inventoried in the estates of young fathers in rural New England through the first half of the eighteenth century was scarcely distinguishable from the mean value of such goods in such estates in Maryland at the earlier point of 1698–1702; see Gloria Main, "The Standard of Living in Colonial Massachusetts," *Journal of Economic History*, 43 (1983), 103–105. For other aspects and other regions, see Carole Shammas, "The Domestic Environment in Early Modern England and America," *Journal of Social History*, 14 (1980–81), 3–24; Sarah McMahon, "A Comfortable Subsistence: The Changing Composition of Diet in Rural New England, 1620–1840," *William and Mary Quarterly*, 3d ser., 42 (1985), 26–65; Jack Michel, "In a Manner and Fashion Suitable to Their Degree: A Preliminary Investigation of the Material Culture of Early Rural Pennsylvania," *Working Papers from the Regional Economic History Research Center*, 5 (1981), 1–83; Cary Carson, "Doing History with Material Culture," in Ian Quimby, ed., *Material Culture and the Study of American Life* (New York, 1978), 41–64; Cary Carson *et al.*, "Impermanent Architecture in the Southern American Colonies," *Winterthur Portfolio*, 16 (1981), 135–96.

13. Shammas, "The Domestic Environment"; McMahon, "A Comfortable Subsistence," 50.

14. Shammas, "The Domestic Environment"; Rodris Roth, *Tea-Drinking in Eighteenth-Century America: Its Etiquette and Equipage* (Washington, D.C., 1961).

15. Walsh, "Urban Amenities," 117; James Habersham to William Knox, June 13, 1772, in "The Letters of Hon. James Habersham, 1756–1775," *Collections of the Georgia Historical Society*, 6 (1904), 186.

16. Walsh, "Urban Amenities," 116; James A. Henretta, *The Evolution of American Society, 1700–1815: An Interdisciplinary Analysis* (Lexington, Mass., 1973), 138–41.

17. G. B. Warden, "The Distribution of Property in Boston, 1692–1775," *Perspectives in American History*, 10 (1976), 98–99; Edmund and Helen Morgan, *The Stamp Act Crisis: Prologue to Revolution* (Chapel Hill, N.C., 1953), 31.

18. Joyce Appleby, "Ideology and Theory: The Tension between Political and Economic Liberalism in Seventeenth-Century England," *American Historical Review*, 81 (1976), 500–501. See also Joyce Appleby, *Capitalism and a New Social Order: The Republican Vision of the 1790s* (New York, 1984); Joseph Ellis, *After the Revolution: Profiles of Early American Culture* (New York, 1979), part 1; J. E. Crowley, *This Sheba, Self: The Conceptualization of Economic Life in Eighteenth-Century America* (Baltimore, 1974).

19. Wood, *Creation of the Republic*; Robert Shalhope, "Toward a Republican Synthesis: The Emergence of an Understanding of Republicanism in American Historiography," *William and Mary Quarterly*, 3d ser., 29 (1972), 70.

20. Pauline Maier, "Popular Uprisings and Civil Authority in Eighteenth-Century America," *William and Mary Quarterly*, 3d ser., 27 (1970), 3–35; John Alexander, "The Fort Wilson Incident of 1779: A Case Study of the Revolutionary Crowd," *William and Mary Quarterly*, 3d ser., 31 (1974), 589–612.

21. "Letter Book of Francis Jerdone," *William and Mary Quarterly*, 1st ser., 14 (1905–1906), 145; Jack Greene, *Landon Carter: An Inquiry into the Personal Values and Social Imperatives of the Eighteenth-Century Virginia Gentry* (Charlottesville, Va., 1967), 63.

22. Gordon Wood, ed., *The Rising Glory of America, 1760–1820* (New York, 1971), 5–6.

23. Rowland Berthoff, "Independence and Attachment, Virtue and Interest: From Republican Citizen to Free Enterpriser, 1787–1837," in Richard Bushman *et al.*, eds., *Uprooted Americans: Essays to Honor Oscar Handlin* (Boston, 1979), 105.

24. Appleby, *Capitalism*, 16–18; Drew McCoy, "Benjamin Franklin's Vision of a Republican Political Economy for America," *William and Mary Quarterly*, 3d ser., 35 (1978), 618–19.

25. Henretta, *Evolution*, 142–43.

26. *Ibid.*, 143.

27. Max Farrand, ed., *The Records of the Federal Convention of 1787* (New Haven, Conn., 1911–37), I, 393; Gerald Weales, "The Quality of Mercy, or Mrs. Warren's Profession," *Georgia Review*, 33 (1979), 889–90.

28. Randolph Klein, *Portrait of an Early American Family: The Shippens of Pennsylvania across Five Generations* (Philadelphia, 1975), 298; Forrest McDonald, *Alexander Hamilton: A Biography* (New York, 1979), 21–22; Appleby, *Capitalism*, 14; Gordon Wood, "Interests and Disinterestedness," 71.

29. Klein, *Portrait of an Early Family*, 320–21; Edmund Morgan, "Royal and Republican Corruption," in *The Development of a Revolutionary Mentality* (Washington, D.C., 1972), 95.

30. Philip Padelford, ed., *Colonial Panorama, 1775: Doctor Robert Honyman's Journal for March and April* (San Marino, Cal., 1939), xi; Washington to John Hancock, September 24, 1776, in John Fitzpatrick, ed., *The Writings of George Washington* (Washington, D.C., 1931–44), VI, 107–108.

31. E. Wayne Carp, *To Starve the Army at Pleasure: Continental Army Administration and American Political Culture, 1775–1783* (Chapel Hill, N.C., 1984), 112–28, denies that corruption in the administration of supply was rampant in actual fact, but he shows that, within the canons of republican ideology, Americans could only account for the undeniable failures of supply by imputing corrupt conspiracies to supply staff officers and their contractors. Even if Carp is correct, then, the widespread conviction of such conspiracies corroded commitment to sacrifice for the commonwealth as surely as widespread realities of corruption could have.

32. John Brooke, "Society, Revolution, and the Symbolic Uses of the Dead: An Historical Ethnography of the Massachusetts Near Frontier, 1730–1820," (unpublished Ph.D. dissertation, University of Pennsylvania, 1982), 272; Sam Bass

Warner, *The Private City: Philadelphia in Three Periods of its Growth* (Philadelphia, 1968), chapter 2; Wayne Bodle, "This Tory Labyrinth: Community, Conflict, and Military Strategy during the Valley Forge Winter," in Michael Zuckerman, ed., *Friends and Neighbors: Group Life in America's First Plural Society* (Philadelphia, 1982), 222–50; Eric Foner, *Tom Paine and Revolutionary America* (New York, 1976), chapter 5; Alexander, "The Fort Wilson Incident"; Marquis de Chastellux, *Travels in North America in the Years 1780, 1781 and 1782*, trans. and ed. by Howard Rice (Chapel Hill, N.C., 1963), 382.

33. Wood, *Creation of the Republic*, 422; Foner, *Tom Paine*, 138.

34. Wood, *Creation of the Republic*, 610, 607.

35. Foner, *Tom Paine*, chapter 5; McDonald, *Alexander Hamilton*, 138.

36. Appleby, *Capitalism*, 96.

37. *Ibid.*, 16; Berthoff, "Independence and Attachment," 107.

38. Crowley, *This Sheba, Self*, 152.

39. Appleby, "Ideology and Theory," 509; Appleby, "Social Origins," 945, 951; Appleby, *Capitalism*, 92.

40. Rhys Isaac, "Dramatizing the Ideology of Revolution: Popular Mobilization in Virginia, 1774 to 1776," *William and Mary Quarterly*, 3d ser., 33 (1976), 378–79.

41. Wood, *Creation of the Republic*, 606–607; L. H. Butterfield, ed., *Letters of Benjamin Rush* (Princeton, N.J., 1951), I, 285–86; Edward Countryman, "Consolidating Power in Revolutionary America: The Case of New York, 1775–1783," *Journal of Interdisciplinary History*, 6 (1976), 672–73; Jacob Cooke, ed., *The Federalist* (Middletown, Conn., 1961), Number 10, 56–65.

42. Robert Wiebe, *The Opening of American Society: From the Adoption of the Constitution to the Eve of Disunion* (New York, 1984), 87–88, 118; Wood, *Creation of the Republic*, 606–607.

43. Rhys Isaac, *The Transformation of Virginia 1740–1790* (Chapel Hill, N.C., 1982); Brooke, "Society, Revolution, and the Symbolic Uses of the Dead," esp. chapters 1, 4.

44. Howard Miller, *The Revolutionary College: American Presbyterianism in Higher Education, 1707–1837* (New York, 1976).

45. Ellis, *After the Revolution*, 26–27.

46. Lonna Malmsheimer, "New England Funeral Sermons and Changing Attitudes Toward Women" (unpublished Ph.D. dissertation, University of Minnesota, 1973); Daniel Blake Smith, *Inside the Great House: Planter Family Life in Eighteenth-Century Chesapeake Society* (Ithaca, N.Y., 1980); Jan Lewis, *The Pursuit of Happiness: Family and Values in Jefferson's Virginia* (Cambridge, England, 1983).

47. Nancy Cott, "Divorce and the Changing Status of Women in Eighteenth-Century Massachusetts," *William and Mary Quarterly*, 3d ser., 33 (1976), 586–614.

48. Lisa Waciega, "A 'Man of Business': The Widow of Means in Southeastern Pennsylvania, 1750–1850," *William and Mary Quarterly*, 3d ser., 44 (1987), 40–64; Linda Speth, "More than Her 'Thirds': Wives and Widows in Colonial Virginia," in Carol Berkin, ed., *Women, Family and Community in Colonial America* (New York, 1980).

49. Michael Hindus and Daniel Scott Smith, "Premarital Pregnancy in America, 1640–1971: An Overview and Interpretation," *Journal of Interdisciplinary History*, 5 (1975), 537–70; Daniel Scott Smith, "Parental Power and Marriage Patterns: An Analysis of Historical Trends in Hingham, Massachusetts," *Journal of Marriage and the Family*, 35 (1973), 419–28.

50. Wood, *Creation of the Republic*, viii.

51. Appleby, "Social Origins," 956.

52. Appleby, *Capitalism*, 93–94, 67–68; Alexis de Tocqueville, *Democracy in America* (1835, 1840; repr. New York, 1945), II, 104–105.
53. Appleby, *Capitalism*, 90; Wood, *Creation of the Republic*, 610–11.
54. Morton Horwitz, *The Transformation of American Law, 1780–1860* (Cambridge, Mass., 1977).

The Transforming Impact of Independence, Reaffirmed
PAULINE MAIER

1. Bailyn, *The Ideological Origins of the American Revolution* (Cambridge, Mass., 1967), x.
2. *Ibid.*, 302.
3. Frederick B. Tolles, "The American Revolution Considered as a Social Move-ment: A Re-Evaluation," *American Historical Review*, 60 (1954), 1–12. Among more recent efforts to address the overall social impact of the Revolution see, for example, James A. Henretta and Gregory H. Nobles, *Evolution and Revolution: American Society, 1600–1820* (Lexington, Mass., 1987).
4. Brody, "The Old Labor History and the New: In Search of an American Working Class," in Daniel J. Leab, ed., *The Labor History Review* (Urbana, Ill., 1985), 1–16, esp. 4–5, 13–15. Several more recent studies also suggest that instances in which American working people manifested a sense of shared identity among themselves and against their rulers and employers, such as Thompson discovered in his study of England between the 1780s and 1830s, were at best brief and transient before the Civil War. See, for example, Jonathan Prude, *The Coming of the Industrial Order: Town and Factory Life in Rural Massachusetts, 1810–1860* (New York, 1983), and also Sean Wilentz, *Chants Democratic: New York and the Rise of the American Working Class, 1788–1850* (New York, 1984).
5. Jeffrey G. Williamson and Peter H. Lindert, *American Inequality: A Macroeconomic History* (New York, 1980).
6. Thompson, *The Making of the English Working Class* (New York, 1966), esp. 9–11.
7. See, for example, Thomas Paine, "The Rights of Man," Second Part (1792), in Philip S. Foner, ed., *The Complete Writings of Thomas Paine* (New York, 1945), I, 354: "The independence of America, considered merely as a separation from England, would have been a matter of little importance, had it not been accom-panied by a revolution in the principles and practise of governments."
8. *Ibid.*, I, 13.
9. David Ramsay, *An Oration Delivered ... the Fourth of July, 1794* (Charleston, [1794]), 7; quotation from the Virginia convention of 1829–30 in Stanley N. Katz, "The Strange Birth and Unlikely History of Constitutional Equality," *Jour-nal of American History*, 75 (1988), 753.
10. Bailyn, *Ideological Origins*, esp. 307–308, and J. R. Pole, *The Pursuit of Equality in American History* (Berkeley, Cal., 1978), esp. 13–58. Note the strikingly modern argument Philadelphia Jews posed against a provision in Pennsylvania's Frame of Government (1776) that required all assembly delegates to affirm the divine origin of both the Old and the New Testament. That requirement, they said, violated the state's bill of rights, by which no man who acknowledged the being of a God could be "deprived or abridged of any civil right." Moreover, by ex-cluding Jews "from the most important and honourable part of the rights of a free citizen," the provision served as a "stigma upon their nation and religion." "Memorial of Rabbi Ger. Seixas of the Synagogue of the Jews at Philadelphia," *The Freeman's Journal* (Philadelphia), January 21, 1784.

11. Pauline Maier, *The Old Revolutionaries: Political Lives in the Age of Samuel Adams* (New York, 1980), 40 (quotation, 1771), 30–32; Crevecoeur, *Letters from an American Farmer and Sketches of Eighteenth-Century America* (New York, 1963), 61 (Letter III); "Philadelphiensis," Letter V, in Herbert J. Storing, ed., *The Complete Anti-Federalist* (Chicago, 1981), III, 118. See also Ramsay's description of the "old world" in *An Oration*, 13 ("A few among [the inhabitants there] are exalted to be more than men, but the great bulk of the people, bowed down under the galling yoke of oppression, are in a state of dependence which debases human nature"), and Joel Barlow's similar description of those "unnatural combinations which in Europe are called Society" in his *Advice to the Privileged Orders in the Several States of Europe Resulting from the Necessity and Propriety of a General Revolution in the Principle of Government* (Ithaca, N.Y., 1956; orig. 1792 and 1795), esp. 79–80.

12. See, for example, Montesquieu, *The Spirit of the Laws* (New York, 1949; orig. 1748), esp. books III, V, and VII; Gordon S. Wood, *The Creation of the American Republic, 1776–1787* (Chapel Hill, N.C., 1969), 46–124.

13. *Ibid.*, 98–99; Crevecoeur, *Letters from an American Farmer*, esp. 61–64.

14. Franklin, "Information To Those Who Would Remove to America" (1782), in John Bigelow, ed., *The Works of Benjamin Franklin* (New York, 1904), IX, 433–34, 437; Aedanus Burke as "Cassius," *Considerations on the Society or Order of Cincinnati* (Philadelphia, 1783), 5; Pinckney speech of June 25, 1787, in Max Farrand, ed., *The Records of the Federal Convention of 1787* (New Haven, Conn., 1911), I, 398. Also Thomas Jefferson, *Notes on the State of Virginia* (New York, 1964; orig. 1785), esp. 156–58 (Query XIX), and the "Federalist Farmer," Letters V and VII, in Storing, ed., *Complete Anti-Federalist*, II, 251, 266.

15. Smith in Jonathan Elliot, ed., *The Debates in the Several State Conventions, on the Adoption of the Federal Constitution.* . . . (Washington, 1836), II, 246; Adams, "A Defence of the Constitutions of Government of the United States of America. . . . ," in Charles Francis Adams, ed., *The Works of John Adams* (New York, 1971; orig. Boston, 1850–56), IV, 271.

16. Jefferson, describing Europe, to Edward Carrington, Paris, January 16, 1787, in Julian P. Boyd, ed., *The Papers of Thomas Jefferson*, XI (Princeton, N.J., 1955), 49; *Pennsylvania Evening Herald*, November 30, 1785, quoted in John K. Alexander, *Render Them Submissive: Responses to Poverty in Philadelphia, 1760–1800* (Amherst, Mass., 1980), 44; Samuel Eliot Morison, ed., "William Manning's 'The Key of Liberty,' " *William and Mary Quarterly*, 3d ser., 13 (1956), esp. 217–20.

17. "Federal Farmer," Letter III, in John P. Kaminski and Gaspare J. Saladino, eds., *The Documentary History of the Ratification of the Constitution* (henceforth *DHRC*), XIV (Madison, Wis., 1983), 31; and see also Melancthon Smith in Elliot, ed., *Debates in the State Conventions*, II, 246–48. Note, moreover, that William Manning's division of American society into two "ordirs of men," the "Few & Many," turned upon distinctions of wealth and labor as well as a real or intended power relationship. The few included those so rich they could live without physical labor, who looked down on the "many" who worked with their hands, and were "ever hankering & striving after Monerca or Aristocracy." Morison, ed., "William Manning's 'Key of Liberty,' " 217–18, 220.

18. Bushman, " 'This New Man': Dependence and Independence, 1776," in Bushman *et al.*, eds., *Uprooted Americans: Essays to Honor Oscar Handlin* (Boston, 1979), 91–92.

19. Archibald S. Foord, *His Majesty's Opposition, 1714–1830* (Oxford, 1964), esp. 37–42; Bernard Bailyn, *The Origins of American Politics* (New York, 1968); Major Wilson, "Republicanism and the Idea of Party in the Jacksonian Period," *Journal of the Early Republic*, VIII (1988), 419–42.

20. Madison to Jefferson, October 24, 1787, in Robert A. Rutland *et al.*, eds., *The Papers of James Madison*, X (Chicago, 1977), 212–13. See also "Brutus," Letter III, and Samuel Chase's "Notes" from his speeches in the Maryland ratifying convention in Storing, ed., *Complete Anti-Federalist*, II, 380, and V, 20.

21. Bailyn, *Ideological Origins*, 299; "Federal Farmer," Letter VII, in Storing, ed., *Complete Anti-Federalist*, II, 266.

22. Quotation from a newspaper essay by William Paterson in John E. O'Connor, *William Paterson: Lawyer and Statesman, 1745–1806* (New Brunswick, N.J., 1979), 213–14. See also François-Jean, Marquis de Chastellux, *Travels in North America in the Years 1780, 1781, and 1782 . . .*, Howard C. Rice, Jr., trans. and ed. (Chapel Hill, N.C., 1963), II, 438–39; Isaac Weld, *Travels Through the States of North America, and the Provinces of Upper and Lower Canada, During the Years 1795, 1796, and 1797* (4th ed.; London, 1807), I, 146; "A Republican" in the *Connecticut Journal* (New Haven) March 31, 1784; Letters of "Agrippa," 1788, in Storing, ed., *Complete Anti-Federalist*, IV, 93–94; David McLean, *Timothy Pickering and the Age of the American Revolution* (New York, 1982), esp. 100, 265; Washington to Madison, March 31, 1787, in John C. Fitzpatrick, ed., *The Writings of George Washington* XXIX (Washington, D.C., 1939), 190; Mercy Warren, *History of the Rise, Progress and Termination of the American Revolution* (Boston, 1805), I, 21–22. For studies of urban poverty in eighteenth-century America, see Gary B. Nash, *The Urban Crucible: Social Change, Political Consciousness, and the Origins of the American Revolution* (Cambridge, Mass., 1979); Alexander, *Render Them Submissive*; Billy G. Smith, "Inequality in Late Colonial Philadelphia; A Note on Its Nature and Growth," *William and Mary Quarterly*, 3d ser., 41 (1984), 629–45 (which conveniently cites the previous literature); and Jack P. Greene's more upbeat conclusions in *Pursuits of Happiness: The Social Development of Early Modern British Colonies and the Formation of American Culture* (Chapel Hill, N.C., 1988), esp. 73–74, 91–92, 136–37, 187–88.

23. "To the Public," the *Independent Chronicle and Universal Advertiser* (Boston), April 8, 1784; William Smith, Jr., *The History of the Province of New York*, ed. Michael Kammen (Cambridge, Mass., 1972; orig. London, 1757), I, 223; "Notice by the Society for the Relief of Distressed Debtors, New York, January 20, 1788," in *American Magazine* (New York), January 1988, 121–22; O'Connor, *Paterson*, 213–14; Alexander, *Render Them Submissive, passim*. These attitudes had roots in earlier English "republican" writings: see Edmund S. Morgan, "Slavery and Freedom: The American Paradox," *Journal of American History*, 59 (1972), 9–12.

24. Franklin, "Information," in Bigelow, ed., *Works of Franklin*, esp. IX, 437–42, 444; Alexander, *Render Them Submissive*, 54–55 (quotation from the Pennsylvania press of the 1780s) and *passim*; Richard Price, *Observations on the Importance of the American Revolution* (Hartford, Conn., 1785), 49. Also Benjamin Rush, "Information to Europeans who are disposed to Migrate to the United States of America," in Rush, *Essays, Literary, Moral & Philosophical* (Philadelphia, 1798), 189–210; Smith, *History of New York*, I, 223–25; and Enos Hitchcock, *The Farmer's Friend, or the History of Mr. Charles Worthy. . . .* (Boston, [1793]). J. E. Crowley, in *This Sheba, Self: The Conceptualization of Economic Life in Eighteenth-Century America* (Baltimore, 1974), 3–4, suggests that the idealization of "middling" levels of wealth made some sense in the eighteenth century: "After a family attained a certain level of affluence . . . increments of wealth did not necessarily correspond with absolute improvements in material well-being; indeed, the medical care, diet, clothing and household facilities of the wealthy may have exacted a toll in physical discomfort which people of more middling means avoided."

25. Franklin, "Information . . . ," in Bigelow, ed., *Works of Franklin*, IX, 437; "To the

Public," *Independent Chroncle and Universal Advertiser*, April 8, 1784; Brewster as "A MECHANIC, not yet a FREE-MAN" and "The MECHANICK ON TAXATION" in the *Norwich Packet* (Norwich, Conn.), September 8, 1791, and May 10, 1792. See also Alexander, *Render Them Submissive*, chapters 4–7, on the efforts in Philadelphia to implement similar policies. Ironically, such "reformist" policies, which were sometimes founded upon an assumption of American distinctiveness, predicted the course England would take a half century later in adopting its own poor law.

26. Weld, *Travels*, I, 127; Warren, *History of the American Revolution*, III, 415.

27. Alexander Hamilton in Elliot, ed., *Debates in the State Conventions*, II, 256; Franklin, "Information," in Bigelow, ed., *Works of Franklin*, IX, 436; John Gardiner, *An Oration, July 4, 1785* . . . (Boston, 1785), 9.

28. "A Farmer," Essay I, February 15, 1788, in Storing, ed., *Complete Anti-Federalist*, V, 19. Also Julian Niemcewicz, *Under Their Vine and Fig Tree: Travels through America in 1797–1799, 1805* . . . , trans. and ed. Metchie J. E. Budka, *Collections of the New Jersey Historical Society at Newark*, XIV (Elizabeth, N.J., 1966), 185–86; Barlow, *Advice to the Privileged Orders*, esp. 79–81.

29. King, R. R. Livingston, and Melancthon Smith, in Elliot, ed., *Debates in the State Conventions*, II, 35, 277–78, 246; Timothy Pickering quoted in McLean, *Pickering*, 265; "Harrington" (probably Benjamin Rush) in *DHRC*, XIII (Madison, Wis., 1981), 116; Fisher Ames to George Richards Minot, November 12, 1794, to Christopher Gore, February 24, 1803, and to Thomas Dwight, October 25, 1796, in Seth Ames, ed., *Works of Fisher Ames* (Boston, 1854), I, 151, 319, 204; Jefferson to John Adams, October 28, 1813, in Lester J. Cappon, ed., *The Adams-Jefferson Letters* (Chapel Hill, N.C., 1959), II, 388; Morison, ed., "William Manning's 'Key of Liberty,'" 247.

30. Hamilton in Elliot, ed., *Debates in the State Conventions*, II, 257, and R. R. Livingston's defense of the rich at 276. Similarily, Gouverneur Morris wrote John Jay that he suspected there were more rogues outside coaches than in them: letter of January 10, 1784, in Jared Sparks, *The Life of Gouverneur Morris* (Boston, 1832), I, 267.

31. Franklin in Farrand, ed., *Records of the Federal Convention*, II, 249. See also Gouverneur Morris's similar remarks in *ibid.*, I, 511–14, and Charles Carroll of Carrollton's earlier assertion that not even wealth and honesty went together, in Peter Onuf, ed., *Maryland and the Empire, 1773: The Antilon-First Citizen Letters* (Baltimore, 1974), 57–58.

32. Timothy Pickering to Charles Tillinghast, Philadelphia, December 24, 1787, *DHRC*, XIV, 194. Pickering argued there that the absence of property qualifications in the federal constitution disproved Antifederalist arguments that it would lead to aristocracy. Hamilton also insisted that, because the Constitution did not "render a rich man more eligible than a poor one," it was founded upon a "broad and equal principle." In Elliot, ed., *Debates in the State Conventions*, II, 256.

33. See Charles Carroll of Annapolis to Daniel of St. Thomas Jenifer, June 14, 1778, quoted in Maier, *The Old Revolutionaries*, 223.

34. Morison, ed., "William Manning's 'Key of Liberty,'" 217; Findley in Mathew Carey, ed., *Debates and Proceedings of the General Assembly of Pennsylvania, on the Memorials Praying a Repeal of the Law Annuling the Charter of the Bank* (Philadelphia, 1786), 130. Also Samuel Adams as "Candidus," *Boston Gazette*, January 20, 1772, in Harry Alonzo Cushing, ed., *The Writings of Samuel Adams* (New York, 1904–1908), II, 316–17.

35. Livingston as "Primitive Whig III" in *New Jersey Gazette* (Trenton), January 23, 1786; Ruth Bogin, *Abraham Clark and the Quest for Equality in the Revolutionary Era, 1774–1794* (East Brunswick, N.J., 1982), 34 and *passim*.

36. Hamilton, "The Continentalist No. VI," July 4, 1782, in Morton J. Fisch, ed., *Selected Writings and Speeches of Alexander Hamilton* (Washington, D.C., 1985), 64; Jefferson to Washington, March 15, 1784, in Boyd, ed., *Jefferson Papers*, VIII (Princeton, N.J., 1953), 26; Cathy Matson and Peter Onuf, "Toward a Republican Empire: Interest and Ideology in Revolutionary America," *American Quarterly*, 37 (1985), 496–531, esp. 516–19, including quotations from Webster's *Sketches of American Policy* (Hartford, Conn., 1785), at 517. See also Drew McCoy, *The Elusive Republic: Political Economy in Jeffersonian America* (Chapel Hill, N.C., 1980), 69–75, 96–100, and *passim*; Bernard Bailyn, *Faces of Revolution: Personalities and Themes in the Struggle for American Independence* (New York, 1990), 261–64.

37. Carole Shammas, Marylynn Salmon, and Michael Dahlin, *Inheritance in America from Colonial Times to the Present* (New Brunswick, N.J., 1987); Lawrence M. Friedman, *A History of American Law* (2d ed.; New York, 1985), 65–68, and Stanley N. Katz, "Republicanism and the Law of Inheritance in the American Revolutionary Era," *Michigan Law Review*, 76 (1977–78), 1–29. There is some evidence, moreover, that partible inheritances were customary in Virginia well before the Revolution. See James W. Deene, Jr., "Patterns of Testation: Four Tidewater Counties in Colonial Virginia," *American Journal of Legal History*, 16 (1972), 154–76.

38. "A Freeman II" (Tench Coxe), 1788, in *DHRC*, XV (Madison, Wis., 1984), 508–509. Also Charles Pinckney in Farrand, ed., *Records of the Federal Convention*, I, 400; [Jonathan Jackson,] *Thoughts upon the Political Situation of the United States. . . .* (Worcester, 1788), 56–57, and Timothy Pickering to Charles Tillinghast, Philadelphia, December 24, 1787, *DHRC*, XIV, 194.

39. See, for example, the veto statements of governors Francis Rawn Shunk and William Freame Johnston in George E. Reed, ed., *Pennsylvania Archives*, 4th Ser., VII (Harrisburg, Pa., 1902), 86–87 (1846), 236 (1846), and 559–60 (1852). In the 1780s, William Findley had used a similar argument against the Bank of North America. See Carey, ed., *Debates of the Pennsylvania Assembly*, 123.

40. Rush Welter, *Popular Education and Democratic Thought in America* (New York, 1962), 24; New Hampshire constitution of 1784 in Ben[jamin] Perly Poore, compiler, *The Federal and State Constitution, Colonial Charters, and other Organic Laws of the United States*, II (2nd ed., Washington, D.C., 1878), 1291; Samuel Knox, "An Essay on the Best System of Liberal Education," 1799, in Frederick Rudolph, ed., *Essays on Education in the Early Republic* (Cambridge, Mass., 1965), 276.

41. Welter, *Popular Education*, and Lawrence A. Cremin, *American Education: The National Experience, 1783–1876* (New York, 1980). Robert Coram, "Political Inquiries," 1791, in Rudolph, ed., *Essays on Education*, 113, and see also Samuel Harrison Smith, "Remarks on Education . . . ," 1798, *ibid.*, 209–11. Coram, a radical equalitarian, confessed a deep indebtedness to the future Federalist Noah Webster: see 125ff. For Webster's writing on education, see Webster, *On Being American: Selected Writings, 1783–1828*, ed. Homer D. Babbidge, Jr., (New York, 1967), which includes his statement that "knowledge should be diffused by means of schools and newspapers." (85).

42. On mobility, see Abell Buell, "The Sequel of Arts and Sciences," c. 1774, in Gordon S. Wood, *The Rising Glory of America, 1760–1820* (New York, 1971), 107 (illustration 2): "Learning advances men of mean degree,/ To high attainments wealth and dignity." Coram, "Political Inquiries," in Rudolph, ed., *Essays on Education*, 82, 143; Webster, essay on education from the *American Magazine*, 1787–88, in Babbidge, ed., *On Being American*, 85. Ramsay, *An Oration*, 18–19, also linked education with the abolition of primogeniture and a broad access to office as antidotes to aristocracy. The general concern with preparing boys for

productive occupations explains the emphasis on practicality in proposed curricula. See, for example, Coram's "Political Inquiries" and Smith's "Remarks on Education" in Rudolph, ed., *Essays on Education*, 139 and 198, and Rush, "A Plan for Establishing Public Schools in Pennsylvania," 1786, in Rush, *Essays*, esp. 15–19.

43. Smith, "Remarks on Education," in Rudolph, ed., *Essays on Education*, 220; Jackson, *Thoughts upon the Political Situation*, 27; Rush, "Of the Mode of Education Proper in a Republic," in Rush, *Essays*, 11; "Of Sufficiency," in the *Pennsylvania Mercury and Universal Advertiser*, October 1, 1784. The last essay, however, also asked readers to "keep fair with those that are above you by their birth or station," which restated earlier colonial attitudes.

44. Bernard Bailyn, *Education in the Forming of American Society* (Chapel Hill, N.C., 1960), 45–47, 113; Welter, *Popular Education and Democratic Thought*, 26–27; Theodore R. Sizer, ed., *The Age of Academies* (New York, 1964); and Donald G. Tewksbury, *The Founding of American Colleges and Universities before the Civil War* (New York, 1969; 1932), esp. 16.

45. Isaiah Thomas, *The History of Printing in America.* . . . (orig. 1810), 2nd ed., vol. II, in *Transactions and Collections of the American Antiquarian Society*, VI (1894; reprinted 1971), 9–10, 199, and, quoting Miller's *Brief Retrospect of the Eighteenth Century* [1803 and 1805], 200–201.

46. Hartz, "The Rise of the Democratic Idea," in Arthur M. Schlesinger, Jr., and Morton White, eds., *Paths of American Thought* (Boston, 1963), esp. 43–44, and *The Liberal Tradition in America* (New York, 1955), esp. 17–18.

47. Introduction to Wood, ed., *The Rising Glory of America*, esp. 3–6; Appleby, "The Social Origins of American Revolutionary Ideology," *Journal of American History*, 64 (1978), 935–58, esp. 935–40. See also Wood, *Creation of the American Republic*, and "Interests and Disinterestedness in the Making of the Constitution," in Richard Beeman *et al.*, eds., *Beyond Confederation: Origins of the Constitution and American National Identity* (Chapel Hill, N.C., 1987), 69–109. Appleby's position is further developed in *Capitalism and a New Social Order: The Republican Vision of the 1790s* (New York, 1984), and in several articles including "Liberalism and the American Revolution," the *New England Quarterly*, 69 (1976), 3–26; "Commercial Farming and the 'Agrarian Myth' in the Early Republic," *Journal of American History*, 68 (1982), 833–49, and "Republicanism in Old and New Contexts," *William and Mary Quarterly*, 3d ser., 43 (1986), 20–34. For a different discussion of the issues raised by these and other recent interpretations of the Revolution that is skeptical of the "civic-humanist" explanation of Independence, see John P. Diggins, *The Lost Soul of American Politics: Virtue, Self-Interest, and the Foundations of Liberalism* (New York, 1984).

48. Wood in *Rising Glory of America*, 6, and *Creation of the American Republic*, esp. 53, 68, and also 61, 63–64; "Ideally, republicanism obliterated the individual," and it justified massive powers of coercion on the part of public and quasi-public bodies. Such a "classical republic" might have provided a functional substitute for that feudal tradition whose absence explained for Hartz the failure of socialism to take root in the United States.

49. Wood, "Interests and Disinterestedness," esp. 83, 85–86, 77–81, 93–102, and *Rising Glory of America*, 9; Appleby, "Social Origins," 949, 952–55, and "Liberalism and the American Revolution," esp. 9–17.

50. *Creation of the American Republic*, esp. 562, 606, and *Rising Glory of America*, 9.

51. "Republicanism in Old and New Contexts"; *Capitalism and a New Social Order*, 3–5 and *passim*.

52. "Republicanism in Old and New Contexts," 26.

53. Stephen Innes, "Introduction. Fulfilling John Smith's Vision: Work and Labor in Early America," in Innes, ed., *Work and Labor in Early America* (Chapel Hill, N.C., 1988), esp. 3–16; and see also James Oakes, "From Republicanism to Liberalism: Ideological Change and the Crisis of the Old South," *American Quarterly*, 37 (1985), esp. 568, which traces the "liberal" rhetoric of slaveholding politicians of the 1850s back to seventeenth-century colonial promotional literature. Greene, *Pursuits of Happiness*, 188, and also Bushman, " 'This New Man,' " 85–89.

54. Warren, *History of the American Revolution*, esp. III, 250–52; Ramsey, *An Oration*, 6, and *The History of the American Revolution* (Philadelphia, 1789), esp. I, 27–34; Findley, *History of the Insurrection in the Four Western Counties of Pennsylvania. . . .* (Philadelphia, 1796), v–vi.

55. Ramsay, *An Oration*, 3, 5; Findley, *History of the Insurrections*, vi; Warren, *History of the American Revolution*, III, 327, 251–52. Ramsay suggested that even the constitutional transformations of the Revolution were almost unnoticed: see his *History of the American Revolution*, I, 350–51, and also 356–57, where he makes clear that those changes were nonetheless of historic significance for the "friends of mankind."

56. Warren nonetheless recognized the inequalities of wealth and knowledge in the South. See her *History of the American Revolution*, I, 21–22, 251, and II, 298.

57. Tocqueville, *Democracy in America*, ed. Phillips Bradley (New York, 1945), esp. I, 14, 27–46, and II, 108 (quotation); Hartz, *Liberal Tradition*, 31, and also 35: for Tocqueville, Hartz said, "the outstanding thing about the American effort of 1776" was "not the freedom to which it led, but the established feudal structure it did not have to destroy."

58. *Democracy in America*, ed. Bradley I, 46–53. See also George Wilson Pierson, *Tocqueville and Beaumont in America* (New York, 1938), 115, 120–31, 163–64. Hartz, *Liberal Tradition*, 61, 52–53.

59. Greene, *Pursuits of Happiness*, 186–87 (quotation), 168, 175–76, 197–98; Timothy Breen, *Tobacco Culture: The Mentality of the Great Tidewater Planters on the Eve of Revolution* (Princeton, N.J., 1985). See also Rowland Berthoff and John M. Murrin, "Feudalism, Communalism, and the Yeoman Freeholder: The American Revolution Considered as a Social Accident," in Stephen G. Kurtz and James H. Hutson, eds., *Essays on the American Revolution* (Chapel Hill, N.C., 1973), 256–68; Murrin, "The Legal Transformation: The Bench and Bar of Eighteenth-Century Massachusetts," in Stanley N. Katz, ed., *Colonial America: Essays in Politics and Social Development* (Boston, 1971), 415–49, and Bailyn, *Ideological Origins*, 274–80. The development of traditionally conservative communities in late colonial America provided for Appleby a foundation for the attractiveness of "civic-humanist" ideas. See *Capitalism and a New Social Order*, 6–12.

60. Lipset, *The First New Nation: The United States in Historical and Comparative Perspective* (New York, 1963), 178, 86–89, and see also Lipset, *Continental Divide: The Values and Institutions of the United States and Canada* (New York, 1990).

61. Bernard Bailyn, *The Ordeal of Thomas Hutchinson* (Cambridge, Mass., 1974), esp. 25–26; Edwin G. Burrows and Michael Wallace, "The American Revolution: The Ideology and Psychology of National Liberation," *Perspectives in American History*, 6 (1972), esp. 298–99; Maier, *The Old Revolutionaries*, esp. 276–77.

62. Morris to a Mr. Penn, May 20, 1774, and speech of May 1776 in Sparks, ed., *Life of Gouverneur Morris*, I, 23–26, 100–105.

63. Pickering letters quoted in McLean, *Pickering*, 265. McLean describes Pickering's "democratic republican ideology" and its development in the course of the independence movement (see esp. 32–34, 51–56, and 263–76). Though Pickering's

views changed in the late 1790s, McLean's book confirms Linda Kerber's observation that there was a "variant of democracy that was Federalism," and even a
distinctive Federalist animus toward aristocracy where it was most firmly established within the United States, among the slaveholding planters of Virginia.
Kerber, *Federalists in Dissent: Imagery and Ideology in Jeffersonian America* (Ithaca,
N.Y., 1970), 207, 185, and chapter 2, "Anti-Virginia and Anti-Slavery," 23–66.

64. Paul Longmore, *The Invention of George Washington* (Berkeley, Cal., 1988), 107–
108, 143, 215–16, 47. Richard Henry Lee is another example: see Maier, *Old
Revolutionaries*, 164–200.

65. Winfred E. A. Bernhard, *Fisher Ames: Federalist and Statesman, 1758–1808* (Chapel
Hill, N.C., 1965), 72.

66. On the last point see Lance Banning, "Jeffersonian Ideology Revisited: Liberal
and Classical Ideas in the New American Republic," *William and Mary Quarterly*,
3d ser., 43 (1986), 3–19, and Isaac Kramnick, "The 'Great National Discussion':
The Discourse of Politics in 1787," *ibid.*, 45 (1988), 3–32.

67. Carey, ed., *Debates of the Pennsylvania Assembly*, 19 (Smilie: unlike the Bank's
defenders, "we on this side have no private interest to serve on the occasion"),
128, 21. The bank's defenders insisted that they also were also concerned for
the public welfare, not their own, narrow interests. If both sides expressed "classical republican" values, they also, according to Crowley, *This Sheba, Self*, 151–
54, both held the same modern ("liberal") economic ideas: the bank's defenders
shared with their antagonists views of "the benign nature of commerce and
wealth, but . . . were more explicit in voicing them and less ambiguous about
their implications. In marking the change from colonial social values, the most
striking feature of their arguments was their forthright assertion that selfishness
was not socially dangerous" (153).

    Note, too, that the "new men" attracted to a "liberal view of society" whom
Appleby identified by name in "Social Origins," 953–55, Christopher Gadsden
and Patrick Henry, both became supporters of the Federalist Party. Gadsden,
whom she cites for his "liberal" views on trade, also espoused a conception of
society that conformed exactly to the regressive vision associated with "classical
republicans." See "A Steady and Open Republican," May 6, 1784, in Richard
Walsh, ed., *The Writings of Christopher Gadsden, 1746–1805* (Columbia, S.C., 1966),
206. Similarly, the New York Sons of Liberty, whom Appleby cites for their
defense of self-interest, condemned corruption in a good "civic-humanist" manner and had little difficulty reconciling "virtue" with their avid pursuit of material
betterment: see Maier, *Old Revolutionaries*, esp. 97–100.

68. *Ibid.*, 3–50.

69. Wilson, "Republicanism and the Idea of Party in the Jacksonian Period." On the
persistence of "classical republican" values see also Rowland Berthoff, "Independence and Attachment, Virtue and Interest: From Republican Citizen to Free
Enterpriser, 1787–1837," in Bushman, ed., *Uprooted Americans*, 97–124.

70. See Appleby, "Social Origins," 952–53: "Radical Whigs like John Trenchard and
Thomas Gordon rejected material progress because it was not based upon the
triumph of virtue. In a frequently quoted passage from *Cato's Letters*, Trenchard
and Gordon criticized charity schools for giving poor children ambitions above
their station and making them unfit for the servant class to which they were
destined." Her source was Staughton Lynd's *Intellectual Origins of American Radicalism* (New York, 1968), 35, which, however, quoted not "Cato" but
J. G. A. Pocock, "Machiavelli, Harrington, and English Political Ideologies in the
Eighteenth Century," *William and Mary Quarterly*, 3d ser., 22 (1965), 575. Pocock
said that in criticizing charity schools, Trenchard and Gordon opposed both
High Church educational activities and social mobility; "they want the children

of the poor left in the servant class where they belong." He cited *"Cato's Letters, passim."* The relevant letter, no. 133, is in Trenchard and Gordon, *Cato's Letters: Essays on Liberty, Civil and Religious, and Other Important Subjects,* 4 vols. in 2 (New York, 1971; reprint of 6th edition, London, 1755), IV, 236–46. It criticizes charity schools "as they are now employed and managed" for the political principles they taught, and for taking children from productive trades and preparing them for positions such as those of servants in which they hope to "earn a comfortable Subsistence . . . without much Labour," *i.e.,* for increasing the supply of servants at the cost of more productive occupations. See esp. 237, 241, 243–44. The essay apparently had little impact on America, where the Revolution provoked, as this essay argues, an enthusiasm for mass education, and, Rush Welter suggests, an expansion of "pauper schooling" (*Popular Education and Democratic Thought,* 26). On other topics mentioned in the text, see esp. letters 38, 45, and 64, in the original vol. II (in vol. I of the reprint), 34–43, 85–90, 267–78.

The mixture of "liberal" and "civic-humanist" ideas in *Cato's Letters* was noted by Isaac Kramnick, *Bolingbroke and His Circle: The Politics of Nostalgia in the Age of Walpole* (Cambridge, Mass., 1968), 243–52. And in "Republican Revisionism Revisited," *American Historical Review,* 87 (1982), 629–64, Kramnick demonstrated that after 1760 the heirs of the English "Country" tradition, with whom Americans often identified, praised achievement and talent, equal opportunity, industry and productivity, and opposed the defenders of a traditional social hierarchy.

71. Bailyn, *Origins of American Politics*; and Pauline Maier, *From Resistance to Revolution: Colonial Radicals and the Development of American Opposition to Britain, 1765–1776* (New York, 1972), esp. 27–48.

72. Bailyn, *Ideological Origins,* 302–305, 318–19; Hutchinson to Lord Hillsboro, March 26, 1770, cited in Vernon L. Parrington, *The Colonial Mind, 1620–1800* (New York, 1927), I, 200. Hartz, *Liberal Tradition,* 52–53, cites the Hutchinson letter as if it revealed a general colonial rather than a specifically Revolutionary development.

73. *First New Nation,* 76. Other more tangible factors were also relevant, including the early establishment of universal manhood suffrage and broad distribution of knowledge in the United States. See Alan Dawley, *Class and Community: The Industrial Revolution in Lynn* (Cambridge, Mass., 1976), esp. 237, 241, and, for comparative purposes, Thompson's *Making of the English Working Class.*

74. Jackson, *Thoughts upon the Political Situation,* 122.

75. "The Factory as a Republican Community: Lowell, Massachusetts," in Kasson, *Civilizing the Machine: Technology and Republican Values in America, 1776–1900* (New York, 1976), 53–106; Sanford, "The Intellectual Origins and New-Worldliness of American Industry," *Journal of Economic History,* 18 (1958), 1–16, esp. 1–2.

76. Faler, *Mechanics and Manufacturers in the Early Industrial Revolution: Lynn, Massachusetts, 1780–1860* (Albany, N.Y., 1981), 186–87; Wilentz, *Chants Democratic,* 62.

77. Foner, *Free Soil, Free Labor, Free Men: The Ideology of the Republican Party before the Civil War* (New York, 1970), esp. 16–18.

78. Linda Kerber, *Women of the Republic: Intellect and Ideology in Revolutionary America* (Chapel Hill, N.C., 1980), esp. 7–8, 15–32.

79. "Political Inquiries," in Rudolph, ed., *Essays on Education,* 127–29.

80. "An Address to the Ladies" signed "Alfonso," in *American Magazine,* March 1788, 244–45; Adams, "Defence of the Constitutions," in Adams, ed., *Works of John Adams,* IV, 301.

81. Jefferson, *Notes on the State of Virginia,* 132–39; Worthman's "Solemn Address"

of 1800 quoted in Philip S. Foner, *The Democratic-Republican Societies, 1790–1800; A Documentary Sourcebook.* . . . (Westport, Conn., 1976), 13; Niemcewicz, *Under Their Vine and Fig Tree*, 9, 104; Chastellux, *Travels in North America*, 439–40.

82. See, for example, Alexander Hamilton's "Report on Manufacturers," 1791, in Jacob E. Cooke, ed., *The Reports of Alexander Hamilton* (Evanston, Ill., 1964), 130–31.

83. Kerber, *Federalists in Dissent*, chapter 2, 23–66; Rush, "Thoughts upon Female Education," in his *Essays*, 92; Webster in Wood, *Rising Glory of America*, 168.

84. Cott, *The Bonds of Womanhood: 'Woman's Sphere' in New England, 1780–1835* (New Haven, Conn., 1977), esp. 205–206.

85. Thomas Dublin, *Women at Work: The Transformation of Work and Community in Lowell, Massachusetts, 1826–1860* (New York, 1979); Dale T. Knobel, *Paddy and the Republic: Ethnicity and Nationality in Antebellum America* (Middletown, Conn., 1986), 88, 76, 126, and *passim*.

86. Oakes, "From Republicanism to Liberalism," esp. 568–69.

87. Klein, *Slavery in the Americas: A Comparative Study of Virginia and Cuba* (Chicago, 1967), esp. 254–64. Klein's portrait of nineteenth-century Cuban race relations has been modified without, I think, undermining the value of his comparison, by Rebecca Scott, *Slave Emancipation in Cuba; The Transition to Free Labor, 1860–1899* (Princeton, N.J., 1985). For an excellent account of the significance of the Revolution in fostering at once the emancipation of slaves and a racism that sought "scientific" proof of blacks' inferiority, see Duncan J. Macleod, *Slavery, Race, and the American Revolution* (London, 1974). Reginald Horsman, *Race and Manifest Destiny: The Origins of American Racial Anglo-Saxonism* (Cambridge, Mass., 1981), sees racism and republicanism as alternatives, in part, I suspect, because he overestimates the extent to which blacks were included in eighteenth-century assertions of men's natural equality. He therefore misses—or rejects—the possibility that republicanism, with its emphasis on the "natural" distinctions among men, might have enhanced Americans' vulnerability to racism.

The Transition to Capitalism in America

JAMES A. HENRETTA

1. Alan Dawley, *Class and Community: The Industrial Revolution in Lynn* (Cambridge, Mass., 1976), 20, 15–16.

2. Paul G. E. Clemens and Lucy Simler, "Rural Labor and the Farm Household in Chester County, Pennsylvania, 1750–1820," in Stephen Innes, ed., *Work and Labor in Early America* (Chapel Hill, N.C., 1988), 106–108. The quoted material is from Brinton's 1781 contract which is cited in 108n.

3. Sarah S. Hughes, "Slaves for Hire: The Allocation of Black Labor in Elizabeth City County, Virginia, 1782–1810," *William and Mary Quarterly*, 3d ser., 35 (1978), 270.

4. Jean-Christophe Agnew, "The Threshold of Exchange: Speculations on the Market," *Radical History Review*, 21 (1980), 115, develops this distinction between a market-place and the market-process.

5. Eric Wolf, *Europe and the People Without History*, (Berkeley, Cal., 1982), 194. For the transforming effect of merchant capital, see note 48 below.

6. Stanley Lebergott, "The Pattern of Employment since 1800," in Seymour E. Harris, ed., *American Economic History* (New York, 1961), 292 and *passim*. For a broader perspective on these issues, see Immanuel Wallerstein, *The Modern World-System: Capitalist Agriculture and the Origins of the European World-Economy in the Sixteenth Century* (New York, 1974), and *The Modern World-System II: Mercantilism*

and the Consolidation of the European World-Economy, 1600–1750 (New York, 1980). Steven J. Stern, "Feudalism, Capitalism, and the World-System in the Perspective of Latin America and the Caribbean," *American Historical Review*, 93 (1988), 829–72, proposes an alternative interpretative framework that is similar, in some respects, to the approach developed in this paper.

7. James F. Shepherd, "British America and the Atlantic Economy," in Ronald Hoffman *et al.*, eds., *The Economy of Early America: The Revolutionary Period, 1763–1790* (Charlottesville, Va., 1988), 10; Robert E. Lipsey, "Foreign Trade," in Lance E. Davis *et al.*, eds., *American Economic Growth: An Economist's History of the United States* (New York, 1972), 554.

8. My contrast between these two systems of political economy draws upon Michael Merrill, "The Anti-Capitalist Origins of the United States" (unpublished paper, 1988; to appear in *Review: The Journal of the Fernand Braudel Center* in 1990).

9. Daniel Vickers, "Working the Fields in a Developing Economy: Essex County, Massachusetts, 1630–1675," in Innes, ed., *Work and Labor*, 52–59.

10. Vickers, "Working the Fields," 59–60, 63–65, 67.

11. Michael Merrill, "Cash Is Good to Eat: Self-Sufficiency and Exchange in the Rural Economy of the United States," *Radical History Review*, 9 (1977), 42–72; Richard S. Dunn, "Servants and Slaves: The Recruitment and Employment of Labor," in Jack P. Greene and J. R. Pole, eds., *Colonial British America: Essays in the New History of the Early Modern Era* (Baltimore, 1984), 185–86.

12. Bettye Hobbs Pruitt, "Self-Sufficiency and the Agricultural Economy of Eighteenth-Century Massachusetts," *William and Mary Quarterly*, 3d ser., 41 (1984) 338, 339–40, 349; Richard L. Bushman, "Family Security in the Transition from Farm to City, 1750–1850," *Journal of Family History*, 6 (1981), 242.

13. Fred Anderson, "A People's Army: Provincial Military Service in Massachusetts during the Seven Years War," *William and Mary Quarterly*, 3d ser., 40 (1983), 499–527.

14. Daniel Vickers, "Nantucket Whalemen in the Deep Sea Fishery: The Changing Anatomy of an Early American Labor Force," *Journal of American History*, 72 (1985), 292–93.

15. Pruitt, "Agricultural Economy," 363; Hamilton quoted in Merrill, "Anti-Capitalist Origins," 27; town meeting quoted in Rowland Berthoff, "Independence and Attachment, Virtue and Interest: From Republican Citizen to Free Enterprise, 1787–1837," in Richard Bushman *et al.*, eds., *Uprooted Americans: Essays to Honor Oscar Handlin* (Boston, 1979), 114.

16. Daniel Vickers, "Competency and Competition: Economic Culture in Early America," *William and Mary Quarterly*, 3d ser., 47 (1990), 4–10; *Gazette* quoted in Gregory H. Nobles, "Hardship in the Hilltowns: Agricultural Development and Economic Conditions in Pelham, Massachusetts, 1740–1790" (paper presented to the Organization of American Historians, Chicago, April 1980), 30.

17. Laurel Thatcher Ulrich, "Martha Ballard and Her 'Girls': Women's Work in Eighteenth Century Maine," in Innes, ed., *Essays on Work*, 90–92. Allan Kulikoff, "The Transition to Capitalism in Rural America," *William and Mary Quarterly*, 3d ser., 46 (1989), 139, argues that "women so disliked this added work that they willingly permitted their daughters to work in textile factories as soon as they were established."

18. Report enclosed in letter of November 10, 1789, from Phineas Bond to the Duke of Leeds, American Historical Association, *Annual Report . . . 1896* (Washington, D.C., 1897), I, 651.

19. On American proto-industrialization, see James A. Henretta, "The War for Independence and American Economic Development," in Hoffman *et al.*, eds.,

Economy of Early America, 45–87, esp. 48–52, 66–68, and 81–86; for Europe, see Peter Kriedte, Hans Medick, Jurgen Schlumbohm, *Industrialization Before Industrialization: Rural Industry in the Genesis of Capitalism*, trans. by Beate Schempp (Cambridge, England, 1981), 99–100, 131–45.

20. Ulrich, "Women's Work," 98.

21. Winifred B. Rothenberg, "The Emergence of a Capital Market in Rural Massachusetts, 1730–1838," in Hoffman *et al.*, eds., *Economy of Early America*, 137–40. Richard D. Brown, "The Emergence of Urban Society in Rural Massachusetts," *Journal of American History*, 61 (1974), Table I, shows that Massachusetts residents founded only seven "profit-seeking" voluntary associations before 1790, but then created thirty in the 1790s and seventy-eight in the following decade.

22. Quoted in Merrill, "Anti-Capitalist Origins," 34.

23. Billy G. Smith, " 'The Vicissitudes of Fortune': The Career Patterns of Laboring Men in Philadelphia, 1756–1798," in Innes, ed., *Work and Labor*, 230; Dunn, "Servants and Slaves," 180–83.

24. Sharon V. Salinger, "Artisans, Journeymen, and the Transformation of Labor in Late Eighteenth Century Philadelphia," *William and Mary Quarterly*, 3d ser., 40 (1983), 71; Stern, "Feudalism, Capitalism and the World System," 838.

25. B. H. Slicher Van Bath, *The Agrarian History of Western Europe, A.D. 500–1850* (London, 1963), 226–33; Mark Egnal, "The Economic Development of the Thirteen Continental Colonies, 1720–1775," *William and Mary Quarterly*, 3d ser., 32 (1975), 208–10.

26. Thomas M. Doerflinger, *A Vigorous Spirit of Enterprise: Merchants and Economic Development in Revolutionary Philadelphia* (Chapel Hill, N.C., 1986), 113–14, 122–24; Doerflinger, "Farmers and Dry Goods in the Philadelphia Market Area, 1750–1800," in Hoffman *et al.*, eds., *Economy of Early America*, 189–90; Doerflinger, "Commercial Specialization in the Philadelphia Merchant Community, 1750–1790," *Business History Review*, 57 (1983), 20–49.

27. John J. McCusker and Russell R. Menard, *The Economy of British America, 1607–1789* (Chapel Hill, N.C., 1985), Table 13.1; Shepherd, "British America and the Atlantic Economy," Table 2.

28. Clemens and Simler, "Rural Labor and the Farm Household," 109–10; Bushman, "Family Security," 240.

29. Clemens and Simler, "Rural Labor and the Farm Household," 127–31.

30. Kulikoff, "Transition to Capitalism," 141–42, likewise contrasts "yeomen" and "capitalist" farmers. The top 13 farmers (of the 67 whose wills were probated in three Delaware Valley counties in 1774) were probably capitalist farmers; the average value of their crops and livestock was £251. Another 14 farmers owned animals and farm commodities worth over £100; some may have been capitalists. The remaining 40 farmers (60 percent) were probably yeomen. See Doerflinger, "Farmers and Dry Goods," 188.

31. Rothenberg, "Capital Market," 161. Also see Duane E. Ball, "Dynamics of Population and Wealth in Eighteenth-Century Chester County, Pennsylvania," *Journal of Interdisciplinary History*, 6 (1976), 634–35 and Table 5; Carole Shammas, Marylynn Salmon, and Michel Dahlin, *Inheritance in America: From Colonial Times to the Present* (New Brunswick, N.J., 1987); Table I.4 and page 68 document the new practice of paying a widow's dower as annual interest on one-third of the value of the husband's landed estate; Doerflinger, *Spirit of Enterprise*, 305–307, notes similar gains in the liquidity of business assets in Philadelphia between 1750 and 1790. The appearance of banks and "commercial paper" allowed merchants "to transact more business with the same amount of property."

32. Shepherd, "Atlantic Economy," 7; Russell R. Menard, "Slavery, Economic

Growth, and Revolutionary Ideology in the South Carolina Lowcountry," in Hoffman *et al.*, eds., *Economy of Early America*, 265.

33. Doerflinger, *Spirit of Enterprise*, 356–65; Lois Green Carr and Lorena S. Walsh, "Economic Diversification and Labor Organization in the Chesapeake, 1650–1820," in Innes, ed., *Work and Labor*, 175–83.

34. Robert D. Mitchell, *Commercialism and Frontier: Agriculture and the Settlement of the Shenandoah Valley* (Charlottesville, Va., 1977); Hughes, "Slaves for Hire," 265; J. R. Wordie, "Rent Movements and the English Tenant Farmer, 1700–1838," *Research in Economic History*, 6 (1981), 193–243, traces the impact of the cereal boom on English agricultural capitalism.

35. Hughes, "Slaves for Hire," 269, 275, 277–79; see, in general, Robert Starobin, *Industrial Slavery in the Old South* (New York, 1970).

36. Philip D. Morgan and Michael L. Nicholls, "Slaves in Piedmont Virginia, 1720–1790," *William and Mary Quarterly*, 3d ser., 46 (1989), esp. 222–38; Dunn, "Servants and Slaves," 179.

37. Philip D. Morgan, "Work and Culture: The Task System and the World of Lowcountry Blacks, 1700–1860," *William and Mary Quarterly*, 3d ser., 39 (1982), 579.

38. Morgan, "Work and Culture," 576; Philip D. Morgan, "Task and Gang Systems: The Organization of Labor on New World Plantations," in Innes, ed., *Work and Labor*, 201.

39. Carr and Walsh, "Economic Diversification and Labor Organization," 159; Morgan, "Task and Gang Systems," 201–202.

40. Morgan, "Task and Gang Systems," 208, 202.

41. Morgan, "Work and Culture," 590–96.

42. Quoted in Rowland Berthoff, "Independence and Attachment," 114.

43. Robert Brenner, "Agrarian Class Structure and Economic Development in Pre-industrial Europe," *Past and Present*, 70 (1976), 52.

44. Quotation from E. Wayne Carp, *To Starve the Army at Pleasure: Continental Army Administration and American Political Culture, 1775–1783* (Chapel Hill, N.C., 1984), 65; Henretta, "American Economic Development," 79–87.

45. Merrill, "Anti-Capitalist Origins," 1–2.

46. James P. Whittenberg, "Planters, Merchants, and Lawyers: Social Change and the Origins of the North Carolina Regulation," *William and Mary Quarterly*, 3d ser., 34 (1977), 225, 226–28. Jacob M. Price, "Reflections on the Economy of Revolutionary America," in Hoffman *et al.*, eds., *Economy of Early America*, 306, notes that high transportation costs increased the impact of falling prices on North Carolina producers.

47. Whittenberg, "Planters, Merchants, and Lawyers," 237.

48. Ordinarily, merchant capital is "conservative," invested in trade among existing producers. But, as Stern argues ("Feudalism, Capitalism, and the World System," 869), "under colonial conditions, which allied merchant capital with imperial political power in the fluid environment of a frontier 'outpost,' merchant capital could exercise an aggressive, organizing, and transformative impact on technologies and social relations of production."

49. Whittenberg, "Planters, Merchants, and Lawyers," 234–35.

50. Dulany quoted in Joseph A. Ernst, "The Political Economy of the Chesapeake Colonies, 1760–1775: A Study in Comparative History," in Hoffman *et al.*, eds., *Economy of Early America*, 213; Robert E. Mutch, "Colonial America and the Debate about the Transition to Capitalism," *Theory and Society*, 2 (1980), 847–63; Oscar and Mary Handlin, *Commonwealth: A Study of the Role of Government in the American Economy* (Cambridge, Mass., 1945), chapters 1–2; Morton J. Hor-

witz, *The Transformation of American Law, 1780–1860* (Cambridge, Mass., 1977), chapter 1.

51. Gary Kulik, "Dams, Fish, and Farmers: Defense of Public Rights in Eighteenth-Century Rhode Island," in Steven Hahn and Jonathan Prude, eds., *The Countryside in the Age of Capitalist Transformation* (Chapel Hill, N.C., 1985), 30–33.

52. *Ibid.*, 39.

53. Handlin and Handlin, *Commonwealth*, 100, 102, 71–72, 82–86; Alan Taylor, " 'A Kind of Warr': The Contest for Land on the Northeastern Frontier," *William and Mary Quarterly*, 3d ser., 46 (1989), 3–26.

54. Cathy Matson, "Public Vices, Private Benefit: William Duer and His Circle, 1776–1792," in William Pencak and Conrad Edick Wright, eds., *New York and the Rise of American Capitalism: Economic Development and the Social and Political History of an American State, 1780–1870* (New York, 1989), 98–99; Doerflinger, *Spirit of Enterprise*, 270–71, 300–301.

55. My argument follows that of Merrill, "Anti-Capitalist Origins," 6, on the distinction between "capitalist" and "agrarian" paths of commercial development. Bingham quoted in Doerflinger, *Spirit of Enterprise*, 333.

56. Quoted in Ruth Bogin, "Petitioning and the New Moral Economy of Post-Revolutionary America," *William and Mary Quarterly*, 3d ser., 45 (1988), 405.

Opening the American Countryside
RICHARD L. BUSHMAN

1. Among the multitude of useful recent books are James A. Henretta, *The Evolution of American Society, 1700–1815: An Interdisciplinary Analysis* (Lexington, Mass., 1973); Gloria Main, *Tobacco Colony: Life in Early Maryland, 1650–1720* (Princeton, N.J., 1982); Carville V. Earle, *The Evolution of a Tidewater Settlement: All Hallow's Parish, Maryland, 1650–1783* (Chicago, 1975); Darrett B. Rutman and Anita H. Rutman, *A Place in Time: Middlesex County, Virginia, 1650–1750* (New York, 1976); Robert Gross, *The Minutemen and Their World* (New York, 1976); James T. Lemon, *The Best Poor Man's Country: A Geographical Study of Early Southeastern Pennsylvania* (Baltimore, 1972); Allan Kulikoff, *Tobacco and Slaves: The Development of Southern Cultures in the Chesapeake, 1680–1800* (Chapel Hill, N.C., 1986); Paul G. E. Clemens, *The Atlantic Economy and Colonial Maryland's Eastern Shore: From Tobacco to Grain* (Ithaca, N.Y., 1980); Stephen Innes, *Labor in a New Land: Economy and Society in Seventeenth-Century Springfield* (Princeton, N.J., 1983); David Grayson Allen, *In English Ways: The Movement of Societies and the Transferal of English Local Laws and Custom to Massachusetts Bay in the Seventeenth Century* (Chapel Hill, N.C., 1981); Joan M. Jensen, *Loosening the Bonds: Mid-Atlantic Farm Women, 1750–1850* (New Haven, Conn., 1986); John J. McCusker and Russell R. Menard, *The Economy of British America, 1607–1789* (Chapel Hill, N.C., 1985). The McCusker and Menard volume lists virtually all of the relevant literature, including articles, for the colonial period. Works on the nineteenth century are analyzed in Allan Kulikoff, "The Transition to Capitalism in Rural America," *William and Mary Quarterly*, 3d ser., 46 (1989), 120–44. Earlier works on agricultural history are listed in John T. Schelebecker, *Bibliography of Books and Pamphlets on the History of Agriculture in the United States, 1607–1967* (Santa Barbara, Cal., 1969), and T. R. Liao, *The History of American Agriculture* (Washington, D.C., 1981).

2. William N. Parker, "The Magic of Property," *Agricultural History*, 54 (1980), 447–89.

3. The English debate with a guide to the literature is summarized in Joan Thirsk, *England's Agricultural Regions and Agrarian History, 1500–1750* (London, 1987), 56–61.

4. Clarence H. Danhof, *Change in Agriculture: The Northern United States, 1820–1870* (Cambridge, Mass., 1969); Wayne D. Rasmussen, ed., *Agriculture in the United States: A Documentary History* (New York, 1975), I, 519.

5. After publishing his *Essay on Field Husbandry* at midcentury, Jared Eliot corresponded with a half dozen other Americans, including Franklin, William Logan, and Peter Oliver, on clover, horse-hoeing, and the drill plow. Jared Eliot, *Essays Upon Field Husbandry In New England and Other Papers, 1748–1762*, ed. Harry J. Carman and Rexford G. Tugwell (New York, 1934); Rodney H. True, "Some Pre-Revolutionary Agricultural Correspondence," *Agricultural History*, 12 (1938), 106–17. In 1785 the Philadelphia Society for Promoting Agriculture was organized, and others soon followed. The English Board of Agriculture, organized in 1793, named seven Americans honorary members. Rodney C. Loehr, "The Influence of English Agriculture on American Agriculture, 1775–1825," *Agricultural History*, 11 (1937), 3–15; Paul H. Johnstone, "Turnips and Romanticism," *Agricultural History*, 12 (1938), 232–33.

6. Americans drained their soil of its nutriments, he reported, until the land yielded a half or a third as much as comparable land in Europe, where more enlightened practices prevailed. W[illiam] Strickland, *Observations on the Agriculture of the United States of America* (London, 1801), 51. G. Melvin Herndon has argued that Strickland had reasons for discrediting American farmers, but offers no persuasive evidence that Strickland's evaluation of the soil was wrong: "Agriculture in America in the 1790s: An Englishman's View," *Agricultural History*, 49 (1975), 505–16.

7. For a comment on the inapplicability of many reforms to English farms, see G. E. Mingay, ed., *The Agricultural Revolution: Changes in Agriculture, 1650–1880* (London, 1977), 12.

8. Clear explanations of the fundamentals of the English agricultural revolution are to be found in the introductions to E. L. Jones, ed., *Agriculture and Economic Growth in England, 1660–1815* (London, 1967); Mingay, ed., *The Agricultural Revolution*; and in B. A. Holderness, *Pre-Industrial England: Economy and Society, 1500–1750* (London, 1976), chapter 3.

9. Samuel Deane, *The New-England Farmer; or Georgical Dictionary . . .*, 3d ed. (Boston, 1822), 130.

10. The American system was not classic shifting agriculture with villages that moved as the fields migrated through the forest. D. B. Grigg, *The Agricultural Systems of the World: An Evolutionary Approach* (Cambridge, Mass., 1974), 57–60, 72–73.

11. Strickland, *Observations on the Agriculture*, 49–50; "An Account of the Present State and Government of Virginia [1696]," Massachusetts Historical Society, *Collections for the Year 1798*, 5 (Boston, 1835), 127. Jared Eliot, advocating reforms in the middle of the eighteenth century, said earlier farmers "depended upon the natural Fertility of the Ground, which served their purpose very well, and when they had worn out one piece they cleared another. . . ." Eliot, *Essays on Field Husbandry*, 29.

12. True, "Agricultural Correspondence," 114. On New England's efforts or failure to maintain soil fertility, see William Cronon, *Changes in the Land: Indians, Colonists, and the Ecology of New England* (New York, 1983), 150–52.

13. Robert D. Mitchell, *Commercialism and Frontier: Perspectives on the Early Shenandoah Valley* (Charlottesville, Va., 1977), 136; Lemon, *The Best Poor Man's Country*, 168–69; Evaluation, 1784/86, *Massachusetts Archives*, vol. 163, Massachusetts State Archives, Boston. The amount of cleared land and uncleared land was calculated by combining categories on the Massachusetts tax valuations for 1784. In the cleared category are tillage, upland meadow, fresh meadow, salt marsh, and pasturage; in the uncleared are woodland, unimproved, and unimprovable. The

median of cleared land in Suffolk towns was 55 percent, and for Berkshire towns between 28 and 30 percent. For a description of the tax valuations, see Van Beck Hall, *Politics Without Parties: Massachusetts, 1780–1791* (Pittsburgh, 1972), 5.

14. Main, *Tobacco Colony*, 43–44. For an imaginative reconstruction by a historical geographer, see Ralph H. Brown, *Mirror for Americans: Likeness of the Eastern Seaboard, 1810* (New York, 1943), 211.

15. G. E. Gifford, Jr., ed., *Cecil County Maryland, 1608–1850, As Seen by Some Visitors, and Several Essays on Local History* (Rising Sun, Md., 1974), 12.

16. Philip Vickers Fithian, *Journals and Letters of Philip Vickers Fithian, 1773–1774: A Plantation Tutor of the Old Dominion*, ed. Hunter Dickinson Farish (Charlottesville, Va., 1957), 89. Samuel Deane, the reformer, objected to the appearance and the wasted space of the worm-rail fence, but conceded "as it is easily made, and soon taken up, it may do best where a fence is wanted only for a short time." Deane also conceded that "rail fence is perhaps as much used as any." Deane, *Newengland Farmer; or Georgical Dictionary . . .*, 2d ed. (Worcester, Mass., 1797), 107, 109.

17. Danhof suggests that the farmers for years may not have realized that their soil was losing fertility, blaming declining yields on the weather or insects, "the normal vagaries of farming." *Change in Agriculture*, 252. The transition to continuous cropping is discussed from a slightly different perspective in Henretta, *The Evolution of American Society*, 18–21, and in Gross, *The Minutemen and Their World*, 87–88.

18. Carville Earle and Ronald Hoffman, "Urban Development in the Eighteenth-Century South," *Perspectives in American History*, 10 (1976), 28–31; Clemens, *The Atlantic Economy and Colonial Maryland's Eastern Shore*.

19. *The Delaware Register* (Dover, Del.), 2 (October 1838), 202.

20. Carl Bridenbaugh, ed., *Gentleman's Progress: The Itinerarium of Dr. Alexander Hamilton, 1744* (Chapel Hill, N.C., 1948), 141–42.

21. Robert Honyman, *Colonial Panorama, 1775: Dr. Robert Honyman's Journal for March and April*, ed. Philip Padelford (San Marino, Cal., 1939), 8–9. Honyman did say the planters sowed timothy and clover in the meadows.

22. Honyman, *Colonial Panorama*, 8.

23. J. B. Bordley, *Essays and Notes on Husbandry and Rural Affairs* (Philadelphia, 1799), 235.

24. Paul G. Bourcier, " 'In Excellent Order': The Gentleman Farmer Views His Fences, 1790–1860," *Agricultural History*, 58 (1984), 546–64; quotes from Gifford, *Cecil County, Maryland*, 12, and as quoted in Clarence H. Danhof, "The Fencing Problem in the Eighteen-Fifties," *Agricultural History*, 18 (1944), 169. Style had always favored alternatives to the ragged worm-rail fence. During his student days in London, John Dickinson wrote home to his mother on their Delaware plantation, inquiring what progress "Hedging is making. My Honoured Father used to talk of it, and I am very fond of it, since I have been in England: If all the Grounds about our House were enclosed with Hedges, it is not possible to conceive how beautiful they would look." Quoted in Harold Donaldson Eberlein, *Historic Houses and Buildings of Delaware* (Dover, Del., 1962), 75.

25. Martin L. Primack, "Farm Fencing in the Nineteenth Century," *Journal of Economic History*, 29 (1969), 288.

26. Mitchell, *Commercialism and Frontier*, 136. Land-usage figures tabulated from "Massachusetts Valuation Returns for Worcester Co. 1781–1860," compiled by the research staff at Old Sturbridge Village, Massachusetts, and available in the Old Sturbridge Village Research Library, hereafter "Massachusetts Valuation Returns."

27. Jay E. Cantor, *The Landscape of Change: Views of Rural New England, 1790–1865* (Sturbridge, Mass., 1976).

28. Strickland thought long fallow was characteristic of New York agriculture in the 1790s. He identified a four-course rotation without a fallow year, "then a repetition of the same, as long as the land will bear any thing; after which it is *laid by* without seed for *old-fields*. . . ." Strickland, *Observations on the Agriculture*, 38. For the five unopened towns, see "Massachusetts Valuation Returns."

29. One observer commented that at the end of the eighteenth century, the practice of rotational agriculture and the introduction of clover on farms near Philadelphia gave "many old farms . . . a new appearance." Quoted in Lemon, *Best Poor Man's Country*, 171.

30. *The Delaware Register* (Dover, Del.), 2 (October 1838), 201.

31. Strickland, *Observations on the Agriculture*, 43; Danhof, *Change in Agriculture*, 254.

32. Timothy Dwight, *Travels in New England and New York*, ed. Barbara Miller Solomon (Cambridge, Mass., 1969), I, 77. For evidence of heavy uses of manures even earlier, see Carl Raymond Woodward, *Ploughs and Politicks: Charles Read of New Jersey and His Notes on Agriculture, 1715–1774* (New Brunswick, N.J., 1941), 138–51.

33. Richard A. Wines, "The Nineteenth-Century Agricultural Transition in an Eastern Long Island Community," *Agricultural History*, 55 (1981), 53–56.

34. George Washington adopted the tone of his English correspondent Arthur Young when he condemned the American system of agriculture as being as "unproductive to the practitioners as it is ruinous to the landholders." Washington blamed the continuation of the old way on innate conservatism. "To forsake it, to pursue a course of husbandry which is altogether different and new to the gazing multitude, ever averse to novelty in matters of this sort, and much attached to their old customs, requires resolution." Quoted in Rasmussen, ed., *Agriculture in the United States*, 285. Jefferson had another view. He was highly skeptical of Arthur Young's proposals as being impractical. Loehr, "The Influence of English Agriculture on American Agriculture," 10.

35. Danhof, *Changes in Agriculture*, 278; see also 256.

36. Marvin W. Towne and Wayne D. Rasmussen, "Farm Gross Product and Gross Investment in the Nineteenth Century," in National Bureau of Economic Research, *Trends in the American Economy in the Nineteenth Century*, Studies in Income and Wealth, 24 (Princeton, 1960), 255–312; Robert Gallman, "Changes in Total U.S. Agricultural Factor Productivity in the Nineteenth Century," *Agricultural History*, 46 (1972), 206, 208–209.

37. Although the extent of its adoption is uncertain, the cradle scythe increased the number of acres a man could reap or mow two or three times, widening the harvest-time bottleneck that had long inhibited production. Percy W. Bidwell and John I. Falconer, *History of Agriculture in the Northern United States, 1620–1860* (New York, 1941), 125, 207–208; Danhof, *Change in Agriculture*, 228.

38. Robert A. Gross, "Culture and Cultivation: Agriculture and Society, in Thoreau's Concord," *Journal of American History*, 69 (1982), 42–61.

39. I have attempted to explain the continuing appeal of farm life in "Family Security in the Transition from Farm to City, 1750–1850," *Journal of Family History*, 6 (1981), 238–56.

40. Clarence H. Danhof, "Agriculture in the North and West," in Glenn Porter, ed., *Encyclopedia of American Economic History* (New York, 1980), I, 361–63.

41. Gross, "Culture and Cultivation," 56.

42. Richard A. Easterlin, "Factors in the Decline of Family Fertility in the United States: Some Preliminary Research Results," *Journal of American History*, 63 (1976), 602, 610.

43. Easterlin, "Farm Family Fertility," 602. The average farm in Northville on Long Island in 1865 was 101 acres. Wines, "The Agricultural Transition," 56.

44. U.S. Department of Commerce, Bureau of the Census, *Historical Statistics of the United States, Colonial Times to 1970* (Washington, D.C., 1959), part I, 201. Contrary to what might be expected, the monthly earnings of farm laborers did not rise by much until after 1850, presumably because the supply of landless laborers in the community remained high until urban and industrial growth pulled them away from rural areas. Stanley Lebergott, *Manpower in Economic Growth: The American Record Since 1800* (New York, 1964), 539.

45. Strickland, *Observations on the Agriculture*, 55; Bordley, *Essays and Notes* (Philadelphia, 1799), 182–83.

46. Quoted in Richard H. Abbott, "The Agricultural Press Views the Yeoman: 1819–1859," *Agricultural History*, 42 (1968), 36–37, 38.

47. Deane, *Newengland Farmer* (1797), 1; and quotation in Gilbert C. Fite, "The Historical Development of Agricultural Fundamentalism in the Nineteenth Century," *Journal of Farm Economics*, 44 (1962), 1206–1207. See also Abbott, "The Agricultural Press," *Agricultural History*, 42 (1968), 44, 45. Initially the antidote for rural boorishness was agricultural science, the very commodity promoted in the journals, the idea being to elevate farm work with mental activity. *New England Farmer and Gardener's Journal* (Boston), 17 (August 1838).

48. E. G. Storke, ed., *The Family and Householder's Guide. . . .* (Auburn, N.Y., 1859), 31, quoting from the *American Agriculturalist*; *The Cultivator, A Consolidation of Buel's Cultivator and Genesee Farmer, Designed to improve the Soil and the Mind* (Albany, 1840), 93; *The Genesee Farmer* (Rochester, N.Y.), 15 (1854), 160; 16 (1855), 158; 16 (1855), 279. Instruction in genteel practices intensified in *The Genesee Farmer* after the addition of a "Ladies' Department" in February 1854.

49. The beginning of this trend clearly appears in household estate inventories around 1750. Lois Green Carr and Lorena S. Walsh, "Changing Life Styles in Colonial St. Mary's County," Regional Economic History Research Center, *Working Papers*, 6 (1978), 73–118; and Lorena S. Walsh, "Urban Amenities and Rural Sufficiency: Living Standards and Consumer Behavior in the Colonial Chesapeake, 1643–1777," *Journal of Economic History*, 43 (1983), 109–117. The information on Kent County comes from a random sample of inventories from the 1770s (N = 48) and the 1840s (N = 50) found in Kent County Probate Inventories, Hall of Records, Dover, Delaware.

50. The beneficiaries of the first phase of the agricultural revolution made up the great market for industrial production in the first decades of the nineteenth century. Diane Lindstrom, *Economic Development in the Philadelphia Region, 1810–1850* (New York, 1978).

51. The exertions of modest farm families to educate their daughters is analyzed in David F. Allmendinger, "Mount Holyoke Students Encounter the Need for Life Planning, 1837–1850," *History of Education Quarterly*, 19 (1979), 27–46.

52. For a detailed description of how one family achieved this ideal, see Gail Emily Nessell, "The Goodale Family: Seven Generations of Continuity and Change in Marlborough, Massachusetts" (M.A. Thesis, University of Delaware, 1985).

53. The lust for gain rather than poverty made small southern farmers willing to sacrifice refinements in order to enlarge their holdings, according to James Oakes, *The Ruling Race: A History of American Slaveholders* (New York, 1982), 81–87.

INDEX

LIST OF CONTRIBUTORS

RICHARD BUEL, JR., is Professor of History at Wesleyan University. He is the author of *Securing the Revolution* (1972); *Dear Liberty* (1980); and, with the late Joy D. Buel, *The Way of Duty* (1984).

RICHARD L. BUSHMAN, Professor of History at Columbia University, is the author most recently of *King and People in Provincial Massachusetts* (1985) and *Joseph Smith and the Beginnings of Mormonism* (1985).

PHILIP GREVEN is Professor of History at Rutgers University and the author of *Four Generations* (1970), *The Protestant Temperament* (1977), and *Spare the Child: The Religious Roots of Punishment and the Psychological Impact of Physical Abuse* (1991).

JAMES A. HENRETTA is Priscilla Alden Burke Professor of American History at the University of Maryland, College Park. His most recent book (with Gregory H. Nobles) is *Evolution and Revolution: American Society, 1600–1820.* He is currently at work on a study entitled "The Rise and Decline of the Liberal State in America, 1800–1920."

MICHAEL KAMMEN is Professor of American History and Culture at Cornell University, where he has taught since 1965. His books include *People of Paradox* (1972), which received the Pulitzer Prize for History, and *A Machine That Would Go of Itself: The Constitution in American Culture* (1986), which received the Francis Parkman Prize and the Henry Adams Prize. His most recent work is *Mystic Chords of Memory: The Transformation of Tradition in American Culture.*

STANLEY N. KATZ has taught at Harvard, Wisconsin, Chicago, Pennsylvania, and Princeton, where he was formerly Class of 1921 Bicentennial Professor of the History of American Law and Liberty. Past President of the American Society for Legal History and the Organization of American Historians, he is currently the President of the American Council of Learned Societies. He is the author of *Newcastle's New York* (1968), and the editor of *The Case and Tryal of John Peter*

Zenger (1963) and *Colonial America: Essays in Politics and Social Development* (3rd ed., 1983).

DAVID THOMAS KONIG is Professor of History and Chair of the Department at Washington University in St. Louis. His publications include *Law and Society in Puritan Massachusetts* (1979), *The Plymouth Court Records, 1686–1859* (16 vols., 1978–1981), and many essays on colonial legal history.

PAULINE MAIER is William R. Kenan, Jr. Professor of American History at the Massachusetts Institute of Technology. She has published two books on the American Revolution—*From Resistance to Revolution* (1972) and *The Old Revolutionaries* (1980)—and a junior-high-school textbook, *The American People: A History* (1986). Her next book is tentatively titled "The Revolutionary Tradition in America: Independence to the Civil War."

MARY BETH NORTON is the Mary Donlon Alger Professor of American History at Cornell University, where she has taught since 1971. She is the author of *Liberty's Daughters: The Revolutionary Experience of American Women* (1980) and other works on women in early America. Her essay in this volume is drawn from her current study of gender in the seventeenth-century English mainland colonies.

JACK N. RAKOVE is Professor of History at Stanford University. He is the author of *The Beginnings of National Politics* (1979) and *James Madison and the Creation of the American Republic* (1990), and editor of *Interpreting the Constitution: The Debate over Original Intent* (1990).

GORDON S. WOOD is University Professor and Professor of History at Brown University. He is the author of *The Creation of the American Republic* (1969), which won both the Bancroft and the John H. Dunning Prize, of many articles on the revolutionary era, and of a forthcoming book, "The Radicalism of the American Revolution."

MICHAEL ZUCKERMAN is Professor of History at the University of Pennsylvania. He is the author of *Peaceable Kingdoms: New England Towns in the Eighteenth Century* (1970) and of a forthcoming collection of biographical studies of the American character, *Almost Chosen People*.

A NOTE ON THE TYPE

This book was set in a digitized version of a type
face called Baskerville. The face itself is a facsimile
reproduction of types cast from molds made for
John Baskerville (1706–1775) from his designs.
Baskerville's original face was one of the forerun-
ners of the type style known to printers as "modern
face"—a "modern" of the period A.D. 1800.

Composed by Crane Typesetting Service, Inc.,
West Barnstable, Massachusetts
Printed and bound by Fairfield Graphics,
Fairfield, Pennsylvania
Designed by Anthea Lingeman